FESTIVAL ACTIVISM

Activist Encounters in Folklore and Ethnomusicology
David A. McDonald, editor

FESTIVAL ACTIVISM

EDITED BY

**DAVID A. McDONALD,
ANDREW SNYDER,**
AND
JEREMY REED

INDIANA UNIVERSITY PRESS

This book is a publication of

Indiana University Press
Herman B Wells Library
1320 East 10th Street
Bloomington, Indiana 47405 USA

iupress.org

© 2025 by Indiana University Press

All rights reserved
No part of this book may be reproduced or utilized in any form or by any means, electronic or mechanical, including photocopying and recording, or by any information storage and retrieval system, without permission in writing from the publisher.

First Printing 2025

Library of Congress Cataloging-in-Publication Data

Names: McDonald, David A., editor | Snyder, Andrew (Ethnomusicologist) editor | Reed, Jeremy (Ethnomusicologist) editor
Title: Festival activism / edited by David A. McDonald, Andrew Snyder, and Jeremy Reed.
Other titles: Activist encounters in folklore and ethnomusicology
Description: Bloomington, Indiana : Indiana University Press, 2025. | Series: Activist encounters in folklore and ethnomusicology | Includes bibliographical references and index.
Identifiers: LCCN 2025019292 (print) | LCCN 2025019293 (ebook) | ISBN 9780253074263 hardback | ISBN 9780253074270 paperback | ISBN 9780253074294 ebook | ISBN 9780253074287 adobe pdf
Subjects: LCSH: Music festivals—Social aspects | Music festivals—Political aspects | Music—Social aspects | Music—Political aspects | Activism | Social justice
Classification: LCC ML3916 .F5 2025 (print) | LCC ML3916 (ebook) | DDC 306.4/842—dc23/eng/20250520
LC record available at https://lccn.loc.gov/2025019292
LC ebook record available at https://lccn.loc.gov/2025019293

CONTENTS

Introduction: Festival Activism / DAVID A. MCDONALD, ANDREW SNYDER, AND JEREMY REED   1

DISRUPTION

1. Carnival Arts and "Freedom Dreams": An Ethnography of Culture, Power, and Black Political Struggle in London's Carnival Scene / DEONTE L. HARRIS   29
2. Rethinking Relational Geometries in Musical Events in Europe: Artistic Devices and Activist Implications / FILIPPO BONINI BARALDI   52

REFUGE

3. An Accessible Carnival: Festivity, Inclusion, and Disability in Rio de Janeiro / ANDREW SNYDER   75
4. The Festivalization of Feminism, DIY Music, and Intersecting Identities at Ladyfests / LOUISE BARRIÈRE   100

RENEWAL

5. Love Songs That Protest: *Sentipensante* Music Making as Postneoliberal Activism in the Neighborhood Tango Festivals of Buenos Aires / JENNIE GUBNER   123
6. Al-Balad Theater: Festivals as Sites of Social Action and Community Development in Neoliberal Jordan / JEREMY REED AND SERENE HULEILEH   144
7. Resignifying Traditional Festive Culture for Progressive Ends in Portugal from Dictatorship to Democracy: Associativism and the Production of Protest / MIGUEL MONIZ   165

DELIBERATION

8. Another Possible World: Transnational Activism at WOMAD / JAMES NISSEN   191

9. *Babaláwo* and *Bataleras*: Translocal Academic and Ritual Activism at the Festival of the Caribbean (Festival del Caribe) in Eastern Santiago de Cuba / RUTHIE MEADOWS   215

10. Festival Study as a Framework for Dialogic Social Justice: A Perspective from Johannesburg / OLADELE AYORINDE   240

FUTURITY

11. Festival Futurity at the Palestine Music Expo / DAVID A. MCDONALD   261

12. "The Many Ways We Are Alike": The Perils of Multiculturalism in Boise's World Village Festival / KIMBERLY J. MARSHALL AND STEVEN HATCHER   280

Afterword: The Work That Music Festivals Do / ERIC FILLION AND AJAY HEBLE   301

List of Contributors   311

Index   317

FESTIVAL ACTIVISM

Introduction

Festival Activism

DAVID A. MCDONALD, ANDREW SNYDER,
AND JEREMY REED

What meaningful differences exist between a festival and a protest, and when might they be one and the same? Under what circumstances, and with what effects, do festivals embody and enact activist potential? Theorizing assembly, Judith Butler posits that "acting in concert can be an embodied form of calling into question the inchoate and powerful dimensions of reigning notions of the political" (2015, 9). Though Butler does not discuss festivals per se, the social and political potentials of collective assembly are enduring motifs of festive studies. In our interrogation of what we call *festival activism*, we focus on the (unintentional) double meaning of the words "in concert."

We seek to understand how assembled bodies express the fluid and porous boundaries between the festive and the activist. By *festival activism*, we refer to a collection of tactics of intervention that arise from elements inherent to festival settings and are mobilized for political ends. We argue that festivals offer possibilities for strategic and critical action at all stages of their development and articulation. Festivals can cloak oppositional politics or stage them explicitly, but, in all cases, they are their own modality of intervention, distinct from more familiar politics of indignation and refusal. As such, festivals are potentially important sites of intervention and inquiry for scholars, practitioners, and performers alike.

In this volume, we offer case studies from around the world that focus on moments when festivals become opportunities for political intervention—sometimes as vehicle, sometimes as generative space, sometimes as direct action. The chapters collectively ask how festival performers, participants, and organizers encounter and challenge myriad forms of violence that frame their worlds. Accessibly written by scholars, activists, curators, and practitioners, this volume is meant to be a resource for critically understanding the potential impact of festivals as strategic tools for political intervention.

Festival Politics

Defining *festival* and the related term *festivity* is a complicated task. Our use of the term festival reflects contributors' various descriptions of ludic, programmed events from around the world. We view *festivity*—and its adjective *festive*—as a broader terrain that includes festivals but also commemorations, holidays, feasts, and other events. We recognize the fluidity between these cultural forms, as well as the diversity of terms used to refer to them. Miguel Moniz, for example, argues in this volume that festivals in Portugal fall more broadly under the term *festa*, which is difficult to translate into English and can signal a variety of festive events beyond *festival* as normally construed (equivalent to Spanish *fiesta* or French *fête*). In this volume, we move forward with the understanding that *festival* and *festivity* are useful concepts for analysis of programmed, ludic social events when contextualized within their unique cultural and political settings. We take a similar approach to the term *activism*. Building from the contributors' diverse understandings and applications of the term, we broadly define *activism* as a configuration of postures and practices aimed at intervention in and transformation of the social and political order.

Theorizing the boundaries between these terms has long been a central concern for scholars in both festive studies and social movement theory. This volume seeks to blur these boundaries altogether, focusing on moments when festivals advance activist agendas and activist groups use festivity for maximum political impact. In these moments, aesthetic and performative dimensions of assembly enhance each endeavor. This is certainly not to say that festivals and protests are necessarily one and the same, rather that their overlapping characteristics, methods, and social effects lend themselves to mutual inquiry and analysis. In this way, we hope to build on and extend the work of scholars and practitioners who approach festivals as meaningful spaces for ordering, maintaining, subverting, or transforming their social and political worlds.

Throughout this literature, we note two predominant approaches to festival study. On the one hand, there are those who view festivals as a mechanism of top-down rule, what Foucault (Foucault et al. 1991) might call an "art of governance." Laurent Fournier (2019), for example, argues that until the eighteenth century, festivals in Europe were widely viewed as safety valves that allowed people to let off steam without damaging the extant political order. In other words, elites channeled transgressive behavior toward ludic activities so as to neutralize and pacify more overt political demands. This approach positions festivals as fundamentally anti-activist—as stabilizing forces in the normative social order. Such views hold festive behavior as acting against, rather than engaging with, subversive political causes.

Festivals are also occasions for ritualistic myth making that forms the social order (DaMatta [1979] 1991). Folklorists of the nineteenth century viewed them as one of many popular expressions vital to emerging notions of national identity (Fournier 2019). We might view the anthropological tradition that begins with Émile Durkheim and his studies of Aboriginal religious behavior as one in which festivals, through their production of "collective effervescence," help structure the social lives of a given community (Durkheim [1912] 1995). In more recent literature, scholars have approached festivals as fundamental to political governance. Depending on who is in power, top-down approaches to festivals are not necessarily conservative reproductions of the social order but rather opportunities for transforming it (Guss 2000; Guilbault 2007).

The focus on top-down approaches is countered by an approach to festivals as subversive, from the bottom up. Sigmund Freud (1913) viewed festivals as potential spaces for transgression and expression of the normally repressed id. Victor Turner's theory of "communitas" as a liminal experience of equality and social intimacy poses that such egalitarian experiences are part of "anti-structure," contrasting the "structure" of official society (Turner 1969). Carnival studies, focused more specifically on the diverse pre-Lenten festive traditions of the Catholic world, often follows carnival's own mythic ideology that portrays festivals as inversions of official hierarchies (Bakhtin [1941] 1984).

In these classic theorizations, festivals operate as spaces within which political action arises—that is, we see something akin to what we term *festival activism*. Our understanding of festival activism is not, however, bound to a particular form or expression. Rather, we draw on Aurélie Godet's useful observations on the politics of carnival that underscore festival as sites of contest between diverse agendas, revealing a politics of "ambivalence and indeterminacy" (Godet 2020, 13–14). This approach denies carnival any intrinsic political meaning or function and instead focuses on how activities are strategically mobilized by specific groups for political benefit. Festivals, like carnival, are no more inherently activist than they are political. It is in their situated and contextualized articulation that we begin an exploration of festival activism.

While festive studies scholars have long engaged with the political, it is worth mentioning that social movement theory scholars have also approached, although ambivalently, creativity, emotion, performance, and festivity. Early social scientists such as Gustave Le Bon viewed crowds and social movements as irrational mobs disruptive to the social order ([1985] 2000). By contrast, Marxist approaches frame social movements as eminently rational; social movement scholars in the 1960s and 1970s tended to reinforce this idea, arguing that activists are rational, politically driven actors. Since the "cultural turn" of the 1980s, many have moved beyond such binaries, and there is a growing tendency to focus on creativity (Jasper 1997) and emotion (Jasper 2018) as well as what Larry Bogad calls "tactical performance," the strategic use of performative arts in protest movements. More generally, the growing prevalence of the term *artivism* points to increasingly collapsed boundaries between artistic and activist dimensions.[1] It is perhaps no surprise that activist vocabularies are increasingly "festivalized," as Andy Bennett (Bennett, Taylor, and Woodward 2014) has suggested that the "festivalization of culture"—the growing tendency to express rituals, artifacts, consumerism, and other facets of social life in festive vocabularies—is a growing part of our contemporary political world.

With this edited volume, we seek to extend these discussions by connecting festive studies and social movement theory. Such an approach, we believe, dovetails with emerging trends in festive studies, which has in recent years witnessed the founding of two dedicated journals: the *Journal of Festive Studies* (2019) and the *Journal of Festival Inquiry and Analysis* (2022). In addition, we note the recent publication of the *Routledge Handbook of Festivals* (2019), which includes a section on the "strategic use of festivals," as well as several other edited volumes and monographs exploring the politics of festival and the festivalization of politics.[2] Indeed, as this volume initially took shape, we were alerted to an upcoming conference sponsored by the University of Guelph and Queen's University called "Curating for Change: What Festivals Do in the World." Bringing together scholars, practitioners, curators, and organizers, this online symposium examined how festivals promote "activist arts-based practices and pedagogies."[3] Based on our shared interest in an increasingly prominent topic, we reached out to the organizers, Ajay Heble and Eric Fillion, who graciously provided an excellent afterword to this book. Their forthcoming book, *Ripple Effects: The Active Histories and Possible Futures of Music Festivals*, complements *Festival Activism* with its sustained focus on how festival curation can make festivals into "insubordinate spaces that activate diverse energies of creativity, awareness, care, and inspiration." One of the contributors to this volume, James Nissen, has consolidated the International Festival Research Network, which held a symposium on "Social Inclusion, Community, and Belonging at International Music Festivals" in 2024.[4] In conversation with the debates arising from these forums, we explore the mechanics of activist intervention in festival practice, examining how, under what conditions, and to what effect festivals may serve as tools and settings for political intervention.

Moreover, the chapters included in this volume demonstrate the transdisciplinary nature of festive studies. Contributors work in diverse areas of public, private, and academic sectors. The assembled chapters reflect the dispositions of multiple disciplinary fields: ethnomusicology, folklore, cultural studies, media studies, performance studies, festive studies, and others. And while each draws from a wide array of theoretical resources and methodological approaches, all engage with central concerns of qualitative humanistic inquiry, carefully exploring tensions that arise in the encounter between individual agency and collective action. Indeed, this theme recurs throughout the volume, framing our theoretical discussion below. Festivals and the interventions they facilitate are important forms of collective action, yet they are conditionally dependent on and products of the agency, values, and aspirations of dedicated individuals. As the case studies demonstrate, the structural impact and embodied politics of festival activism arise from the desire of individuals and communities to transform their worlds. The approach represented here thus tacks dutifully between these two frames, charting how engaged individuals work collectively and collaboratively toward the creation of larger forms of community and how those communities further contour individuals' shared values and dispositions. Many of the case studies include compelling stories of individual acts of artistic expression and cultural empowerment as the basis for collective action and structural change. They demonstrate the impact that affective, embodied politics can have at various levels from the local to regional, national, and transnational.

These insights are reinforced by the volume's near-global reach. Contributors provide case studies from countries across five continents, including Brazil, Argentina, England, France, Germany, Jordan, Portugal, Cuba, South Africa, Nigeria, the United States, and Palestine. But perhaps more importantly, contributors examine a wide array of intersectionally diverse communities from each of these countries, demonstrating how communities are ritually defined, redefined, and transcended through festival practice.

Approaching Festival Activism

In approaching festival activism, this volume attempts to provide a resource for thinking about the various ways in which festivals are mobilized for political intervention. It does not propose a universal theory but rather curates an array of case studies that, in their accumulation, form a composite understanding of festivals as significant tools for activism. As a first step in thinking through these connections and surveying the case studies included in this volume, we note four *key resources* for political action inherent to festival activity: *participatory action, pleasure, assembly,* and *appearance.* In varying configurations, these four resources offer an orienting framework for thinking about the dynamics of festival activism. How these resources are strategically mobilized for political impact through festival activism's tactics of intervention is discussed subsequently.

Participatory Action

As Thomas Turino eloquently demonstrates, participatory action, especially coordinated sonic and gestural action, is among a variety of activities that can catalyze social change, alternative citizenship, and long-term political transformation (Turino 2016, 298). According to Turino, participatory music making and dance are key to social transformation for a number of reasons: they operate according to values and practices often opposed to the dominant capitalist ethos; they engender a kind of egalitarian consensus building; they are pleasurable, leading to continuity of involvement; and they become "the basis for special social cohorts (voluntary social groups drawn together by enthusiasm for the activity and by shared, pre-existing tendencies toward the broader values that underlie the activity)" (Turino 2016, 298).

While Turino's case studies focus on subtle, long-term effects of participatory music making, his model proves useful as a starting point for theorizing more direct and immediate activist interventions such as those exhibited in festival settings. Indeed, festive studies scholars have often attended to ways in which participatory dynamics elicit the profound feelings of communitas necessary for successful festival experiences (Rutherdale 1996; Van Heerden 2009). Roxy Robinson goes further, arguing that participatory dynamics directly influence the activist potential of any festival event (Robinson 2015, 11). According to Robinson, participatory festival models elicit a meaningful mode of social and political celebration in that they afford audience members a sense of control and, hence, a feeling of being part of the performance. When barriers separating performers and spectators dissolve, a more egalitarian ethos emerges, which is crucial in the creation of flow states and new forms of community. As Robinson suggests, participatory dynamics enhance political action across festival contexts. Insofar as participants experience pleasurable egalitarian modes of interaction (communitas), and insofar as these experiences facilitate the enactment of new coalitional communities, so too might we imagine participatory action as a significant resource through which historically marginalized, vulnerable, or oppositional groups might feel and act as if "part of the performance" (Robinson 2015, 11). In this way, participatory action plays an important (if not essential) role in both successful festival practice and political transformation.

Pleasure

What makes participatory action such an important resource for festival activism is the way it engenders egalitarian social interactions through pleasurable experience. The pleasures of participation lead to a continuity of involvement and enthusiasm for collective action. Pleasure, in this sense, is more than a fortuitous byproduct of participatory festival experience: it is a key resource for political intervention. As several contributors to this volume note, festival activism emerges from the creation and manipulation of public intimacies through a politics of pleasure. Similarly, Jocelyne Guilbault writes, live performances "do cultural work in ways that cannot be reduced solely to the grid of resistance or solely to the outcomes of capitalist reproduction" (2010, 17). Rather, "the political" in festival practice arises from the "politics of pleasure" that animates "distinct skills, knowledges, and civic values" (2010, 17). "Pleasure is not innocent," Guilbault argues, "it transforms audience members . . . into subjects of community and . . . in so doing, pleasure then becomes a productive force of power" (2010, 22).

Guilbault's insight is shared among the contributors to this volume. Pleasure holds activist potential in that it facilitates and sustains the coalitional intimacies necessary for collective action. And while pleasure (like festivity) is often dismissed as ephemeral escapism, we argue that ephemeral escapism is not trivial. As the authors in this volume demonstrate, pleasure brings people into public spaces, calls them to action through feelings of collective intimacy, and sustains enthusiasm beyond festival spaces and into daily life. The politics of pleasure may be subtle, but they nevertheless remain effective tools for activist intervention, for it is in moments of pleasure that political desire and egalitarian thinking can be articulated.

Assembly

The inherent pleasure of the festival experience entices crowds to assemble in novel, often fortuitous, configurations. And it is in that act of assembly that festival holds its greatest potential for activist intervention. Just as political demonstrations and other protests take place conspicuously in public spaces, in festival practice, bodies assemble; they move, act, and speak collectively; and, in so doing, they performatively define a public and lay claim to the spaces they occupy. At times, these spaces are provided (through permits, agreements, legal authorization), and at other times they are spontaneously taken or occupied. In each instance, there is an inescapable though limited claim of sovereignty. Festivals by their very nature are acts of assembly, and assembly is an act of sovereignty. As Butler writes, the concept of assembly captures how "embodied actions of various kinds signify in ways that are, strictly speaking, neither discursive nor pre-discursive. In other words, forms of assembly already signify prior to, and apart from, any particular demands they make. Silent gatherings, including vigils or funerals, often signify in excess of any particular written or vocalized account of what they are about.... The gathering signifies in excess of what is being said, and that mode of signification is a concerted bodily enactment, a plural form of performativity" (2015, 8).

Simply in their assembly, festival participants embody a kind of coalitional politics and activist potential. The spatial proximity of participants, the movement of bodies, gives a sense of public intimacy and collective belonging. Indeed, as Butler notes, when festival participants assemble, they exercise a plural form of performativity. Their assembly enacts and defines the contours of the (provisional) public, asserts a fundamental right for that public to appear, and, in occupying public space, makes demands on its behalf. These demands are made prior to and apart from any musical/linguistic gesture, statement, or claim. They may be explicit or implicit. Yet in each case, the signifying effect of assembly lies in the constitution and legitimation of those assembled. Coordinated action is its own form of political action. Especially when it involves bodies normatively excluded from public appearance, assembly can be a particularly effective form of calling into question dominant hierarchies of exclusion and privilege. Probing the dynamics of assembly, the chapters in this volume offer an opportunity to explore unique relations, interdependencies, and discourses that inform festival practice. What does it mean for particular bodies to assemble in particular spaces at particular times? What types of interventions are made in the act of assembly?

Appearance

Through assembly, newly constituted (provisional) publics appear—and in their appearance, festival participants can make significant political demands. In this way, appearance is a political effect of assembly and a significant resource for festival activism. As the chapters in this volume note, the public appearance of festival participants is in many cases a political act, rendering visible unique configurations of marginalized bodies normatively denied public recognition while disrupting the discourses responsible for their exclusion. A festival's activist potential is not only to facilitate feelings of solidarity or belonging among diverse participants, nor is it to enable the articulation of transgressive ideas and values. Rather, the activist potential of a festival lies in the constitution and legitimation of transgressive bodies, the manipulation of the external gaze on those bodies, and the reclamation of public space on behalf of those bodies. In this way, the signifying potential of a festival activism lies in its capacity to define communities and legitimize their appearance within and against conflicting (and often violent) conditions of erasure (Arendt 1958; Rancière 1999; Butler 2015). As curated public spectacles, festivals inherently engage in the politics of appearance, and appearance is a powerful resource for intervention. Staging artists, choosing venues, and soliciting audiences are curatorial acts that manipulate the appearance of bodies and the ideas they signify.

Tactics of Intervention

In surveying the case studies presented in this volume, we have come to understand that festival activism emerges from the strategic mobilization of inherent festival key resources (participation, pleasure, assembly, and appearance) for a desired political effect. Indeed, these festival resources do not necessarily translate into festival activism and can be manifested for other ends. Festivals can be commercialized and commodified, restricting a community from engaging in activism through festivity that is not directed toward a profit motive (though activism can itself be commercialized). They can be co-opted by dictatorial regimes or channeled toward right-wing activism, a topic largely unexamined in this book but deserving of its own analysis. And, while we show how festivals are spaces in which activist projects can be articulated, it is important to recognize the fragile and precarious ecosystems of festivals, especially those attempting to embrace noncapitalist logics or those of marginalized communities. In many cases, activism is directed at guaranteeing the conditions for a festival's very existence—the foundation for allowing communities to assemble and appear that is the basis for articulating other activist projects (Snyder forthcoming).

But we suggest that, when these four resources are mobilized in response to situated social, cultural, and political circumstances, they manifest festival activism through various tactics of intervention, which we summarize in five interrelated and overlapping concepts: *disruption, refuge, renewal, deliberation,* and *futurity*. We find these five tactics of intervention to be a useful organizing framework for understanding and analyzing how festivals can directly engage and transform political fields. We stress that this list is not comprehensive, nor are these terms necessarily used by the contributors themselves. These are recurring themes worthy of reflection and are starting points for critical inquiry and analysis.

Disruption

Writing about experimental festivals that challenge musical life in Paris, Filippo Bonini Baraldi asks a fundamental question: "How can art produce ruptures in [the] consensual habitus of being in the world?" (p. 66). The answer, he argues, lies not in straightforward political messages or demands but rather in the activation of "dissensual regimes of sensoriality" (p. 66). Quoting Rancière, Bonini Baraldi describes "the efficacy of disconnection" in festival activism as "a rupture in the relationship between the productions of artistic activity and defined social ends, between sensible forms, the meanings that one can give to them, and the effects that they can produce. We can put it another way: the *efficacity of dissensus*. What I mean by dissensus is not the conflict of ideas or feelings. It is the conflict of several regimes of sensoriality. It is through this that art, and the regime of aesthetic separation, finds itself touching on politics" (Rancière 2008, 66, qtd. on pp. 66–67; emphasis added). For Bonini Baraldi, reconfiguring musical space, movement, and interaction "can be the fundamental fuel for activating changes in socio-political domains" (p. 67). Activist potential is linked to, and the product of, "dissensual dispositions and sensorial experiences" (p. 67).

Bonini Baraldi's argument captures a fundamental tactic of festival activism: for festivals to make any kind of sociopolitical intervention, they must first intervene in fields of normative dispositions and sensorial experiences. That is, they must cause a disruption. This first order of intervention may occur across several fields. Festivals intrinsically involve a kind of disruption of everyday life. In the act of assembly, they constitute disruptions to public space, and, in the ephemeral emergence of coalitional communities, they disrupt spheres of appearance governing which bodies may appear. But Bonini Baraldi's argument goes further, citing the strategic disruption of "relational geometries" in musical space, movement, and experience as the "fuel" for sociopolitical change.

Deonte Harris similarly argues that activist intervention in London's Notting Hill Carnival celebration emerges first from disruptions caused by Black cultural visibility and audibility. London's carnival celebrations are politically contentious sites, he writes, given that they are predicated on and emerge from Black presence in Britain. In taking over public spaces and in the appearance of Black bodies in those spaces, carnival celebrations index Britain's history of large-scale migration and resettlement of Caribbean and African peoples in relation to the very precarious position of Black people and Black culture in contemporary British society. The disruptions caused by Black cultural visibility and audibility throughout festival season create opportunities for "individuals or collectives . . . to bring critical awareness of particular political issues and injustices" to distinct audiences within the festival space, and "ultimately advocate for social change of some sort through art or performance" (pp. 29–30).

In each case study, festival activism emerges from an act of disruption, opposition, or disturbance to the dominant social (or sensorial) order. Festivals are mechanisms through which marginalized groups assert their presence through the appropriation of public spaces and resources. For the artists chronicled in Harris's chapter, festival performance enacts a disruptive intervention into the spheres of appearance by constituting and legitimizing Black culture; enabling the visibility and audibility of Black bodies; and manipulating the public gaze on those Black bodies. The resulting visibility and audibility solicit support by drawing attention to their concerns, raising awareness of their presence, and displacing dominant relations under the guise of festivity. Disruption occurs in both form and content. The festival itself is a mechanism of disruption along with its performative content.

Given that festivals are often viewed as pleasurable, positive, and (ideologically) harmless escapes from daily life, their ensuing disruption is often positively construed and tolerated. Moreso than traditional protest marches or antagonistic occupations of public space, festivals are surreptitious means of drawing attention to and galvanizing support for the concerns of marginalized communities. Festivity often cloaks its disruptive politics. And, just as Black carnival street performers entice revelers to participate, they compel their predominantly white interlocutors "to reckon with the historical continuum of Black trauma: the legacies of slavery, colonialism, and Empire, as well as the realities of contemporary Black oppression in the UK" (p. 46). Playful, performative, and creative resistance illuminates "the history of trauma that Black people in the UK have had to endure... while also affirming Black humanity and the potency of Black cultural and political presence in postwar Britain today" (p. 47). These festival activists intend to oppose exploitation and oppression through disruption of the status quo, appropriation of public space, and pleasurable disturbance of dominant discourse.

Refuge

While the disruption of public space invariably involves the establishment and demarcation of oppositional boundaries, those boundaries form a kind of protective enclosure wherein marginalized, excluded, targeted, and other precarious groups may seek refuge from everyday forms of violence. Indeed, the refuge provided by festival is an often-overlooked tactic of intervention; as such, it is a theme that extends across many of the chapters in this volume.

Filippo Bonini Baraldi's discussion demonstrates how festivals may provide refuge to musicians marked with illegal citizenship status. Festival organizers hosted workshops to stimulate "dialogue among different communities that [are] victims of social stigma, in order to produce cohabitation, recognition, reciprocity, and exchange of good practices" (p. 63). Transylvanian Roma and Italian transgender performers quite literally took refuge from authorities within festival spaces, simultaneously seeking resources to challenge public stigma and blatant prejudice.

Within the chaotic street carnival scenes of Rio de Janeiro, Brazil, Andrew Snyder documents ways in which the ensemble Orquestra Voadora, made up of around four hundred performers, has sought to provide refuge to participants with disabilities. Organizing with disability rights groups and adopting a public stance of anti-ableism, the group has argued that it must not accommodate people with disabilities only on the margins but rather must fundamentally transform festive practices by adapting pedagogies, designating accessible spaces in parades, and directly advertising participation in the group to people with disabilities.

For carnival participants like Camila Alves, who is blind, Orquestra Voadora's moves toward greater accessibility solicit powerful feelings of belonging and community: "To be in the middle of the band, amid the stilt walkers, to be among other people with disabilities too . . . this was all very powerful—this sensation of belonging in carnival" (pp. 85–86). Furthermore, as Voadora participant Fernanda Shcolnik argues, the building of a culture with a structure of accessibility has positive, practical, and political effects for everyone. Accessible festival spaces are inherently democratic spaces, she says, in that they encourage participation and facilitate inclusive engagement among diverse groups. Such acts of refuge redefine the contours of the carnival community for all.

Similar acts of refuge arise in Louise Barrière's chapter on Ladyfest festivals in Western Europe, where transinclusive and feminist politics shape festival practice. Ladyfest organizers give priority to cisgender women, trans people, and nonbinary and intersex people, who have less access and opportunity within male-dominated music spaces. Privileging underrepresented female and queer musicians on stage is a key element to Ladyfest organizers' "festivalization of feminism" (p. 100) and part of a larger effort to militate against patriarchy within the public sphere and DIY music scenes. Ladyfest's feminist politics are intended to provide safe festival experiences to women and sexual minorities; as Barrière argues, these efforts coalesce into a politically determining context or atmosphere that forcefully enacts feminist politics and notions of community. Here refuge is provided not only to precarious bodies but also to the transgressive ideas they represent.

This idea of refuge is what James Nissen articulates in his study of the 2017 WOMAD Festival. Nissen notes that within festival spaces intercultural interactions can also forge intimate connections of empathy, which may offer emotional support for those struggling against social oppression and collective shelter for invisible and unheard marginalized voices (p. 203). In one interactive moment, Nissen evocatively describes how the Tanzanian Albinism Collective spoke against persecution in Ukerewe. As children in the audience jumped onstage to dance alongside the band, social stigmas prohibiting such contact dissolved. This moment of transgression and performative solidarity had an emotional and psychological effect on the band members. But, perhaps more importantly, such interactions "have a 'tremendous' capacity to empower because they can make artists feel safe while they are performing... and potentially mobilize international support beyond the event" (p. 204). Nissen suggests that refuge extends beyond the interactions of festival participants, as WOMAD provides "refuge for cosmopolitan worldviews that transgress everyday realpolitik to challenge racist nationalism and thus disrupt the global political order, offering a safe and welcoming space that maximizes cooperation and empathy and minimizes confrontation and harm. By empowering, transforming, questioning, and imagining, WOMAD discursively insists that another world is possible and experientially prefigures another possible world" (p. 210).

In each of these examples, activist intervention arises in the refuge provided to participants normatively marked as precarious. Refuge is an act of protection, an affordance of safety, and an invitation to participate. Transgressive ideas, worldviews, and perspectives are equally provided refuge within festival spaces, whether through public performance, informal workshops, or collective political action. Opportunities for visibility, legibility, and action arise both within and beyond festival spaces. But, for many festival participants discussed in these chapters, refuge means more than temporary safety. Rather, refuge is an act of survival. As the authors demonstrate, brief moments of collective legitimation, recognition, and safety have an empowering effect, a political salience, and a psychological impact long after the festival ends.

Renewal

While festivals necessarily disrupt everyday life and, in that disruption, create ephemeral spaces of refuge for transgressive bodies and ideas, an effort to revive, renew, or sustain communities and cultural practices against external threat often lies within these spaces. As several contributors to this volume note, local grassroots festivals offer unique social spaces within which to preserve or sustain traditional values, perspectives, and ideals. Renewal, in this sense, takes on two very important activist meanings: first, it endeavors to safeguard communities and environments against displacement and erasure;

and second, it includes the artful adaptation of traditional forms, practices, and ideas for contemporary political needs. In acts of renewal, past and often beloved performance repertories sentimentalize and hence mobilize the political needs of vulnerable communities and the spaces they occupy. People, place, and politics are renewed through festival practice. The efficacy of this form of intervention results from the aggregation of sentimental attachment to tradition, community-based participatory social action, and resulting forms of intimacy.

Jennie Gubner, for example, explores *"sentipensante"* performances of tango in Buenos Aires in which traditional, sentimental performance practices are strategically layered with carefully curated political messages. She shows how intimate and romantic music-making experiences become affective vehicles through which to critique neoliberal urbanism and export-oriented entrepreneurial politics. Against the backdrop of neoliberal efforts to monetize Argentinian tango as a tourist commodity, Gubner describes how local tango artists promote new ways of experiencing tango by relocating it within local neighborhood imaginaries, aesthetics, and everyday practices. In the promotion of neighborhood tango festivals, organizers mobilize romantic feelings connected to "neighborhoodness" to advocate for alternate models of cultural production. As Gubner eloquently argues, the intimacy of emotional, romantic, and nostalgic music-making experiences has significant political potential: "Using nostalgia and romanticized imagery to discuss neighborhood life is common in the classic tango lyrics. By applying these techniques [to the contemporary scene, festival organizers were] able to cultivate an air of sentimentalism and romance to promote a localizing politics of tango music in the urban landscape. By rebuilding affective connections between tango and neighborhood life, these kinds of narratives promote both [sentimental] and post-neoliberal ways of imagining tango and city life. In these contexts, sentimentalism becomes a tool for activism" (p. 138).

Sentimental and nostalgic attachments to neighborhood politics factor heavily in al-Balad Theater's social action against neoliberal development in Jordan. As Jeremy Reed and Serene Huleileh describe, acceleration of neoliberal discourse in the past two decades has transformed Amman into what Jordanian scholars have apocalyptically, if exaggeratedly, called a "decentered, fragmented, and privatized" cityscape of "empty buildings . . . and the skeletal remains of speculative development" (p. 147). Al-Balad Theater's various festivals intervene by helping artists and audiences navigate shifting neoliberal conditions and dynamics of inclusion and exclusion. More than providing refuge in the form of safe and accessible spaces for artists to present their work, these festivals shape individual and collective identities and relationships to place. Al-Balad Theater's approach is multimodal, promoting music, murals, and storytelling. But it is also multitemporal in the way it looks to revive, renew, and reimagine Amman's downtown neighborhoods as accessible and inclusive spaces for future generations.

The renewal of established protest vocabularies and narratives can also work as an effective tool of recruitment, an instrument of community building, and a lens through which to imagine and enact possible desired futures. This point is articulated by Miguel Moniz in his examination of Portuguese *festas*, a capacious term that includes public village and saint day festivities, examining creative resignifications of traditional repertoires for contemporary aims from the early twentieth-century dictatorship to the present. Though the symbology of *cultura popular*—that is, traditional and folkloric representations of "authentic" Portuguese culture—was produced, consolidated, and controlled during forty-eight years of fascist rule until 1974, Moniz shows that festas featuring traditional vocabularies have become central to Portugal's postdictatorship political sphere. In stark contrast to the tactic of intervention we have termed *disruption*, or explicitly oppositional politics, "these creative aesthetic and structural changes occur not by rejecting but by adapting older forms to meet progressive circumstances, refashioning ritualized cultural behavior, and creating space for older institutional practices to remain relevant" (p. 183).

Adapting and resignifying traditional elements of the popular, he argues, can be particularly efficacious for activist projects because of their conciliatory guise. By adopting elements of traditional parade forms (*marchas populares*), for example, alternative brass bands create social spaces that "teach, inform, and transform local communities and larger audiences without rupturing expectations for the public display of popular culture" (p. 170). Finding novel ways to perform within traditional cultural forms, Portuguese festas create "norm-rupturing sonic and social spaces that challenge political hierarchies. However, they do so while generally supporting expectations for performative structures and folk practices" (p. 169). Gubner and Reed and Huleileh reinforce this point. They each demonstrate how tradition is mobilized to reframe public debate on the past, influence people's views toward present political issues, and enact a desired vision for the future. Hence, nostalgia for traditional forms and practices can bring the public into festival spaces, where it can be recruited in the pursuit of activist goals.

Deliberation

If Moniz, Gubner, and Reed and Huleileh point to the various ways festival organizers pursue political action by repurposing traditional repertoires for progressive aims, it is in festival spaces that nostalgia, romance, and sentimentalism become tools for deliberation: emotional cues aimed at transforming participants' consciousness and recruiting support. Insofar as festivals are "fields of action in which both dominant and oppressed are able to dramatize competing claims" (Guss 2000, 10), they are also psychosocial spaces where disparate identity formations, cultures, and geographies historically kept and mapped separately are allowed to interact.

As many of the authors in this volume note, festivals are significant sites of encounter. Through participation, pleasure, assembly, and appearance, festival participants are solicited to engage in deliberative action: to accommodate difference, negotiate potential compromise, and seek common ground in the pursuit of collective goals. Deliberative tactics of intervention may occur explicitly in pronounced political content (Harris, Nissen, and Barrière) or implicitly in subtle interactions (Ayorinde), performative dialogue (Meadows), or structural forms (Bonini Baraldi). And while deliberation may arise in both form and content, in each instance it signals a larger intent to inform, educate, and transform political consciousness.

James Nissen's analysis of the 2017 WOMAD festival, for example, considers three main strategies to engage with transnational politics: protest music, intercultural interaction, and activist coordination. WOMAD's artists perform songs with direct activist messages, offer impromptu social commentary between songs, and engage with transnational politics through workshops, talks, and interviews. Artists further participate in deliberative action by facilitating intercultural interactions, which, Nissen argues, can challenge and resignify racially marked sounds and identities. In their encounter, artists and audiences communicate political worldviews, participate in translocal coalition building, and share transnational vocabularies of social justice. His interviews with festivalgoers "suggest that the processes that underpin these protest events have the potential to festivalize activism by disrupting alienation and complacency, raising consciousness, and mobilizing participants to get involved in transnational activism beyond the festival" (p. 207). Nissen concludes that WOMAD engenders activist sensibilities by providing meaningful spaces to forge horizontal connections across diverse constituencies.

The resolution of difference and forging of transnational consciousness through deliberative action is a central theme in Ruthie Meadows's chapter on Ifá-Òrìṣà ritual practice. Meadows underscores the role of eastern Cuban academics in developing the Festival del Caribe in Santiago de Cuba, attesting to the ways scholar-practitioners utilize festival spaces to assert and validate controversial forms of ritual and gendered revisionism. Meadows notes that, for Cuban practitioners, looking to contemporary Yorùbáland in West Africa as the original homeland for Regala de Ocha-Ifá opened up novel possibilities for women to be priestesses (*iyánífá*) and *òrìṣà* ritual drummers.

She documents how, in 2015, female percussionist Nagybe Madariaga Pouymiró used the academic spaces of the Festival del Caribe to assert the right of women to play the consecrated *batá* drums under the tenets of Nigerian-style Ifá. Through festival, Pouymiró directly intervened into Cuban ritual practice and, as a result, collapsed boundaries between ritual praxis and academic study of Afro-Cuban religion. By harnessing the academic legitimacy of the state-sponsored festival to reimagine a ritual practice inclusive of female practitioners, Pouymiró legitimated Nigerian-style forms of knowledge and her own authority as a *babalao* (priest) within and beyond the spaces of the festival.

Meadows's analysis points to the importance of festivals in shaping public consciousness through deliberative action. The Festival del Caribe served as a vehicle to legitimate African-inspired ritual practices and practitioners through its public visibility and state-sponsored events and institutions. As Meadows notes, the Festival del Caribe underscores the idea that academic participation and agency can be a key component of festival activism. She further illustrates the important role scholar-practitioners play in festival organization and performance, dismantling the boundaries between festival performance, academic inquiry, and ritual praxis.

Oladele Ayorinde makes a similar argument in his thoughtful reflection on the Wits Festival Study Group (WFSG). Founded by a team of nine scholar-practitioners in 2019, the WFSG sought to raise awareness, exchange scholarly ideas, and develop new and more inclusive models of festival practice. The festival the group created, Jazz Cosmology: Not Another Jazz Festival, was meant to militate against conventional forms of exclusion and inclusion in standard South African jazz festivals by directly involving local communities in all aspects of festival practice. Ayorinde and his collaborators sought to revive "the collective experience and sensibilities of the cross-class alliances that incubated jazz in South Africa for much of the previous century" (p. 245; cites Pyper [2016, 117]).

Despite facing considerable obstacles, the Cosmology Festival succeeded in bringing together a diverse audience of "jazz aficionados," the majority of whom were provided transportation from peripheral townships and villages to attend. Ayorinde describes how, in a beautiful moment of deliberative festival activism, several audience members spontaneously ascended the stage to perform *Diga*, a solo improvised dance associated with urban township popular culture. Through this brief embodied performance on the stage of one of South Africa's most exclusive theaters, the inclusive and deliberative logic of the Cosmology Festival was fully realized. On stage, the artists performed different and at times contradictory messages. They expressed diverse beliefs, attitudes, and commitments, offering competing visions of South Africa's body politic. In this moment, deliberation occurred within performance itself, signaling traditional forms of exclusion while compelling a new and more inclusive understanding of the community and its needs. The festival created a dialogic space for rethinking and reimagining the national community. Ayorinde's argument not only demonstrates the important role academics can play in festival practice, as does Meadows's, but further documents how festival planning and organization present opportunities for future political intervention.

Futurity

As Ayorinde notes, festivals' sometimes radical disruption of societal norms allows organizers to performatively implement goals and values that aim to transform what society might one day become. Indeed, many of the chapters presented in this volume draw attention to the aspirational and critical character of festival activism. Insofar as the various case studies explore themes of disruption, refuge, renewal, and deliberation, each indexes the ways festivals, in both form and content, move collectively toward aspirational futures. Indeed, as many of the authors in this volume note, there is world-making potential in festival practice. Festival participants collectively imagine and enact (im)possible future aspirations, whether strategically incorporated into festival design, performed on stage, or seized in public spaces. Disruption opens spaces of refuge, which in turn facilitate transgressive imaginings of self and other. Such collective imagining articulates a form of possibility that, while ephemeral, nevertheless moves toward a desired political alternative. In festival practice, participants collectively embody the unimaginable as a possible, perhaps even inevitable, reality.

This is what we mean by festival futurity: the diverse ways of collectively imagining and enacting a desired future through festival practice, as well as the spatial, logistical, and material resources required to experience that future in the present moment. Festival futurity is a central theme in David A. McDonald's analysis of the Palestine Music Expo (PMX), where organizers and performers strategically articulate aspirational visions of Palestine beyond the carceral violence of Israeli occupation. Andrew Snyder similarly shows how Orquestra Voadora's efforts to improve accessibility for carnival participants is "focused on planting the seeds of a more accessible world," as the group expressed through its 2023 carnival parade theme, "The future is anti-ableist" (p. 95). Ruthie Meadows writes that festivals' inclusion of ritual practitioners and academics opens up "novel spaces of possibility otherwise unthinkable within the landscape of Cuban ritual practice" (p. 216). Deonte Harris considers how Afro-diasporic carnivals are important Black "world-making projects" that serve as "critical spaces where the freedom dreams of Black people are expressed through carnival arts" (p. 48). "Protest and activism are not only a means for artists to speak truth to power in the here and now," Harris writes, "they are, in and of themselves, unique articulations of potential future worlds that are more free and just for people of African descent" (p. 48). And Kimberly Marshall and Steven Hatcher demonstrate the ways festival organizers create aspirational spaces of festival futurity in early design and programming phases of festival production. As Idaho state folklorist, Hatcher strategically recruits participants into the World Village Festival for their potential to disrupt white nationalist politics. In so doing, Hatcher hopes to produce a "heterotopia" where "performers, vendors, audience, and the geography of the festival combine to create a space ... that models an alternative to the politically divisive and antagonistic realities of Idaho" (p. 281). In each of these examples, festival organizers, performers, and participants create spaces for collectively imagining beyond the limits of the present moment. They endeavor to show the potential of what could one day be and reveal an activist intent to not only imagine society's potential but also, more importantly, actively participate in its becoming. Each of these case studies documents futurity as a tactic of intervention and an opportunity to imagine, embody, and enact something radically new.

In its experimental, disruptive, and transgressive pursuit of the yet to come, festival futurity points to (and advances toward) new political horizons. These case studies demonstrate the agential world-making capacities of festival practice, moving beyond traditional models that conceptualize festivals as either microcosms of society or instruments of communitas and instead positioning them as forms of direct action and political intervention. Marshall and Hatcher indeed see their work "to build broad, multicultural coalitions in the face of rising divisiveness and hate" as a form of direct action (p. 281). They argue that approaching festivals as direct action allows better understanding of the deliberate, intentional, and strategic forms of world making at the heart of festival practice.

Direct action is also a central concept in McDonald's analysis of the Palestine Music Expo (PMX). McDonald argues that the greatest impact of PMX, held under nearly impossible political circumstances, is as a form of direct action against local Islamist authoritarians as well as the Israeli military. Citing David Graeber and others, McDonald describes how festival organizers, performers, and participants use PMX as "a way of actively engaging with the world to bring about change, in which the form of action—or at least the organization of the action—is itself a model for the change one wishes to bring about" (Graeber 2009, 206). As both a means and an end, PMX imagines Palestinian sovereignty through its enactment. It disrupts and displaces the overdetermining effects of the occupation through a joyful celebration of what Palestine might one day become: ignoring the logics of occupation; assembling Palestinian bodies; and collectively, joyfully imagining Palestine beyond the limits of the present moment.

This notion of festival futurity as a kind of direct action rests on the idea that small moments of ephemeral escapism or aspirational world making are not trivial. Indeed, as the contributors to this volume argue, festival futurity has both immediate and long-term effects. In seeking new relational and sensorial notions of community, festivals can be crucial instruments of political transformation, not merely through the content of performances (lyrics, chants, social interactions) but as structural forms manifest in the participatory, pleasurable enactment of a desired future. In their participatory politics and the pleasures that ensue, festivals have the capacity to sustain enthusiasm for imagined political realities long after performances have concluded. Assembling bodies for collective appearance, festivals offer multisensorial opportunities for the impossible, the nonexistent, or the ideal to be imagined and enacted. This tactic of intervention reorients thinking away from a politics of anger, indignation, and refusal and instead captures and mobilizes pleasure, participation, and assembly for maximum political impact. This desire-based performance of futurity collectively manifests new possible worlds beyond festival spaces. And it is in these efforts that we focus our collective attention to festival activism.

Notes

1. See, for example, Monika Salzbrunn's application of the term to carnivals in her European Research Council–funded project "Super-diversity, Creativity and Political Expression."

2. Philip Auslander (2002); Lorenzo Ferrarini and Nicola Scaldaferri (2020); Christine Garlough (2013); Reebee Garofalo, Erin Allen, and Andrew Snyder (2020); Eileen Hayes (2010); Fabian Holt (2021); Isabel Machado (2023); Andrew Mall (2020); George McKay (2015); Dylan Robinson (2020); Roxy Robinson (2015); Matt Sakakeeny (2013); Andrew Snyder (2022); Miguel Valerio (2022); Steve Waksman (2022); Jonathan Wynn (2015).

3. For details about the conference, see "Curating for Change: The Work That Music Festivals Do in the World," June 23, 2022, https://www.whatmusicfestivalsdo.ca/.

4. For more information on the International Festival Research Network and its symposium on June 14, 2024, see https://www.festivalresearchnetwork.org/events/report-1st-ifrn-symposium-on-social-inclusion-community-and-belonging.

Bibliography

Arendt, Hannah. 1958. *The Human Condition*. Chicago: University of Chicago Press.
Auslander, Philip. 2002. *Liveness: Performance in a Mediatized Culture*. London: Taylor and Francis.
Bakhtin, Mikhail. (1941) 1984. *Rabelais and His World*. Translated by Helene Iswolsky. Bloomington: Indiana University Press.
Bennett, Andy, Jodie Taylor, and Ian Woodward. 2014. *The Festivalization of Culture*. Farnham, Surrey: Ashgate.
Bogad, Larry. 2016. *Tactical Performance*. London: Routledge.
Butler, Judith. 2015. *Notes toward a Performative Theory of Assembly*. Cambridge, MA: Harvard University Press.
Csikszentmihalyi, Mihaly. 1990. *Flow: The Psychology of Optimal Experience*. New York: Harper & Row.

DaMatta, Roberto. (1979) 1991. *Carnivals, Rogues, and Heroes: An Interpretation of the Brazilian Dilemma*. Translated by John Drury. Notre Dame, IN: University of Notre Dame Press.
Durkheim, Émile. (1912) 1995. *The Elementary Forms of Religious Life*. New York: Free Press.
Ferrarini, Lorenzo, and Nicola Scaldaferri. 2020. *Sonic Ethnography: Identity, Heritage and Creative Research Practice in Basilicata, Southern Italy*. Manchester: Manchester University Press.
Foster, Susan Leigh. 2003. "Choreographies of Protest." *Theatre Journal* 55(3): 395–412.
Foucault, Michel, Graham Burchell, Colin Gordon, and Peter Miller. 1991. *The Foucault Effect: Studies in Governmentality, with Two Lectures by and an Interview with Michel Foucault*. Chicago: University of Chicago Press.
Fournier, Laurent Sébastien. 2019. "Traditional Festivals: From European Ethnology to Festive Studies." *Journal of Festive Studies* 1: 11–26.
Freud, Sigmund. 1913. *Totem und tabu*. Leipzig: Hugo Heller.
Garlough, Christine. 2013. *Desi Divas: Political Activism in South Asian American Cultural Performances*. Jackson: University Press of Mississippi.
Garofalo, Reebee, Erin Allen, and Andrew Snyder. 2020. *HONK! A Street Band Renaissance of Music and Activism*. New York: Routledge.
Godet, Aurélie. 2020. "Behind the Masks, the Politics of Carnival." *Journal of Festive Studies* 2: 1–30.
Graeber, David. 2009. *Direct Action: An Ethnography*. Edinburgh: AK Press.
Guilbault, Jocelyne. 2007. *Governing Sound: The Cultural Politics of Trinidad's Carnival Musics*. Chicago: University of Chicago Press.
Guilbault, Jocelyne. 2010. "Music, Politics, and Pleasure: Live Soca in Trinidad." *Small Axe* 14(1[31]): 16–29.
Guss, David. 2000. *The Festive State: Race, Ethnicity, and Nationalism as Cultural Performance*. Berkeley: University of California Press.
Hayes, Eileen. 2010. *Songs in Black and Lavender: Race, Sexual Politics, and Women's Music*. Chicago: University of Illinois Press.
Heble, Ajay, and Eric Fillion. Forthcoming. *Ripple Effects: The Active Histories and Possible Futures of Music Festivals*. Philadelphia: Temple University Press.
Holt, Fabian. 2021. *Everyone Loves Live Music: A Theory of Performance Institutions*. Chicago: University of Chicago Press.
Jasper, James. 1997. *The Art of Moral Protest*. Chicago: University of Chicago Press.
Jasper, James. 2018. *The Emotions of Protest*. Chicago: University of Chicago Press.
Le Bon, Gustave. (1895) 2000. *The Crowd: A Study of the Popular Mind*. Ontario: Batoche Books.
Machado, Isabel. 2023. *Carnival in Alabama: Marked Bodies and Invented Traditions in Mobile*. Jackson: University of Mississippi Press.

Mair, Judith. 2019. *The Routledge Handbook of Festivals*. London: Routledge.
Mall, Andrew. 2020. *God Rock, Inc. The Business of Niche Music*. Oakland: University of California Press.
Manabe, Noriko. 2019. "Chants of Resistance: Flow, Memory, and Inclusivity." *Music and Politics* 13(1): 1–19.
McKay, George. 2015. *The Pop Festival: History, Music, Media, Culture*. New York: Bloomsbury.
Rancière, Jacques. 1999. *Dis-agreement: Politics and Philosophy*. Minneapolis: University of Minnesota Press.
Rancière, Jacques. 2008. *Le spectateur émpancipé*. Paris: La Fabrique.
Robinson, Dylan. 2020. *Hungry Listening: Resonant Theory for Indigenous Sound*. Minneapolis: University of Minnesota Press.
Robinson, Roxy. 2015. *Music Festivals and the Politics of Participation*. London: Routledge.
Rutherdale, Robert. 1996. "Canada's August Festival: Communitas, Liminality, and Social Memory." *Canadian Historical Review* 77(2): 221–49.
Sakakeeny, Matt. 2013. *Roll with It: Brass Bands in the Streets of New Orleans*. Durham, NC: Duke University Press.
Salzbrunn, Monika. 2020. "The Twenty-First-Century Reinvention of Carnival Rituals in Paris and Cherbourg: Extending the Boundaries of Belonging via Politicized Ritual." *Journal of Festive Studies* 2(1): 105–27.
Silverstein, Shayna. 2019. "On Sirens and Lamp Posts: Sound, Space, and Affective Politics." *Music and Politics* 13(1): 1.
Snyder, Andrew. 2022. *Critical Brass: Street Carnival and Musical Activism in Olympic Rio de Janeiro*. Middletown, CT: Wesleyan University Press.
Snyder, Andrew. Forthcoming. "The Struggle for Lisbon's Brazilian Carnival and against Structural Xenophobia." *Music and Minorities*.
Tilly, Charles. 2010. *Regimes and Repertoires*. Chicago: University of Chicago Press.
Turino, Thomas. 2008. *Music as Social Life: The Politics of Participation*. Chicago: University of Chicago Press.
Turino, Thomas. 2016. "Music, Social Change, and Alternative Forms of Citizenship." In *Artistic Citizenship: Artistry, Social Responsibility, and Ethical Praxis*, edited by David J. Elliott, Marissa Silverman, and Wayne D. Bowman. 297–313. New York: Oxford University Press.
Turner, Victor W. 1969. *The Ritual Process: Structure and Anti-structure*. London: Routledge.
Valerio, Miguel. 2022. *Sovereign Joy: Afro-Mexican Kings and Queens, 1539–1640*. Cambridge: Cambridge University Press.

Van Heerden, Esther. 2009. "Liminality, Transformation and Communitas: Afrikaans Identities as Viewed through the Lens of South African Arts Festivals: 1995–2006." PhD diss., Stellenbosch University.

Waksman, Steve. 2022. *Live Music in America: A History from Jenny Lind to Beyoncé*. Oxford: Oxford University Press.

Wynn, Jonathan. 2015. *Music/City: American Festivals and Placemaking in Austin, Nashville, and Newport*. Chicago: University of Chicago Press.

DISRUPTION

ONE

Carnival Arts and "Freedom Dreams"

An Ethnography of Culture, Power, and Black Political Struggle in London's Carnival Scene

DEONTE L. HARRIS

The Notting Hill Carnival (NHC) is an annual street celebration that takes place in London over the August bank holiday weekend. It features several dozen masquerade bands parading in the streets, mobile and static sound systems emitting music, concert stages for performing artists, and a plethora of merchant stalls selling food and other festive items to carnival attendees. With nearly 1.5 million attendees and revenue close to £400 million each year, the NHC is one of the largest and most lucrative cultural events in the UK today.[1]

Despite its mainstream popularity and commercial success as a premier tourist attraction in the UK, annual production of the NHC and its broader cultural scene does not transpire without societal tension. As social geographer Peter Jackson attests in "Street Life: The Politics of Carnival" (1988), London's carnival has historically manifested as a "contested event that expresses political and ideological conflict" (214). By and large, this conflict is the direct result of the politicization of race in postwar Britain and continued contestations over Black presence and culture in contemporary British society.[2] Due to the high concentration of Black cultural visibility and audibility during carnival, as well as the large scale occupation of the streets by Black people, the NHC epitomizes this ongoing historical conflict, physically and symbolically. Moreover, as this ideological and cultural clash unfolds annually, the NHC also becomes a generative platform for Black carnivalists to create artistic responses to highlight and combat their experiences of xenophobia, racism, and other forms of discrimination in Britain.

As a politically contentious site, the NHC is a space where distinct forms of festival activism manifest in creative ways. By "festival activism," I refer to intentional acts within the festival space by individuals or collectives seeking to bring critical awareness to particular issues and injustices, ultimately advocating for social change through art or performance. There is, of course, a historic precedent in the African diaspora for the use of carnivals to critique and protest governing bodies, politicians, and societal structures that engender inequalities (Rohlehr 1990; Dunn 1992; Cowley 1996; Burton 1997; Liverpool 2001; Guilbault 2007; Henry 2008; Henry and Plaza 2019; Arnaud 2020). Within carnival contexts, creative forms of subversion, protest, and activism are sometimes shrouded in code and intended to be legible among cultural insiders; other acts are more overt and transparent, such as the 2017 "Green for Grenfell" campaign at NHC.[3] Regardless of the form of the act, whether masquerade, song (especially calypsos), or other, I have always been mesmerized by the creativity of Black carnivalists who are able to shed light on some of the most pressing issues of the times through their art in compelling ways.[4]

The 2016 calypso performance by Gerry Archer, aka G-String, at NHC is one example. On the World Music Stage at Powis Square on Carnival Sunday, Archer performed an original calypso titled "Referendum." Envisioning himself as an MP (Member of Parliament) representing "the Calypso Party," Archer sang a musical manifesto to the crowd, centering the wants, needs, and desires of Black people in the UK and those in the diaspora affected by British politics past and present.

In three of his verses, Archer sang about the power and importance of calypso as a political art form for social commentary. He rendered blistering critiques of European colonialism and British imperialism and expressed his desire for the reallocation of funds in the UK to create institutions that acknowledge the social, economic, and cultural contributions Black people have made to Britain. Below is a sample of lyrics from his calypso:

VERSE 3:
Well in my opinion
We need a calypsonian MP
To run up the country
Giving them social commentary
Giving them the truths and the rights,
Letting all of the whole world know
The contribution that we play
Through the music of calypso, I tell you . . .

VERSE 5:
When you say Referendum
How come they don't mention King Leopold?
Who went to the Congo
Kill all the people and steal all we gold
The next criminal I'm talking about
It is the one that they call Cecil Rhodes
So when I reach in the power
We giving Africa back all they gold, I tell you . . .

VERSE 8:
When I get in power
I'm closing down the London Dungeon
Then I'm running round the corner
And then I'm shutting down the Tower of London
And then I'm building a Black museum
For the whole world to see
The contributions that Black people made
To build this motherfucking country, I tell you . . .

I present this brief ethnographic performance excerpt to elucidate how the cultural politics of London's carnival is not only specific to local contexts and conditions of Black Britons but also connected to a much larger history of political struggle in the global Black diaspora. As such, this chapter argues that the production of carnival and carnival arts in London must be understood in terms that go beyond theorizations of liminality, communitas, and carnivalesque ritual inversions (Bakhtin 1984; Turner 1967, 1977, 1988) to account for the specificities of the interplay between Black consciousness, Black diasporic politics, and Black cultural production in the carnival realm. While Mikhail Bahktin's and Victor Turner's writings and theories often serve as the entry point for much of what has become known as carnival studies (Crichlow and Armstrong 2010), I argue that the literature on the Black radical tradition (Robinson [1983] 2000; Kelley 2002) offers an alternative and arguably better model for analyzing the cultural activities of Black carnivalists and the complex web of diasporic relations and politics in which they are situated.

Theorizing the Black Radical Tradition

In *Black Marxism: The Making of the Black Radical Tradition* ([1983] 2000), Cedric Robinson conceives of the Black radical tradition (BRT) as a means of reorienting how we might understand radical thought, practices, and revolution in ways that do not continue to privilege Europe and white Westerners. In doing so, Robinson produces a critical theory of revolutionary thought and struggle centered on the experiences, activities, and political projects of people of African descent. With attention to the impacts and consequences of European colonial expansion, the transatlantic slave trade, and racial capitalist exploitation on the lives of people of African descent from the Middle Ages to the late twentieth century, Robinson argues that these served as crucial sites for the development of a new, collective political consciousness that birthed Black radicalism and engendered distinct genealogies of Black struggles for freedom and liberation, past and present.

The roots of Black radicalism, according to Robinson, began with the "rejection of European slavery and revulsion of racism in its totality" by Africans and their descendants in the New World ([1983] 2000, 310). From there, Robinson argues that the BRT was nurtured in Africa and the Americas through a range of social, cultural, and political responses to the conditions of slavery, colonialism, and racial capitalism. Rather than simply accepting subjugation and the anti-Black social systems intended to relegate them to nonbeings, chattel, and/or colonial subjects, Africans on the continent and in the diaspora actively resisted these oppressive systems whenever and wherever possible; in doing so, they forged alternative ways of doing and being in accordance with their dreams of future worlds free of slavery, colonialism, racism, and heteropatriarchy.

Among the acts of resistance Robinson cites as evidence of traditions and genealogies of Black radicalism are the numerous uprisings, rebellions, and insurrections by enslaved Africans (such as the Haitian Revolution), the creation of self-liberated African communities in the Americas by runaways and fugitives (maroon societies), and the formation and practice of a number of syncretized Afro-Atlantic religions (e.g., Santería, Haitian Vodou, and Brazilian Candomblé) by Africans in the Americas. Contained in these acts, beliefs, and practices are what Robinson refers to as "the raw materials of the BRT." In other words, they contain "the values, ideas, conceptions, and constructions of reality from which resistance was manufactured" by African-descended peoples' "ability to imaginatively re-create a precedent metaphysic while being subjected to enslavement, racial domination, and repression" ([1983] 2000, 309). While Robinson does not directly discuss the rise of Afro-diasporic carnival practices and musics, the theoretical and historical groundwork he lays makes clear that they are part of the unfolding world of Black radical politics and cultural activity, as I show later in the chapter.

Robin D. G. Kelley's writings on the BRT pick up the foundation laid by Robinson but also take it in new directions, particularly relating to linkages between imagination, collective action, and social movements. In *Freedom Dreams: The Black Radical Imagination* (2002), Kelley interrogates disparate sociopolitical and cultural movements involving Black radical activists, freedom fighters, and artists and privileges the role of imagination in the formation and development of those movements. According to Kelley, the book was conceived as a "preliminary effort to recover ideas—visions fashioned mainly by those marginalized black activists who proposed a different way out of our constrictions" (xii). What started out as an effort to recover ideas by marginalized Black activists evolved into a book that illuminates distinct histories of Black freedom dreaming, connecting nineteenth- and twentieth-century social movements and political struggles in the African diaspora to those of today as processes in a larger, collective effort for Black liberation.

Building from Robinson and Kelley on the BRT, I extend their theorizations to the domain of carnival by asking several questions: What unique insights can be gained by situating Afro-diasporic carnivals within histories and traditions of Black radicalism? How has London's carnival scene in particular served as a unique arena for the development and cultivation of Black political consciousness and collective action against racism and other discriminatory forms of oppression in the UK? And lastly, what can analyses of carnival arts in London reveal about the contemporary freedom dreams of Black Britons today?

To explore these questions in greater detail, I begin with an overview of the historical development of London's carnival arts scene between the 1950s and '70s and discuss how Black radical politics have always been at the heart of the movement. Following this overview, I share two ethnographic examples based on fieldwork conducted in London between 2013 and 2017 that illustrate the continuation of the legacy of Black radicalism and activism in London's contemporary carnival arts scene. The first example is centered on a carnival-inspired painting by Stacey Leigh Ross titled *We Jammin' Still* (2017). The second example focuses on an interactive art installation by Ishmahil Blagrove at NHC 2015 called *Spirit of Resistance*. I use these ethnographic examples to illuminate how carnival artists imagine alternative social worlds for marginalized and oppressed peoples through creative works, with the desire to ultimately bring those worlds in being.

London's Carnival as an Artistic Manifestation of the Black Radical Tradition

London's post-WWII carnival movement was born out of political struggle, emanating from the denigration of Britain's working-class poor and violence toward Black migrant communities in the 1950s and '60s to the mobilization of creative collective action and organizing in response. An accounting of this history is a central feature of much of the existing literature on London's contemporary carnival scene and its political undercurrents. This literature includes research on the carnival that focuses on the politics of the streets and the right to space for Black Britons (Jackson 1988; La Rose 1989; Cohen 1993); the intersectional race, class, and gender politics that envelops its annual production and execution (Race Today Collective 1977; Cohen 1980, 1982; Gutzmore 2000); and the continued struggle over cultural representation, ownership, and economic control of the festival (Alleyne-Dettmers 1997, 1998, 2002, 2005; Nurse 1999; Burr 2006; Ramnarine 2007; Ferdinand et al. 2013; Blagrove Jr. and Busby 2014).

In reviewing this literature, what becomes apparent is that theorizations of liminality, communitas, and carnivalesque ritual inversion fail to adequately encapsulate the meaning and significance of Black cultural activities during carnival, let alone the political ethos and stakes of London's carnival movement. This is primarily because the carnival, then and now, is a product of Black radical activism invested not in the temporary suspension or inversion of social relations but in the commitment to fundamentally change society and the world for the marginalized and oppressed through sustained action. Such was the case for the development of the earliest postwar Caribbean carnivals in London (1959–64), organized by activist Claudia Jones (Sherwood 1999; Davies 2008). This can also be seen in the ways carnivals throughout the African diaspora were transformed into creative spaces for Black political engagement and struggle at the height of the Black Power Movement during the 1970s (Hill [1972] 1997; Manning 1978), as was the case in London as well (Race Today Collective 1977; Cohen 1993). In the ethnographic sections that follow, I show how the BRT continues to manifest in the carnival scene as evidenced by the political imaginations of contemporary Black British carnivalists and the articulation of their freedom dreams through carnival arts.

We Jammin' Still: *Empowering Black Women through Carnival Arts*

A radical Black feminist spirit of resistance has been an indelible feature of London's carnival scene since the earliest organizational efforts of Claudia Jones and her Caribbean carnivals. In the souvenir program for the 1959 carnival, Jones declared that "A People's Art is the Genesis of their Freedom" (Davies 2008, 167). This spirit has continued to reverberate in London's carnival scene over the years, inspiring new iterations of protests and activism through carnival arts. One example of this can be seen in the work of Stacey Leigh Ross, who blends her art with radical politics and creative forms of activism.

Ross is a forty-plus-year-old Black woman of Trinidadian heritage who began working as a freelance artist in the UK after moving there from Trinidad in 2003. I first met Ross in London at Carnival Expo 2017, a two-day event that can be described as everything you'll ever see related to carnival under one roof (costumes, food, music, art, etc.). Ross was one of the registered vendors selling her art pieces at the event. After surveying her items on display, I began to talk to Ross about specific works that piqued my interest, most notably a painting titled *We Jammin' Still*, which features a full-figured Caribbean woman dressed in "pretty mas" (bikini style) as the centerpiece of the painting. On closer inspection of the piece, I became fascinated with the multilayered collage of images and texts surrounding the woman, which I did not see from afar. As Ross began to provide general information about the painting and insights into its production process, I immediately wanted to learn about the life of the artist, the motivation for her work, and as much about the *We Jammin' Still* painting as possible. So I purchased the piece and set up an interview with her to talk about it in more depth.

In the week following Carnival Expo 2017, Ross and I met near Kings Cross Station in London for our interview. In the nearly two-hour interview, Ross discussed her upbringing in Trinidad and the role carnival and carnival arts have played in her life since she was young. She also provided insights into her development as an artist, including the central role that both women and carnival play as inspirational material for making her pieces. And finally, Ross revealed what led to her political transformation into an activist and how she came to produce art that serves as social commentary on issues concerning Black communities, especially Black women.

During the interview, Ross informed me that she was always very conscious of her Blackness in Britain, as she worked and lived in a rural English town with few Black residents (Royston, Hertfordshire). Additionally, she told me that she felt a certain kind of pressure to suppress aspects of who she was in order to "get ahead" in the UK. However, in 2016, everything changed for her. One of the most significant factors for the change was her participation in Carnival Expo for the first time, which helped her connect to her Trinidadian/Caribbean roots. In our interview in 2017, she shared the following about her experience at Carnival Expo:

> I remember standing at my booth and looking around at all these first- and second-generation Caribbean people, and how colorful they were. And how, you know, their hairstyles, their makeup . . . they were strutting around in their bad suit like we still in Port of Spain [Trinidad]. And I remember thinking to myself, "When did you forget who you were?" It was like roll back the years and think, "You were that person. You used to be like that . . . What the fuck, Stacey?" And then I made a commitment to myself . . . to be Caribbean. I love bright colors. WEAR BRIGHT COLORS! And to bring my sunshine with me wherever I am going regardless of the weather . . . And that was kind of the first stage of "remember who you are."

Prior to Carnival Expo and her return to her roots, Ross spent several years in the UK working odd administrative jobs and not producing art. After she and her husband moved from London to Royston, she went back to making art. Ross became a member of the local arts society and started participating in the Royston Arts Festival. While Ross loved getting back into painting and producing creative works, she told me during the interview that she started to get somewhat bored with her work. She did not feel completely satisfied with what she was producing.

> At first I was just painting to disappear into the painting and to reconnect with the fact that I used to paint and then stopped for eight years. But then, you know, there comes a point when, ok, it's all well and good to experiment with techniques and . . . it's pretty. But my whole ethos of doing art ever since I've known myself has always been to do something that is more than just pretty. *It should serve a purpose.* You know art is a language . . . It's a weapon. And I just wasn't using it . . . So, I started to get quite restless, which is never a bad thing. It just means you're moving up to the next level. And I started realizing, ok, I wanted to do some more community-based

stuff... But it wasn't quite enough. And then there was the whole Stanford rape case thing. And that was in the news. (Emphasis added)

The high-profile case that caught Ross's attention, in which Stanford University student Brock Turner was charged for sexually assaulting an unconscious woman on the school's campus, was broadcast worldwide and covered extensively in the news for months. Though Turner was found guilty of rape, the judge presiding over the case sentenced Turner to only six months in jail; he served just three months of his sentence. Like the #MeToo movement that gained global traction one year later, the results of the Stanford rape case brought glaring attention to the ways in which society and the criminal justice system continue to fail victims of sexual assault, especially women.

The Stanford rape case, including the letter the victim wrote to her assailant during court proceedings,[5] was one of several incidents in 2016 that shook Ross to her core. Other events she shared with me were the buildup to and aftermath of the EU referendum vote in the UK (leading to Brexit) and the widespread reports of police violence against Black American citizens throughout the summer of 2016. She called the latter the "Great Black Manhunt" of 2016.

In the interview, Ross called this period of deep introspection her "awakening"; she chose from that moment onward to no longer be silent about the perpetuation of injustices against marginalized peoples.

> I had quite a few sledgehammers slam into my life... Oh, I cried and bawled my eyes out, but once that excess of emotion was gone I was left in a state of numbness, or so I thought. Turns out it was really deep introspection. I managed only one painting and a handful of doodles in seven months. I just couldn't find the will to paint. It took one year, four life changing events, a trailer-load of lower-level angst, and me paying a lot of attention to my instincts to finally figure it out. It was time for CHANGE. Things started popping up on my radar—violence, rape culture, social injustice, lack of empathy, hate mongering, dirty politics, hate crimes, sex crimes, refugee crises, abuse... And the list goes on.

To bring awareness to these issues, Ross uses her life experiences as a Black woman and her expertise in Caribbean carnival arts as cornerstones of her activist-oriented paintings: "I come from a Caribbean island where the mas' [masquerade] is an art form that speaks each individual's truth. Old calypsos, kaiso and ole mas' used to be THE newspapers of my people. Pretty art is pretty, but powerful art is unforgettable and life changing. And so it began."

The first piece she produced while on this journey is called *We Jammin' Still* (2017). It explicitly addresses abuse and sexual violence against women and girls and combines themes from the Caribbean and traditions of carnival as its foundation.[6]

Ross's *We Jammin' Still* is an adaptation of the hit 2017 soca song by the Ultimate Rejects titled "Full Extreme."[7] The tune was released in December 2016 in advance of the 2017 Trinidad Carnival in February, where it won the Road March title for most played song on the road during carnival that year; the song was also played extensively during Caribbean-styled carnival celebrations around the world, including at London's NHC in August 2017. While "Full Extreme" was the carnival party anthem of the year, the song is infused with social commentary pertaining to the ways vulnerable people in society survive in the face of adversity, as seen in many of the song's lyrics.

> **VERSE 2:**
> Recession doh [don't] bother we
> Promote a fête [party] and you go see
> How we go party to the full extreme
> And light it up with kerosene
> Oh God, the Treasury could burn down
> We jammin' still, we jammin' still
> The economy could fall down
> We jammin' still, we jammin'!

In my interview and follow-up conversations with Ross, she pointed out the song's brilliant use of double entendre to reflect aspects of Trinidadian society.

> Yes, Trinbagonians [people from Trinidad and Tobago] are happy, joyful people who carry on in the face of adversity, BUT we are also people who will bury our noses in our backyards, and so long as *our* party is still going we will ignore everything that is falling down around us. Our greatest strength is also our greatest weakness. And that's true! Trinidadians are so obsessed . . . On one hand, it's a beautiful thing, and on the other hand, it's the thing that's holding us back. We're so obsessed with the party that unless the party stops, people will not rise up. Interrupt the party and then you will see chaos [laughs]. "They do what?! They stop di party?!" That will lead to revolution. And maybe carnival needs to go where it's going to stop the party so that we can start the party again.

With this conceptual backdrop, Ross adapted the tagline "we jammin' still" to provide her own social commentary, which not only addressed cases of domestic violence and sexual abuse against Black women and girls within the context of women's experiences in the modern carnival but also celebrated Black women's agency, femininity, and sexuality.

To begin *We Jammin' Still*, Ross researched cases of abuse and sexual violence against women and girls in the Caribbean and UK and attached statistics and newspaper clippings from cases on the background of the canvas. Some examples of clippings she compiled read: "1 in 5 Jamaican women has experienced physical or sexual violence from her partner in her lifetime"; "42.8% of women's first sexual experience in the Eastern Caribbean was forced"; "1 in 4 children suffer abuse in the eastern Caribbean"; "In the UK, 250,000 teenage girls are suffering from abuse at any one time"; and "10,000 women a year file for restraining orders in T&T [Trinidad & Tobago]." The choice to orient the piece with statistics and newspaper clippings was inspired by the work of London-based photographer and activist Fiona Compton, who started the powerful #NotAskingForIt and #SinceItsNudesYouLike social media campaigns. Portions of the letter written by the victim in the Stanford rape case were placed alongside the statistics and headlines, which Ross burned and discolored using tea bags to symbolize what she described as the "irrevocable damage [in the aftermath of rape] that violently changes a person's life, attitude, [and] body."

In the shadow of these sprawling headlines are three figures strategically placed around the canvas, each a different depiction of women and girls who have suffered some form of abuse: in the bottom-right corner of the painting, a figure of a seated woman has her knees positioned against her chest as if bracing for an attack; in the top left, an image of a woman bends over to comfort an abused child; and just left of center in the painting is the fading image of a traditional Caribbean woman wearing a flowy blue and white dress with a matching headscarf. Finally, there is the figure of the modern Caribbean woman "playing mas" at the center of the painting. Posed with one hand behind her head and the other in the air with a clenched fist, the modern Caribbean woman sports a bikini-style (pretty mas) carnival costume that accentuates the curves of her body, complemented with a gold necklace and bracelets on her wrists and ankles. These accessories (or "glitz," as Ross calls them) operate as a double entendre. On the one hand, her glitz are decorative accent pieces for her carnival costume. On the other hand, Ross revealed to me that "her glitz . . . acts like the shackles

[of] old because she is still shackled by the modern obsession with 'sexy,' by the violence of the past that has stretched into the present, by the teachings of the women before her... Our historical acceptance and expectation of certain behaviors from Caribbean men still shackles us, and them. Unless we understand it and actively work to stop it, we ALL perpetuate it." At the end of the production process, Ross finalized the piece with a red banner with the words "We Jammin' Still"; the banner is held up by the modern Caribbean woman who, despite the barrage of abuse and degradation leveled at her, is empowered to reclaim her agency, her body, her sensuality/sexuality, and her sense of worth.

Like the glitz Ross applied to the costume of the masquerade figure, the banner too is a form of double entendre. It signifies a celebration of self, rooted in enjoyment and pleasure, while also encouraging collective action against sexual violence and abuse: "Yea, I came back and I just cut out that and I put it... and I thought, 'Yea. Now we're jammin.' And for me 'We Jammin' Still' is... we jammin' in spite of all this stuff going on cuz we're strong. But we're [also] jammin' in spite of all this because we refuse to do something about it. And we're still obsessed with pretending it's not happening... So, yea, hopefully in my next forty years, we'll be very, very awake and doing stuff about it."

In sum, *We Jammin' Still* by Stacey Leigh Ross is firmly rooted in a Black radical ethos that points to what feminist scholar Patricia Hill Collins cites as "alternatives to the way things are [and how they are] supposed to be" (2000, 286). In her carnival-inspired, feminist art piece, Ross depicts the Black female body as suspended between histories of oppression and struggles for liberation simultaneously. On the one hand, the Black female body is represented as a unique site of contempt, violence, and exploitation. This can be seen in the volume of statistics and quotes that covers the entire canvas of the work, indicative of the ever-present realities of misogyny, sexism, heteropatriarchy, domestic abuse, and sexual harassment/assault that women face in society. On the other hand, the Black female body is celebrated in the work as a site of knowledge, pleasure, and power, actively subverting racist and heteropatriarchal ideologies that attempt to denigrate Black women's sense of worth through hegemonic forms of control. Finally, insights from the interview with Ross illustrate links between her own political imagination and the development of the *We Jammin' Still* work, where the value of the piece lies not so much in how much she sold it for (I bought it for £130 in support of the artist) but in her personal conviction to use her art as a form of activism to empower Black women and promote social justice for victims of abuse and sexual assault.

Figure 1.1. *We Jammin' Still* (2017). Picture courtesy of Stacey Leigh Ross.

"Appropriate This, Motherfuckers!": On Black Trauma and Creative Resistance

On Carnival Sunday at NHC 2016, I witnessed a man pushing a decorated shopping cart through the congested crowds and giving out rum shots to carnival attendees who engaged him on the street. He was not part of any official NHC performance units and was operating of his own accord. When I spotted him, he was near the intersection of Powis Mews and Talbot Road, just in front of a club called The Globe, where a performance stage for DJs and live musicians had been assembled specifically for carnival. The stage was designed in the shape of a huge white ship, with bold black letters on its side that read "Empire Windrush," and just underneath, "London." The makeshift stage, modeled after the historic *Windrush* ship that brought nearly five hundred passengers from the Caribbean to London in 1948, was intended to celebrate the fiftieth anniversary of the NHC.

The man pushing the shopping cart, Ishmahil Blagrove Jr., is a radical Black activist, resident of Notting Hill, and long-time community organizer in London. He is also an editor for RiceNPeas, an independent film and book publishing company. I first met Blagrove in the summer of 2014 at a launch event for a book he coedited commemorating the history of the NHC. When I got the opportunity to interview him in 2015 and again in 2017, I learned not only the story behind the man but also about his commitment to uplifting the Black communities of Britain and beyond.

Blagrove is of Jamaican parentage and was born in the UK in the late 1960s. For more than thirty years, he has regularly been on the frontlines combatting injustices Black and ethnic minority communities face in the Notting Hill community—most recently the horrific tragedy that befell the Grenfell Tower in June 2017.[8] Discussing his childhood in our initial 2015 interview, Blagrove told me that during the 1960s and '70s, his generation represented the first postwar British-born Black population. They were the children of the *Windrush* and African immigrants. He acknowledged how incredibly diverse these newly established Black communities were culturally (hailing from different Caribbean islands and African countries), at times connecting only on the level of their Blackness. This meant that these groups all faced prejudice and discrimination as racial and ethnic minority communities in Britain. For example, it was in Birmingham, Blagrove recalled, that he was called a "wog," "N-word," and "coon" for the first time; he was only nine years old. He continued, stating that such experiences were instrumental in the "jour-

Figure 1.2. Ishmahil Blagrove (white shirt) pushing his installation piece, *Culture Clash*, at NHC 2016.

ney of formulating and shaping that sense of 'Blackness,'" including "coming back to London [at] about [the age of] ten or eleven and being stopped by the police for just wearing a silver ring," his first personal encounter of police harassment. These incidents were fundamental in shaping how he came to know himself and his precarious situation in Britain—born of this society yet rejected by it, existing in a kind of "limbo space," he told me. Consequently, experiences of racism and police harassment and an awareness of widespread inequalities led to his participation in a number of grassroots social justice organizations from his youth through adulthood. These have spanned several continents, including North America (the Caribbean specifically), Africa, and Europe. Regarding his activism, Blagrove stated: "I believe that even now, to this very day, my whole lifeblood is about the Black struggles, the Black experience, about bettering and improving who we are as a people. And I don't believe it should always be about protest, you know what I mean. It shouldn't be when someone is getting their head top lick off by police that you're out on the streets. There are other ways that we could be doing this even in times

Figure 1.3. Carnival attendee receives free shot of rum at Blagrove's interactive installation, NHC 2016.

of peace, or not even peace cuz there's never peace, through film, media, etc., you know what I'm saying." One way Blagrove has attempted to bring attention to these issues and address them is through the exhibition of interactive art pieces at NHC. Blagrove's 2015 carnival piece, *Spirit of Resistance*, is one example.

Spirit of Resistance is a compilation piece of African diasporic spirituality explored through themes of ritual, remembrance, and resistance. Two components of the art installation give the piece its unique characteristics. One is a thematically designed shopping cart that has been repurposed for carnival. The other is the "rider" himself (i.e., Blagrove, who journeys through the streets with the cart on carnival day). The shopping cart is designed with various artifacts, images, and symbols of ritual, remembrance, and resistance from across the African diaspora. For example, on the front of the cart, one finds the unification of several Afro-Atlantic religious orders displayed: *Regla de Ochà*, *Vodun*, *Candomblé*, *Abakua*, and *Ifá*, each of which is practiced among descendants of enslaved Africans throughout the Americas today.

In addition to these, there is a silver soprano saxophone turned upright with yellow flowers in its bell and the names of deceased pioneers of NHC on its keys, as well as a Red Stripe beer banner on the side of the cart with the names of important figures of NHC who were still alive in 2015. Around the frames of the cart are the words "freedom," "resistance," and "anti-establishment," and a gambling table placed on top of the cart has a sign that reads "any double wins free shot."

Beyond the cart, the other crucial component of *Spirit of Resistance* is Blagrove himself. His attire consists of an African hunter's jacket with the names "Dutty Boukman," "Nat Turner," and "Tate & Lyle" (the sugar company) inscribed on the back.[9] He also has the word "Free" on his cuffs. Finally, in the interior of his jacket are various stitchings of African symbols, as well as a British passport and the phrases "Listen to the universe," "Feel the energies around you," and "Surrender to nature."

Regarding the ideology behind the *Spirit of Resistance* carnival piece, Blagrove stated the following in our 2015 interview:

> It's about a continual struggle, the battle being passed on [he shows me a calendar with images of Black freedom fighters titled *Spirits of Resistance*] . . . It's about the characters of the struggle. It's not just about THE Black struggle. It's a universal struggle, you know what I'm saying? There is crossover . . . I believe there is a connection within a certain movement or a message that can be learned from their own struggles [the different struggles of Black freedom fighters] and incorporated into present-day Black struggles . . . We connect the dots through this constant theme of resistance.

In the interview, Blagrove also informed me that the piece is designed to be interactive, and the entire endeavor—researching material, collecting artifacts, assembling the piece, and exhibiting it on the streets—is a personal, "spiritual journey" for him. It is interactive in the sense that carnival attendees, most of whom are white, directly engage with Blagrove and his presentation on the streets. They stop to talk to him and take pictures of and with him, and he gets them to participate in his game—roll a double, win a free shot of alcohol (see fig. 1.3). For the general carnival attendee looking to drink, dance, and have a good time, this game is very enticing. However, the game is a recoding of the centuries-long oppression and denigration of people of African descent at the hands of Europeans and the British, and Blagrove persuades white carnival revelers to consume the pain (figuratively speaking) completely unbeknownst to them. This is achieved through the symbolism of the items on the cart, including rum and sugar, where Blagrove transfers the strife of enslaved Africans and their descendants on white carnival attendees by getting them to drink his rum for "free."

> This is a subtle piece of work. It might be in your face; it does seem blatant. But when I'm out in the carnival, and I'm serving white people, you know what I mean. I'm giving them refined sugar. And they're thinking, "Oh this is great! Oh, this is wonderful!" And then people come up to me and say, "Well, why you giving this to people for free?" Cuz I'm giving them [white people] rum for free. I don't charge them. "I'm giving it [centuries of exploitation and oppression] back." ... This is a spiritual journey, for me. It's a part of the energy; they won't even understand the context, stuff like ... [pointing], you know what I mean, Tate & Lyle, the sugar producer. They won't understand the significance of that. It's just a logo for them. But Tate & Lyle was one of the largest sugar producers. They didn't necessarily participate in the essence of slavery, but they came off the back of slavery ... It still comes out of colonialism.

Continuing about the significance of symbolism in his piece, Blagrove shared:

> There is so much symbolism in here ... me riding this coat with a British passport. If you're going to go traveling, you need a passport, yea? You can't get as far without a passport. For me, it's about symbolism and references. And of course you get people saying, "Well, what does that mean?" or "What a pretty jacket!" "Ah, that's really nice!" "I really like it!" Then, there will be those people who will be appreciating it aesthetically and going, "Ah, that is really fantastic!" You get that all the time when you come out with a piece and everything else. And again, *they don't understand ... our conceptions of art. They are not valued ... So yea, this is a challenge to that. Appropriate this, motherfuckers!* (Emphasis added)

The latter portion of his statement speaks to how the carnival space has been co-opted over the years by mostly white middle-class attendees, who in Blagrove's estimation have no idea what carnival is or why it even exists; it is treated as just a "jump up" in the streets. For Blagrove, the meaning and value of carnival have become corrupted through the continued lack of cultural understanding regarding the purpose behind NHC and the lack of acknowledgment of its particular historical development in the context of rampant anti-Black racism in Britain. Blagrove's art piece, however, jolts those in proximity to his presentation out of their comfort zone of simply partying in the streets and forces the predominately white attendees to reckon with the historical continuum of Black trauma: the legacies of slavery, colonialism, and empire, as well as the realities of contemporary Black oppression in the UK. In a conversation in 2017, Blagrove explained to me that:

The piece embod[ies] our history. It speaks of all of those experiences, from slavery to the present condition ... It is saying we are still here. It is saying we're not giving up. It is saying that there's still fighting, there's still pushing, there's still the challenge of inequality, and we're still fighting for equal rights, and to be represented and recognized as human beings, you know what I mean, and on planet Earth as equal owners, with an equal destiny and an equal vision. That needs to be seen. We need to be seen. We are not seen. And that I think, to me, is what it represents.

Insights from Blagrove on the intention and aims of his piece reveal the depths to which his artistic creativity and sensibilities are linked to his radical political imagination. In transforming the streets into an interactive gallery, Blagrove attempts to reconstruct power relations that exist between himself and white carnival attendees in the London carnival space. In the process of this reconstruction, Blagrove uses forms of creative activism to not only make visible the historical continuum of trauma that Black people in the UK have had to endure due to legacies of slavery, colonialism, and empire but also affirm Black humanity and the potency of Black cultural and political presence in postwar Britain today.

Conclusions

This chapter has investigated manifestations of festival activism in London's carnival scene as distinct, artistic renderings of Black radicalism. In doing so, it has showed how the political imagination of Black carnivalists in the UK is connected to Black liberation struggles, past and present, and their desires to bring new social worlds into being. As such, Black British carnivalists have historically used carnival art, music, and performance as means to convert the legacies of trauma, marginality, and exploitation into forms of solidarity and empowerment; they continue to do so today in radically creative ways.

In both ethnographic examples of contemporary artworks by UK carnivalists Stacey Leigh Ross and Ishmahil Blagrove Jr., it is evident that the past is never truly the past. Instead, it exists as traces of history that continue to inform the present. In this way, the legacies of chattel slavery, the plantation complex, colonialism, and empire are understood not as far-gone experiences that are behind us but as ever-present specters that reanimate into new forms of anti-Black racism. This, I argue, is why literature on the BRT is so important and why it is particularly useful for analyses of Afro-diasporic carnival art and festival activism among Black carnivalists. The BRT provides a crucial lens for understanding Black people not simply as victims of history but as some of its many complex agents. Moreover, by interrogating history from below, centered on the perspectives and experiences of people of African descent, the BRT shines an important spotlight on Black politics and culture as foundational tools in Black world-making projects.

Afro-diasporic carnivals are microcosms of these world-making projects and serve as critical spaces where the freedom dreams of Black people are expressed through carnival arts. Considering this, scholarship on the BRT has much to contribute to carnival studies by offering tools and frameworks for analyzing the interrelationship between Black political struggle and diasporic relations, connections, and cultural production. In the Afro-diasporic carnival complex, protest and activism are not only a means for artists to speak truth to power in the here and now; they are, in and of themselves, also unique articulations of potential future worlds that are more free and just for people of African descent.

Notes

1. For information on the economic impact of the carnival, see the 2024 online article written by Vic Montune for *The Voice*, https://www.voice-online.co.uk/news/uk-news/2024/08/02/carnival-generates-396-million-for-londons-economy/.

2. The politicization of race in postwar Britain can most notably be seen in relation to Black immigration. Examples of this can be seen in a number of instances, including the following: The "Keep Britain White" campaigns of Oswald Mosley in the 1950s; the "if you want a n*gger for a neighbor, vote Labour" slogan used during the 1964 general elections; Enoch Powell's infamous "Rivers of Blood" speech (1968) regarding his detestation of Black immigration and fears of white minoritization in Britain; Prime Minister Margaret Thatcher's comments on Britain being "swamped by an alien culture" (1978); and Prime Minister David Cameron's criticisms of "state multiculturalism" as perpetuating radicalization and terrorism (2011).

3. "Green for Grenfell" was a campaign launched by the organizing entity of the NHC in which many carnival bands, such as London's KCS band, showed solidarity for the seventy-two victims of the Grenfell Tower fire who died in June 2017. At exactly 3 p.m. on Carnival Sunday and Monday in 2017, the entire festival ceased normal operations and observed a moment of silence for the victims. This is the only time in my five-year experience of attending NHC that the festival grounds were ever unilaterally quiet.

4. Masquerade and calypso are two of the most important performance arenas in Caribbean carnivals. Masquerade is simultaneously a carnival art form, performance, and cultural practice that combines costuming with theater, drama, sculpture, music, and dance. Calypso is a folk-turned-popular-music genre that developed

in the Caribbean in the late nineteenth to early twentieth century in the context of carnival. Calypso songs, sometimes referred to as "kaisos," feature elements of topical commentary whereas calypsonians use different communicative devices such as humor, satire, innuendo, word play, double entendre, and protest to share knowledge, observations, or views on various subjects through artful storytelling.

5. For the letter written by the victim in the Stanford rape case, see Baker 2016.

6. Ross also disclosed to me that she was working on an exhibition titled *Some Lives Matter*. The title of the exhibition-in-progress serves as a direct critique to the slogan "All Lives Matter," itself a repudiation of Black Lives Matter as a philosophy and movement. For further details, see Ross, "#somelivesmatter," April 7, 2018, https://www.byleigh.com/somelivesmatter/.

7. Soca is a popular music genre in the Caribbean associated with the celebration of carnival. It is one of the primary styles of music one hears on the road during carnival and at Caribbean fêtes.

8. For a news report on the Grenfell Tower fire tragedy, see "Grenfell Tower: What Happened," *BBC News*, October 29, 2019, https://www.bbc.com/news/uk-40301289.

9. Boukman and Turner are legendary freedom fighters who instigated slave insurrections of significant import in the Americas. Boukman was a vodou priest and leader who took part in the Haitian Revolution (1791–1804), while Turner led a slave revolt in Southampton County, Virginia, in 1831.

Bibliography

Alleyne-Dettmers, P. 1997. "'Tribal Arts': A Case Study of Global Compression in the Notting Hill Carnival." In *Living the Global City: Globalization as a Local Process*, edited by John Eade, 161–78. London: Routledge.

Alleyne-Dettmers, P. 1998. "Ancestral Voices: Trevini—A Case Study of Meta-masking in the Notting Hill Carnival." *Journal of Material Culture* 3(2): 201–21.

Alleyne-Dettmers, P. 2002. "Black Kings: Aesthetic Representation in Carnival in Trinidad and London." *Black Music Research Journal* 22(2): 241–58.

Alleyne-Dettmers, P. 2005. "The Relocation of Trinidad Carnival in Notting Hill, London and the Politics of Diasporisation." In *Globalisation, Diaspora, & Caribbean Popular Culture*, edited by Christine G. T. Ho and Keith Nurse, 64–89. Kingston, Jamaica: Ian Randle.

Arnaud, Lionel. 2020. "Carnival as Contentious Performance: A Comparison between Contemporary Fort-de-France, Pointe-à-Pitre, and London Carnivals." *Journal of Festive Studies* 2(1): 179–202.

Baker, Katie J. M. 2016. "Here Is the Powerful Letter the Stanford Victim Read Aloud to Her Attacker." *BuzzFeed News*, June 3, 2016. https://www.buzzfeed.com/katiejmbaker/heres-the-powerful-letter-the-stanford-victim-read-to-her-ra.

Bakhtin, Mikhail. 1984. *Rabelais and His World*. Translated by Hélène Iswolsky. Bloomington: Indiana University Press.

Blagrove Jr., Ishmahil, and Margaret Busby. 2014. *Carnival: A Photographic and Testimonial History of the Notting Hill Carnival*. London: RICENPEAS.

Bunce, Robin, and Paul Field. 2014. *Darcus Howe: A Political Biography*. London: Bloomsbury Academic.

Burr, Angla. 2006. "The 'Freedom of Slaves to Walk the Streets': Celebration, Spontaneity, and Revelry versus Logistics at the Notting Hill Carnival." In *Festivals, Tourism, and Social Change*, edited by David Picard and Mike Robinson, 84–97. Clevedon: Channel View.

Burton, Richard D. E. 1997. *Afro-Creole: Power, Opposition, and Play in the Caribbean*. Ithaca, NY: Cornell University Press.

Cohen, Abner. 1980. "Drama and Politics in the Development of a London Carnival." *Man* 15(1): 65–87.

Cohen, Abner. 1982. "A Polyethnic London Carnival as a Contested Cultural Performance." *Ethnic and Racial Studies* 5(1): 23–41.

Cohen, Abner. 1993. *Masquerade Politics: Explorations in the Structure of Urban Cultural Movements*. Berkeley: University of California Press.

Collins, Patricia Hill. 2000. *Black Feminist Thought: Knowledge, Consciousness, and the Politics of Empowerment*. 2nd ed. New York: Routledge.

Cowley, John. 1996. *Carnival, Canboulay and Calypso: Traditions in the Making*. New York: Cambridge University Press.

Crichlow, Michaeline A., and Piers Armstrong. 2010. "Carnival Praxis, Carnivalesque Strategies and Atlantic Interstices." *Social Identities* 16(4): 399–414.

Davies, Carole Boyce. 2008. "Carnival and Diaspora: Caribbean Community, Happiness, and Activism." In *Left of Karl Marx: The Political Life of Black Communist Claudia Jones*, 167–90. Durham, NC: Duke University Press.

Dunn, Christopher. 1992. "Afro-Bahian Carnival: A Stage for Protest." *Afro-Hispanic Review* 11(1/3): 11–20.

Ferdinand, Nicole, et al. 2013. *Carnival Futures: Notting Hill Carnival 2020*. London: King's Cultural Institute.

Guilbault, Jocelyne. 2007. *Governing Sound: The Cultural Politics of Trinidad's Carnival Musics*. Chicago: University of Chicago Press.

Gutzmore, Cecil. 2000. "Carnival, the State and the Black Masses in the United Kingdom." In *Black British Culture and Society: A Text Reader*, edited by Kwesi Owusu, 361–76. London: Routledge.

Henry, Francis, and Dwaine Plaza, eds. 2019. *Carnival Is Woman: Feminism and Performance in Caribbean Mas*. Jackson: University Press of Mississippi.

Henry, Jeff. 2008. *Under the 'Mas': Resistance and Rebellion in the Trinidad Carnival*. Trinidad: Lexicon.

Hill, Errol. (1972) 1997. *The Trinidad Carnival: Mandate for a National Theatre*. London: New Beacon Books.

Jackson, Peter. 1988. "Street Life: The Politics of Carnival." *Environment and Planning: Society and Space* 6(2): 213–27.

Kelley, Robin D. G. 2002. *Freedom Dreams: The Black Radical Imagination.* Boston: Beacon Press.

La Rose, Michael. 1989. *"Police Carnival" 1989: A Report on the 1989 Notting Hill Carnival.* London: Association for a People's Carnival.

Liverpool, Hollis. 2001. *Rituals of Power and Rebellion: The Carnival Tradition in Trinidad and Tobago, 1763–1962.* Chicago: Frontline Distribution.

Manning, Frank E. 1978. "Carnival in Antigua (Caribbean Sea): An Indigenous Festival in a Tourist Economy." *Anthropos* 73(1/2): 191–204.

Nurse, Keith. 1999. "Globalization and Trinidad Carnival: Diaspora, Hybridity and Identity in Global Culture." *Culture Studies* 13(4): 661–90.

Race Today Collective. 1977. *The Road Make to Walk on Carnival Day: The Battle for the West Indian Carnival in Britain.* London: Race Today Collective.

Ramnarine, Tina K. 2007. *Beautiful Cosmos: Performance and Belonging in the Caribbean Diaspora.* London: Pluto Press.

Robinson, Cedric. (1983) 2000. *Black Marxism: The Making of the Black Radical Tradition.* Chapel Hill: University of North Carolina Press.

Rohlehr, Gordon. 1990. *Calypso & Society in Pre-independence Trinidad.* Port of Spain, Trinidad: Gordon Rohlehr.

Sherwood, Marika. 1999. *Claudia Jones: A Life in Exile.* London: Lawrence and Wishart.

Turner, Victor. 1967. "Betwixt and Between: The Liminal Period in *Rites de Passage.*" In *The Forest of Symbols: Aspects of Ndembu Ritual,* 93–111. Ithaca, NY: Cornell University Press.

Turner, Victor. 1977. *The Ritual Process: Structure and Anti-structure.* Ithaca, NY: Cornell Paperbacks.

Turner, Victor. 1988. *The Anthropology of Performance.* New York: PAJ.

TWO

Rethinking Relational Geometries in Musical Events in Europe

Artistic Devices and Activist Implications

FILIPPO BONINI BARALDI

One of the most important achievements of ethnomusicological research has been to show that music is able to create many different *relational geometries*, by which I refer to the ways in which human bodies relate to other human bodies or other types of agents in a determined context. In Seville, people walk together for hours during an Easter procession, addressing *saetas* chants to the Christ; in Balinese *kecac*, dozens of men form a circular, collective body, performing interlocking rhythmic formulas; during *Toraja* funerals in Indonesia, several groups of peasants sing in the same space, but in a highly asynchronized fashion. Any valuable ethnography shows that the ways of being together in music are manifold, and each responds to particular social and existential needs.

What is remarkable, however, is not the fact that we can find this variety in different regions of the world but rather that such diversity generally exists within one group of people. To give an example I know closely, in a small Roma village of Transylvania, the performance modes, relational geometries, and social configurations engendered by the musical act vary according to the season, context, and public and can take the form of a point, line, triangle, square, or circle, so to speak (Bonini Baraldi 2021).[1] In my view, this is what defines a rich musical culture: one in which the musical act allows a variety of possible dynamics of being together, a multitude of relational geometries, an affirmation of the individual as a multiple social being. As Beaudet writes, "thus, by their contrasts, the different *wayãpi* musics [of French Guiana] allow the expression of several personalities, several simultaneous personalities for the same individual; they define the person as a multiple social being.

Indeed, the acts of music even appear as so many places of passage of the person; and, among these, wouldn't the *tule* be the ones which, above all and in a more profound way, bring into play the contradiction inherent in these passages?" (1997, 137).

Conversely, I view an impoverished musical culture as one in which the relational geometries people can experience through music are slim, always the same, frozen into a static pattern—one in which the individual's movement and development are flattened into a predictable, normative pathway.

In the first part of this chapter, I argue that Parisian musical life at the beginning of the twenty-first century is, contrary to what one may think, an example of an impoverished musical culture in many respects. I suggest that, despite the enormous variety of musical genres one can find in the city, most musical acts feature highly standardized relational geometries and highly normative dispositions of bodies, which are essentially the same for almost every type of music played. Following Jacques Rancière's critical thoughts on political art (2008), I propose that this impoverishment is a fundamental issue that reduces society into a "regime of consensus" in which we perceive the same things and give them the same meaning. I further suggest that ethnomusicologists, now that the discipline has become more applied and engaged, should combat this trend toward impoverishment. But how? Certainly not by constraining more "traditional" musical forms into the configuration of the Western concert format, as often happens in world music festivals—instead, we should learn from the relational geometries we have observed in the world and create new spaces, situations, and opportunities where music can foster multiple dispositions of bodies and heterogeneous sensible experiences.

In the second part of this chapter, I describe two festival projects in which we sought to concretely address these concerns.[2] In an event called Bal des Pianos, organized in the Parisian suburb of Montreuil, we experimented with an ensemble of counterdevices that allowed us to contrast the dominance of the presentational (Turino 2008), "frontal" geometry of musical acts and, more widely, the norms of Parisian musical life. These same counterdevices—as far as they allowed the expression and experience of values of difference, margins, heterogeneity, and multiplicity in reaction to those of the norm, center, consensus, and uniformity—resonated with activist concerns in areas other than the arts. In the EU-funded project European Festival of Diversities and Antidiscrimination, we joined LGBTQI+, migrant women, and Roma activists and organized the Bal of Diversities in several European cities.

In the final section, I discuss how these musical and ethnomusicological experimentations, besides providing direct, musical support in defense of specific activist concerns, have broader political, even utopian, implications.

Paris at the Beginning of the Twenty-First Century: An Impoverished Musical Life

Having been involved in Parisian musical life for over fifteen years, I have progressively developed quite a pessimistic view on how music is performed, acted, and lived on a day-to-day basis. Three fundamental issues are at the center of my concerns.

The first issue goes well beyond music and ethnomusicology and concerns contemporary life in neoliberal urban centers. As in other metropolitan cities, in Paris everyone seems perpetually busy, caught up in a thousand things, and spending a great amount of time in transport. The rhythm of daily life, dependent on high costs of living and therefore on salaried work, gives the impression of never having time to propose, invent, or simply participate in life's collective moments, whether conveyed by music or not. Naturally, people meet and communities form, but these communities tend to bring together similar cohorts of people, who share the same skin color, social status, ideas, and tastes. The multiculturalism that Paris boasts is not necessarily synonymous with interculturalism, and communities are often, in reality, closed singularities: groups that remain impermeable to each other, closed on themselves. Music venues can exacerbate this separation. Each one, attempting to differentiate itself from the others and attract paying spectators, specializes in a genre (rock, French song, experimental music, etc.), favoring the formation of communities of tastes (rockers, nerds, folkies, etc.) that rarely mix. How can we hope, in this environment, to weave new relationships, to see the emergence of new, active, and critical communities?

A second critical point concerns the ultraregulated, ultrastandardized way in which life in general, and musical life in particular, is governed in neoliberal urban centers like Paris. When music becomes primarily a commodity, everything must fit into a clearly identifiable box, each with specific standards and procedures. Transversal paths, multiple identities, and the occupation of interstices are perceived as suspicious, escaping labeling and control. Music is by no means excluded from these norms and restrictions. It is forbidden to play music in public space, with the exception of some touristic spots. Even if you want to play in the subway, you need to pass an audition and obtain authorization. Established in 1982, the *fête de la musique*, during which everyone meets in the streets on June 21 to play, is quite a carnivalesque paradox: we are invited to celebrate, one day a year, what we cannot do throughout the rest of the year. While we know that public space is a privileged place to perform music, we have decided to confine music to places explicitly provided for it: theaters, clubs, bars, and the like (e.g., Watt 2016). In addition to restrictions in space, we add restrictions in time. The time limits for making music are excessive, and antinoise laws are rather antidemocratic: one vote "against" (a neighbor who calls the police because musicians are playing in the street) is worth more than a hundred votes "for" (neighbors who are happy that something is happening in their neighborhood). To all these factors, we add the gentrification of working-class neighborhoods, traditionally more open to common use of space and time (e.g., Sakakeeny 2013; Cardoso 2019; Martin 2021; Snyder 2022). Here, more and more prohibitions are gradually introduced to satisfy the new inhabitants (e.g., Clerval 2013). From my point of view, all these norms and restrictions impede the development of a more creative and varied artistic life.

The third critical point has to do with the performance mode (or model, or device) characterizing most musical events in Paris, as in other urban centers. This mode—what has been called the Western "presentational" (Turino 2008) or "frontal" concert—is basically the same for any musical genre, and it can be briefly described as follows. Musical performances are confined to the space and time for leisure, generally on weekend evenings. Their duration is always between one and two hours. The performance space is always organized with a clear separation between artists and public, in a frontal relationship. The stage becomes an essential element of musical performance; its size reflects the prestige of the event and the artists. The sound system is often exaggerated, with a predilection for high volume. The management of musical venues is in the hands of private corporations, aiming for nothing other than profit, and entrance fees exclude those who cannot afford them. The security of the clubs is entrusted to private companies, which often operate excessively, if not aggressively.

This performance mode is linked to the history of Western music (Italian-style theater, technology, the emergence of the bourgeoisie, etc.) and the outcome of a process that, in European cities, saw art become autonomous from other human activities (work, rituals, religion, etc.; see Artaud [1938] 1964; Goehr 1989). As this performance mode is a product of a specific culture, it would be naive to attempt to replace it with another model or even to suppress it. It would be naive as well to argue that our musical life has become impoverished because we no longer sing while harvesting wheat. Indeed, the problem is not so much the device as the fact that every musical act, every type of music, conforms and is systematically reduced to this performance mode. This is what I mean when I say that we are living an impoverishment of relational geometries—the ways in which bodies relate to other bodies in a determined space-time are strongly reduced. Through repeated participation in the same performance mode, we develop a specific listening habitus, a set of physical and emotional dispositions that are inscribed in our bodies, often implicitly, and inform acceptable forms of behavior in a given situation (Bourdieu 1980, Becker 2001). When musical acts, regardless of formal differences between genre, always generate the same relational geometry, then emotions conform, bodies freeze, relationships crystallize, consensus and passivity set in. We have lost the possibility of experiencing a multitude of relational geometries, a plurality of configurations of being together, an ensemble of situations in which the person develops as a multiple social being. A dominant, normative performative model dictates any musical act, limiting participants' actions, expectations, and physical and emotional dispositions. This is what I view as the impoverishment of our musical life, which needs to be denounced and changed. As Jacques Rancière (2008) puts it:

> The problem of political art does not concern the moral or political validity of the message transmitted by the representative device. It concerns the device itself. Its fissure reveals that the effectiveness of art does not consist in transmitting messages, giving models or counter-models of behavior or learning to decipher representations. It consists, first of all, in the disposition of bodies, in the division of singular spaces/times that define ways of being together or separated, in front of, or in the middle of, inside or outside, close or distant (60). . . . The political question is, first of all, that of the ability of anybody to seize its destiny. (88)

If we agree with this analysis, we may ask, Should this impoverishment call for action, and who is best positioned to propose concrete solutions? What can or should ethnomusicologists do? How can actions in the musical domain meet with other activist concerns, other social preoccupations?

Ethnomusicologists and the Problematic Staging of the World's Musical Traditions

Since the works of renowned figures of our discipline (Merriam 1964; Blacking 1973; Rouget 1980), we—ethnomusicologists—have convincingly shown that music, beyond a simple acoustic matter, is a tool to manage human interactions, to question the place of the individual in the group, to accompany the "becoming-other" of the subject (Beaudet 1997), and to foster different dynamics of being together. Having documented the importance of music for human beings, we should therefore be in a good position to counteract and denounce the impoverishment that strikes urban European musical life and propose alternatives. However, when we leave the academy and observe how we contribute to the musical life of the *cité*, or urban community, it seems to me that we often only participate in its impoverishment. The most obvious example is the way ethnomusicologists, at least in France, stage the world's musical traditions. More and more festivals and concerts request our mediation and expertise. In some cases, they offer us the opportunity to invite musicians we have met in the field, which gives us the impression of rebalancing a power relationship intrinsic to the discipline (the Westerner who travels to study the "other"). I have operated in this capacity, accompanying Roma musicians from Transylvania to French world music festivals. But why is this problematic?

To find a place on the program of a traditional or world music festival, any "other," or foreigner, must necessarily be distinguished from another "other." Consequently, people are hyperethnicized: their cultural or ethnic identity is often displayed in an exaggerated, even grotesque way. To give an example, images on a festival website display Croatian villagers who, during village meals, get up in small groups of three or four to sing short songs (*ganga*) of about thirty seconds, glass in hand. When the same people are invited to perform at the prestigious Maison des Cultures du Monde in central Paris, they wear traditional attire and carry an "ethnic" glass in hand.[3] Here, the performance consists of an hour and a half of singing on stage in front of an audience seated in a concert hall. The original relational geometry (a collective banquet in public space) is violently transplanted into a performance mode that stands still (a concert on stage). The entire social process, the set of social interactions that gives life and meaning to these sound forms, is left in place under the pretext that it is not adaptable to our venues. Why are we not capable, as ethnomusicologists and active, critical citizens, to stop the car traffic in Boulevard Raspail, where the Maison des Cultures du Monde is located, and organize a banquet in the public space, where we would invite the Croatian peasant to eat, drink, and sing? Even worse, the original process, the Croatian village banquet, becomes endangered: singers get into the habit, once they get home, of asking for a stage and a sound system, perceived as a sign of prestige.

Of course, this problem is not new, and those who have organized world music concerts or festivals know well that the Western performance format is unsuitable for many musics of the world. In a short text published in 1999, Bernard Lortat-Jacob imagines an alternative theater room where it would be possible to disseminate differently—and, therefore, to understand differently—the artistic expressions of other cultures. He imagines a modular space able to break down the frontal character of performance, where the public would be free to move around, lie down, eat a meal, and so on. A venue of this type would undoubtedly be a step forward, since the good intentions that motivate the programming of world musics do not justify such submission to a typically Western conception of musical performance (the concert format).

However, the problem I point to is not an architectural one but a social one. The standardization of listening habits, of the musician-spectator relationship, of the space and duration of musical performances; the increasing control over participants' movements and actions; the tendency toward simplification rather than complexification of musical acts—all are the consequence of a logic of power and profit, which generates distances and hierarchies rather than encounters and equity (see also Kheshti 2015). Antonin Artaud ([1938] 1964), in a chapter emblematically titled "En finir avec les chefs-d'œuvres" (Enough with the masterpieces), denounces this problem loud and clear, but his cry has gone generally unheard. Neither have been heard the hypotheses of Merriam (1964), Blacking (1973), or Rouget (1980), which can be summarized with the famous adage: "Music is much more than music." The theoretical message of ethnomusicology, when confronted with the way world music is (dis)played in festival and concerts, has no practical existence. We ethnomusicologists continue to disseminate musical and ethnic forms hollowed of the social processes and relational geometries that generate them. We believe we are enriching ourselves with more and more images and sounds, whereas I suggest we are impoverishing the quality of human relations music has the power to generate. We are cannibals of cultures: what matters to us are ethnic representations and the sound representations that go with them (see also hooks 1992).

Experimenting with Counterdevices: The Bal des Pianos

In response to this standardized, normative, impoverished way of experiencing music—including in genres marketed as world musics—we urgently need to advance countermodels, counterproposals, counterstrategies. I am certainly not the only one to sound the alarm. For many years now, contemporary composers have been looking for alternatives to the presentational mode of sound diffusion and the architecture of musical venues. In a different domain, free parties and rave parties have opened possibilities for the musical act (abandoned factories, rural areas, etc.) that go beyond the restrictions of urban dance clubs (see Kosmicki 2010). As for our collective, we organized an event called Bal des Pianos, which took place in a disused piano factory of Montreuil, a Parisian suburb. For several years (2005–2011), we experimented with a set of counterdevices inspired by musical and social processes that exist in other regions of the world. My role as an ethnomusicologist was to provide examples (ethnographic descriptions, pictures, videos, films) that allowed us to put into practice new relational geometries, new ways of experiencing space, time, movement, interactions in the musical act. Here I briefly describe the work topics that stood at the heart of our action over the years.

Temporality

We wanted to give the musical event a broader temporality, circumventing the rules governing live performances in Paris. Indeed, in many societies, musical events (rituals, feasts, processions, etc.) have a much longer duration than the one hour and thirty minutes or two hours generally accorded in most European cities. Our balls lasted about twelve hours, usually at night, between 7 p.m. and 7 a.m. The time necessary for the preparation of the ball was also a fundamental concern. We asked for venues to be available throughout the week preceding the ball. Long-term occupation of the space allowed us to not only prepare the venue but also collectively discuss political and social questions at the heart of the project. It provided a way of meeting closely with the foreign musicians we regularly invited. Having attended world music festivals, we knew that "traditional" musicians are often tossed about from one concert or festival to another without really having time to forge relationships with their hosts, the public, or other musicians present. This temporality allowed us to open a reflective time, to create a space of life rather than a space of show, to put the music at work rather than make a work of music.

Scale, Density

On average, the number of musicians involved in the ball was eighty, but we also worked with extremes ranging from ten to one hundred and fifty musicians. The number of spectators was seven hundred on average, with at most fifteen hundred people. Why these numbers? Our aim was to create a popular gathering open to all that maintained proximity between the musicians and public. More than the number of spectators or musicians, the ratio between the two interested us. With time, we found that the ideal density allowing music to work, so to speak, was one musician for every twelve to twenty people. This was a critical response to events commonly organized in the music industry where four or five musicians play in front of hundreds or even thousands of people.

Space, Scenography, Sound System

These crowds required fairly large locations, so space was another fundamental line of reflection and action. The basic idea was to erase any focal, definitive, or unambiguous center: no specific space was attributed to any function (playing, watching, eating, drinking, sitting, etc.). We were continually reconfiguring the venue, abnormalizing the flow of people in order to avoid the stillness of bodies, perceptions, and relationships. Scenographers, architects, manufacturers, and light engineers were associated with the project from the beginning. Rather than organizing the venue as a setting for a concert, their role was to design devices allowing the reconfiguration of the space in real time according to needs, desires, densities, and above all, the type of music played. This work included, among other things, the creation of mobile stages, retractable walls, and objects of uncertain use, such as inflatables structures.[4] Reconfigurations of the space were meant to break expectations and disrupt flows. Everything was not constantly moving, but everyone could occupy any place for an indefinite period for the deployment of a particular action (playing, talking, eating, etc.). The variability of paths and multifunctionality of the space resulted in a heterogeneity of lived experiences, stimulating the participants' encounters, debates, and stories.

The musicians were invited to take a critical look at the unfolding of the event and occupy empty, marginal spaces rather than a central stage. The intent was to favor circulations and multiply possible perspectives, thus avoiding the centrality and unidirectionality of the gaze and ear. We did not acoustically isolate the various spaces where musicians were playing; on the contrary, we left them permeable to each other. As a result of this particular configuration, the ball offered moments of sound superposition where different musics mingled voluntarily. These intersecting acoustic spaces had the same interest for us as each musical performance itself, and we worked them out just as if we were working out a specific repertoire.

The balance of musicians and audience allowed us to work with minimally invasive sound systems. Although we favored acoustic sound, we allowed amplified sound when it was part of the musical work. The stage was an object of work without systematic evidence. In other words, we did not refuse it, but we did not make regular use of it. Musicians sometimes performed on a stage, sometimes around a table, on the floor, on a mobile cart, or on the bleachers where spectators usually sit. The site was always open to creative proposals that could surprise without becoming anecdotal or sacrificing the quality of sound.

Musicians

Some bands were formed within our own collective, and others were already existing. Most musicians played repertoires from various regions of the world with the intent of making people dance. Among others, we worked with Roma musicians from Moldavia, Transylvania, Epirus; Tsapiky bands from Madagascar; Malian griots; and Algerian Gnawa. However, it was important for us to work with a multiplicity of musical genres: contemporary music, improvised music, free jazz, punk rock, and the like. This mixture of genres was a way of mixing audiences—communities of tastes—but also of questioning our listening habits. A chamber music trio or Roma fanfare could trigger completely different responses depending on the time, space, and mirror effect generated by the simultaneous presence of other types of music. We wanted to avoid any overspectacularization, overethnicization, or overexoticization of the musical performance and the musicians themselves. In the eyes of the public, the Roma, Malian, or Malagasy musicians were not exotic foreigners, just musicians among other musicians. In the Bal des Pianos, cultural otherness was caught in an ensemble of multidimensional, multipolar relationships and interactions, limiting the danger of an exotic, distancing gaze.

Program, Scenario

How could we coordinate one hundred musicians in a collective, twelve-hour musical event? Our goal was to avoid any predetermined program as much as possible. In other words, the musicians could jump into action whenever they wanted. We tried to counter the habits of show business, such as the tendency of musicians to perform only in the central phase of the night, when the audience is larger. Indeed, music festivals often generate hierarchies (the least famous groups performing at the beginning and the more famous at the end) and stereotypical behaviors (musicians waiting their turn backstage). The challenge was to invite musicians to be present throughout the duration of the night and to provoke them to question the right time and place for action. This did not mean playing nonstop for twelve hours but rather being ready to perform at any time, depending on how the event unfolded.

Roles and Hierarchies

Our ambition was to erase the boundaries between the different roles at play in live musical events (musician, technician, cook, bartender, security, etc.) as much as possible to avoid fixed, predictable, hierarchical relationships. A musician could be at one moment performing but also welcoming the public or cleaning the kitchen floor. Overall, the "do it yourself" philosophy was preferable to hierarchical, predetermined roles and functions. In principle, everyone could move from place to place, from one function to another. The border between musicians and nonmusicians, as well as between professional and amateur musicians, was also open and permeable, as some bands were formed specifically for the ball.

Economy

The economics of the event was also a subject of reflection and debate. We offered lower admission prices than most music clubs or festivals, often paying the musicians more than these places do. Production costs were kept to a minimum because there was no need to hire specific professional figures (turner, producer, coach, administrator, cultural mediator, publicist, etc.). Profits were shared equally among all participants. The ball was fundamentally an illegal event, since any request for a subsidy or authorization would have come up against the law (noise legislation, safety legislation, labor law legislation, etc.).

Bridging Musical and Social Activism: The European Festival of Diversities and Antidiscriminations

Over the years, our efforts produced numerous encounters and collaborations with social activists involved in other areas. In particular, fruitful partnerships with civic associations working with migrant women, Roma, and transgender and LGBTQI+ communities resulted in a project called European Festival of Diversities and Antidiscrimination.[5] After describing the general framework of this event, I explain why our ball allowed a sort of embodiment or sonic implementation of the fundamental issues at stake in this project.

During the years 2007–2013, the European Union (EU) launched a program called Europe for Citizens: Promotion of Active European Citizenship (later renamed EUCROWD) as a tool to "foster European citizenship and to improve conditions for civic and democratic participation at Union level by gradually transforming the relationship between EU citizens and EU decision-makers into more of a partnership, thus contributing to the creation of an engaged citizenship."[6] In particular, the program sought to provide "support to projects initiated by civil society organizations,"[7] funding activities (workshops, seminars, cultural events, etc.) that could foster the dissemination and valorization of EU achievements, including in the fields of human rights and antidiscrimination.[8]

The basic aims of our project were twofold: to encourage meeting of and discussion among communities that face strong discrimination and that are rarely in contact one with each other; and to disseminate and celebrate the values of difference and antidiscrimination through music and dance. Hence, the activities we organized in various EU cities—Paris, Granada, Palermo, Porto, Bologna, Ljubljana, Linz—encompassed both workshops on causes of prejudice and strategies for change and musical events called Balls of Diversities.

The workshops were organized in seminar format, allowing us to create a fruitful interface between members of marginalized communities and experts (lawyers, sociologists, psychologists, politicians) who could provide strategies for active citizenship. In other, more informal meetings, we stimulated dialogue among different communities that were victims of social stigma to foment cohabitation, recognition, reciprocity, and exchange of good practices. To give an example, Transylvanian Roma and Italian transgender people elucidated reciprocal beliefs and misbeliefs, deconstructing stereotyped images. Both communities progressively displayed increasing openness and awareness of the other's condition based on a common experience of suffering from stigma and prejudice.

We further organized Balls of Diversities, events strongly inspired by the Bal des Pianos described above. Through these events, our aim was to ensure visibility for the project and attract larger sectors of citizens. We also wanted to offer a space where participants could meet in a more informal and festive way, complementing daytime meetings and workshops. But more importantly, the Ball of Diversities, due to its radical reelaboration of the norms usually at stake in music events, was intended as a sort of sonic implementation of the values at the core of the project. In other words, the counterdevices developed in the Bal des Pianos, as described in the previous section, proved useful in conveying an embodied experience of the notions discussed in meetings and workshops: diversity, marginality, multiplicity, and antidiscrimination.

As the title of the project suggests, our intent was to valorize, empower, and celebrate the idea of diversity. The deconstruction of the frontal concert format and the copresence of radically diverse musical genres—bringing together a punk-rock band and a baroque string trio—mirrored participants' activist efforts toward a more inclusive society where no dominant sexual orientation or ethnic origin should prevail. Discussions on gender fluidity were reflected in our search for permeable sonic spaces and musical genres. Equality and equity in the social domain resonated with our artistic concerns about building a collective based on nonhierarchical interactions and multivaried functions. Furthermore, we discussed and experimented with actions and strategies to prevent ethnic or gender discrimination. The opposition of margin versus center, which the communities involved in the project recurrently expressed as problematic, was also a main concern; we eliminated any point that could stand as a center (a stage) and favored a multiplication of peripheral, often simultaneous, presences and actions. Finally, the illegal status of some partners of the project, such as migrant women, and the illegal status of our events reflected a joint effort to subvert antidemocratic laws and rules.

Broader Activist and Political Implications

An urban life that confines us in closed communities, excessively framing the musical act, and a performance mode that imposes a single relational geometry are symptoms and derivatives of our *"société du spectacle"* (Debord 1967), which collectively impoverish our musical life and which I portray as an ensemble of relational geometries between musicians themselves, musicians and the public, and citizens and cultural institutions. I further argue that ethnomusicologists are well placed to counteract this tendency—if we stop thinking that inviting traditional musicians on the stages of world music festivals is the only option available. As an alternative approach, I described how, in the Bal des Pianos, we experimented with an ensemble of counterdevices, inspired by various musical processes (as opposed to musical forms) existing in the world, that allowed participants to experience a plurality of relational geometries, a multiplicity of dispositions, and a variety of sensitive perceptions.

In the framework of the European Festival of Diversities and Antidiscriminations, these same counterdevices proved useful to express—or rather, deploy—a number of conceptual oppositions central to the concerns of discriminated communities: uniformity versus diversity; monofocal versus polyfocal; impermeable versus permeable; center versus margins. In this conclusive section, my aim is to point to a few implications of these artistic actions that are wider, even utopian, beyond questioning musical impoverishment and empowering marginalized communities.

A first topic of reflection concerns the mechanisms of decision making, and therefore of organization, developed in these events. The ball was not governed by a global plan of action or a hierarchical organization of leaders and subleaders with specific functions and subfunctions. There were no common goals or rules for accomplishing them other than to make people dance. Musicians, manufacturers, scenographers, cooks, and others collaborated to carry out a common action at a local level without having a plan or instructions at a more global level. They shared an artistic act based on the affinities of the moment and the intensities of the relationships experienced. Groups and bands could dissolve once an action of shared interest was accomplished or waned in intensity. Any action was guided, within limited time frames, by leaders whose authority could be subverted at any time. In a certain way, our collective looked like a microsociety based on self-organization, where the global order is not fixed in rules but rather emerges spontaneously from a set of local interactions. To borrow Oudeyer's vocabulary of self-organization theory, the ball was a context in which "macrostructures emerge from microstructures that do not contain the global plan" (2013, 10). According to connectionist theories in cognition, the human brain in contact with the environment could function in the same way: "In such a system, each constituent functions only in its local environment, so that the system cannot be actuated by an external agent which would somehow turn the handle. But thanks to the transformational nature of the system, global cooperation emerges spontaneously" (Varela 1996, 61). What would a society of this type look like?

A second topic of reflection is related to the concept of polymusics. Our way of thinking about interactions, organization, and decision making generated a playing habit based on the uncoordinated superimposition of several bands in the same sound space. We made numerous interventions in this sense: stable occupation of the same room by a dozen groups playing at the same time; musicians seeking to go through the sound of another group; quests for musical interstices and sound intersections; scenographic work allowing the acoustic permeability of separate spaces. Indeed, we practiced a social and musical process some ethnomusicologists call polymusic, "the deliberately uncoordinated superimposition of sound productions" (Beaudet et al. 2005, 3).[9] Polymusic has been observed in different regions of the world, motivated by reasons including defense of territory, competition, rivalry, ceremonial euphoria, sound offering, cult of chaos, and affirmation of multiple identities (Seeger 1987; Beaudet 1992; Martínez 1996; Rappoport 1999). Polymusic is present as well in some Western musical works and practices, carnivals, or techno-parades.[10] In all cases, "the different constituent parts of polymusic are together without being welded to each other. They can come apart, be put together in a different way, and so forth. Finally, the aim in polymusic is indeed to allow several voices to be heard and that really means that not only one voice is heard" (Beaudet et al. 2005, 5).

The ball was a polymusical party driven by the desire to make heard several voices, cries, words, and sounds at the same time in the same space. Contrary to so-called fusion or world music, or even to the idea of the jam session, practicing polymusic was for us a way to criticize the unity of form; to fight against the norms generally at stake in our (Western) musical practices; to let in the same space beings that are both similar and different coexist.

The activist, political, utopian potential of polymusical acts emerges more clearly when we consider a third key concept: dissensus (from the French *dissensus*). As Jacques Rancière has observed, the contemporary era is marked by consensus, the image of a homogeneous world in which we give the same meaning to all we see or hear: "What happens to critical art when this dissensual horizon has lost its obviousness? What happens to it in the contemporary context of consensus? The word consensus means much more than a 'modern' form of government giving priority to expertise, arbitration and negotiation between the 'social partners' or the different types of communities. Consensus means the agreement between meaning and meaning, that is, between a sensible mode of presentation and a regime of interpretation of its data. It means that, whatever our differences of ideas and aspirations, we perceive the same things and we give them the same meaning" (2008, 75).

How can art produce ruptures in this consensual habitus of being in the world? Art has a political efficacy not when it conveys a straightforward political message or gives instructions on how to behave but rather when it is able to activate what Rancière calls "dissensual regimes of sensoriality": "The aesthetic rupture has thus brought a singular form of efficacy: the efficacy of a disconnection, of a rupture in the relationship between the productions of artistic activity and defined social ends, between sensible forms, the meanings that one can give to them and the effects that they can produce. We can put it another way: the efficacity of dissensus. What I mean by dissensus is not the conflict of ideas or feelings. It is the conflict of several regimes of sensoriality. It is through this that art, in the regime of aesthetic separation, finds itself touching on politics" (2008, 66).

In this conceptual framework, polymusical action can be seen—and we indeed conceived it this way for the ball—as a way of "musicking dissensus": taking action against the impoverishment of our musical lives.[11] Expanding relational geometries through continuous reconfigurations of space, movements, and interactions goes hand in hand with the emergence of a multiplicity of sensory regimes, which in turn can be the fundamental fuel for activating changes in sociopolitical domains. If the ball had an activist efficacy beyond its own context, it was precisely in allowing a multitude of different, dissensual corporeal dispositions and sensorial experiences.

This leads to the fourth and final topic of reflection, given by the concept of commons. In one of the first articles calling for a more applied and engaged ethnomusicology, Charles Keil (1998) invites us to put into practice the egalitarian musical processes we have observed in other cultures to stimulate musical, motor, performative—and therefore reflexive, critical, political—skills: "No question that there is still plenty of urgent ethnomusicology to do, making common cause with indigenous peoples around the world as they defend themselves against oppressive governments in alliance with greedy corporations. Saving the rainforests and their peoples—and all of the other ecologically niched traditions, of course—is a high priority, probably the highest. But if that is all we do, we will probably fail. Having learned from 'them,' I believe we must make our own music, and based upon 'their' most egalitarian musicking processes at that" (306).

Concretely, Keil's proposal is to promote situations where one learns, with music, to build up "the local human rites that will serve us well in the future by helping us to resist commodification, consumerism, and the power-over syndrome in the only way they can be resisted, through pleasure, joy, meditation, compassion, and intensified local participation" (306–307).[12] Keil's wish is to see musically active citizens emerge everywhere, singing and drumming together. If we want to build a better society, we must multiply, he tells us, the occasions by which we coordinate ourselves rhythmically with other people.

This participatory dimension, this working together, this transformation of the citizen from passive spectator to active participant, echoes the idea of the commons, a concept which for Dardot and Laval (2014) must be thought "as a co-activity, and not as co-belonging, co-ownership or co-possession" (48).[13] According to these authors, it is from this co-activity, this co-obligation, this coparticipation that new ways of thinking, and, consequently, new forms of radical democracy, can arise.[14] Music can be seen as an ideal ground for experimenting with new forms of coaction precisely because it has the intrinsic and immediate potential to coordinate several people (their bodies, their intentions, their emotions) around a common task. In general, this coordinated coaction is based on an agreement of gestures, grammars, intentions, and emotions. But is this search for agreement, for the principle of unity, for common characteristics, the only way of thinking about the commons?

In our Bal des Pianos, and later in the Ball of Diversities, we defended a rather different kind of collective action, which gave rise to a different set of implications on the political domain. Rather than seeking uniform, coordinated, agreed on, synchronized actions, we created a terrain of heterogeneity, a space of multiple perspectives, fragmented trajectories, where differences, contradictions, and uncoordinated and asynchronized actions, intentions, and emotions were valorized. It is this polymusical, dissensual, and heterogeneous coaction that brought us to together in multiple ways, according to the desires and intensities experienced. It was also what allowed each of us to exist in multiple ways, that is to say, to be free in our transformations, free to be transformed by the action of others. Hopefully, it is from these ways of being together in music—a multiple commons—that new relational geometries may emerge and new forms of radical democracy may arise.

Acknowledgments

Many of the ideas presented in this chapter were developed through conversations with the people involved in the organization of the Bal des Pianos and the Festival of Diversities and Antidiscriminations, which I would like to acknowledge. Some of the ideas presented here were previously published in a French article (Bonini Baraldi and Manneveau 2015). I would like to thank the editors, David A. McDonald, Andrew Snyder, and Jeremy Reed, for their valuable comments.

Notes

1. During funeral wakes, musicians address the dead by playing his or her favorite melodies near the coffin. On All Saints' Day, at the cemetery, they go around the graves playing a few melodies for each deceased. On the cold and snowy Christmas Eve, they play for dozens of minutes in front of the closed doors of their friends' small houses to wish them a happy New Year in exchange for a glass of wine. When hired for weddings, they accompany the procession by foot for miles with their violins, accordions, and double basses. When they play for the banquets of Hungarian or Romanian peasants, they approach the tables and choose the most suitable tunes for every client. In each of these cases, the performance mode and the relational geometries are different.

2. I use the plural "we" since this has been a collective project, realized within the cultural associations Plug-in-Circus and Kouzmienko. To read more about the project, see "PIC," Plug-in-Circus, http://plugincircus.fr/.

3. Images can be accessed at Plug-in-Circus, http://plugincircus.fr/.

4. For more images and videos of the balls, see "*Les Bals*" and "*Grand Bal des Différences*," Plug-in-Circus, http://plugincircus.fr/.

5. The project included the participation of Movement for Transgender Identity (MIT, Bologna, Italy), the association Arcilesbica Lady Oscar (Palermo, Italy), the LGBT Monitoring Centre of the City Council of Venice (Italy), the Autonomous Center of and for Migrant Women (Linz, Austria), and the Roma association Nadara (Tîrgu Mureș, Romania).

6. "EUCROWD," *ECAS* (blog), accessed September 28, 2023, https://ecas.org/projects/eucrowd/.

7. "Action 2: Active Civil Society-European Commission," accessed September 28, 2023, https://ec.europa.eu/citizenship/about-the-europe-for-citizens-programme/overview/action-2-active-civil-society/index_en.htm.

8. In recent years, the EU has been extremely active in the field of antidiscrimination: it has put in place a new and evolving legislative framework and funded numerous activities, including training seminars at the Academy of European Law, information campaigns, and studies and analyses. The EU declared 2007 the Year of Equal Opportunities for All and supported many initiatives to strengthen awareness. Furthermore, in the same year, the EU Fundamental Rights Agency came to life. These actions aim to create not only a regulatory and institutional framework but also a general climate favorable to equal treatment, respect for diversity, and human dignity.

9. "Incoordination does not affect the musical elements but rather their superimposition. More than a musical product, polymusic is a musical act" (Beaudet et al. 2005).

10. See, for instance, Charles Ives's *Three Places in New England, Orchestral Set No. 1* or John Cage's *Musicircus*.

11. This expression (in French, *musiquer le dissensus*) has been proposed by Florent Manneveau. See Bonini Baraldi and Manneveau 2015.

12. "School by school, community center by community center, district by district, county by county, watershed by watershed, region by region" (Keil 1998, 306).

13. These authors tell us that the commons "is not in the ownership of things but in that of actions"; it is a "co-obligation born of participation in the same task" (Dardot and Laval 2014, 23).

14. The development of free software and commons copyrights (creative commons) is an example of this process.

Bibliography

Artaud, Antonin. (1938) 1964. *Le théâtre et son double*. Paris: Gallimard.
Beaudet, Jean-Michel. 1992. "Musique et alcool en Amazonie du Nord-Est." *Cahiers de sociologie économique et culturelle* 18: 79–88.
Beaudet, Jean-Michel. 1997. *Souffles d'Amazonie: Les orchestres tule des Wayãpi*. Nanterre: Société d'Ethnologie.
Beaudet, Jean-Michel, Rosalia Martínez, Dana Rappoport, and Pierre Salivas. Unpublished. "Composing Multiplicity." Last modified 2005.
Becker, Judith. 2001. "Anthropological Perspectives on Music and Emotion." In *Music and Emotion: Theory and Research*, edited by P. N. Juslin and J. A. Sloboda, 135–60. Oxford: Oxford University Press.
Blacking, John. 1973. *How Musical Is Man?* Seattle: University of Washington Press.
Bonini Baraldi, Filippo. 2021. *Roma Music and Emotion*. New York: Oxford University Press.
Bonini Baraldi, Filippo, and Florent Manneveau. 2015. "Pour un commun multiple: L'expérience du Bal des Pianos en région parisienne." *Filigrane: Musique, esthétique, sciences, société. Édifier le Commun, I, Tiers-Espaces*. https://revues.mshparisnord.fr/filigrane/index.php?id=725.
Bourdieu, Pierre. 1980. *Le sens pratique*. Paris: Éditions de Minuit.
Cardoso, Leonardo. 2019. *Sound-Politics in São Paulo*. Oxford: Oxford University Press.
Clerval, Anne. 2013. *Paris sans le people: La gentrification de la capitale*. Paris: La Découverte.
Dardot, Pierre, and Christian Laval. 2014. *Comun: Essai sur la révolution au XXe siècle*. Paris: La Découverte.
Debord, Guy. 1967. *La société du spectacle*. Paris: Buchet/Chastel.
Goehr, Lydia. 1989. "Being True to the Work." *Journal of Aesthetics and Art Criticism* 47(1): 55–67.
hooks, bell. 1992. "Eating the Other: Desire and Resistance." In bell hooks, *Black Looks: Race and Representation*, 21–39. Boston: South End Press.
Keil, Charles. 1998. "Applied Sociomusicology and Performance Studies." *Ethnomusicology* 42(2): 303–12.

Kheshti, Roshanak. 2015. *Modernity's Ear: Listening to Race and Gender in World Music*. New York: New York University Press.
Kosmicki, Guillaume. 2010. *Free parties: Une histoire, des histoires*. Marseille: Le Mot et le Reste.
Lortat-Jacob, Bernard. 1999. "Du côté des spectacles, ou comment améliorer les conditions de diffusion des musiques du monde? Éléments de réflexion." *Internationale de l'imaginaire* 11 (Les musiques en question): 156–71.
Martin, Alison. 2021. "Plainly Audible: Listening Intersectionally to the Amplified Noise Act." *Journal of Popular Music Studies* 33(4): 104–25.
Martínez, Rosalia. 1996. "El Sajjra en la música de los Jalq'a." In *Cosmologia y Música en los Andes*, edited by M. P. Baumann, 311–22. Berlin: International Institute for Traditional Music, Vervuert Ibero-Americana.
Merriam, Alan P. 1964. *The Anthropology of Music*. Evanston: Northwestern University Press.
Oudeyer, Pierre-Yves. 2013. *Aux sources de la parole: Auto-organisation et évolution*. Paris: Odile Jacob.
Rancière, Jacques. 2008. *Le spectateur émpancipé*. Paris: La Fabrique.
Rappoport, Dana. 1999. "Chanter sans être ensemble: Des musiques juxtaposées pour un public invisible." *L'Homme* 152: 143–62.
Rouget, Gilbert. 1980. *La musique et la trance: Esquisse d'une théorie générale des relations de la musique et de la possession*. Paris: Gallimard.
Sakakeeny, Matt. 2013. *Roll with It: Brass Bands in the Streets of New Orleans*. Durham, NC: Duke University Press.
Seeger, Anthony. 1987. *Why Suyà Sing: A Musical Anthropology of an Amazonian People*. Cambridge: Cambridge University Press.
Snyder, Andrew. 2022. *Critical Brass: Street Carnival and Musical Activism in Olympic Rio de Janeiro*. Middletown, CT: Wesleyan University Press.
Turino, Thomas. 2008. *Music as Social Life: The Politics of Participation*. Chicago: University of Chicago Press.
Varela, Francisco J. 1996. *Invitation aux sciences cognitives*. Paris: Seuil.
Watt, Paul. 2016. "Editorial—Street Music: Ethnography, Performance, Theory." *Journal of Musicological Research* 35(2): 69–71.

REFUGE

THREE

An Accessible Carnival

Festivity, Inclusion, and Disability in Rio de Janeiro

ANDREW SNYDER

Carnival has many animating myths—it is ideally a subversive, democratic experience of freedom—but perhaps none is as aggressively defended in Rio de Janeiro as the belief that carnival is a space of free participation for a wide variety of diverse communities. Carnival *blocos*—mobile, participatory music ensembles—are especially valorized in this respect. Their performances are financially free, as they occur in public space at no charge, and often theoretically anyone is invited to participate in the ensembles. But saxophonist André Ramos, who helps organize the efforts of Orquestra Voadora's bloco to include people with disabilities (*pessoas com deficiências*), questions this myth: "I reject this idea that this carnival that we here in Rio call 'free' [*livre*], the street carnival, is really free.... Imagine that everyone you know is going to street carnival and having fun, and you can't be there because that space has excluded you in some way."[1] As he writes in the declaration of the broader accessibility project with which Voadora partners, "carnival's essence is its democratic nature, but for the ideal to be truly achieved, it must be equally accessible to all and include people with disabilities" (Ramos, Dornelles, and Jardim 2020).

Indeed, from the perspective of people with disabilities, "street carnival" (*carnaval de rua*), an enormous community of blocos not associated with the city's famous and elaborate samba schools,[2] has many barriers to access. Voadora's gigantic bloco, which plays on the Tuesday of carnival, involved approximately 350 performers playing brass and percussion and practicing circus arts under Rio's baking sun for an audience of over 200,000 in 2024, numbers that have grown every year since its founding in 2008 (outside of the pandemic). This multitude is jammed with revelers aiming to get as close as possible to the rope (*corda*) that separates them from the musicians to better hear the music and witness the spectacle that includes stilt walkers, puppets, flags, standards, and a variety of imaginative costumes (*fantasias*). Ramos explains that, in such a setting, a person with a disability might have to put in Herculean effort to be part of the event. He muses that on seeing a person in a wheelchair at a crowded bloco, one might react with "a first line of thought that is 'how cool that guy is here,' and, yes, it is very cool individually. But there is nothing cool about something that requires a major overcoming of barriers [*superação*] to be there—that really is something that the collective has to change. We have to find a way to welcome these people."[3]

Since 2018, Orquestra Voadora has developed an "accessibility group" (*núcleo de acessibilidade*) made up of band members, participants with disabilities, and accessibility professionals devoted to creating what the group calls an "accessible carnival." This internal group, in which Ramos was a principal participant, has worked separately and in partnership with Acessibilifolia. This latter project, which ended in 2023, was organized by Projeto Um Novo Olhar (New View Project), fought for accessible participation in the arts for people with disabilities, and was supported by Brazil's National Arts Foundation (FUNARTE) and the School of Music at the Universidade Federal do Rio de Janeiro, where Ramos completed a master's degree in music. *Acessibilifolia* is a neologism that unites the Portuguese words for accessibility and revelry, *acessibilidade* and *folia*; the project has sought to promote accessibility in various forms of celebration throughout Brazil.[4]

In alliance with Acessibilifolia, Voadora's accessibility group has sought to make logistical and social changes in the broader world of Voadora to make participation at all levels more accessible to people with disabilities, including playing an instrument, sound engineering, participating in event organization, and simply celebrating as a *foliona/folião* (audience member or reveler). Voadora's project highlights the right of people with disabilities to cultural engagement, in particular to a form of street festivity that is volatile and relatively uncontrolled, distinct from spaces of high culture where some progress at accessibility has been made, such as concert halls and museums. Camila Alves, one of the participants with disabilities in Voadora, draws attention to the importance of making festive events accessible and going beyond accessibility in terms of navigating the practicalities of everyday life: "This is an important initiative for us to push for the idea that people with disabilities can be in all spaces. We need more than medical actions ... but places of culture, happiness, and festivity" (Projeto UNO, episode 7).[5] In an effort to "provoke people to think about the accessibility or lack thereof of cultural and educational spaces as well as the city as a whole," Ramos produced a series of short documentaries of testimonies of people with disabilities who participated in Voadora called *Inclusion and Revelry* (*Inclusão e Folia*), which was also the first action of the larger Acessibilifolia project (Ramos, Dornelles, and Jardim 2020).[6]

Based on the testimonies of participants in these videos and interviews with Ramos from 2021 to 2024, this chapter examines Voadora's strategies to make carnival more accessible, as developed from 2018 to 2024. It expands and updates an article (Snyder 2022b) published when the project's initial efforts had been cut short by the pandemic and, like all social life, shifted online; this chapter considers the bloco's postpandemic projects as well. Looking back on six years of antiableist engagement, the chapter offers an opportunity to reflect on the challenges of realizing such ambitious dreams, a dynamic inherent to festival activism itself.

For Voadora's accessibility group, creating an accessible carnival requires structural change and a collective confrontation with ableism (*capacitismo*), what disability rights activist TL Lewis defines in the first part of a working definition as "a system of assigning value to people's bodies and minds based on societally constructed ideas of normalcy, productivity, desirability, intelligence, and fitness" (2022). In a text explaining the project, Voadora argues that, rather than festivities making the world more free for people with disabilities, "the ableism and inaccessibility that characterize life in cities are reproduced and often accentuated in festivities" (Ramos, Dornelles, and Jardim 2020). Only conscious structural transformation can combat ableism in festive practices. As disability studies scholars broadly argue, disability, like other social categories such as race and gender, is a category created by an ableist society that normalizes exclusive practices and discrimination based on individual capacities.[7] For Ramos, deconstructing these norms requires constant attention to how groups like Voadora naturalize culturally constructed oppressive practices. For him, this work is a condition for creating a distinctly anti-ableist carnival culture.

I argue that, beyond promoting the rights to culture of people with disabilities in an ableist world, Orquestra Voadora rejects a separatist model of disability arts and music,[8] one Alves describes as encompassing "events tailored to people with disabilities who knows where, with a ton of people with disabilities" (Projeto UNO, episode 1). Its project can, for example, be distinguished from Bloco Senta que Eu Empurro (Sit While I Push Bloco), founded in 2008 in Rio specifically for people with disabilities. While Voadora recognizes this group and others like it as engaging in an important form of festive disability activism, the group embraces an inclusive model within groups not defined as primarily destined for people with disabilities. This model, however, does not aim to be inclusive at the margins but rather demands structural changes for all—even if this goal remains to be fully realized, as Voadora has over time reconciled itself to the need for separate, safe spaces within the bloco. Indeed, Ramos characterizes the participation of people with disabilities in Voadora as a "meeting" (*encontro*) of people with diverse experiences and needs. He stresses that this is not a "perfect meeting—it's one that has many questions remaining to be resolved—but it is a powerful encounter with a great deal of potential" (Projeto UNO, episode 1).

This imperfection or incompleteness might be understood through the distinction between *accommodation*, which generally refers to an individualized change granted to a person with a disability contingent upon a burden of proof of the disability, and *access*, which provides structural changes making a space accessible without a person with a disability needing to request accommodation. Much of Voadora's initial work has been based on finding solutions to include particular people based on their individual needs in ways that might be considered closer to accommodation, but these steps point toward a larger goal of accessibility represented in the project name, Acessibilifolia. An ultimate goal for the bloco could be understood as akin to the concept of *universal design*, a term coined by Ronald Mace and principally applied to architecture, to describe "barrier-free" environments freely usable by anyone (Mace, Story, and Mueller 1998), yet this notion remains a platonic ideal not yet in reach. Ultimately, Voadora rejects a zero-sum framework whereby the gains of rights by people with disabilities are seen as limiting those of nondisabled people. The group suggests instead that efforts to promote access will create a more inclusive, empowering, and caring culture for all participants to thrive.

More broadly, I develop an argument I have made elsewhere (2022a) that suggests that classic carnival theories celebrating festivity's resistant potential, such as Bakhtin's ([1941] 1984), are more useful when we understand how such beliefs in carnival's liberatory potential animate and inspire the ethical practices of a community rather than simply applying these theories as interpretative models to diverse carnival practices.⁹ In other words, it is in engaging in this critical work of remaking carnival to be inclusive for disabled people that Ramos and the Voadora community believe they are bringing carnival closer to its ideals of freedom, subversion, and democracy. Embracing the belief that festive experiences can resonate beyond the ephemeral, they hope that participants' experiences in these events will make broader changes in the social culture of Voadora, participants' personal lives, and festive events in Brazil more broadly.

Though the data for this research was collected between 2021 and 2024, the chapter is also based on my ethnomusicological research since 2013 on Orquestra Voadora and Rio's larger street carnival community of which the group is a part (Snyder 2022a), including teaching in Voadora's music classes (*oficinas*) to prepare musicians to participate in the annual carnival bloco. This research was particularly intense during my doctoral fieldwork from 2014 to 2016, when I did not witness disability as a foremost concern to participants. An early draft of this chapter was distributed by Ramos to those who participated in the documentary, and they were encouraged to give feedback, which was incorporated into the final version in a process of "dialogic editing" (Feld 1987). Though I do not (currently) identify as disabled, my thinking on anti-ableism has been strongly influenced by the anti-ableist organizing work of my wife and our relationship with her brother, who has Down syndrome.

Orquestra Voadora: Band, Bloco, Class, Movement

Orquestra Voadora was founded in 2008 and first participated in street carnival in 2009. The band continued to participate annually until the pandemic's unprecedented cancelation of carnival in 2021 and 2022, coming back in full force in 2023. Influenced both by revivalist brass blocos of street carnival that played traditional Brazilian carnival genres and by eclectic styles of brass and popular music from New Orleans to the Balkans, Voadora's repertoire is a unique Brazilian twist on world music (Snyder 2022a). Orquestra Voadora (Flying Orchestra) refers both to a presentational performance band of approximately ten members who play gigs professionally and to a participatory bloco theoretically open to anyone with an instrument, availability, and interest in learning the bloco's repertoire to perform on carnival Tuesday in a massive spectacle. The bloco rehearses every Sunday afternoon for about five months before carnival, and, in 2013, the band also opened an *oficina*, a band-led class of around three hundred participants devoted to instrumental instruction and open to beginners that runs throughout the year on a weekly basis (Snyder 2019b).

The bloco, and later its oficina, led to an exponential expansion of new musicians and bands playing a wide variety of repertoires in Rio's public spaces. This community grew into an increasingly definable movement known as *neofanfarrismo*, of which Orquestra Voadora is one of the most popular, professional, and influential representatives. As brass bands from other countries, especially France and the United States, began to visit the city in the 2000s, the movement increasingly connected with a transnational network of alternative brass bands that had consolidated around the HONK! Festivals of Activist Brass Bands, which had emerged in the Boston area in 2006 and spread around the world (Snyder, Allen, and Garofalo 2020). In 2015, Rio's brass band movement held the first annual HONK! Rio Festival of Activist Brass Bands, which gave the movement a definitively activist identity, and the HONK! festival network has since spread around Brazil with six HONK! festivals in the country as of this writing. The neofanfarrismo movement has defined its avowedly leftist activism in diverse ways, including participating in protests, playing for free in public spaces, and adopting inclusive strategies that promote the musicianship of those with no experience in music, especially from marginalized communities.

In line with the HONK! ethos, the band has from its inception offered a critique of the concept of musical ability. Unlike the earlier brass ensembles that revived traditional repertoires of Rio's street carnival, not all of Voadora's band musicians were professionally trained. The bloco they manage includes a wide range of interested musicians, from professionals to amateurs to beginners. By rejecting the notion that a certain kind of musical ability is required to participate in Rio's iconic festivity, the band and movement opened the door to many people engaging in musical projects for the first time.

However, this revision of musical ability did not necessarily offer access to marginalized communities, as Voadora and the neofanfarrismo movement are manifestations of one of the more privileged communities in Rio de Janeiro—what many during my fieldwork referred to as the "alternative middle class." Many *neofanfarristas* are university educated, the movement is much whiter than other popular scenes such as samba schools, and it has been largely male led. As the movement has taken on an increasingly activist identity, however, it has diversified impressively in the past decade—all-women groups were born out of Voadora's oficina as the ranks of female musicians exploded, and brass band projects from favelas and peripheral areas of the city were founded

(Snyder 2022a). One could see Voadora's concern with including people with disabilities as a logical extension of the band's interest in creating an ever-more diverse and democratic bloco and living up to a conception of a truly free carnival. Until 2018, however, disability rights were largely not on the community's radar, a problem Ramos associates with a broader neglect of the issue in the left's more fixated focus on class, race, and gender.

Voadora's Accessibility Group

In the introduction to the documentary series *Inclusion and Revelry*, Ramos explains that the bloco had always attracted a wide range of people and saw itself as facilitating "carnival's power of encounter" between diverse communities. It had also always included the participation of people with disabilities in the bloco and oficina in small numbers; they were welcomed in a "natural and spontaneous way" but without a conscious, collective approach. In 2018, the group resolved to take "structured action" (Projeto UNO, episode 1). Founding an accessibility group, the members began to conduct interviews with participants with disabilities to better understand what kinds of barriers to access they faced. The group started to think about logistical questions for the carnival bloco and pedagogical questions for the oficina. They put out public calls specifically inviting people with disabilities to take part and explaining their willingness to put in the work to make carnival an accessible space for those who wanted to participate.

A principal preoccupation in this endeavor has been thinking about how to increase the "representivity" (*representividade*) of people with disabilities in Voadora's social sphere—that is, how to break what Ramos calls the "vicious cycle of exclusion" that occurs when lack of people with disabilities becomes a self-fulfilling prophecy. How can one create a space in which people with disabilities are not "excluded a priori? Since there is no one with disabilities in a [given space], a person with disabilities might believe that any such events are exclusive to begin with."[10] To break the cycle, the accessibility group agreed, this effort must be led by and in coordination with people with disabilities, in alliance with the well-known disability rights movement slogan "Nothing about us without us." Nondisabled participants of the band could not effectively apply their own frameworks for accessibility without people with disabilities.

In this work with people with disabilities, they aimed to move from the realm of the abstract to concrete actions. For Ramos, this shift from abstract to concrete had a personal dimension marked by the birth of his niece, who has the rare chromosomal condition of 5p-, or "cri du chat," in 1999: "When she was born, I felt remorse—how could I not have thought about this before? Why was it that I only started to think about this when it happened to a person close to me? ... Unfortunately, we live in a situation of such great exclusion [of people with disabilities] that when there is no one on your radar, it remains abstract." In the case of carnival blocos, as Ramos explains, "You can imagine what a person with a disability might need in the abstract, but this changes completely when this person is a concrete person whom you know and have exchanged with.... These days, it's no longer something abstract, like, 'What do we do if there is a person with a disability at the bloco?' No, that person is Fernanda, it's Antônio."[11] As the numbers of disabled people increase in participation, the group hopes that presence will build on itself exponentially, bringing concrete questions to be resolved and accommodated to make the space more accessible.

This concretization has been especially important in the group's thinking about the actions necessary to welcome people with such a diverse range of needs. Disability, as Ramos explains, is a word that "encompasses many different realities" (Projeto UNO, episode 1)—visual, auditory, physical, locomotive, cognitive—and "within each of these disabilities there is also an individual with their specific capacities, needs, and desires."[12] Building an accessible carnival culture requires both general structural changes, including physically changing the spatial layout of carnival events and creating legible materials through sign language, braille, audio captioning, and reading text aloud, as well as responding to individual needs. In the group's text explaining the project, it is clear that the aspiration to make carnival more accessible does not stop at accommodating a few people who might be interested in taking part. Rather, it encompasses an entire structural transformation of the group's roles and activities in search of accessibility: "Making carnival accessible means facilitating the participation of people with disabilities in all the spaces that make up this environment. We must guarantee their representivity not only in the audience of carnival but equally in the organization of blocos and parades, in the production of music, dance and other forms of art, as well as in the world of work created by carnival" (Ramos, Dornelles, and Jardim 2020). But how do these lofty goals manifest in practice?

Inclusion and Revelry

The documentary video series *Inclusion and Revelry* that Voadora released in partnership with Um Nova Olhar offers the perspectives and testimonies of

Figure 3.1. Screenshot of "Um Novo Olhar" with braille. Used with permission of André Ramos.

some of the people with disabilities most involved in these efforts. The videos themselves are meant to be accessible to people with auditory and visual disabilities. Each video opens with visuals that are explained simultaneously by a voice-over: "At the center of the white screen, the title in braille appears and letters flash 'Um Novo Olhar.' Confetti on the screen. At the top of the screen emerges in red 'Acessibilifolia.'" The video often pauses so that the voice-over can describe each person's physical features and surroundings as well as footage of interviewees participating in carnival and Voadora's bloco. Audio captioning in Portuguese appears at the bottom of the screen along with a sign language interpreter, and all written text, such as the credits at the end, is also read aloud. This section examines the testimonies and perspectives offered in the videos regarding Voadora's aim to create an accessible carnival bloco.

Inaccessible Carnival

The documentary testimonials describe the many ways carnival is an inaccessible space for people with disabilities. Connecting the physical attributes of the street to practices of street carnival, interviewees argue that inaccessibility is not limited to blocos' social and cultural practices but extends to the physical architecture of the street and city more broadly. Foliona Fernanda Shcolnik, who has low vision, describes Rio de Janeiro as a city where the "sidewalks are badly kept, and there are holes in the street and varying levels [of pavement]" (Projeto UNO, episode 3). Foliona Camila Alves, who is blind, argues that "street carnival brings with it the mark of inaccessibility. . . . Street carnival is as inaccessible as the street is inaccessible" (Projeto UNO, episode 3). Diverse forms of urban inaccessibility interact with the needs of each person with a disability in different ways.

Saxophonist Heitor Luiz, a wheelchair user, notes that in a city as unequal as Rio, "accessibility is widely variable from neighborhood to neighborhood, which has a lot to do with socioeconomic conditions" (Projeto UNO, episode 6). Indeed, accessibility equipment can be expensive; middle-class neighborhoods with more accessibility infrastructure, including those that line the Bay of Guanabara (such as Ipanema and Copacabana), are generally flat, offering radically different challenges from the hilly, poorer, not up-to-code favelas that jut up between middle-class neighborhoods. Orquestra Voadora, like much of the street carnival, remains predominantly an expression of the city's middle class despite its many efforts to diversify, and the interviewees with disabilities appear to be primarily middle-class and toward the whiter end of Brazil's racial spectrum. Without broader structural efforts to radically remake the architecture of the city and the extreme inequalities woven into it, cultural practices like those of the city's blocos are limited in their impact. They seek to better navigate inaccessible architecture over which they have limited power, while broader political fights push for structural advances for disability rights.[13]

When based in an unexamined ableist worldview, the blocos' cultural practices, as Ramos argues, can accentuate an already inaccessible city. Interviewees speak especially of the problems of crowding at street carnival events, which, unlike the samba school parades that have assigned seats,[14] involve an almost entirely uncontrolled competition to get closer to the music. Joana Vargens recounts that when her daughter Maria, who uses a wheelchair, was smaller, they went to participate in Voadora in the early days of the bloco, but "it got really mega big, really crowded, tons of people, and I basically quit. I told myself, no, it's impossible; it's a hassle. And there were two years when we just didn't even stay in Rio during carnival" (Projeto UNO, episode 5). Finding a place away from crowded areas left them far from the sound and energy of the event, and taller people would block Maria's view. André Rola, photographer of carnival events and father of Bárbara, who also uses a wheelchair, relates that they had to "force" themselves to be present at carnival events, what Ramos describes as "overcoming barriers" in inaccessible events.

Crowding is, of course, a problem for everyone—I often felt almost crushed in masses of bodies at street carnival events, unable to make my way through a crowd to exit. One way blocos have sought to reduce crowding is by limiting information about the whereabouts of events, relying on word of mouth and secrecy instead of public advertisement. But Ramos argues that if "you parade with a secret bloco and you don't tell anyone except your friends that you will roll at 4:30 in the morning at a distant location, you will create something limited to only a small sector with your group of people."[15] In other words, this strategy of withholding information to create less crowded events is also ableist and creates other barriers to accessibility. He notes that some blocos even revel in inaccessibility, holding events in the middle of the night and sometimes involving crowd antics, such as mass running, that involve dangers for all.

Making Orquestra Voadora (More) Accessible

Voadora's first public, major action to include people with disabilities, resulting from the formation of the accessibility group in 2018, was to create an accessibility section (*ala de acessibilidade*) for the 2019 carnival bloco. *Alas* refer to differentiated sections of carnival parade groups, which reach a high degree of complexity in the samba schools in particular. In Voadora, there are alas for each instrument as well as for stilt walkers, sound car managers, and other participants. The aim was for this accessibility section to be primarily for foliões with disabilities who wanted to enjoy the experience in an uncrowded space inside the rope that separates the bloco from the audience, with others accompanying them as needed. Joana Vargens and her daughter Maria, who had stopped participating in carnival as described above, heard about the ala and participated in 2019. Joana relates with delight, "It was the greatest carnival.... We were inside the bloco, next to the sound, and we managed to dance, participate, and move around. To be with all the people in tranquility.... Maria loved it.... She was glued to the music and the vibrations, enchanted with the stilt walkers" (Projeto UNO, episode 5).

Foliona Camila Alves, who is blind, likewise reflects emotionally about her experience participating in the accessibility section: "To be in the middle of the band, amid the stilt walkers, to be among other people with disabilities too, which I hadn't experienced in carnival until then, this was all very powerful—this sensation of belonging in carnival" (Projeto UNO, episode 2). She was accompanied to that carnival by three friends who had pledged to help her experience the blocos, but, because of Voadora's accessibility section, her experience there was distinct from her experience in spaces where her friends had to help and protect her amid the carnival chaos: "To be with them inside the rope, have fun with them, and not be in this alternation of who is going to have fun and who is going to take care of me, this was also very powerful" (Projeto UNO, episode 2). The bloco also included sign language and audio descriptions during the parade.

The accessibility section received similar praise from other interviewees, but, after the first year, the accessibility group raised questions about having a distinct section for people with disabilities. They worried that this practice reinforced separation, even segregation, between participants with disabilities and the nondisabled. But the question of mixing foliões into band spaces brought other logistical concerns. Ramos notes that, if he, as a saxophonist, were to enter the space of the percussion, it would cause disturbances: "the 'free space' of the band isn't really free. . . . Circulation is already quite limited."[16] Beyond this issue, the diversity of needs of the foliões with disabilities shifted the practice of maintaining a separate accessibility section somewhat the following year, when foliões with disabilities were dispersed according to their needs and interests, requiring the group to find "solutions that are completely individual and can't be generalized."[17]

Ultimately, the accessibility section has been consolidated as an intrinsic element of the bloco, while the group remains committed to involving people with disabilities in other elements of the bloco should they desire to participate, as Ramos explains: "What if you want to simply go to the bloco, without doing anything, without playing, without walking on stilts, not doing anything? This space, for people with disabilities, is very difficult to attain, and the accessibility section is necessary for this reason. . . . One thing isn't a detriment to the other. You don't need to abolish this space in order to incentivize people to participate in other ways."[18] In 2024, the ala was organized by Camila Alves and paraded to its own theme of "Assexybilidade," putting the English word *sexy* into the Portuguese word for accessibility. She aimed to make the bloco more *assexível*, playing on the almost exact sounding of the world *accessible* (*acessível*). The theme was an homage to the film *Assexybilidade* by Daniel Gonçalves, which argues for the right of people with disabilities to sexual pleasure.

Figure 3.2. Assexybilidade parade. Photo by André Rola.

In line with the goal of integrating people with disabilities in other bloco spaces, Voadora has sought to provide music education at the oficina to people with disabilities to prepare them to participate musically in the bloco. These efforts have required oficina teachers to combat the ableist naturalization of music pedagogy concerning how the body should interact with an instrument to produce music. Heitor Luiz, who is interviewed in the film and uses a wheelchair,

Figure 3.3. Screenshot of documentary featuring Fernanda Shcolnik walking with small group of Voadora musicians. Used with permission of André Ramos.

chose the saxophone to play in the bloco and became Ramos's student. Ramos describes his work with Luiz as a "change of the prism" through which Ramos sees the world, as he shifted his standard pedagogy. "Instrumental pedagogy," he argues, "presupposes a normalization of the body. You have to be open to new and different ways to hold the instrument, how to breathe. You have to be open to another conception of the instrument, sound, and space."[19] This insight reflects a desire to not only accommodate his pedagogy to Luiz but also create a more accessible pedagogy for all.

Participants with disabilities offered other practical advice to Voadora's planning group to make the space more accessible. Luiz, for example, gave the simple idea of having access-support people ready to accompany wheelchair users from the metro to bloco practice areas and the parade starting point. Folião Antônio Bordallo, who uses a wheelchair and participates in Voadora, argues that blocos need to not only develop accessibility sections but also use the internet to publicize them so that people with disabilities can become aware of them and sign up to participate.

Beyond general and individualized responses that facilitate the participation of people with disabilities, interviewees argue that it is necessary to develop a "culture of accessibility" among participants that is fundamentally receptive to diverse needs that can never be fully anticipated. Foliona Fernanda Shcolnik, who has low vision, refers to the need for Voadora to develop "attitudinal accessibility" (*acessibilidade atitudinal*), which "confronts the question of the people's attitudes. For example, crossing the street is a situation when it is great when people help, or at least offer help. You can ask, 'Do you want help?' 'What do you want me to do?' Often people don't feel they know how to help or even how to ask—'How would I know how to help a blind person? I don't know what to do.' Well, you can speak to them normally. They might not see, but they will talk to you" (Projeto UNO, episode 4). Attitudinal accessibility aims to shift responsibility for accommodation from the individual with the disability to the collective culture's concern with reducing barriers to access.[20]

"Everybody Wins with Accessibility"

As described above, the strategic effort to include people with disabilities follows several other efforts to diversify the bloco of Orquestra Voadora, which began as a primarily middle-class, whiter, and predominantly male group but has become much more diverse along lines of class, race, and gender. Interviewees connect the accessibility group's work to a larger preoccupation with intersectional inclusion of all marginalized communities in the contemporary left. This effort connects to the second part of TL Lewis's working definition cited above, which argues that ableism promotes "constructed ideas [that] are deeply rooted in eugenics, anti-Blackness, misogyny, colonialism, imperialism, and capitalism. This systemic oppression leads to people and society determining people's value based on their language, appearance, religion and/or their ability to satisfactorily re/produce, 'excel' and 'behave.' You do not have to be disabled to experience ableism" (2022). Similarly, interviewees suggest that the creation of an accessible bloco improves not just the lives of people with disabilities; as Fernanda Shcolnik argues, "everybody wins with accessibility."

Camila Alves notes a "synchronicity" in Voadora's 2019 carnival parade, which was the first after the formation of the disability group and the year the bloco made a public homage to councilwoman Marielle Franco. Franco was a Black, lesbian member of the Socialism and Freedom Party (PSoL) who had been assassinated the year before, possibly by those allied with extreme-right president Jair Bolsonaro, in power between 2018 and 2022. Her image appeared all around Rio as the left mourned her loss, and she became the face of persistent resistance to Bolsonaro's dismissal of the rights of marginalized communities. In 2019, Voadora placed a massive banner of her face on its

Figure 3.4. Orquestra Voadora parade. Photo by Marcelo Credie.

sound car; bloco participants were encouraged to visually commemorate her; and Franco's partner, Mônica Benício, spoke to the crowd in remembrance of Franco and her work, ending her speech with the fullhearted claim that "carnival is resistance" (Projeto UNO, episode 6). Though Voadora had already been concerned with diversification and activism, the 2019 carnival was a heightened space for these concerns—as Alves explains, "we were already talking a lot about the rights of minorities and resistance" (Projeto UNO, episode 6). Heitor Luiz notes that with "all the discourses against feminism, against Black people, against the LGBT+ movement, the responses impact the movements of people with disabilities as well" (Projeto UNO, episode 6).[21]

Beyond this intersectional convergence of movements fighting for the inclusion of diverse marginalized communities within the world of Orquestra Voadora, Fernanda Shcolnik argues that accessibility has positive, practical impacts for everyone involved. For example, a sidewalk that is broken, as many are in Rio, might be an insurmountable barrier for a person with a disability, but it is also a danger and burden for anyone trying to use it. Antônio Bordallo notes that if blocos constructed corridors through crowds of foliões for people with disabilities to securely reach the bloco, these corridors could also be used by anyone in case of "emergency or someone having a difficult time with heat or alcohol" (Projeto UNO, episode 4). Many blocos leave a littered landscape in their wake, and, while throwing trash on the ground is especially disruptive for the mobility of people with disabilities, it is a problem for everyone. For Shcolnik, "when you have an accessible space, it is a democratic space for everyone because accessibility doesn't harm people who don't have disabilities. It often helps them too because accessibility is not only for people with disabilities, but for a mother with a stroller or an older person with a cane.... This is good for everybody" (Projeto UNO, episode 6).

Recent Projects and Challenges

Orquestra Voadora's work to include people with disabilities initially focused on creative solutions to promote the integration of diverse peoples in physical space. But of course, as with any effort to physically draw people together in space, Voadora's accessibility efforts, along with almost all its other activities, were drastically disrupted by the pandemic, which descended in 2020 right after Voadora's second carnival parade since the formation of the accessibility group. Initially, Ramos explains, the group had aimed to "use the period of isolation to further plan accessibility strategies ... [as] all the debates about carnival after the pandemic ... must include people with disabilities in the discussion" (Projeto UNO, episode 1). Though the pandemic was not "a moment as full of potential that we thought it could be," as everyone experienced crisis, death, and deprivation from the sociality of musical community—which could make thinking about carnival feel less relevant—some work toward the goal of creating an accessible carnival was accomplished during this period.

As with so many elements of life, the accessibility group's efforts shifted online. While many blocos and bands simply ceased operating, others produced live virtual performances. Though several started to use sign language interpreters, Ramos noticed how few videos used any accessibility materials and publicly pushed other blocos to add them, and he continued to work with Um Novo Olhar to make Voadora's carnival materials more accessible. During the 2021 carnival—which was mostly conducted online, as in-person activities were banned—many of these accessibility tools were adopted for the online offerings (Snyder 2021). The pandemic, of course, limited physical contact with local communities but provided an unprecedented opportunity for new conversations, networking, and reflections between diverse communities (Snyder, Allen, and Garofalo 2022). Voadora aimed to spread the idea of making cultural activities beyond Rio's carnival community accessible through the various global communities of which it is a part. This has included connecting with festive groups engaging with accessibility from around Brazil and networking within the Brazilian HONK! Festival circuit, which links bands like Voadora all over the world in alliance with diverse conceptions of musical activism. As Ramos relates, "it was really during that time that we went to establish these contacts and these bridges and act on other fronts."[22] By early 2022, the networking of the accessibility group had led to a new manifestation of festival activism.

Festival Acessibilifolia, which took place in Rio de Janeiro over four weeks in April 2022, brought together several carnival groups focused on carnival and disability for workshops, debates, and performances. The work of Orquestra Voadora had inspired Um Novo Olhar to amplify its Acessibilifolia project on accessibility and carnival, as well as other festive manifestations in Brazil, aiming to create bridges between diverse carnival groups focused on creating an accessible carnival as well as with schools and institutions serving disabled people. Though carnival was canceled for the second year in a row, the city allowed a postponed version in April, taking advantage of a lull in the pandemic after the first omicron wave. Festival Acessibilifolia coincided with the first major carnival mobilization since the pandemic, known as "Carnabril" (for "Carnival in April").

Along with Voadora, the festival included participation from Embaixadores de Alegria, the first samba school for people with disabilities; Senta Que Eu Empurro and Bloco Eficiente, blocos for people with disabilities; and Loucura Suburbana, Bloco Zona Mental, and Bloco Tá Pirando, Pirado, Pirou!, blocos focused on mental health. Taking place twice a week during the month, the festival's events included conversations about mental health and accessible revelry; workshops on carnival costume design, creation of musical instruments from recycled materials, and percussion; and musical performances by Embaixadores da Alegria, Sento Que Eu Empurro, and Voadora. Bringing together up to two hundred people, by Ramos's estimation, the festival was offered for free, with funds from FUNARTE providing food and transport to and from the historic theater where events took place. Ramos described the theater as physically accessible, and the festival also used visual captions and sign language.

Similar to the logic of Voadora's inclusive approach, the festival allowed registration by people with and without disabilities, prioritizing the former. Ramos explained, "I think the participation of people with and without disabilities is very necessary and welcome because we want all blocos to be accessible. It wouldn't be very productive to create a festival just for people with disabilities. It would reinforce the idea that there is need for a special, reserved space and not a space for everyone. Our idea is to promote spaces where these people can be, but not a space just for them, a space in which they can be together with other people experiencing carnival, not having another carnival."[23] However, people without disabilities outnumbered those with disabilities at the festival, an outcome Ramos views as revealing the necessity of further planning in order to create a better balance regarding how to make such an event accessible, attractive, and welcoming to people with disabilities: "You can't just have a festival about accessibility and revelry and suddenly expect a bunch of people to arrive at once. Bringing new people to the world of carnival is slow work."[24] Though the festival worked with other institutions that had the means to transport people to the event, Ramos recognized the continued need to create more of a network of information to reach disabled communities, which might view anything related to carnival as exclusive by its very nature.

In my most recent conversation with Ramos in 2024, he described the many challenges of creating a more accessible carnival culture over the years, especially in the postpandemic world, as the work of "little ants" (*formiguinhas*). Festival activism, like all activism, attempts to transform entrenched hierarchies and hegemonies of power and necessarily involves challenges, frustrations, and disillusionment. Even as elements of an activist vision are actualized, the gap between these actions and the dream's full realization can be palpable.

Hoping in the initial years for an "explosion" of interest and transformation of Rio's street carnival, Ramos described a generally supportive reception to the concept but ultimately a lack of committed people to put principles into action: "Come November, December, everyone is crazy overworked with a thousand things, and you come talking about accessibility, it's like, 'Great, cool, let's go talk with so and so.'" He emphasized the continued necessity and challenge of creating networks of people to collectively realize these goals. Finding people with disabilities who are willing to take on leadership positions has notably taken shape in Camila Alves taking full responsibility for the accessibility section. Yet the scope of Voadora's accessibility activities has become focused on the accessibility section despite genuinely wanting "to make the bloco more accessible beyond creating a section." Ramos lamented that involvement of people with disabilities in the oficina, in other roles of the bloco, and at other times of the year has currently dropped off. Recently, the group has only managed to mobilize people around accessibility in the context of carnival, illustrating the importance of major festivities as privileged opportunities for activism that may be more difficult to actualize in other spaces and occasions.[25]

A More Accessible Carnival Future

These shortcomings notwithstanding, Ramos's conviction has been steadfast over the years that the work of creating an accessible carnival should not stay as just an inward project of Orquestra Voadora but needed to spread its message beyond the world of the bloco. Before it ended in 2023, Acessibilifolia had intended to design a course on creating accessible carnivals to be offered asynchronously online called Anti-ableist Revelry (*Folia Anticapacitista*) and wanted to replicate the festival with local partners in other cities in Brazil, including São Paulo, Belo Horizonte, Recife, and Salvador, to forge a genuinely national movement. Though these projects are currently on hold, Voadora's internal efforts continue, and other blocos in Rio's street carnival have begun to develop their own accessibility sections and engage Voadora in learning how to make their projects more accessible.

Ramos readily recognizes that many elements of increasing accessibility for people with disabilities in Orquestra Voadora remain to be confronted. The video series prominently features people with physical and visual disabilities, but it does not engage with people with cognitive disabilities. Another world of people with disabilities in the city is almost entirely absent due to the socioeconomic and racial divides that characterize life in Rio de Janeiro. Making Voadora a truly welcoming space for people with disabilities to play any role remains a work in progress. Voadora often begins by learning how to accommodate individual people before conceiving of how to build a more accessible culture for all, and the need for separatist safe spaces within inclusive projects continues to be felt despite the desire to create a fully accessible bloco.

Nevertheless, in its militance for the cultural rights of people with disabilities, Orquestra Voadora's accessibility group is ultimately focused on planting the seeds of an accessible world in a much more ample sense than disability rights groups often strive for in their focus on the logistical. Indeed, this futurity was reinforced in its first full carnival parade following the pandemic in 2023, the theme of which was "The future is antiableist," a line that resonates with what we have defined as *festival futurity* in the introduction of this book: the "world-making potential in festival practice.... In festival practice participants may collectively embody the unimaginable as a possible, perhaps even inevitable, reality" (McDonald, Snyder, and Reed, p. 19). Citing participant Camila Alves in an Instagram post about the parade, Voadora wrote, "Access is love, access is a question of justice."

Indeed, though Voadora views engaging in festivity as a right in itself, the group also advances an argument about the efficacy of festive experience in confronting the ableist world more broadly. As Ramos states in an article about Acessibilifolia, "It's a gateway. Revelry has the potential to be very democratic. But we also want to take this [conversation to broader] society" (Anon 2022a). Based on all these experiences, Ramos has been fundamentally optimistic through our conversations through the years, redoubling these efforts and, despite the challenges, combatting "the cycle of exclusion. As we bring more and more people together, this will increase the representivity of people with disabilities," he asserts. "This will feed on itself, and so I see a possibility of advancement, of an improvement much greater than where we are now."[26]

More recently, as a postdoctoral researcher in Lisbon, Portugal, I witnessed an instantiation of the tangible spread of including people disabilities in festivities and social movements. Held in the first weekend of July (Disability Pride Month) as the last action of the June Pride Month, Lisbon's 2024 LGBTQIA+ Pride march was led by Lisbon's Brazilian street carnival bloco Colombina Clandestina (see Snyder 2023), which happened to have hosted Orquestra Voadora in Portugal in 2022. In front of the percussion and horn players were stilt walkers, and, in front of them, visually juxtaposing the physically high to the low, were four people in wheelchairs, opening this parade of fifty thousand marchers. Directly influenced by Orquestra Voadora or not, Lisbon Pride's intersectional manifestation represents a growing demand to include and highlight people with disabilities and their access needs in festive, carnivalesque, and protest spaces in the Portuguese-speaking world and beyond.

Figure 3.5. Lisbon 2024 Pride parade. Photo by author.

Notes

1. André Ramos, interview by author, Rio de Janeiro, Brazil, July 28, 2021.

2. Though Rio's important samba school tradition has received the bulk of scholarly attention, resurgent street carnival festivities are increasingly being studied. Rio's street carnival blocos have experienced a momentous revival since Brazil emerged from its military dictatorship in 1985, with an ever-increasing number of blocos appearing in the streets, often numbering over five hundred (Snyder 2022a; Fernandes 2019). More broadly, carnival in Brazil is a national obsession—with particular fervor in Rio de Janeiro, Salvador, and Recife—and Voadora seeks to use its accessibility project as an example to this broader carnival world.

3. 2021 Ramos interview.

4. See project website: https://artedetodagente.com.br/um-novo-olhar/uno-acessibilifolia/.

5. This is a point Alves develops in her book *E Se Experimentássemos Mais* (*And If We Experienced More*, 2020), in which she theorizes "aesthetic accessibility" specifically in the context of making museum spaces more accessible. More broadly, there are various attempts globally to make festivals more accessible and to create festivals focused on disability (see Snyder and Mitchell 2008; Cripps, Lyonblum,

and Small 2022), though the subject of disability and festivity is poorly studied. Voadora's efforts at including people with disabilities in an event as raucous as Rio's street carnival is without parallel in the literature I have surveyed.

6. See the series here: https://artedetodagente.com.br/uno-acessibilifolia /episodio-01-o-poder-do-carnaval-e-possibilitar-o-encontro/.

7. Growing out of the disability rights movement, the interdisciplinary field of disability studies offers a sociopolitical analysis of disability as a constructed category and critiques the medical interpretation of disability as deficit and disorder to be normalized. See Davis 2016; Shakespeare 2016.

8. The intersection of disability studies and music/performance is a growing focus of research. See, for example, Howe et al. 2016; Bakan 2015a, 2015b; Lerner and Straus 2006; Straus 2006; Sandahl and Auslander 2005.

9. See Godet 2020 on the history of debate on the politics of carnival.

10. 2021 Ramos interview.

11. 2021 Ramos interview.

12. 2021 Ramos interview.

13. See Maior 2015 for context on the history of disability rights in Brazil.

14. Outside of the scope of this article, the samba schools have been working to make their events more accessible as well, which is in some ways easier due to their higher level of organization and control. The high level of chaos of street carnival—for many, a crucial element of the event's carnivalesque authenticity—presents a different array of accessibility questions.

15. 2021 Ramos interview.

16. André Ramos, interview by author, Rio de Janeiro, Brazil, June 7, 2022.

17. André Ramos, interview with *Batuques e Confetes*, Rio de Janeiro, Brazil, December 2022. https://open.spotify.com/episode/77I8fghaUQoK9lT54kFKlb?si =e27ffeebe38c4397.

18. André Ramos, interview by author, Rio de Janeiro, Brazil, April 23, 2024.

19. 2021 Ramos interview.

20. Shcolnik's insight points toward disability justice movement leader Mia Mingus's concept of "access intimacy," "that elusive, hard to describe feeling when somebody else 'gets' your access needs.... Disabled people's liberation cannot be boiled down to logistics. Access intimacy is interdependence in action." See Mingus 2011.

21. This intersectional analysis points toward a framework of disability justice, which considers disability and ableism in relation to other forms of systemic oppression, such as racism, patriarchy, and capitalism. Conceived by queer, disabled women of color, disability justice critiques previous disability rights movements, such as those that led to the Americans for Disabilities Act in 1990, for their limited focus on physical disabilities over intellectual disabilities. Similarly to the depictions of second-wave feminists by third-wave feminists, they argue that the advocacy of previous disability rights movements is limited to people with disabilities who have other privileged racial, class, and gender identities. See Sins Invalid 2019.

22. 2022 Ramos interview.
23. 2022 Ramos interview.
24. 2022 Ramos interview.
25. 2024 Ramos interview.
26. 2021 Ramos interview.

Bibliography

Alves, Camila. 2020. *E se experimentássemos mais: Contribuições não técnicas de acessibilidade em espaços culturais*. Curitiba: Appris Editora.

Anon. 2022a. "Accessibilifolia 2022: Festival da folia disponível no Rio acontecerá de cinco a 27 de abril." *Mousart*, April 6, 2022. https://mousart.com/accessibilifolia-2022-festival-da-folia-disponivel-no-rio-acontecera-de-cinco-a-27-de-abril/.

Anon. 2022b. "Rio lança festival de folia acessível que engloba festas diversas." *AgênciaBrasil*, April 5, 2022. https://agenciabrasil.ebc.com.br/geral/noticia/2022-04/rio-lanca-festival-de-folia-acessivel-que-engloba-festas-diversas.

Bakan, Michael B. 2015a. "Being Applied in the Ethnomusicology of Autism." In *The Oxford Handbook of Applied Ethnomusicology*, edited by Pettan and Titon, 278–316. New York: Oxford University Press.

Bakan, Michael B. 2015b. "'Don't Go Changing to Try and Please Me': Combating Essentialism through Ethnography in the Ethnomusicology of Autism." *Ethnomusicology* 59(1): 116–44.

Bakhtin, Mikhail. (1941) 1984. *Rabelais and His World*. Translated by Helene Iswolsky. Bloomington: Indiana University Press.

Cripps, Jody, Ely Lyonblum, and Anita Small. 2022. "Signed Music in the Deaf Community Performing the Black Drum at Festival Clin d'Oeil." *Journal of Festive Studies* 4: 191–215.

Davis, Lennard J., ed. 2016. *The Disability Studies Reader*. New York: Routledge.

Feld, Steven. 1987. "Dialogic Editing: Interpreting How Kaluli Read Sound and Sentiment." *Cultural Anthropology* 2(2): 190–210.

Fernandes, Rita. 2019. *Meu bloco na rua: A retomada do carnaval de rua do Rio de Janeiro*. Rio de Janeiro: Civilização Brasileira.

Godet, Aurélie. 2020. "Behind the Masks, the Politics of Carnival." *Journal of Festive Studies* 2: 1–30.

Howe, Blake, Stephanie Jensen-Moulton, Neil Lerner, and Joseph Straus. 2016. *The Oxford Handbook of Music and Disability Studies*. Oxford: Oxford University Press.

Lerner, Neil, and Joseph N. Straus, eds. 2006. *Sounding Off: Theorizing Disability in Music*. New York: Routledge.

Lewis, Talila A. 2022. "January 2022 Working Definition of Ableism." *Talila A. Lewis* (blog), January 1, 2022. https://www.talilalewis.com/blog/january-2021-working-definition-of-ableism.

Mace, Ronald, Molly Story, and James Mueller. 1998. *The Universal Design File: Designing for People of All Ages and Abilities*. Raleigh: North Carolina State University.
Maior, Isabel. 2015. *Breve trajetória histórica do movimento das pessoas com deficiência*. São Paulo: Secretaria de Estado dos Direitos da Pessoa com Deficiência. http://violenciaedeficiencia.sedpcd.sp.gov.br/pdf/textosApoio/Texto2.pdf.
McDonald, David A., Andrew Snyder, and Jeremy Reed. 2025. "Introduction." In *Festival Activism*, edited by David A. McDonald, Andrew Snyder, and Jeremy Reed, 1–25. Bloomington: Indiana University Press.
Mingus, Mia. 2011. "Access Intimacy: The Missing Link." *Leaving Evidence* (blog), May 5, 2011. https://leavingevidence.wordpress.com/2011/05/05/access-intimacy-the-missing-link/.
Projeto Um Novo Olhar: Acessibilifolia. 2021. *Inclusão e Folia*. YouTube video series, episodes 1–7. July 1, 2021. https://www.youtube.com/playlist?list=PL5mP5ut65rSLvjuwsh NMUWOF7M6FR3VMS.
Ramos, André, Patrícia Dornelles, and Marcelo Jardim. 2020. "Acessibilifolia." Unpublished manuscript.
Sandahl, Carrie, and Phillip Auslander, eds. 2005. *Bodies in Commotion: Disability and Performance*. Ann Arbor: University of Michigan Press.
Shakespeare, Tom. 2016. "The Social Model of Disability." In *The Disability Studies Reader: Fifth Edition*, edited by Lennard J. Davis, 195–203. New York: Routledge.
Sins Invalid. 2019. *Skin, Tooth, and Bone: The Basis of Movement Is Our People, a Disability Justice Primer*. USA: Primedia eLaunch.
Snyder, Andrew. 2021. "Carnaval em casa: Activist Inversions in Rio de Janeiro's Street Carnival during the COVID-19 Pandemic." *Journal of Festive Studies* 3: 17–46.
Snyder, Andrew. 2022a. *Critical Brass: Street Carnival and Musical Activism in Olympic Rio de Janeiro*. Middleton, CT: Wesleyan University Press.
Snyder, Andrew. 2022b. "Revelry, Inclusion, and Disability in the Street Carnival of Rio de Janeiro." *Journal of Festival Culture Inquiry and Analysis* 1: 94–109.
Snyder, Andrew. 2023. "Affective Aspirations of Activist Musical Diplomacy at the Bicentennial Celebration of Brazilian Independence in Lisbon." *Yearbook for Traditional Music* 55(1): 1–31.
Snyder, Andrew, Erin Allen, and Reebee Garofalo. 2020. *HONK! A Street Band Renaissance of Music and Activism*. New York: Routledge.
Snyder, Andrew, Erin Allen, and Reebee Garofalo. 2022. "HONK!United: A Virtual Global Festival of Activist Brass Bands during the COVID-19 Pandemic." *Music and Politics* 16(1): 1–28.
Snyder, Sharon, and David Mitchell. 2008. "'How Do We Get All These Disabilities in Here?': Disability Film Festivals and the Politics of Atypicality." *Canadian Journal of Film Studies* 17(1): 11–29.
Straus, Joseph. 2006. "Normalizing the Abnormal: Disability in Music and Music Theory." *Journal of the American Musicological Society* 59(1): 113–84.

FOUR

The Festivalization of Feminism, DIY Music, and Intersecting Identities at Ladyfests

LOUISE BARRIÈRE

This chapter interrogates the articulation of DIY (do-it-yourself) music and marginalized gender identities in the context of a network of feminist DIY music festivals called Ladyfests. While Ladyfests can surely be considered music festivals, their programs almost always also comprise debates, conferences, and workshops on political issues, gender politics, and LGBT movements and identities. The first Ladyfest was organized in Olympia, WA (US), in 2000 under the impulse of former members of the feminist-punk Riot Grrrl movement. The idea spread around the world in the following years, mainly through the internet, leading to local adaptations of the festival's model (Zobl 2004). In this chapter, I specifically focus on the French and German branches of the Ladyfest network. Despite some variations across the entire network, most of the analyses presented in the following pages apply to the practices of other Ladyfests in the Global North.

The global spread of the Ladyfest network enacts what I call a "festivalization of feminism" within the DIY music scene. Here, I understand festivalization as "a current trend to rename as 'festivals' all kinds of traditional forms of gatherings, celebrations and festivities, from calendar to historical events, religious to secular rituals, markets, fairs, commemorations and anniversaries" (Ronström 2015, 72). More precisely, Ladyfests celebrate feminism and the presence of women and sexual minorities in a music scene dominated by heterosexual men. Ladyfests consequently also militate against male dominance and patriarchy, within both the public sphere and DIY music scenes. As Jodie Taylor highlights, "such festivals are considered to be a means to reinforce the shared values, identities, histories, ideologies and mythologies that bind a community, testifying to the longevity and triumph of a community while also indulging in spectacle and celebration" (Taylor 2014, 27). This articulation between community, politics, and spectacle stands at the forefront of Ladyfests. I suggest that feminist festival activists understand culture in a Gramscian sense—that is, as a site where the struggle for hegemony takes place (Williams 1973). As argued by Taylor, "festivals can function as politicized cultural practices and sanctioned forms of collective dissent, offering a limited means of defying hegemonic culture and social norms of the time" (Taylor 2014, 27).

Ladyfests were not the first feminist music festivals; however, they differ generationally from their precursors. So-called women's music festivals were notably organized across the United States in the 1970s (Staggenborg, Eder, and Sudderth 1994; Browne 2011a). At the same time, West German feminists organized *Frauenfest*, which, though similar to women's music festivals, have been investigated less than their American counterparts. German feminist bands of the time include the Flying Lesbians and Lysistrara. Several academic accounts of women's music festivals highlight a lack of trans inclusivity in these earlier festivals (Browne 2011b; Currans 2020). But Ladyfests developed after the spread of queer theory and third-wave feminism in the 1990s and 2000s, which broadened the scope of sexual and gender categories and also critiqued the privileged class and racial limitations of earlier movements (Möser 2007). Importantly, Ladyfests describe themselves as transinclusive—some of their activities remain unavailable to cisgender men but are accessible to a coalitional group of cisgender women, trans people (men and women), as well as nonbinary and intersex people. Ladyfest organizers consider all these groups as having less access to male-dominated popular music spaces: they struggle to access music education and find bandmates and are less represented on stage. Furthermore, Elizabeth K. Keenan and Sarah Dougher suggest that Ladyfests embrace an intersectional understanding of social relationships and appear more welcoming for Black people and people of color than traditional music festivals (Keenan and Dougher 2012). However, this political commitment does not always have a clear effect on the demographics of audience and performers alike.

Despite the self-positioning of Ladyfests in a history of feminist music, I have often been asked, "What makes their music feminist?" This is indeed a tricky question. Most of the bands I have seen play live do not present a politicized discourse. Their lyrics often comprise less political content than the festivals' statements. And while Ladyfest lineups showcase more marginalized musicians than the usual popular or DIY music festival lineup does, some traditional gender roles persist. In mixed-gender bands, women sing more often than they play drums, reflecting a common breakdown in the gendering of instruments. Maybe then, as Eileen Hayes suggests, feminist music at Ladyfests "is less a type of music than it is a site of women's thinking about music, a context for the enactment of lesbian feminist politics and notions of community" (2010, 1). I argue that because of this specific performance context, a feminist implication pervades the acts performed on stage despite their generally depoliticized lyrics and the maintenance of normative gender roles. Even in situations characterized by a lack of politicized lyrics or performance, Ladyfests manage to craft a feminist atmosphere. This has much to do with the context and conditions in which Ladyfests happen: gathering a wide range of female and queer musicians within a male-dominated music scene has political and feminist implications, even when such musicians do not systematically play with the usual elements of feminist performances.

This chapter sheds light on the multiple ways in which Ladyfests encourage and make musicians articulate their art as situated within feminist practices. Using the concept of mediation, I argue that the context of a musical performance modifies its meaning and shapes its political impact. For Antoine Hennion, the concept of mediation aims to overcome the binary relationship between the artwork and its spectator. Hennion stresses the existence of "the reciprocal, local, heterogeneous relations between art and public through precise devices, places, institutions, objects and human abilities" (2003, 80). However, Hennion's theory of mediation hardly takes into account the power relationships that organize chains of intermediaries. Bruno Latour advanced the concept of translation, close to Hennion's concept of mediation, while working on the construction of scientific facts (Hennion and Latour 1993). Latour defines translation as "the interpretation given by the fact-builders of their interests and that of the people they enroll" (Latour and Woolgar 1986, 108).[1] Latour explains how more-or-less powerful groups of scientists oppose each other during controversies, negotiating to "enroll," or recruit, each other in their projects. In the scientific field, not all these groups weigh the same: the chains of mediators contain strong and weak associations.

In this chapter, I suggest applying this theory to the mediation of music in Ladyfests. Latour's concept of translation underpins the ways in which Ladyfests draw on the marginalization of women and LGBT people in the DIY music scene to attract nonspecifically feminist bands based on the musicians' gender identities. In the context of a self-avowedly feminist festival, bands and musicians come to see their performances as serving a feminist agenda by feminist implication—that is, I argue that Ladyfests' organizers act as mediators striving to build a political atmosphere. However, weaker associations also appear in the social field of Ladyfests, considering that musicians of color remain underrepresented. I also take a further look at the ways in which marginalized BIPOC musicians contribute to the Ladyfest network by valorizing their own subjectivities in the festival space.

I draw on methodologies inspired by ethnomusicology and cultural and media studies to track political references in Ladyfest lineups, political heritage, statements, and stage performances. Subsequently, I develop my argument that Ladyfests act as feminist mediators of DIY music. Indeed, the atmosphere of Ladyfests is so fueled with politics that it encourages the audience to focus on the gendered dimension of showcased musical acts. Finally, I analyze the processes of marginalization that remain at work in feminist music festivals. I discuss the ways in which Black, African-European female musicians—and women of color more broadly—use visual or musical elements to celebrate identities beyond those of the dominant white group.

Festivals, Mediations, and Digital Media

Ladyfests are known as live music ventures, and live music is often perceived as unmediated, especially compared to recorded music, which relies heavily on various technologies for its production, diffusion, and consumption (Holt 2010, 244). Yet Philip Auslander (2008) has theorized "liveness" to refute the traditional opposition between live and mediatized performance. Auslander defines "classic liveness" by the "physical co-presence of performers and audience" and the "temporal simultaneity of production and reception experience in the moment" (2008, 61). He stresses that "almost all live performances now incorporate the technology of reproduction, at the very least in the use of electric amplification" (2008, 183). Moreover, despite being naively perceived as unmediated, live music engages many intermediaries—from the musicians themselves to the sound and light engineers, the stage managers, and the event organizers to the people who build the stage before the event ever occurs and those who clean the site afterward (Small 1998). By acting as mediators, they impact the ways in which live performances and spectacles are understood.

This chapter first relies on ethnography of a dozen of Ladyfests and likeminded festivals organized in France and Germany between 2017 and 2019.

Working on a network of festivals, I conducted multisited ethnography, which George Marcus (1995) understands as responding to changes in the organization of the world in the process of globalization. For researchers, it means following people, things, metaphors, stories, lives, conflicts, and ideas across places scattered around the world.

Besides multisited ethnography, I also analyzed a body of more than five hundred Ladyfest websites and social media pages on Myspace, Facebook, Instagram, and Twitter (now X). Starting my ethnographic study in mid-2017, I was in the middle of conducting fieldwork when the COVID-19 pandemic struck in early 2020. All festivals canceled their upcoming editions, and I had to find another data source to analyze. I chose web archives due to the nature of mediations and mediatizations on which contemporary popular music festivals rely. Here, I understand mediatization as a specific kind of mediation: one that relies on informational media. As such, the media becomes another intermediary in the chain of mediators that links the musical object and its consumer.

Contemporary festivals increasingly rely on digital media for promotion. Online content allows them to maintain a connection with attendees and fans. Festivals are not only mediations of music; they are also themselves mediated by online presences, as the internet accompanies and extends participants' experiences (Danielsen and Kjus 2019). When advertising for a new edition, contemporary festivals often post links to bands' digital audio and audiovisual recordings, making the artists' music available to the target audience of the events. In other words, the presence of festivals on the internet serves the propagation of recorded music. In the case of activist festivals, such as Ladyfests, the internet extends the social and political impact of events by giving them a wider and longer dimension. Ladyfests' online pages spread a feminist discourse that surrounds and shapes the interpretation of music. Their webpages thus participate in associating the artists they program with feminism even if feminism is not the primary cause of the artists themselves.

Criticizing the Gendered Division of Musical Labor

Ladyfests' intention to transform the gendered division of musical labor is especially explicit in the organizers' public statements. For instance, the 2008 Ladyfest Mülheim website claims that

> From our [the organizers'] point of view, society as a whole is still male dominated. This is not limited to specific areas and can also be found in

subcultural contexts. Concretely, it means that we still observe, especially in the rock, hardcore and punk scenes, that most concert organizers are men, that most musicians on stage are men (apart from a few female singers and bass players), and that the audience is also male dominated. Meanwhile, women often sit at the entrance or behind the counter. This is why organizing a Ladyfest means so much to us: we want to give [female and queer] musicians a platform.[2]

Booking more women and gender minorities on stage is key to the feminist activism of Ladyfests organizers. Most of the festival organizers I have met are keen to book women-only bands or FLINT bands (female, lesbian, intersex, nonbinary, and trans people) (Barrière 2022).

Yet this is not always possible, and many festivals book mixed-gender bands. More marginally, some work with all-male bands known for their antisexist stance. In 2017, Miette and Coralie, the organizers of the Empowering Festival based in western France, disclosed to me their booking policy: "First of all, we try not to book male bands. But it's not that easy, because there are fewer and fewer female bands in the area. And sometimes, they are not available, so yeah, we're screwed.... So, for festivals, we're mostly looking for feminist or feminist (friendly) bands, because we don't want to hear sexist discourses during the shows."[3] While this booking policy is due to a scarcity of female musicians, it also indicates that Ladyfest organizers consider men as potential allies in the fight for equality. However, as I have highlighted elsewhere (Barrière 2022), including men in lineups tends to reinforce a traditionally gendered division of musical roles previously analyzed by feminist ethnomusicologist Ellen Koskoff (1995, 2014). Within mixed-gender bands, women remain predominantly singers, while men play a variety of instruments. Gender roles and stereotypes are not easy to transform if traditional gender roles play out even at Ladyfests.

Feminist Lineages and Contemporary Social Movements in Ladyfest Networks

Moreover, female and queer artists are not necessarily feminist. Therefore, I sought to unravel the political influences of the German and French Ladyfest networks. I explored how these networks place themselves in relation with local and global feminist histories as part of a reflection on the globalization of feminist thoughts and movements.

References to previous feminist movements appear on Ladyfests' websites and social media pages. The most evident reference connects the contemporary Ladyfest network to the 1990s punk-feminist Riot Grrrl movement. Born in the US in the 1990s, the Riot Grrrl movement went on to reach Canada and the UK and constituted the first translocal, if primarily anglophone, punk-feminist network to reject a male-dominated history of rock music. Though there were already central female figures in the punk scenes of the 1970s, Riot Grrrls openly politicized their gender identity, relying on zines such as *Jigsaw*, *Girl Germs*, and *GUNK* and founding bands such as Bikini Kill, Heavens to Betsy, and Bratmobile to encourage their peers to think about gender power relationships in the punk scene and beyond. Some pioneering Riot Grrrls, including Bratmobile's Alison Wolfe, took part in the organization of the first Ladyfest in Olympia, WA, in 2000 (Downes 2007).

However, the connection between the two movements is less visible in most European countries, where the Riot Grrrl movement hardly developed in the 1990s (Peglow 2011). Knowledge of the Riot Grrrl movement most likely spread with the development of the internet, allowing French and German Ladyfest organizers to claim this feminist and punk lineage. References to the Riot Grrrl movement are particularly obvious in statements that Ladyfest organizing committees publish on their websites. For instance, in 2015, Ladyfest Kassel's organizers wrote: "The first Ladyfest took place in 2000, in Olympia, USA, and stemmed from the Riot Grrrl movement of the beginning of the 90s. From there on, the concept found supporters and organizers all over the world. In Germany, Ladyfests were and are also organized in Göttingen, Aachen, Berlin, Mainz, Leipzig, Darmstradt, Lüneburg, Frankfurt, among many other cities."[4] However, musically, the Ladyfests I have studied tend to distance themselves from Riot Grrrl's punk aesthetics. The connection claimed by French and German Ladyfest organizers is thus more political than musical. Indeed, most of them book bands from a variety of genres, including hip-hop and electronic dance music (as analyzed by Elizabeth Bridges in 2005). Indeed, Elizabeth Bridges argues that the popularity of electronic dance music in Berlin specifically, and in Germany more broadly, shapes the music tastes of local Ladyfest organizers, and through them, festival lineups.

On the political side, some German Ladyfests claim a heritage from the 1970s and 1980s women's marches that took place across Germany under the name *Walpurgisnächte* (see Barrière 2020). As the Walpurgisnächte remain a matter of German national feminist history, French Ladyfests do not claim this reference. More curious, though, is the absence of reference to previous national feminist music initiatives such as Frauenfest or rock bands like the

Flying Lesbians. All in all, it seems that the global spread of certain references, such as the Riot Grrrl movement, has made parts of local feminist history vanish.

On the other hand, some festivals and artists also make connections to contemporary feminist social movements. Among them, German rapper Sookee is one of the most popular artists in the German Ladyfest scene. She appears in the lineups of eight festivals between 2010 and 2012. In 2012, the Ladyfest Aachen website introduces her most recent album, *Bitches, Butches, Dykes & Divas*, as such: "With 'bitches, butches, dykes & divas,' [Sookee] released in 2011 her third solo album. The title track became the soundtrack of the SlutWalk march in Berlin and accompanies the SlutWalk movement in the entire German-speaking area."[5]

The SlutWalk is a global feminist movement that was launched in Toronto in April 2011. Based on spectacular street demonstrations, SlutWalk protests aim to fight rape culture, slut shaming, and victim blaming. Protestors are often scantily dressed to signify that no individual should experience sexual violence regardless of how they dress, as one of their slogans says: "A dress is not a yes."[6] Sookee's song "Bitches, Butches, Dykes & Divas" echoes through its lyrics the fights and concerns of the SlutWalk movement. The audience can for instance hear "Keine klamotte war je zu knapp" (No clothes were ever too tight) or "Reclaiming, embracing, die Schlampe entzieht sich" (Reclaiming, embracing, the slut reveals herself). Yet, paradoxically, the SlutWalk movement and Sookee draw on very different modes of action. Encouraging protestors to undress, the SlutWalk movement plays with the male gaze. Sookee could claim a similar tactic on stage, yet she refuses to sexualize herself in her musical practice (Spiers 2015). As Spiers highlights, Sookee is highly critical of the hypersexualization of women in hip-hop culture, and her use of sophisticated, almost academic language in her lyrics sheds light on her politics more than her visual presentation does.

The Feminist Body on Stage: Parody and Disidentification

Unlike Sookee, however, and despite the explicitly feminist lineages traced by festival organizers, most of the artists and bands booked by Ladyfests hardly write any political texts. If no political message was found in their lyrics, I then hypothesized that it might appear elsewhere, such as in bands' stage performances and uses of the body. When performing on stage, musicians of course use their bodies to play an instrument; they use their bodies literally as an instrument in the case of vocal performance. But their bodies also allow them to embody a "stage persona," which Auslander defines as "a person's representation of self within a discursive domain of music" (2006, 102). In other words, "when we hear a musician play, the source of the sound is a version of that person constructed for the specific purpose of playing music under particular circumstances" (2006, 102). Using specific costumes, makeup, accessories, language, or gestures on stage, musicians build various personae, and such elements may serve a feminist discourse.

As many performance scholars argue, voices, instruments, and clothes are gendered, and musicians may use them to subvert or contravene gender norms. Artists caricature features deemed feminine and draw on parody, sometimes relying on exaggerated body parts. The Brazilian funk singer MC Xuparina, for instance, transformed herself into a gigantic vulva during her performance at LaDIYfest Berlin in 2012.[7] In so doing, she relied on a sense of the grotesque similar to Bakhtin's definition of the carnivalesque (Bakhtin 1984; for an application to popular music, see, for instance, Kattari 2020). Bakhtin's carnivalesque is highly referenced in academic studies on festivals and festivalization. In this context, carnivals and festivals are considered "spaces for the articulation of alternative, liminal forms of identity" (Bennett and Woodward 2014, 11). During such events, participants often "engage in revelry, hedonism and other forms of anti-hegemonic behavior not generally regarded as legitimate forms of social conduct in everyday life" (Bennett and Woodward 2014, 11).

As shown in YouTube videos of the spectacle, during LaDIYfest Berlin, MC Xuparina's transformation into a human-sized vulva relies on a simple accessory she wears as a skirt or scarf. The pinkish piece of cloth is circling her waist when the MC pulls it up to her shoulders and drapes herself in it, singing, "Ich liebe meine Vagina" (I love my vagina). Halfway through the song, Xuparina puts her microphone down. She inserts her arms in a fold that the fabric is forming on her shoulders. She then moves part of the fabric behind her head, leaving another part to hang behind her back. As a recording of her voice continues to sing the text, the singer vigorously moves the fabric with her arms above her head. Bending her knees in rhythm, jumping from one side of the stage to the other, she is now disguised as a vulva—echoing the song's title.

As Jodie Taylor writes, "In Bakhtinian terms, festivals can temporarily facilitate the playful transgression of authority and the symbolic inversion of social hierarchies through carnivalesque ritual and spectacle" (Taylor 2014,

27). One of these symbolic inversions involves revealing what is usually hidden, such as orifices and genitals. In MC Xuparina's show at LaDIYfest Berlin, the staging of the genital orifice takes a particular meaning. Beyond the carnivalesque, embodying female genitals also conveys a feminist meaning. MC Xuparina is replying, humorously, to the dominant sexist and heteronormative discourse of carioca funk. As highlighted by Caitlin E. Wolfe Liblong, women who attend funk *bailes* in Rio de Janeiro are expected to dance in hypersexualized ways on stage or in the audience: "The dancing fuels the sexual atmosphere and the erotic dimension of the baile includes moves like the bundinha and the cachorrão, simulating sex.... Girls are handpicked at a show to go up on stage and dance with the male performers. They dance back to front, some girls facing the crowd and swiveling their hips as the men make pelvic thrusting moves towards their buttocks. Some dance front to front with the men, occasionally picked up by the hips and held so that the crotch areas make contact" (2008, 24).

As she dresses as an oversized vulva while singing an ode to her vagina, MC Xuparina reclaims these stereotypes and rearticulates them through parody and exaggeration. Her gesture appears akin to José Esteban Muñoz's concept of "disidentification" (1999), a survival and negotiation strategy that helps minoritarian subjects negotiate their trajectories in a normative public space. In embodying a vulva, MC Xuparina plays with the normative and stereotyped phantasms of both the dominant public sphere and the Brazilian funk music scene. She offers the audience a parody of gender stereotypes and essentialization in an incongruous, humorous, and ironic manner. It is precisely the humorous yet critical dimension of the MC's stage performance that conveys her "ability to disidentify with the mass public and instead, through this disidentification, contribute to the function of a counterpublic sphere" (Muñoz 1999, 5).[8]

Ladyfests as Feminist Mediators of DIY Music

Though MC Xuparina's performance is intentionally feminist, the feminist context of Ladyfests also influences the interpretation of acts that are not as clearly so. One key example is the synth-punk band GYM TONIC, which comprises three female and one male musician. During fieldwork, I saw GYM TONIC performing at the Dresden-based Böse & Gemein Festival in 2018. On this occasion, the four members of GYM TONIC performed on stage wearing Boy Scout uniforms. While the choice of scout costumes seems uncanny enough for a punk band, the fact that these are *boy* scout costumes appears as a subversion of gender roles. Moreover, in an interview for Berlin-based musical webzine *Schmutz*, Stephanie, one of the musicians, explains that her band plays in "boy scout" costume, insisting on the term *boy* and even specifying "not girl scout."[9] She highlights that the costume choice did not stem from a conscious choice to criticize or play with gender stereotypes. But as they have been invited to feminist festivals more often, band members have noticed that for the festival organizers and audiences, their costumes carry a different meaning: "Three of our four members are female, and we wear Boy Scout uniforms [not Girl Scout] uniforms when we perform. I don't think of us as a girl band, but because we are invited to a lot of feminist festivals I think others think we are.... Wearing Boy Scout costumes as females, playing with this idea, was not a gender conscious decision, but rather an accident found at Humana [a local second-hand shop] that kept on developing as we found more patches online."[10] The staging practices of GYM TONIC have thus become associated with ideas the musicians do not consciously or explicitly express (at least in this context). Consequently, feminist festivals shape the meanings of stage performances. In so doing, they act as mediators of music. Indeed, in Latour's theories, mediators are not neutral intermediaries but rather actors that "transform, translate and modify the meaning of the elements it [the mediator—in our case, the festival] is supposed to carry," as Eriksson, Fleischer, Johansson, Snickars, and Vondereau (2019) aptly summarize. In this case, the feminist festival context translates the stage performance of GYM TONIC into a feminist discourse on gender roles regardless of the performers' lack of intent. The festival shapes the way in which the audience perceives, understands, and engages with the music on stage.

When Ladyfest organizers formulate discourses on feminist lineage, the gendered division of musical labor, or gender stereotypes, they construct and assert ideological material that influences the ways in which the audience will "decode" stage performances' meanings (Hall 1973). Studying television discourses and popular culture, Stuart Hall asserts that there is no unequivocal interpretation of a message. Members of an audience will not necessarily decode a message in the same way it was encoded. In other words, one message often means different things to different people. Stepping away from television studies, the example of GYM TONIC stresses the importance of context for the reception and decoding of a message. If the band had refused to play for a feminist festival, its performances would likely not have been interpreted as playing with gender roles. Ladyfests add feminist value to performances independent of the original discourse promoted by the musicians. The feminist festival and the festivalization of feminism therefore allow musicians to cross the lines between "female" and "feminist" in diverse ways.

If we go back to Latour and Woolgar's definition of translation as "the interpretation given by the fact-builders of their interests and that of the people they enroll" (1986, 108), it appears that Ladyfest collectives recruit female or mixed-gender music bands to build their lineups. These bands serve the interests of the Ladyfests feminist agenda, as they afford the celebration of women and queer identities subject to male dominance and marginalization both within DIY music scenes and society writ large. Furthermore, the Ladyfest collectives provide a feminist interpretation of these bands' interests. Musicians, organizers, and activist discourses seem mutually constitutive: they draw on each other to construct different potential interpretations of stage performances and music.

Fragmented Identities and Intersectionality in the Ladyfest Network

But questioning the power relationships of gender is not the sole concern of Ladyfest feminist activism. Intersectionality is also often mentioned in the discourses of Ladyfest organizers. In festival announcement statements from 2017 onward, Ladyfest Heidelberg organizers repeatedly mention that "intersectional approaches are an essential part of our queer-feminism. In our analysis, we always try not to focus only on white, straight, cisgender, middle-class women, and to address and shed light on the intersections [of gender] with other power relationships such as disability, nationality, body norms, class, and many more."[11] Black feminist scholars such as Kimberlé Crenshaw (2017) and Patricia Hill Collins and Sirma Bilge (2020) coined the term *intersectionality* to highlight that power relationships such as gender, race, and class are not separate categories but intersect with each other in different ways for every person. In other words, the way in which a person experiences their gender identity is always informed by their race and class identities and vice versa: the ways in which they experience racialization is informed by their gender and class identities. An individual and their social experiences cannot be defined by a single parameter. Therefore, individual and collective identities are never fixed nor essential but stem from the multiple power relationships that shape our experiences.

Yet despite the importance of intersectional theories in the Ladyfest statements, when asked to describe festival audience members, organizers often present them as (predominantly) white. For instance, one explained to me that she saw the audience as "almost exclusively white. Between eighteen and thirty-five-year-old mostly—queer people of all genders and some straight cis women, mostly university educated or from university educated families." This statement does not reveal the actual and precise composition of the audience; however, it sheds light on the ways in which festival organizers tailor programs with specific ideas of their audience in mind. Indeed, during the various Ladyfests I attended, very few spaces were dedicated to women and queer people of color, and very few artists of color were performing on stage.

Though marginalized within the festival space, artists of color sometimes use music to showcase their identities beyond gender. The aforementioned Brazilian funk singer, MC Xuparina, for instance, surely criticizes the sexist discourse of funk bailes through her performance as a human-sized vulva. But in so doing, she also criticizes the hypersexualization of Black and Brazilian bodies (see Brooks 2010). The process of disidentification staged during her show at LaDIYfest Berlin concerns not solely her female identity but also a more complex identity as a Black Brazilian lesbian in Germany.

The same year that MC Xuparina performed at LaDIYfest Berlin, Ladyfest Aachen hosted a concert by the African European singer and musician NOISEAUX. When that concert happened, NOISEAUX had just released her second album, *SPECTRUM*. NOISEAUX's music is often characterized as hybrid. Her Bandcamp page reads: "Artist/Activist Noah Sow is no stranger to shattering musical pigeonholes, and in *SPECTRUM*, she brings elements of West African textures, Disco, and Euro-Electro - with notions of 80's and 90's pop, creating a sonic current beneath multi-layered lyrics."[12] NOISEAUX also claims a punk sensibility, yet she does not make punk rock music and even criticizes the whiteness and masculinity of the genre. In 2012, NOISEAUX gave an interview to *Live Unchained*, a former blog dedicated to women of African descent who work in creative industries. During this interview, NOISEAUX expressed that she does not feel in line with punk as a music genre and scene. Nevertheless, she claims a punk-inspired, independent, deviant attitude:

> Punk has different aspects. One is a musical genre. The second and more important one for me is that it is an attitude. I'd call it being deviant, living on one's own account. Not accepting society's stereotypes and pigeonholes—that can definitely result in a way of life.... I could always relate

to some of the punk rock elements: openly expressed emotion, explicit resistance against societal norms, I experienced this as very freeing. Some other elements of "punk rock" I never quite understood . . . like, how did they manage to turn it into this 90% white scene?[13]

NOISEAUX thus fights against the whiteness of punk, which turns a blind eye to its Black influences. To do so, she claims punk as "Black music." It should be noted that the expression *Black music* has been put into question by Philip Tagg (1989). But in his text, Tagg is especially critical toward white musicologists who use this category to essentialize and reify Blackness and Black music in their analyses. In NOISEAUX's case, *Black music* as a term has not been imposed on a type of music by an academic expert. Rather, it is claimed by the artist herself as a gesture of strategic essentialism (Eide 2016).

Musically, NOISEAUX is clearly opposed to any kind of essentialization. She mixes music forms from various areas of the world. For instance, the first track of *SPECTRUM* is an a cappella song entitled "Bavaropeulhfrancohanseate." In singing this word NOISEAUX claims a composite identity with roots in Western Africa and Europe. In the second song of the album, "I Have a Loaded Voice," she calls back to this "hyphenated identity" (Stokes 2004), especially in her use of rhythm. "I Have a Loaded Voice" is particularly interesting since its rhythm is not binary—as is usually the case in punk of electronic dance music—but not ternary either. The song relies on an asymmetrical rhythmic pattern composed of two divisions of three quavers and one division of two (3+3+2) (see fig. 4.1).

Such patterns have been identified by ethnomusicologist Simha Arom (2007) in traditional music from western and central Africa, and these elements have further circulated with colonization and migration, as underscored by Mark Slobin in *Subcultural Sounds: Micromusics of the West* (1992). Paradoxically, syncopation and polyrhythms are used to essentialize African music in colonial contexts. But, at the same time, French ethnomusicologist and political scientist Denis-Constant Martin highlights that rhythm is one of the most useful elements for artists to trace an African music lineage. Denis-Constant Martin also warns ethnomusicologists against the potential essentialization of such rhythmic forms, insisting that "putting the stress on heritage or filiation . . . amounts to denying black people . . . the ability to cope with a new environment, to adapt to it—that is, to create a new but truly black culture and, consequently, to transform their new environment" (1991, 19). While drawing on electronic dance music and pop music influences,

NOISEAUX's music also uses rhythmic patterns that commonly appear in African and Afro-diasporic music genres. She thereby distinguishes herself from many white artists who perform less syncopated music during Ladyfests. In "I Have a Loaded Voice," rhythm is only one layer of the song. Other layers comprise crescendos of synth chords and pop-inspired singing. Moreover, the following titles of the album are inspired by Caribbean music ("Resonate My Dance") and country music ("There Can be Home"), as the musician herself explains. Some of the songs mention the singer's autism ("I Am So Reaching Out Right Now"), while others refer to migration. All these characteristics—lyrics, instruments, rhythm—blend together in such a way that NOISEAUX's identity cannot be defined from a single point of view. Just as her music seeks to escape genre categories, NOISEAUX's album *SPECTRUM* constantly reminds the listener that the musician's identity cannot be summarized by her experiences of migration, gender, descent, or autism.

In sum, Ladyfests often claim the influence of intersectional theory. However, their lineups, audiences, and organizing crews remain predominantly white. Openly speaking of migration, gender, and autism allows NOISEAUX to claim her own musical and political position within the Ladyfests' feminist space and further materialize the intersectional discourse of the organizers into reality.

By celebrating the various dimension of their identities, MC Xuparina and NOISEAUX position themselves as "outsiders within" in the German Ladyfest scene. The figure of the outsider within has been conceptualized by Patricia Hill Collins "to describe individuals . . . who occupied the edges between groups of unequal power. . . . The outsider-within construct spoke to the ambiguities of belonging, yet not fully belonging" (Collins 2012, 66–67). As outsiders within, BIPOC musicians might appear to not fully belong in predominantly white feminist music scenes. Still, they "can draw on a creative tension of being on the margins within intersecting systems of race, class, gender, sexual, and national oppression. . . . As border crossers and boundary markers, people in outsider-within spaces contest the meanings of the categories themselves" (Collins 2012, 67–68). NOISEAUX specifically keeps moving from one facet of her identity to another, from one song to another. Her music offers a valuable and important critique of the power relationships within contemporary feminist spaces. This critique is not only visible in her lyrics; it is also prevalent within the musical structures of her songs, which creatively depart from the most common conventions of punk rock.

Figure 4.1. Musical example.

Conclusions

In French and German Ladyfests, bands and musicians articulate gender identity and feminist activism in various ways. Some musicians do conceptualize the staging of their performances to advance an explicit political discourse. Beyond lyrics, using costumes allows them to play with gender roles in different ways. As they reverse or parody stereotypes, artists engage in a process of disidentification, claiming their refusal to see their identity essentialized by dominant discourses both within the scene and in the global public sphere.

I have argued, however, that it is most importantly the context of the festival itself that conditions the decoding of performances. As I have shown, while women and queer people compose the majority of Ladyfest lineups, only a few bands highlight political statements in their lyrics, as the Riot Grrrl movement did before them. The discourses displayed in festivals' political statements nonetheless afford the identification of feminist lineages and connections with broader feminist lineages and social movements, such as Walpurgisnächte or the SlutWalk marches. As such, Ladyfests indeed act as feminist mediations of DIY music. With the help of political discourses in presentation texts, workshops, and conferences, the festivals suggest feminist readings of musical performances regardless of artists' intent. In other words, Ladyfests translate the stage performance into feminist discourses. While celebrating the representation of women and queer people in DIY music, Ladyfests encourage a feminist interpretation of their discourses, performances, and interests. As feminist festival organizers gather a majority of female and queer musicians, the absence of female and queer musicians in other circumstances becomes much more noticeable. In consequence, their mere presence on stage sounds like a feminist statement. This process is part of the festivalization of feminism that characterizes Ladyfests as feminist mediations of music.

Finally, one of the ways Ladyfest collectives have sought to define the feminist context of the events more recently has been by bringing intersectionality within their range of concern, aiming at distinguishing themselves from previous white feminist music movements (see Hayes 2010 on women's music festivals). Yet this project too is often more discourse than reality, as Ladyfests tend to include very few artists of color in their lineups. Their attempts at diversifying the people represented on stage has so far largely failed at subverting power relationships within the feminist DIY music scene. The minority of BIPOC musicians who participate and promote their interpretation of intersectionality still embody the position of outsiders within the festival. They put their Afropean or African American identity at the core of their music and performance and stress the necessity of taking multiple facets of identity into account when navigating power relationships. They call into question the predominant whiteness of DIY music scenes and feminist movements, arguing that feminist music and festival scenes cannot be built at the expense of women of color.

Common to these various strategies of a feminist festival, we see a theme of responding to lack. For the organizers, there are not enough explicitly feminist acts to fill a program, not enough female instrumentalists to completely avoid programming male ones, and not enough people of color in the DIY scene to create the intersectional public of their aspirations. We might even see this lack as a condition of activist festivals, as they indeed critique the hegemonic world from their own position of marginality. But in the various ways Ladyfests translate and curate the festivalization of feminism, they seek to bring this aspirational world more fully into being.

Notes

1. In the case of music festivals, booking a band could be an equivalent to enrolling it in a project.

2. For the original text, see "Ladyfest Mülheim 2008," accessed September 12, 2023, https://web.archive.org/web/20080924142144/http://www.ladyfest-muelheim.net/?page_id=2. All translations from German and French to English are the author's.

3. Interview by author, March 11, 2017. Names of the festival and interviewees have been changed on their request to remain anonymous.

4. "Lady*fest Kassel," *Tumblr*, accessed September 12, 2023, https://ladyfestkassel.tumblr.com/2015_about.

5. For the original text, see "Ladyfest Aachen," http://ladyfestaachen.blog sport.de/ldyfest/#konzertfreitag (site discontinued).

6. For more information on the SlutWalk movement, see Mendes 2015.

7. I recommend readers watch "Ich Liebe Meine Vagina - MC Xuparina Live @ SO36," YouTube video, October 2012, https://www.youtube.com/watch?v=HnMDMHi2SVE.

8. Muñoz's definition of the concept of "disidentification" relies on Nancy Fraser's concept of "counterpublic sphere." Fraser described counterpublic spheres as "parallel discursive arenas where members of subordinated social groups invent and circulate counterdiscourses, which in turn permit them to formulate oppositional interpretations of their identities, interests, and needs" (Fraser 1990, 67). The Ladyfest network as a whole could be deemed "counterpublic" within DIY music scenes because it allows women and gender minorities to formulate and claim their own interests and needs in a male-dominated space. Ladyfests afford them spaces to gather, debate, and stand up against the patriarchal structure they observe in their daily lives and in their participation in music scenes.

9. Tara Meyer, "A (Gendered) Work in Progress," March 1, 2021, https://web.archive.org/web/20210301034319/https:/www.schmutzberlin.com/gendered-work-progress/.

10. Meyer, "A (Gendered) Work in Progress."

11. See "Selbstverständnis Lady*fest 2018," accessed September 30, 2023, https://ladyfesthd.wordpress.com/wer-wir-sind/selbstverstaendnis-ladyfest-2018/.

12. "SPECTRUM | NOISEAUX," May 1, 2013, https://web.archive.org/web/20130501045046/http:/noiseaux.bandcamp.com/album/spectrum.

13. "Live Unchained Blogozine," accessed September 12, 2023, https://web.archive.org/web/20120314182438/http:/www.liveunchained.com:80/blog.

Bibliography

Arom, Simha. 2007. *La boîte à outils d'un ethnomusicologue*. Montréal: Les Presses de l'Université de Montréal.

Auslander, Philip. 2006. "Musical Personae." *Drama Review* 50(1): 100–19.

Auslander, Philip. 2008. *Liveness: Performance in a Mediatized Culture*. London: Routledge.

Bakhtin, Mikhail. 1984. *Rabelais and His World*. Bloomington: Indiana University Press.

Barrière, Louise. 2020. "Se réapproprier la nuit: Politiques et représentations musicales de la nuit urbaine, de la Walpurgisnacht aux festivals punk-féministes." *MUSICultures* 47: 139–263.

Barrière, Louise. 2022. "Faire entendre les voix de contre-publics féministes des scènes DIY: Emplois vocaux et musicaux dans les Ladyfests en Allemagne." *Semen* 51: 19–37.

Bennett, Andy, and Ian Woodward. 2014. "Introduction." In *The Festivalization of Culture*, edited by Andy Bennett, Jodie Taylor, and Ian Woodward, 1–11. Farnham: Ashgate.

Bridges, Elizabeth. 2005. "Love Parade GmbH vs. Ladyfest: Electronic Music as a Mode of Feminist Expression in Contemporary German Culture." *Women in German Yearbook: Feminist Studies in German Literature & Culture* 21(1): 215–40.

Brooks, Siobhan. 2010. "Hypersexualization and the Dark Body: Race and Inequality among Black and Latina Women in the Exotic Dance Industry." *Sexuality Research and Social Policy* 7(2): 70–80.

Browne, Kath. 2011a. "Lesbian Separatist Feminism at Michigan Womyn's Music Festival." *Feminism & Psychology* 21(2): 248–56.

Browne, Kath. 2011b. "Beyond Rural Idylls: Imperfect Lesbian Utopias at Michigan Womyn's Music Festival." *Journal of Rural Studies* 27(1): 13–23.

Collins, Patricia Hill. 2012. *On Intellectual Activism*. Philadelphia: Temple University Press.

Collins, Patricia Hill, and Sirma Bilge. 2020. *Intersectionality*. New York: John Wiley & Sons.

Crenshaw, Kimberlé W. 2017. *On Intersectionality: Essential Writings*. New York: New Press.

Currans, Elizabeth. 2020. "Transgender Women Belong Here: Contested Feminist Visions at the Michigan Womyn's Music Festival." *Feminist Studies* 46(2): 459–88.

Danielsen, Anne, and Yngvar Kjus. 2019. "The Mediated Festival: Live Music as Trigger of Streaming and Social Media Engagement." *Convergence* 25(4): 714–34.

Downes, Julia. 2007. "Riot Grrrl: The Legacy and Contemporary Landscape of Feminist Cultural Activism." In *Riot Grrrl: Revolution Girl Style Now!*, edited by Nadine Monem, 12–50. London: Black Dog.

Eide, Elisabeth. 2016. "Strategic Essentialism." In *The Wiley Blackwell Encyclopedia of Gender and Sexuality Studies*, edited by Nancy A. Naples, 2278–80. Hoboken: Wiley & Sons.

Eriksson, Maria, Rasmus Fleischer, Anna Johansson, Pelle Snickars, and Patrick Vondereau. 2019. *Spotify Teardown: Inside the Black Box of Streaming Music*. Cambridge: MIT Press.

Fraser, Nancy. 1990. "Rethinking the Public Sphere: A Contribution to the Critique of Actually Existing Democracy." *Social Text* 25/26: 56–80.

Hall, Stuart. 1973. "Encoding and Decoding in the Television Discourse." Paper for the Colloquy on Training in the Critical Reading of Televisual Language. Council and Centre for Mass Communication Research, University of Leicester. http://epapers.bham.ac.uk/2962/1/Hall%2C_1973%2C_Encoding_and_Decoding_in_the_Television_Discourse.pdf.

Hayes, Eileen M. 2010. *Songs in Black and Lavender: Race, Sexual Politics, and Women's Music.* Champaign: University of Illinois Press.

Hennion, Antoine. 2003. "Music and Mediation: Towards a new Sociology of Music." In *The Cultural Study of Music: A Critical Introduction,* edited by Martin Clayton, Trevor Herbert, and Richard Middleton, 249–60. London: Routledge.

Hennion, Antoine, and Bruno Latour. 1993. "Objet d'art, objet de science: Note sur les limites de l'anti-fétichisme." *Sociologie de l'art* 6: 7–24.

Holt, Fabian. 2010. "The Economy of Live Music in the Digital Age." *European Journal of Cultural Studies* 13(2): 243–61.

Kattari, Kimberly. 2020. *Psychobilly: Subcultural Survival.* Philadelphia: Temple University Press.

Keenan, Elizabeth K., and Sarah Dougher. 2012. "Riot Grrrl, Ladyfest and Rock Camps for Girls." In *Women Make Noise: Girl Bands from Motown to the Modern,* edited by Julia Downes, 260–319. Twickenham: Supernova Books.

Koskoff, Ellen. 1995. "When Women Play: The Relationship between Musical Instruments and Gender Style." *Canadian University Music Review/Revue de musique des universités canadiennes* 16(1): 114–27.

Koskoff, Ellen. 2014. *A Feminist Ethnomusicology: Writings on Music and Gender.* Urbana: Illinois University Press.

Latour, Bruno. 2005. *Reassembling the Social: An Introduction to Actor-Network-Theory.* New York: Oxford University Press.

Latour, Bruno, and Woolgar, Steve. 1986. *Laboratory Life: The Construction of Scientific Facts.* Princeton: Princeton University Press.

Mackay, Finn. 2015. *Radical Feminism: Feminist Activism in Movement.* New York: Springer.

Madden, David. 2011. "Crossdressing to Backbeats: The Status of the Electroclash Producer and the Politics of Electronic Music." *Dancecult* 4(2): 27–47.

Marcus, Sara. 2011. *Girls to the Front: The True Story of the Riot Grrrl Revolution.* New York: Harper Perennial.

Martin, Denis-Constant. 1991. "Filiation of Innovation? Some Hypotheses to Overcome the Dilemma of Afro-American Music's Origins." *Black Music Research Journal* 11(1): 19–38.

Mendes, Kaitlynn. 2015. *Slutwalk: Feminism, Activism and Media.* New York: Springer.

Montoro-Pons, Juan D., and Manuel Cuadrado-García. 2020. "Music Festivals as Mediators and Their Influence on Consumer Awareness." *Poetics* 80: n.p.

Möser, Cornelia. 2007. "Aspekte der Gender-Debatte in Frankreich und Deutschland." *Trajectoires* 1: n.p.

Muñoz, José Esteban. 1999. *Disidentifications: Queers of Color and the Performance of Politics.* Minneapolis: University of Minnesota Press.

Peglow, Katja. 2011. "Warum Riot Grrrl in Deutschland still blieb." In *Riot Grrrl Revisited: Geschichte und Gegenwart einer feministischen Bewegung*, edited by Katja Peglow and Jonas Englemann, 166–70. Mainz: Ventil Verlag.

Ronström, Owe. 2015. "Four Facets of Festivalisation." *Puls-Journal for Ethnomusicology and Ethnochoreology* 1(1): 67.

Slobin, Mark J. 1992. *Subcultural Sounds: Micromusics of the West*. Middletown: Wesleyan University Press.

Small, Christopher. 1998. *Musicking: The Meanings of Performing and Listening*. Middletown: Wesleyan University Press.

Spiers, Emily. 2015. "Performing the 'Quing of Berlin': Transnational Digital Interfaces in Queer Feminist Protest Culture." *Feminist Media Studies* 16(1): 128–49.

Staggenborg, Suzanne, Donna Eder, and Lori Sudderth. 1994. "Women's Culture and Social Change: Evidence from the National Women's Music Festival." *Berkeley Journal of Sociology* 38: 31–56.

Stokes, Martin. 2004. "Musique, identité et 'ville-monde.'" *L'Homme* 171–72: 371–88.

Tagg, Philip. 1989. "Open Letter: 'Black Music,' 'Afro-American Music' and 'European Music.'" *Popular Music* 8(3): 285–98.

Taylor, Jodie. 2014. "Festivalizing Sexualities: Discourses of 'Pride,' Counter-discourses of 'Shame.'" In *The Festivalization of Culture*, edited Andy Bennett, Jodie Taylor, and Ian Woodward, 27–48. Farnham: Ashgate.

Williams, Raymond. 1973. "Base and Superstructure in Marxist Cultural Theory." *New Left Review* 82: 3–10.

Wolfe Liblong, Caitlin Elizabeth. 2008. *Mulheres do Morro: The Representation of Women in Brazilian Funk*. Master's diss., Institute for the Study of the Americas, London.

Zobl, Elke. 2004. "Revolution Grrrl and Lady Style, Now!" *Peace Review* 16(4): 445–52.

RENEWAL

FIVE

Love Songs That Protest

Sentipensante *Music Making as Postneoliberal Activism in the Neighborhood Tango Festivals of Buenos Aires*

JENNIE GUBNER

While tango is internationally well known as a type of music and dance, it has rarely been recognized as a music of protest. Similarly, the idea of people performing songs about love, nostalgia, and heartbreak in picturesque neighborhood bars and plazas may not sound like a recipe for activism. However, in residential neighborhoods across Buenos Aires, artists have transformed sentimental, romantic, and nostalgic tango music and dance practices into an affective form of activism to contest the tourist-oriented entrepreneurial cultural politics of the city government. In this chapter, I explore how grassroots tango festivals have harnessed the neighborhood as a rich aesthetic vocabulary through which to advocate postneoliberal approaches to, and experiences of, tango and urban life. My goal is to encourage further thinking about the politics and poetics of festival activism in Latin America—specifically, festivals as platforms to critique neoliberal cultural policies.

From 2011 to 2014, I lived in Buenos Aires, conducting extensive ethnographic research about the politics and poetics of neighborhood tango scenes. During this time, I watched as musicians in neighborhood venues became increasingly organized around common struggles affecting the local tango community. In particular, I came to understand how independently organized neighborhood tango festivals played a central role in that politicization process. Over the course of my fieldwork, I attended at least eleven independently organized tango festivals as a performing violinist, photographer, videographer, volunteer organizer, audience member, and ethnographer.

How Can Love Songs Protest?

In his *Book of Embraces*, Uruguayan activist writer Eduardo Galeano writes about the act of being *sentipensante*, combining feeling and thinking into one action (Galeano 1989, 89). He explains that the term comes from Colombian fishermen, who used it to describe how rational thinking and emotional feeling cannot—and should not—be separated from one another.[1] This concept has been used by Latin American grassroots intellectuals to inform radical approaches to social justice pedagogy in Latin America (Rappaport 2020; Rendón 2009). I borrow this term to describe what I have observed as sentipensante music-making practices, where sentimental performance practices are combined strategically with carefully curated political messages. Neighborhood tango festivals, or *festivales barriales de tango*, offer one example of sentipensante music making in Buenos Aires: they harness intimate and romantic music-making experiences as vehicles through which to affectively critique neoliberal urbanism and export-oriented, entrepreneurial cultural politics. In my fieldwork, I found it particularly interesting that the artist organizers and performers involved in these festivals were acutely aware of the emotional capital the idea of *neighborhoodness* carried in relation to these events. In Argentine Spanish, the term *barrial* means something located in a neighborhood or possessing a quality of neighborhoodness. It denotes activities or places that hold aesthetic, sentimental, and often nostalgic qualities of neighborhood life. References to lo barrial are common in tango culture, and tango lyrics often tell nostalgic stories of love and loss set in early to mid-twentieth-century Buenos Aires neighborhoods. Festival organizers were able to strategically mobilize romantic feelings connected to lo barrial to advocate for alternate models of cultural production and critique government policies related to promoting tango as a tourist industry. Framed in this way, this is not a story of how neighborhood festivals transformed tango from a romantic genre into a political one, but instead of how artists learned to use romantic cultural practices as a vehicle for conveying activist ideas. This process of turning everyday affective experiences and imaginaries of neighborhood tango culture into fuel for critiquing neoliberal cultural policies is what I frame as a form of postneoliberal festival activism.

The idea of *postneoliberal* comes from the writings of Grimson and Kessler (2005), who use the term to talk about movements that emerge explicitly in reaction to, and are informed by, the negative effects of neoliberalism. I see neighborhood tango festivals as examples of postneoliberal activism not because Argentina is "post" the effects of neoliberal economic models—far from it. Rather, artists intentionally framed these festivals as acts of resistance to the ways neoliberal politics were shaping cultural practices in Buenos Aires, thereby envisioning a postneoliberal future. As Manuel Kanai writes, while "neoliberal urbanism may remain hegemonic in innumerable world cities . . . it is far from monolithic and unchallengeable" (Kanai 2014, 1116). Using sentipensante approaches to music making and grassroots organizing, I explore how a popular love song genre saturated in symbolism and imagery from early twentieth-century Buenos Aires can offer one approach to voicing that challenge.

Framing the Politicization of Tango Festivals in Buenos Aires

In Argentina, grassroots social movements informed by anti-imperialist and anticapitalist ideologies grew rapidly following the country's major economic crash in 2001 (Sitrin 2012). These movements emerged across all sectors of society, fomented by the left-leaning national politics of the Kirchner presidencies (Nestor Kirchner from 2003 to 2007 and Cristina Fernández de Kirchner from 2007 to 2015, reelected as vice president in 2019). In dialogue with movements occurring in other sectors of Argentine society and across Latin America, grassroots arts and culture movements played a key role in promoting collective and cooperative alternatives to what were largely seen as failed neoliberal policies—and in engaging young people in these processes (Ugarte 2008).

In the case of tango, much of the politicization I observed during my fieldwork emerged in response to the official cultural politics of the right-wing PRO party, led at the time by Mayor Mauricio Macri, who later became president from 2015 to 2019. In a departure from previous cultural politics surrounding urban tango practices, the PRO party heavily promoted tango as a tourist commodity, source of revenue, and city brand while simultaneously making it difficult to open and sustain neighborhood music venues for everyday use. Macri's decision to designate a hotel manager, Hernan Lombardi, as minister of culture in 2008 was just one of many steps taken to support this agenda and promote neoliberal approaches to urban cultural policy (Sanjurjo and Sanjurjo 2013). Among other actions, Lombardi merged the Festival BA Tango (a primarily music-based festival) and the Campeonato Mundial de Baile del Tango (the city's annual tango dance competition) into a megafestival heavily marketed to foreigners called the Tango Buenos Aires Festival y Mundial. This change occurred following the 2009 UNESCO declaration of tango as a Masterpiece of the Oral and Intangible Cultural Heritage of Humanity, a title that continues to be utilized by city government in advertising campaigns for the city's official annual tango festival (Morel 2009).

Frustrated with what was colloquially referred to as tango "for export," tango artists began utilizing different grassroots methods to promote tango music and dance as localized cultural practices explicitly *"not* for export."[2] These efforts—taking many forms across the city—promoted new ways of thinking about and experiencing tango, distancing the genre from the glossy, staged aesthetics of downtown tourist shows and relocating it within local imaginaries, aesthetics, and practices of everyday life in contemporary Buenos Aires. As part of this process, many artists began positioning neighborhood tango practices, referred to locally as *tango barrial*, as a counterpoint to what they saw as tango-for-export tourist industries. Through this process, tango barrial, traditionally associated with intimate, romantic, and nostalgic neighborhood music and dance practices, was reimagined as a rich aesthetic vocabulary and stage for the cultural politics of the present.

Another major point of tension between tango artists and the cultural policies of the city government during my years of fieldwork in Buenos Aires involved frequent closures related to permit issues around live music venues. This issue can be traced back to the 2005 fire in the underground rock club Cromañon, where 197 people, most of whom were teenagers, died. The year following the tragedy, Macri campaigned against the opposition by promising to clean the city of unregulated live music venues, a mission many saw as an excuse to execute strict sound policing across the city. When Macri became mayor, the PRO party made it illegal to have any kind of live music, even a guitarist in a café, without a live music permit. Obtaining and maintaining permits became a long and painful bureaucratic nightmare for artists and small venue owners, often ending in under-the-table payoffs (Corti 2009).

What musicians found most frustrating was the PRO government's lack of interest in passing legislation to provide permits to small performance spaces like tango bars or cultural centers, which pose very different risks than large rock venues. When venues did obtain permits, inspectors frequently would shut them down and fine them on what seemed like trivial and absurd details. One article from the newspaper *Página 12* from July 2014 states that over fifteen bars and cultural centers—most offering free programming—were shut down that month alone around Buenos Aires.[3] Most of the bars were shut down because of outdated signatures on their evacuation plans. These bars all

Figure 5.1. An orchestra plays at the first neighborhood tango festival of Villa Crespo, November 2013.

had legal and displayed evacuation plans but were lacking updated signatures, which were hard to obtain due to the bureaucratic hurdles of city government.

The disconnect between city-wide marketing campaigns to celebrate the UNESCO declaration and brand Buenos Aires as "The Tango City" and the lack of support for artists, who struggled to find places to perform given so many venue closures, led to widespread anger in the tango community. Artists criticized the PRO party's interest in culture as a commodity and not a vital and sustainable part of everyday urban life. Responding to the touristification of tango alongside routine venue closures, independent movements began mobilizing to fight for a place for their music in the city landscape. With a lack of resources and lack of support from the city government, artists increasingly turned to alternative and independent forms of cultural production and activism to create spaces and disseminate knowledge about local and not-for-export tango movements around the city.

Although not all the musicians who participate in neighborhood tango festivals think of their music as an expression of protest, festivals frame experiences of neighborhood music making as collective and embodied expressions of postneoliberal activism. In the context of these events, references to tango as an expression of locality, urban intimacy, and neighborhood culture become politicized because they are positioned in contrast to the export-oriented cultural politics of the city government. Thus, festivals offer a place to not only bring visibility to what artists colloquially call not-for-export tango scenes across the city but also invite artists to become active and participatory agents in the production of an activist approach to contemporary tango politics. These processes involve both talking about and making music.

Neighborhood Tango Festivals

Festivales barriales de tango, or neighborhood tango festivals, are community-organized and community-run events put on by different tango organizers within a given neighborhood of Buenos Aires. While El Festival de Tango Independiente (the Independent Tango Festival) occurs across multiple neighborhoods, the rest of the festivals discussed in this chapter are confined within the boundaries of individual neighborhoods. Festivals are predominantly held in working-and middle-class neighborhoods, some very close to the city center and others up to an hour bus ride from downtown. They are primarily organized by middle-class musicians, dancers, and tango activists. Festivals tend to last from two to seven days and feature daily free and accessibly priced concerts, dances, and debates organized by independent tango artists. Although many of the concerts are held in already functioning tango venues as a way of bringing publicity to local tango scenes, other events are held in public plazas, schools, libraries, and cafés and restaurants considered symbolic and valued neighborhood locations. Festivals typically culminate in a public outdoor closing ceremony featuring dancing and live bands in a plaza on a Sunday afternoon.

Because these events are collective efforts by artists from different neighborhood scenes, neighborhood tango festivals feel like celebratory community gatherings. Early on, they tended to feature bands from a given neighborhood. As the years passed, festival organizers started inviting musicians from different scenes to come and participate in events, promoting solidarity between neighborhoods. The gigs are rarely paid and, as such, tend to feature well-known artists committed to socially engaged music making or friends of organizers, as well as newer artists eager to find performance opportunities that can bring visibility to their groups. Since none of the festivals are organized with the goal of making money and instead emphasize community building, cultural activism, and social solidarity for tango musicians, artists

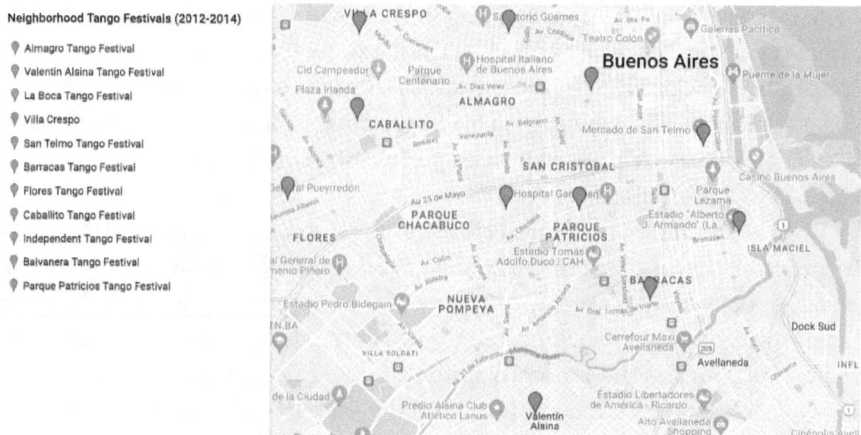

Figure 5.2. A map of Buenos Aires illustrating neighborhoods that hosted independently organized tango festivals between 2012 and 2014. Google Maps.

generally donate their time willingly; I never heard any complaints about lack of payment for participation.

During the years I lived in Buenos Aires from 2011 to 2014, my Facebook feed would start to fill up with daily announcements about upcoming festivals starting around October (spring in the Southern Hemisphere)—first Valentín Alsina, then Flores, then Caballito, San Telmo, La Boca, Almagro (all names of different neighborhoods). Festival season grew so vibrant that from October to December, there was a festival almost every weekend in the city. It turned springtime into a particularly celebratory time of year for the neighborhood tango scenes, simultaneously reclaiming, decentering, and relocalizing tango practices in the city landscape.

Festivals and Counterfestivals: The "Anti-Postcard" Tango Festival

The first Independent Tango Festival (Festival de Tango Independiente) was organized in 2010 as a joint effort by members of Fractura Expuesta and the Unión de Orquestas Típicas (Union of Typical [Traditional] Orchestras, commonly abbreviated as UOT). Fractura Expuesta is a politically activist underground tango radio station founded by two young journalists, Maximiliano Senkiew and Hernan Marcos.[4] The radio station broadcasts on the *Radio Madre* AM530 frequency from its headquarters at the Madres de Plaza de Mayo and has as its goal to bring visibility and publicity to independent tango scenes across the city The UOT is a union of tango orchestras founded in 2005 by a collective of new orchestras. This union was formed to unite and organize the rapidly growing mass of upcoming tango orchestras in the city with goals of improving working and performing conditions for a new generation of tango musicians.

Both organizations maintain close ties to preexisting leftist political organizations in the city. Fractura Expuesta takes much of its political orientation and support from the renowned legacy of the Mothers of the Plaza de Mayo (strong supporters of the Kirchner governments). The UOT, on the other hand, exists under the umbrella union of the Union of Independent Musicians, or UMI, created in 2001 to serve the interests of independently managed musicians across Argentina. Both Fractura Expuesta and members of the UOT collaborate frequently with El Centro Cultural de la Cooperación Floreal Gorini (the Floreal Gorini Cooperative Cultural Center), a publishing house and cultural center dedicated to researching and promoting knowledge about cooperative movements and critical, leftist, anticapitalist scholarship.[5] The politicization of tango movements in recent years has been influenced not only by the broader political climate of the city and nation but also by direct relationships between tango musicians and specific influential activist organizations in the city.

The first Independent Tango Festival came as a reaction to the city government's decision in 2010 to move the new Tango Buenos Aires Festival y Mundial annual tango festival from the middle of the Argentine summer to mid-August (the middle of winter) to coincide with North American and European summer tourism seasons. Further solidifying his interest in tango as more of an export commodity than a form of popular culture, Macri commented during the 2010 festival that tango was the soy of Buenos Aires (soy being Argentina's primary export crop). In the opening speech of the festival, he stated: "The agricultural sector is one of the most dynamic of our economy.... The city, obviously, cannot grow soy, there's no room. So, I say that the city has its own soy, its own green gold, that is tango" (Marcos 2010). Throughout my fieldwork, this reference was often repeated by cultural activists as proof that Macri had little interest in tango as a form of popular culture and saw the genre as a for-export commodity.

The decision to move the festival escalated tensions between the Buenos Aires city government and local artists, who accused politicians of exploiting tango as a major tourist commodity while ignoring the needs of local artistic communities. Frustrated with the increasing touristification of the tango industry by the municipal government, the ideological tone set by the organizers of the first Independent Tango Festival was far from neutral. In a promotional YouTube clip for the festival, a deep voice announces the event over the sounds of a woman singing, backed by one of the new tango orchestras: "From the sixth to the tenth of March, the first festival of independent tango. The Buenos Aires tango scene that doesn't get printed on postcards."[6] In the festival manifesto, published on the Fractura Expuesta website, the organizers outline the goals of their clearly not-for-export festival:

> Because there is a tango that builds identities without declarations, that lives in the neighborhoods, that resists the closures of live music venues, that imagines tango in primary and secondary schools, that runs through the city and the suburbs, and because there is a tango that should also be made visible, the Unión de Orquestas Típicas (UOT) along with Fractura Expuesta Radio Tango are organizing the first Independent Tango Festival.... The proposal is simple. Across the city, contemporary tango scenes share essences, ideas, styles, and different forms of conceiving tango that live among us but are isolated.... The organizers conceived of the festival as a week to bring visibility to that which already is, that which exists, to the concert series, the spaces and artists that contribute to the contemporary tango scene.... In the words of Alorsa from La Guardia Hereje—"another tango is possible, one without hair gel. A tango that once again sings to who we are." This is a festival envisioned for neighborhood residents as an antipostcard festival.[7]

This manifesto established a foundation for a new model of tango activism, one that used independently organized local music festivals to bring visibility to artists while simultaneously creating a platform where debates about the cultural politics of the city could occur. While the festival primarily focused on places where tango *music* was performed regularly, some events also offered places for tango dancing.

Juxtaposed against the city's annual festival, which the PRO government had been organizing in the Expo Center in Recoleta—the richest neighborhood in town—the decision to organize the independent festival around already functioning bars and theaters within the city advocated tango as a dynamic and living expression of everyday urban culture. The first Independent Tango Festival was not only a major success within the independent tango community but also received coverage across social media and in newspapers around the city.

One of the festival's primary goals was to politicize musicians around the city. The festival set out to raise awareness about the venue closures, the changes to the annual official tango festival, and the importance of mobilizing solidarity to fight for local tango artists, venues, and tango scenes. Integral to the atmosphere of this festival was the message that if tango was to be reclaimed as a form of local urban culture, artists and other cultural activists would have to do their part in becoming active agents of social change. Festivals sent the message that artists around the city were going to need to work together to rebuild places for tango in the urban landscape and bring visibility to these cultural practices year round.

While many artists had already been organizing in bars and venues around the city in a more underground fashion, the Independent Tango Festival advocated solidarity between these efforts and framed underground movements within a broader, shared activist agenda. The kind of politics and critical consciousness promoted by these organizers encouraged artists across Buenos Aires to become active participants in grassroots cultural events and to shape culture and society through concrete actions, reactions, and ongoing public debate. Following the Independent Tango Festival, more festivals started popping up across the city.

"Shut up and Play the Bandoneon—Tango Isn't Politics!": The Valentín Alsina Neighborhood Tango Festival

One neighborhood that responded to the call for more independent festivals was Valentín Alsina, a small working-class neighborhood in the province of Great Buenos Aires, just outside the Buenos Aires city limits and about forty minutes by bus from downtown. Valentín Alsina is a quiet neighborhood with low houses and many longtime residents. Whereas the neighborhood was once known as a place with many tango events, nowadays most tango venues are closed and the neighborhood soundscape reflects the musical tastes of working- and middle-class youth, a mix of rock music, cumbia, and other mainstream popular musics. It was a neighborhood I knew well because my first tango violin teacher and mentor, Roberto Abal, lived there his entire life. When he was alive, I would go to his house on weekends, listen to old tango cassettes, and play along with them while talking about tango history. He used to tell me that there was not much tango life left in his neighborhood, and that is why, when he retired from his day job, he went to play in the touristy downtown port neighborhood of La Boca in a restaurant on weekends.

Returning to the neighborhood for the first time since Roberto passed away in 2009, I found it wonderful to see older adults coming out to dance and listen to tango performances, all with a mixture of surprise and curiosity at how tango was returning to the streets of their neighborhood after many years of absence. What also surprised many older adults was the political subtext present in almost all the events occurring over the weekend. As many people associated tango with a form of nostalgic, neighborhood social life, the mainstream music and dance genre of their younger years, they did not share the contemporary understanding of tango as a vehicle for political critique and activism.

On the first night of the festival, the organizers hosted an event in the neighborhood's public library featuring a *charla-debate* (talk and debate) followed by two tango music performances. The talk was titled "Neighborhood Tango Festivals: An Alternative to the Institution? A Result of Cultural *Autogestión* [Self-Organizing]?" The speakers featured two independent journalists of the online tango magazine and radio show *Chamuyo Web* and Alejandro Szwarcman, a renowned poet, tango lyricist, and independent journalist. The moderator was Alberto "Pata" Corbani, a local musician and one of the festival organizers. The groups to perform were Marisa Vázquez, a local singer from the neighborhood, and the Quinteto Negro La Boca, a politically engaged tango group from the nearby Boca neighborhood whose members organized La Boca neighborhood's tango festival. The following is a transcription of some sections of the evening debate.

> "PATA" CORBANI (musician/festival organizer): There is nothing more gratifying than being joined by so many neighbors. In this case, neighbors from Valentín Alsina, such a beloved neighborhood... What motivates us as musicians, as journalists, fundamentally as cultural laborers, is our desire to be recognized by the administrative governments and to react to the difficulties we had in 2009 and 2010 when so many [tango] venues were shut down. These closures, headed by the authorities of the city government of Buenos Aires, were often carried out aggressively and even violently, often in the middle of performances. In the face of these injustices, we came up with the utopian idea to make a [tango] festival [with the slogan] *El Tango No Se Clausura*—"Tango Will Not Be Shut Down"—and here we are, continuing that adventure. Perhaps it was a bit adolescent, but we decided,

why not? Our goal as artists and cultural workers is to establish an exchange with you neighbors, to create permanent spaces for artistic expression and communication, because ultimately everything we do we see as a product of our shared culture, a culture that is no more and no less than a part of everyday life... This is where the [independent tango] festivals come from, and we are going to need you to participate in this one and others. Each year there are more neighborhoods organizing... and all of this has been made possible by grassroots efforts [*autogestión*] in the neighborhoods, with the help of neighbors, and with a spirit of solidarity that has been such a force in making these events possible. I believe that artists must act in solidarity; if not, we aren't going to get anywhere. We all lived through a decade where individualism reigned and caused so much damage, and we don't want that anymore. We want something else.

HERNÁN BUODO (independent journalist): Good evening. Continuing the discussion of the city's festival and the neighborhood festivals, I think the clear difference that sets one apart from another relates to a question of market, specifically, the fact that the city [tango] festival is marketed to foreigners. The tango festival of the city of Buenos Aires used to be held in summertime. It was a festival intended for the people of the city of Buenos Aires and surrounding areas where people could come and walk through the streets. I remember going to the festival in the middle of Corrientes Street downtown. It was really something marvelous. You could walk between one stage and the next; it was summertime, and the entire festival and the relations between the people had a different feel.... As of a few years ago, the festival of Buenos Aires is now held in wintertime and behind closed doors. It is held in wintertime behind closed doors because the largest tourist influences are European foreigners who come looking for tango. That is why it is held in wintertime, in the middle of the Argentine winter. The festival is intended for them. It is no longer intended for the citizens of Buenos Aires. I think that the neighborhood festivals arise with a different character and with different objectives in an effort to make up for what is missing from the cultural politics of the city... The goals of these festivals are different and the love that's put into them is different, really this is what it comes down to.

Later in the debate, Pata Corbani took the mic again and began to describe in detail two circumstances in which inspectors, along with a group of policemen, came into a venue where he was playing and violently closed down the bar, threatening to take away musicians' instruments and money

Figure 5.3. Violentango performing a free concert for an international audience during the 2012 Almargo Neighborhood Tango Festival.

made from the concert. As he mentioned how scared he felt, older adults from the audience in the library began to shout angrily. Some stood up and walked out:

"What is going on here!?"
"We came to hear tango, not this!"
"We want tango not politics!"
"Tango isn't politics!"
"Why don't you just shut up and play the bandoneon!"

ALEJANDRO SZWARCMAN (tango lyricist): I apologize to those I upset and to those who left . . . I hope I didn't come to the wrong conference, but I thought we were here to talk about contemporary debates in tango . . . We can't emphasize enough that in the last thirty or forty years, tango as a popular and cultural expression has been marginalized with clear intentions to promote other cultural industries with specific economic and even political interests.

ANONYMOUS OLDER MAN: I was born and raised here in Valentín Alsina. I think that Argentina has problems. It had problems. There have been problems, and there will be more problems, but they are not going to get resolved in one day. But the countries around us, they have more problems, and honestly, today I came here to hear tango.

After a lively argument with a series of frustrated patrons in the community library, the speaking portion of the event came to an end. It was followed by a concert featuring a local singer, Marisa Vázquez, and the Quinteto Negro La Boca singing old and new tangos.

I find this transcript rich from many perspectives. It offers clear examples of the way artists and organizers deliberately positioned grassroots tango events as a reaction to the negative effects of neoliberal cultural policies and practices. The tone is consistent with messaging from the first Independent Tango Festival, illustrating the growth of this movement into diverse neighborhoods in the city. It also illustrates how, despite rising solidarity between politicized underground tango movements across the city, the activist underpinnings of the festivals were not shared or understood by all participating members, especially older neighborhood residents who had not been following debates in the tango communities. While these overt criticisms of the governing political party at the Valentín Alsina festival led to tensions with individuals not already a part of these underground scenes, the tango concerts and dances held across the neighborhood in places like the central plaza were warmly received by this same population. In these other events, intentionally curated collective and shared sentimental and sentipensante experiences of neighborhood music making and tango barrial allowed similar values to be conveyed in an embodied, intimate, and nonconfrontational way. Of the many festival debates I attended in my years in Buenos Aires, this was the only event that ended in conflict. Most of the time, politicized debates were attended by activists and artists already involved in not-for-export tango movements or interested to get involved. In this context, events generated fruitful dialogue, enthusiasm, and solidarity among organizers, artists, and activists helped define and spread activist values and discourses informing the festivals themselves.

Cultivating Belonging in the Imaginary Neighborhood: The Almagro Neighborhood Tango Festivals

On October 2, 2011, I landed in Buenos Aires to begin fieldwork. That same day, I heard that the second annual tango festival of the Almagro neighborhood was celebrating its finale in Plaza Almagro. I had spent countless nights on the corner of that plaza in an iconic tango bar called El Boliche de Roberto (Roberto's Bar), but this was my first time attending the neighborhood's tango festival. Arriving at the plaza, I found a bunch of young people I did not know cleaning up the blocked street where the festival had taken place. I also saw the familiar face of Osvaldo Peredo, the renowned singer from Roberto's Bar, who was eighty-one at the time. He was stacking white plastic chairs into the back of a neighborhood tango bar owner's brightly colored Volkswagen van, which was completely covered in brightly painted images of tango paintings featuring the faces of iconic tango musicians like Carlos Gardel and Rubén Juárez. I was delighted to see him still so engaged in music making in a community of enthusiastic younger artists who valued him as a teacher, mentor, and friend. That day, he introduced me to one of the festival organizers, Lucas Furno, and a tango researcher from France, Elsa Broclain.

A few weeks later, I sat with Lucas and Elsa in their apartment some blocks from Plaza Almagro. Over the course of a few hours, Lucas explained to me the long history of his relationship to tango in Almagro and how he came to be one of the main organizers of the contemporary Almagro scene. Talking at length about neighborhood festivals, he explained that he and his artist friends had started a weekly tango music series called ConCiertos Atorrantes at a local venue called Sanata to bring visibility and solidarity to new tango formations. In 2010, the city shut down the event multiple times with no clear justification. Frustrated by the city politics, the members of ConCiertos Atorrantes and the organizers of Sanata decided to host the first Almagro neighborhood tango festival to celebrate the neighborhood's music scene. The festival was envisioned to celebrate iconic bars like El Boliche de Roberto and others like Sanata, showcase local bands, and send a message to the city that neighborhood scenes like Almagro were an integral and vibrant part of the city's contemporary tango culture. The philosophy behind the initiative was that the festival would be done completely *a pulmón* (an Argentine phrase meaning from your lungs, indicating an entirely grassroots effort).

That was 2010. The first Almagro festival was a huge success in the neighborhood. The next year, the Almagro festival celebrated the ConCiertos Atorrantes concert cycle alongside other independent concert cycles around the city, a choice intentionally made to create solidarity and connections between neighborhood movements. Each year in preparing for the Almagro festival, organizers would make a website and flyers promoting the event, which were circulated around the neighborhood and especially through Facebook. On the 2011 flyer, Lucas wrote a romantic story of a neighborhood that breathes tango and a music scene that started in El Boliche de Roberto and grew as musicians organized and fought for the right to have a place in the city for their art. He wrote of bars full of nocturnal magic and bohemia, of late-night tango refuges that acted as classrooms for tango; he wrote about how, over time, musicians had come together to organize, to represent the neighborhood, and to tell the story of countless musical nights and the shared sense of pride of a local music scene rooted in the old historic cafés, warehouses, plazas, and side streets of the Almagro neighborhood.

When I asked Lucas about the flyer, he told me that he wrote it like a fairytale and wanted to fuel an imaginary of neighborhood belonging. He said he did not care if the people who went to the bars were really from Almagro. What mattered was that people went to the bars and supported the scene. He explained that creating romanticized imaginaries of the Almagro neighborhood was helpful in uniting people and in creating a story where people felt like they belonged to something and felt loved, because this kind of love acts as a motor that motivates and makes people believe in what they are doing. For him, the neighborhood of Almagro was as much an idea as a place. This way of using nostalgia and romanticized imagery to discuss neighborhood life is common in classic tango lyrics. By applying these techniques to the new bars instead of references to the 1920s or 1930s, he was able to cultivate an air of sentimentalism and romance to promote a localizing politics of tango music in the urban landscape. By rebuilding affective connections between tango and neighborhood life, these kinds of narratives promote both sentipensante and postneoliberal ways of imagining tango in city life. Sentimentalism becomes a tool for activism.

Exactly a year later, I found myself back in the Almagro neighborhood plaza on another Sunday afternoon at the third annual Almagro tango festival. This time, instead of arriving late, I spent the evening on stage with my violin, playing with the Orquesta Típica Conciertos Atorrantes, backing Osvaldo Peredo as he sang a selection from his upcoming orchestral CD release, which Lucas and his friends had recorded with him that year. That day, I also filmed the festival, looking to use my camera to evoke the social aesthetics of neighborhood festival activism. The resulting short film, *Sunday in Plaza Almagro* (2014), illustrates sentipensante music making and postneoliberal activism in action.[8] As singers poetically describe stories of iconic neighborhood bars and local legends alongside the need for visibility and representation for tango artists year round, they root tango to local and specific histories and remove the genre from exoticizing generalizations. As they interpret tangos like the 1941 song "Tres Esquinas" by Enrique Cadicamo, nostalgic references to neighborhood life from the early twentieth century are recontextualized as a celebration of locality and urban intimacy connected to the neighborhood and its contemporary tango scenes in 2011. Even if, as Lucas says, neighborhood residents are not as interconnected as they once were, when Ardit sings these lyrics to an intergenerational crowd from a stage set up by local musicians in the neighborhood plaza, neighborhood imaginaries are brought to life and reified through song. Alongside the performances, speeches about the grassroots nature of the festival remind everyone that these efforts result from local initiatives and not those of the city government. The feeling that day in the plaza event was intimate; the emotion of the organizers and performers came through in every performance and every speech, and each performer and speaker was received with rowdy and enthusiastic applause. By weaving together powerful evocations of neighborhood life with speeches about the importance of local culture and celebrations of the neighborhood's rich recent musical history, this affective—or as Galeano would say, sentipensante—approach to politics becomes a subtle yet important tool through which to raise critical consciousness about current debates surrounding the city government's cultural agendas.

Experiencing Neighborhood Festivals versus Megafestivals

Since 2011, I have attended many tango festivals in Buenos Aires, both official and unofficial. I have also performed in three official tango festivals and four independent neighborhood tango festivals. Having had the opportunity to perform in these festivals, I have seen how they foster very different musical and social experiences both for audiences and for performers. The major difference I have observed between official and independent festivals involves questions of intent and ownership. Many artists perform in both official and independent festivals, although often in different formations and/or showcasing different repertoire. Yet what really distinguishes the independent festivals are the social aesthetics and contexts of their musical sounds—the emphasis on creating local spaces of encounter where live tango music can be embraced as an integral, everyday part of city life. Independent neighborhood tango festivals are all about the production of locality. They grow from grassroots efforts and treat tango as a creative, social, and political form of expression built into the city landscape. Although some efforts have been made by the city festival to include references to local cultural tango practices and scenes that exist throughout the year (mainly in response to artists advocating for this kind of representation), the official festival would need to make many changes in its politics to be perceived by artists as a local celebration of tango culture and not a staged mega-event intended primarily for export and foreign consumption.

My experiences in the city's official tango festival are not so different from what one might expect playing in any kind of megafestival. Big festivals bring more media coverage, larger audiences, and the opportunity to be heard by major artists and organizers in the city. Thus, my string orchestra's preparations for the annual performances at the city festival were always accompanied by a certain amount of stress and pressure. Neighborhood tango festivals, however, are places where music performances are conceptualized at the intersection of musical, social, and activist practices. Because tango lyrics do not usually carry overtly political messages, the activist messages of these festivals are constructed through discourses that emerge in and around them and through the embodied experiences of the festivals themselves. In this case, feelings of locality, neighborhood sentimentality, and belonging become symbolic counterpoints to the glossy marketing and aesthetics of the official festivals (often held in a convention center far from popular local tango venues).

At the 2013 neighborhood tango festival organized in the Villa Crespo neighborhood, members of *La Cámpora*, Cristina Kirchner's youth activist organization, came to talk about the importance of *comunas* (leftist political neighborhood organizations) and the role these entities play in helping foster neighborhood events like festivals. In this case, the tango festival opened itself up as a space for sharing broader political initiatives.

After observing and performing in multiple independent festivals, I have realized that some of these events' most important accomplishments occur before the festivals even begin. In my final year of fieldwork, members of the festival in Valentín Alsina began promoting their November festival in February. Each month, they hosted an event called a "pre-festival," featuring local bands and trying to create hype about the upcoming event. Under the frame of the festival, these events not only supported the political goals of the festivals but also brought needed visibility to tango performances year round. Far beyond only offering a platform for political critique and debate, these year-round events illustrate how festivals have succeeded in promoting solidarity and support for independent artists and cultural organizers.

Conclusions

Neighborhood tango festivals intentionally use romantic sounds, imaginaries, and narratives of neighborhood life as tools to advocate what I frame as a postneoliberal urban cultural politics. This festival activism is manifested not only through experiences of romantic, sentipensante music making but also through targeted political discourse before, during, and surrounding music-making moments. This kind of activism encourages audience members and festival participants to both feel and think about the role of tango as an everyday motor for producing culture, community, and belonging in the city. In the context of independent neighborhood tango festivals, feel-thinking—or sentipensante—approaches to tango performance and cultural activism have acted and continue to act as a powerful discursive and affective means for critiquing neoliberal cultural politics in Buenos Aires and promoting alternative models of urban cultural practices.

In the contemporary neighborhood tango scenes of Buenos Aires, tango music is experienced in many ways. It is a form of socialization, a form of employment, a vehicle for political resistance and activism, and a form of social intimacy and sentimentality. In fact, depending on the individual subjectivities of performers and audience members, tango music events can be experienced as many of these things at the same time. Whereas I used to understand these categories as somewhat separated, I have learned through fieldwork that the lines between politics, sentimentality, employment, and socialization in music scenes are usually quite blurry. As such, the politics of activism in neighborhood tango scenes must be understood alongside the personal needs and goals of artists struggling for visibility and economic sustainability in the city. Motivated by a complex cocktail of personal, community-based, and political aspirations, neighborhood tango festivals have thrived in Buenos Aires. In 2022, as I conclude this chapter, old and new neighborhood festivals continue to emerge each year, signifying both the successes of what is now a highly interconnected city-wide movement and the need to continue challenging the hegemony of neoliberal urban agendas.

Notes

1. The renowned Colombian scholar and activist Orlando Fals Borda, one of the pioneers of Participatory Action Research, also references this concept, which he says he learned from a community of Colombian fishermen. See Rappaport 2020.

2. The term *for export* (rendered in English) started appearing in the tango community on CD titles in the 1970s and '80s, when artists were trying to promote their music to foreign and tourist audiences. With tango's popularity waning in Argentina at that time, efforts were made to rebrand tango as a genre for global consumption. As tourist industries grew in the wake of the 2001 crash, this term was revitalized with a negative connotation in reference to tango shows and products created to feed and fulfill exoticized global imaginaries of tango not for local con-

sumption. At a time of decolonial movements across Latin America, the choice to define underground tango scenes as *not for export* aligned these cultural practices with larger Pan–Latin American political and activist movements.

3. Laura Guarinoni, "Para defender la cultura," *Página 12*, July 9, 2014.

4. The official website for Fractura Expuesta Radio Tango can be found at "Fractura Expuesta—Tango!," September 23, 2016, https://www.fracturaexpuesta.com.ar

5. The official website for Centro Cultural de la Cooperación Floreal Gorini can be found at "Centro Cultural de la Cooperación," accessed September 15, 2023, https://www.centrocultural.coop/.

6. "Primer Festival de Tango Independiente," Orquestastipicas, YouTube video, 00:35, March 2, 2010, https://www.youtube.com/watch?v=cZPF2FHoIss.

7. "Llega el Festival de Tango Independiente," Fractura Expuesta, March 2, 2010. Translated by author.

8. For further discussion, see Jennie Gubner, "Domingo en Plaza Almagro (Sunday in Plaza Almagro)," *Journal of Audiovisual Ethnomusicology* (2022): 1, https://javem.org/domingo-en-plaza-almagro.

Bibliography

Corti, Berenice. 2009. "Redefiniciones culturales en la Buenos Aires post Cromañon: El debate sobre el vivo de la música independiente." In *Actas de la VIII Reunión de Antropología del MERCOSUR*, 1–15. Buenos Aires: Universidad Nacional de San Martin.

Galeano, Eduardo. 1989. *Libro de los abrazos*. Mexico: Siglo XXI.

Grimson, Alejandro, and Gabriel Kessler. 2005. *On Argentina and the Southern Cone: Neoliberalism and National Imaginations*. New York: Routledge.

Kanai, Miguel. 2014. "Buenos Aires, Capital of Tango: Tourism, Redevelopment and the Cultural Politics of Neoliberal Urbanism." *Urban Geography* 35(8): 1111–7.

Marcos, Germán. 2010. "Macri: 'El tango es la soja porteña.'" *Fractura Expuesta.com.ar*, August 4, 2010. https://www.fracturaexpuesta.com.ar/noticias/20100804.html.

Morel, Hernán. 2009. "El giro patrimonial del tango: Políticas oficiales, turismo y campeonatos de baile en la Ciudad de Buenos Aires." *Cuadernos de Antropología Social* 30: 155–72.

Rappaport, Joanne. 2020. *Cowards Don't Make History: Orlando Fals Borda and the Origins of Participatory Action Research*. Durham, NC: Duke University Press.

Rendón, Laura. 2009. *Sentipensante (Sensing/Thinking) Pedagogy: Educating for Wholeness, Social Justice and Liberation*. Sterling, VA: Stylus.

Sanjurjo, Luis, and Eugenia Sanjurjo. 2013. "Políticas de Olvido: La gestión neoliberal de los patrimonios históricos y culturales." In *La Ciudad Empresa: Espacios, ciudadanos y derechos bajo lógica de mercado*, edited by Javier Marín, 213–22. Buenos Aires: Ediciones del CCC.

Sitrin, Marina. 2012. *Everyday Revolutions: Horizontalism and Autonomy in Argentina*. New York: Zed Books.

Ugarte, Mariano, ed. 2008. *Emergencia: Cultura, música, politica*. Buenos Aires: Ediciones del CCC.

SIX

Al-Balad Theater

Festivals as Sites of Social Action and Community Development in Neoliberal Jordan

JEREMY REED AND SERENE HULEILEH

When al-Balad Theater opened in 2005, it was located in the old Cinema al-Urdun (Jordan Cinema) building, which the founders of al-Balad Theater had spent over two years renovating. The idea to rehabilitate disused spaces as alternative theater locations in major Arab cities had been spearheaded by the Young Arab Theater Fund, led by Tareq Abou el Futouh, and the Arab Theater Training Center, led by Raed Asfour. The first such project was The Garage in Alexandria, Egypt, which opened its doors to the public in 2000. Two years later, during the Amman International Theater Festival, Raed Asfour organized a workshop for architects called "Rehabilitating Alternative Theater Spaces" to identify a space in Amman similar to that of The Garage. After visiting several locations, the workshop group agreed that the size and layout of Cinema al-Urdun was the most suitable to turn into a multipurpose space. Equally special about the building was its strategic location between Jabal Amman and Wasṭ al-Balad (Amman's downtown district), between the increasingly gentrified First Circle area of Jabal Amman and the older *sūq* (market) area of downtown Amman. More than simply creating an alternative space, the renovation of Cinema al-Urdun was an intervention into the reterritorialization of Wasṭ al-Balad.

While the Wasṭ al-Balad area of Amman marks the old administrative district of the city, it is not a centralized *madīna* (old city) or a "traditional urban quarter" (Shami 2007). The sequestered nature of Wasṭ al-Balad, in a valley in between hills, is both an example and a consequence of Amman's fragmented, stitched-together urban sprawl. Older city neighborhoods, initially anchored by community settlements, are woven into and in some ways trapped by privatized development driven by Jordan's neoliberal turn. As "neoliberal urbanism" (Hourani 2014) in Amman continues, more and more sites of Ammani public life—cinemas, cafés, bus stations—are being disrupted, displaced, or destroyed (Abu Khafajah and Al-Rabady 2013).

The reframing of the Waṣṭ al-Balad valley floor as a heritage tourism zone in 1996, coupled with the enactment of investment and landlord-tenant laws, has encouraged property developers to align with state tourism initiatives and empowered landlords to renegotiate lease agreements and challenge rent control (Hourani 2014). These conditions unfortunately led to al-Balad Theater's downstairs neighbor, who had bought the building and turned part of it into a café and Turkish bath, to demand the theater's eviction. The landlord wanted to expand his tourism-focused café. Despite arguing that al-Balad Theater had concretely contributed to the cultural life (and thus, touristic potential) of Amman and the Waṣṭ al-Balad district, al-Balad Theater lost its court case. Since the eviction, al-Balad Theater has made its home in another cinema space, although the sunk cost of renovating its previous space has resulted in an uphill financial battle.

Despite the eviction and slow rebuilding process in its new location, al-Balad Theater has continued its core programming through three festivals: al-Balad Music Festival, the Baladk Street and Urban Arts Festival, and the Hakaya Storytelling Festival. In fact, these three festivals have been part of al-Balad Theater's programming since its early years and serve as extensions of the theater's mission to create spaces for restoring vital relationships among and between artists and their communities. The city itself is an integral part of each festival program. Al-Balad Music Festival is located in the Roman and Odeon Amphitheaters in the heart of Waṣṭ al-Balad, offering an alternative sounding of Waṣṭ al-Balad; the Baladk Festival is located in various neighborhoods in and around the city, creating novel ways of seeing and experiencing urban space; and the Hakaya Festival's opening night is organized around a ceremony at the Saḥa al-Hāshemīyya (Hashemite Square/Plaza) in Waṣṭ al-Balad, while the rest of the program spans all of Jordan, focusing on the intersection of storytelling, art, and community education. Each festival constitutes a space of intervention, whether generating sonic disruption, reimagining urban visual aesthetics, or creating safe spaces for individual and collective expression.

A fruitful way of thinking about these festivals is to consider the distinction between the meanings of *sha'bīyya* (popular) and *jumāhīrīyya* (populist) that describe festivals and artists alike (Huleileh 1996). Both reflect notions of "gathering together" from a grassroots perspective—in contrast to *nukhbawīyya*, "elitist," or *tijārīyya*, "commercial." *Sha'bī* festivals cater to popular and profitable taste, whereas *jumāhīri* festivals tap into the critical taste and collective experience of their audience. It is difficult to situate al-Balad Theater's festivals completely within either of these perspectives because the festivals are enmeshed in multiple categories at the same time. In some ways, these categories point to an unexpected field of contestation. Of course, the three festivals that al-Balad Theater produces are not the only ones in Jordan. Al-Balad Theater has sought to define itself on its own terms, yet at various points, other entities, such as the Ministry of Culture, have made efforts to block events like al-Balad Music Festival (and festivals produced by other organizations), citing competitive potential with state festivals happening in the same season. Al-Balad Music Festival is not a competitor to events like the state-produced Jerash Festival of Culture and Arts or municipal Amman Summer Festival, which are premised on the optics of political spectacle and tourism. Defending the festivals of al-Balad Theater as necessary events within the Jordanian public cultural sphere has only served to reinforce the community-driven mission of the theater.

In this chapter, we examine al-Balad Theater's use of festivals as a modality of social action within a neoliberalizing Jordan. We argue that the framework of festival—with its intensive occasions for symbolic and participatory experience—enables al-Balad Theater, on behalf of itself and its artists, audiences, and volunteers, to navigate the shifting neoliberal conditions that are unevenly reconfiguring Ammani urbanization and Jordanian cultural policy via market-driven priorities of privatization and commodity value. As such, we assert that festivals are crucial sites of intervention and possibility in the broader Ammani public sphere.

Much of the scholarship based in and about Amman has emphasized its changing and contentious urban development (Ababsa 2013; Abu Hamdi 2016; Corbett 2011; Daher 2013; Musa 2013; Parker 2009). The acceleration of the Jordanian iteration of neoliberal discourse in the past two decades has resulted in a city transformed by malls, villas, and condos, along with updated transportation infrastructure that has reinforced concentrations of wealth and stratified access. The notion of public space in Amman is part and parcel of analyses of the city's urban changes. A great deal of focus has been directed toward the ways in which Ammanis of varying socioeconomic backgrounds negotiate spaces of exclusion and alienation (Parker 2009; Daher 2007; Yaghi 2019) brought about by Amman's neoliberal reconfiguration and "shifting patterns of work and leisure" (Schwedler 2010). Amro Yaghi contends that Amman is characterized by "pseudo public space," that is, conditionally accessible space (2019, 249). More critical still are somber analyses of Amman as "a landscape marred by empty buildings, gaping holes and the skeletal remains of speculative development gone bust" (Hourani 2014) and "a postmodern cityscape: decentered, fragmented, privatized" (Shami 2007).

Our argument is that the form of festival itself is not merely an example of al-Balad Theater's institutional survival but an integral tool in its broader mission of creating safe and accessible spaces for artists and cultural actors. The festivals are sites of intensive, intentional communal experience that shape individual and collective identities and their relationships to place. Each festival highlights not only a different form of creative expression but also different relationships between creative expression, audience, and space.

The thoughts presented in this chapter are drawn from Serene Huleileh's seventeen years of experience with al-Balad Theater and lifetime of cultural activist and management work in Jordan and Palestine, as well as Jeremy Reed's dissertation fieldwork in Amman from 2017 to 2021, including close participant observations of al-Balad Music Festival in 2017 and 2019 (as a volunteer) and the Baladk Festival in 2019. We draw on our shared experiences, community connections, and distinct but complementary points of view. Additionally, we conducted interviews between February 2022 and September 2023 virtually and on-site with key individuals involved with the three festivals discussed here.

Al-Balad Theater: A Cultural Hub for Jordan

Al-Balad Theater is a multipurpose art and community organization that provides space and opportunity for artists and cultural actors to present their work. The fundamental mission of the theater is to "contribute to artivism and weave the social fabric of the city and the region to develop an environment that is supportive, enriching, and inspiring for independent artists of all ages, and provide safe community spaces for expression and independent artistic production that is attuned to people's concerns."[1] When it was established, al-Balad Theater was one of few organizations in the Jordanian cultural sphere operating as an independent not-for-profit organization. Even today, almost two decades later, there are precious few spaces for relatively unrestricted artistic and intellectual activity in Amman. More than providing a space for free and creative expression, al-Balad Theater provides logistical support and mediates interactions between artists and the bureaucratic hurdles of funding conditions and state regulations. The space it provides, particularly in contemporary Amman, is more than simply a physical venue.

The need for such a space was rooted in the political and economic climate at the time of the theater's founding. The reverberations of the second Palestinian Intifada (2000–2005) animated decades-old social tension between Jordanian and Palestinian identities that has always characterized the struggle for a single national identity in Jordan. The intensity of the protest in the streets prompted a slew of state restrictions on the public sphere and political expression, many of which linger today. Simultaneously, the influence of conservative Islamists continued its steady rise, expanding its reach within the education sector and leadership of professional associations (Schwedler 2003). Framing all of this was an acceleration of Jordan's neoliberal reorganization. While the streets of Amman were flooding with protestors, land in and around Amman that had previously been the domain of the state was steadily being sold to private developers.

Against this changing political and social backdrop, al-Balad Theater started navigating its way through the cultural and artistic life of the city, soon becoming a local and regional hub for young artists, up-and-coming and established musicians, and the community at large. It was—and still is—the only space in Amman governed by artists for artists. The theater at first organized one-off events covering all artistic genres: music, theater, dance, film, poetry and literature, storytelling, etcetera. After a few years, however, its focus coalesced around three main areas: urban street art, music, and storytelling. Even though its programming faced a lot of competition, it managed to sustain its work and vision year after year without interruption and built a network of collaborations across the country and the region. Gradually, it developed its own framework of festival to contend with both neoliberal and conservative forces in the volatile political landscape of Jordan.

Volunteers: A Note from Behind the Scenes

For al-Balad Theater, festival is not restricted to the performance-audience nexus. Volunteers constitute the backbone of all three festivals. The work of the theater is focused on volunteerism from all age groups and walks of life. In fact, most of the theater staff started as volunteers; some have moved on to similar projects while remaining closely connected to the theater. Al-Balad Theater places a large emphasis on empowering its staff and volunteers as the next generation of cultural practitioners and activists in Amman.

The former al-Balad Theater staff members we interviewed in the course of this project Aya Nabulsi, Mu'ath Iseed, and Lubna Juqqa—in addition to current staff members Yazeed Iseed, Mohammad Amireh, and Rita Akroush—range in age from late-twenties to mid-thirties. Unlike the founders of al-Balad Theater, they grew up in an iteration of Amman in full neoliberal swing, characterized by a selective reduction of civil liberties across the board. Volunteering and working with al-Balad Theater connects them to community-oriented opportunities that the world they live in does not promote. Mohammad Amireh recalls:

> I started working with al-Balad Theater when I was fifteen years old, and since then it has become a staple in my professional and personal development. I worked with all three festivals since 2011 till today. I can't forget that moment at the Roman Amphitheater during the concert of Umaima Al Khalil. I was looking from the top of the amphitheater and felt at that moment that this is where I want to be for the rest of my life. I always felt, even as a young man, that my voice was heard by the theater staff and administration; they believed in me—us—and always wanted to be inclusive rather than exclusive. Today I am working with the theater, and I follow the same model when working with volunteers.[2]

The responsibilities and guidance—as well as mutual learning opportunities—that staff and volunteers receive through producing these three festivals stand as significant assets in their present and future work. Mohammad Amireh continues to explain, "The most important thing we learned from working with the theater is to work collectively and not necessarily seek to be the rising star. We all need recognition, for sure, but we also need the space to make mistakes and learn from them, and that's what al-Balad Theater provides." This chapter is as much about their work and contributions as it is about al-Balad Theater itself. In what follows, we consider the ways in which al-Balad Theater's three festivals navigate and intervene in Ammani public space and Amman's cultural sphere.

The Baladk Festival: Visual Aesthetic Reconfiguration of a Cement and Stone City

The Baladk Street and Urban Arts Festival (first held in 2013) focuses on Jordanian street artists and muralists. Often in collaboration with visiting international artists, local participating artists in the Baladk Festival are assigned sites in cooperation with local property owners and the Greater Amman Municipality (GAM). Festival sites are spread out across the city and serve as tableaus for murals that engage social issues such as gender, class, and cultural identity through specific themes like "The People," "Our City," and "Otherness." Aspiring artists can sign up to observe festival artists as they work, and participants come together in workshops to network and discuss their techniques. Many of the sites feature art pieces that are multiple stories tall and are as provocative in their visual appearance as they are in the issues with which they engage. Linked together under the banner of the festival, these sites gesture toward a reimagined cityscape that engages both the community in the vicinity of the murals and transient passersby.

Lubna Juqqa was the project coordinator at al-Balad Theater at the time of the inception of the Baladk Festival. Her involvement with both the theater and festival stemmed from her interest in visual arts programming and the work of local graffiti and street artists like Mike Derderian and Wissam Shadid. When we interviewed her, Lubna told us that she understood street art as a form of "public arts activism" that was direct, politically engaged, and used "one's neighborhood and country as an artistic medium."[3]

What started as a single-street event located outside of al-Balad Theater evolved into a sprawling program with dozens of murals across Amman, Zarqa, and Al-Ruseifa. More recently, the Baladk Festival even found its way across the Jordan River into Palestine. Al-Balad Theater director Raed Asfour saw the potential for this festival to expand into a full-fledged, country-wide annual festival. In its following iterations, the Baladk Festival scaled up to promote Jordanian, regional, and international artists in a mutually enriching experience for artists and citizens. Mu'ath Iseed took over management of the festival in 2015 and recalled: "I personally had an interest in curating interventions and seeing public reactions to them. I saw that Amman had almost no public interactions with applied culture or applied arts, and I felt like I had the opportunity to do that with the Baladk Festival. Soon enough, my interest in the festival became less about the Baladk Festival and more about the city itself."[4]

At the same time, Mu'ath Iseed and Lubna Juqqa both realized that the festival could not achieve its objectives without engaging in honest communication around prospective sites with both the community and structures of power that govern public space in Amman. After the first few editions, it became evident that only through consistent communication with property owners and adjacent residents could participants and organizers arrive at a better appreciation of Amman as a city. As Lubna Juqqa observed, the street art that forms the basis of the Baladk Festival is part of a critical relationship between artist and location. The Baladk Festival not only encourages new aesthetics in public space but also questions the public's relationship to space in Amman. Recalling an early iteration of the Baladk Festival, Lubna remarked that "We had paint and brushes for whoever wanted to join from the neighborhood. And that happened . . . We had kids, and we had young people joining and drawing on the walls. But then the next day . . . people in the neighborhood just painted all over this mural. Yeah. So I learned that maybe they are feeling that I'm in this neighborhood, it's their neighborhood, and we are a bunch of complete strangers to them."

For Jordanian artists, the Baladk Festival has become a pivotal event in the development of their artistic vision and career. As Jordanian muralist Yazan Mismar comments:

> Because it's a festival and an annual event, it is curated differently every year, moving from a small event to a huge festival . . . The same festival repeated every year gains experience. For me, the festival [offers] rare infrastructure for street visual arts in Jordan; some artists paint their first mural through this festival, and it's an eye-opener for them. Baladk added playfulness to my work; we as artists need this space to play and experiment and express ourselves freely in a way that we cannot do when we work with clients who commission us to paint subject-specific murals.[5]

In 2020, al-Balad Theater created a map that pinpoints the location of the Baladk Festival's various murals, creating an alternative map of the city generated by these festive and creative interactions. The inclusion of sites in Amman's eastern neighborhoods and less-visited streets suggests a broader

Ammani experience—even if the sites are fragmented pieces within the Baladk Festival cartography.⁶

Looming large in the background, however, are state actors and institutions that oversee public activity in Amman and from which permission must be acquired. In particular, the Greater Amman Municipality (GAM) is a major player in all al-Balad Theater's activities. Working with GAM is the only way al-Balad Theater can access public sites like the saḥa al-hāshemīyaa and the Roman and Odeon Amphitheaters. Formal approval from GAM for installation sites and mural concepts bolsters al-Balad Theater's position in case of public or police disruption. The negotiations between al-Balad Theater and state institutions that support and cosign the theater's festivals are as much about content as they are about access. What is and is not allowed to be presented in public vis-à-vis the values of the kingdom is one matter, but also of concern are political topics that might agitate the public sphere. We follow Delanty, Giorgi, and Sassatelli (2011) in considering festivals as instances of the cultural public sphere that offer opportunities for aesthetically and effectively negotiating collective and individual relationships to the personal, public, and political. However, as Hanan Toukan observes, the relationship between the regime and civil society in Jordan—a "benevolent autocracy" simultaneously selectively tolerant and repressive—complicates the potential of counterhegemonic contemporary arts production (Toukan 2021, 170).

Jordanian cultural policy often "operates through broad recommendations and guidelines rather than through any real distribution of resources" (Khamis 2018). Cultural plans are heavily influenced by the current political moment and department official operating the desk. As with many of the functionary offices in Amman, GAM has a labyrinthine and redundant bureaucratic structure. Even more challenging is negotiating the broad institutional posture of GAM that favors development projects to the point of marginalizing its own administrative efficacy (Daher 2013; Malkawi 1996). However, on an individual basis, specific officials have served as key allies of the theater, such as the former head of GAM's cultural affairs department, Shima al-Tal. When considerate officials are not on the other side of the desk, planning for events like the Baladk Festival becomes substantially more challenging.

Once the Baladk Festival transitioned to focus on murals, a prominent conflict arose centered on a mural painted on a multistory wall towering over the city center. The concept that artists Jofre Oliveras and Dalal Mitwally pitched to the Baladk Festival and GAM in 2021 depicted a construction worker[7] beneath a Nabatean column. Their aim was to create a statement about the relationship between the individual and society. For Jofre Oliveras, "this mural talks about our individual responsibility in society. It has opposite interpretations depending on the beholder, because the same image can oppress or empower people."[8] From one vantage point, social identity and shared heritage is the outcome of individual labor, and, from another, the spectacle of heritage can be read as an oppressive weight on the shoulders of daily life. The Nabatean column represents the use of Petra as the de facto shared heritage site in Jordanian state iconography (Corbett 2013; Katz 2005). More than just a celebration of the working-class labor that supports Jordanian society, the subtext of the mural implicitly contains the contentious politics of identity and visibility in Jordan. The objection from GAM focused on the fact that the column was resting on a red and white *keffiya*, or scarf.

"You know, the red and white *shemagh* [scarf] means something very specific in Jordan, and we don't want to exclude anyone," explained Shima al-Tal, head of the GAM cultural affairs department, when we asked her about GAM's objection. Shima insisted that her intention was to "simply suggest a neutral and inclusive option—white—to avoid unnecessary social disturbance." The red and white shemagh frequently denotes a distinct Jordanian identity in national branding campaigns such as Jordan First (2002) and We Are All Jordan (2006). The Palestinian iteration of the keffiya is typically black and white. The concern at play is the relationship between Palestinian and Jordanian identities. The coherence of Jordanian national identity has long been a third rail of Jordanian politics. Not only did Jordan absorb a mass number of Palestinians fleeing during the 1948 *nakba* (catastrophe), but both the Jordanian state and the Hashemite monarchy have played key roles in the trajectory of the Palestinian-Israeli conflict. While there is significant cultural overlap between the two identities, they have historically occupied distinct domains in Jordanian social life, often represented through material and symbolic means (Layne 1994). However, the rationale given to Oliveras and Mitwally was that the red and white shemagh suggested Palestinian Marxist affiliation, which made the color choice a sensitive issue.

Al-Balad Theater director Raed Asfour defended Jofre Oliveras and Dalal Mitwally in their meeting with GAM, insisting that they should go ahead with their plans and that he would help them navigate any repercussions. Mitwally observed that GAM's outrage "highlighted the fear of artistic expression and its power to even slightly loosen the grip of control that the authority has. This cultural regulation ends up creating a linear and uncontested image of the culture in Jordan."[9] At the very least, the installation highlights the Baladk Festival's impact at an institutional level. While the white scarf may represent a compromise, it also represents a point of contact and friction between art and authority. As long as the murals remain on the walls of the city, they serve as markers of the efforts of Baladk Festival's artists and organizers to reimagine the aesthetic contours of urban Amman.

Hakaya: Stitching the Community Fabric

The Hakaya Storytelling Festival grew out of an organic collaboration between several organizations, led by the Arab Education Forum and al-Balad Theater, that have a strong, rooted belief in "the centrality of stories to learning, art, and life." Through this long-term and strategic collaboration, which started in 2007, the Hakaya Festival has managed to carve a position at the nexus of art and community education, challenging formal education at the same time that it strengthens the link between art and learning. Turning to storytelling is also a way to thrust forward focus on the power of community and the performing arts.

The Hakaya Festival focuses on reclaiming the centrality of stories to learning, art, and life. The festival is not about storytelling as heritage but rather as a local praxis and integral part of Jordanian life. The Hakaya Festival celebrates storytelling—*hakaya*—as intangible cultural heritage and works to situate storytelling as a modality of learning and artistic expression. It brings together artists, oral historians, storytellers, and educators in residence for workshops and performances by professional and vernacular storytellers in an itinerant festival that moves through seasons and locations. By presenting storytelling in various forms, the Hakaya Festival enriches the community by reminding it of the strength of its individual and collective stories in stitching the social fabric of society and creating a healthy basis for individual and collective growth. To create an easily accessible program, the Hakaya Festival is produced across multiple sites within Amman and in cities around Jordan. When the festival first started, organizers could not find a single Jordanian storyteller to perform to the public. Fifteen years later, there are at least six professional Jordanian storytellers who perform year-round, and for some, storytelling has become a full-time career.

As Munir Fasheh, founder of the Arab Education Forum, describes, "[the Hakaya Festival] is about regaining harmony, wisdom, wellbeing, and pluralistic attitudes in living. It builds on abundance and not scarcity; and on transforming perceptions of self and one's relation to the world. It is about regaining what was made invisible. In stories, we live the present in its fullness and depth, and through stories we converse with people who lived 1000 years ago and who will live in the future" (Fasheh 2008). The festival challenges attitudes in Jordanian formal education that privilege Western modes of knowledge production over local ways of knowing and communicating (Hashem and Starr 2022). In this context, storytellers become precious community assets for the linguistic, expressive, intellectual, social, cultural, and spiritual growth of children. The shift in oral interaction among people, including the disappearance of stories from community interaction as a result of outdated literacy campaigns and Western models of education, is part of the ongoing damage to community spirit and social fabric to which the Hakaya Festival is responding.

In fact, it was the Hakaya Festival that highlighted in its 2015 edition the extent to which art, broadly speaking, is being boxed out from the school curriculum. In a seminar titled "The Hidden Curriculum That Prohibits the Arts," educators and researchers discussed various attempts, both declared and hidden, to remove art and critical thinking from schools and the educational process. An analysis of textbooks, curricula, and education policies clearly showed that an extremist wave has influenced all aspects of the educational process the regime has either endorsed or ignored.

The Hakaya Festival intervenes not only in the educational sphere but also in public space. The first two editions of the festival were primarily held in al-Balad Theater, al-Hussein Cultural Center, and at the Ruwwad Center in Jabal Natheif. However, it soon became necessary to expand the network of performance spaces outside Amman. The festival regularly organizes opening and closing nights in central squares in the cities of Irbid, al-Salt, Karak, and Aqaba, where families from less privileged areas of the city can gather to enjoy open spaces away from their apartments.

Over the years, the Hakaya Festival has worked tirelessly to mend the fabric of the Jordanian community, which is being torn to pieces by globalization, neoliberal policies, and turbulent identity politics exacerbated by a regular influx of refugees. Through performances, workshops, hikes, and film screenings, the Hakaya Festival seeks to create a convivial setting in different locations around Jordan. However, given that its main objective is to show and promote the power of people's stories, the festival shifted in its tenth edition to focus more on encouraging attendees to tell their stories rather than remain passive spectators. That is when the Masawīyya ma' al-Ḥakawātiyya, "An Evening with Storytellers," started: one storyteller tells a short story, and then audience members are invited to tell their stories. Over the years, so many stories have been exchanged in places like Karak, Irbid, Madaba, and al-Salt in addition to Amman. When al-Balad Theater was evicted, an outpouring of comments flooded the theater's social media account—many cited Hakaya as the program that meant the most to them. One commenter attested that they felt that their story was one of many embedded in the legacy of the theater and that their identity had been formed in that space as a result.

Al-Balad Music Festival: Sounds of Resistance

Al-Balad Music Festival is a celebration of Jordanian and regional Arab musical groups that takes place in the Roman and Odeon Amphitheaters framing the Saḥa al-Hāshemīyya in Wasṭ al-Balad. Established in 2009 and occurring biannually, al-Balad Music Festival is not just a platform for local artists; it is also an alternative sounding of the Wasṭ al-Balad district. While Wasṭ al-Balad remains a popular historic area of the city, successive urban renewal and regeneration projects—many of which have targeted the Saḥa—have either disrupted or displaced existing social hubs in favor of enhancing the touristic potential of the area (Abu Khafajah and Al-Rabady 2013; Corbett 2011). Al-Balad Music Festival is intended to be a public hub, a space of celebratory and sonic possibilities amid shifting urban geographies.

While performances in the two amphitheaters are now regular occurrences, this was not the case in 2009, when the festival was first produced. Further, the Saḥa al-Hāshemīyya area of the Roman Complex underwent a dramatic renovation between 2009 and 2015, with the ostensible aim of reviving the area as a gathering hub for Ammanis and tourists. Both the Baladk Festival and al-Balad Music Festival are situated within, and draw on, Amman's changing urban dynamics. As such, they offer opportunities for creative and collective expression, enrichment, and entertainment through the arts, but they also propose alternative senses of place through festive experience.

Much like the production process for the Baladk Festival, to present al-Balad Music Festival, the theater needs to interface with GAM and the Ministry of Tourism and Antiquities (MOTA). Ironically, to produce events in Wasṭ al-Balad or anywhere else in the city, al-Balad Theater must find ways of collaborating with the same entities that are facilitating the parceling of Ammani land for private and international investment. The Saḥa al-Hāshemīyya itself was renovated with funding support from the Japanese International Cooperation Agency (JICA), which also backed early stages of the Downtown Tourism Zone. Property owners were encouraged to sell their land (Hourani 2014), and though the Saḥa al-Hāshemīyya was named in honor of the royal family, residents of the area were shocked to see administrative buildings and structures from the earliest days of the kingdom demolished (Abu-Khafajah and Al-Rabady 2013). The renovation project also included the demolition of the nearby Raghadan bus station and its adjacent garden. What is left is an open plaza space that "emphasizes the Roman over the Jordanian" (189).

The transformation of the Raghadan bus station underscores an observation that al-Balad Theater staff mentioned in our interviews, namely that residents of West Amman were reluctant to travel downtown. It was difficult even for theater staff to convince friends to attend al-Balad Music Festival. Negotiating with Uber and the parallel Jordanian app Careem to offer discounted service rates were necessary incentives to attract west Ammani audience members. In place of the bus station is a planned boutique hotel, a project arranged between GAM and a transnational hotel developer (Daher 2013). As the area is a tourist district, visitors are likely to stay within a walkable or taxi-rideable vicinity of key sites such as the Saḥa al-Hāshemīyya. However, it is substantially more difficult for Ammanis who live outside the immediate neighborhood vicinity to access.

Al-Balad Music Festival focused on what it loosely described as "alternative Arabic music." As such, the festival became a springboard launching several musical projects in Jordan and the region. The term *alternative Arabic music* has become a catchall for a wide range of music by "musicians and their audience producing a politicized counter-culture that innovatively fuses local and international musical expressions as a form of protest that aims to challenge external and internal impositions of structural oppression and othering" (Karkabi 2013, 310). However, the term is in many ways more of a stance than a genre, one conditioned by position and privilege. It is a term that applies to many of the artists who perform at al-Balad Music Festival—although for some, it is a necessary evil, a label useful in marketing but otherwise empty. Tareq Abu Kwaik, one of the Jordanian alternative scene's default figures who has performed at al-Balad Music Festival with the groups el-Morabba3

(Jordan) and 47Soul (Jordan/Palestine), describes the term as an "expression of the youth's identity crisis and way for them to process that crisis."[10] Considering the mounting constraints on expressive freedoms and public gathering in Jordan, it is remarkable that al-Balad Music Festival is able to use Ammani public space—the Roman Complex and Saḥa al-Hāshemīyya—to host music that challenges the norm.

Hanan Toukan's inquiry into the conditions of public art in Amman suggests that the politics of the Jordanian state accommodates some subversive public arts performances while censoring others (2021). Toukan proposes that niche modes of artistic expression—"experimental work" that draws on a "global conceptual language"—are perceived by the state as alienating to the public and therefore not worth ministry funds. A case in point is to contrast the mural incident above with the lack of state reaction to al-Balad Music Festival's programming. Aya Nabulsi, the director of al-Balad Music Festival from 2011 to 2019, described to us how "the moment of alternative music changed things . . . People became more mature about accepting each other, accepting the differences . . . And when I'm talking about acceptance, it's on both parties. It's not only about western Amman."

At the festival in 2019, a young Jordanian band called Ayloul sang about the treatment of Syrian refugees in the band's northern home city of Irbid. In the same festival space that year, globally recognized veteran Palestinian ensemble Trio Joubran underscored the horrors of the Israeli blockade of Gaza by reinterpreting the poetry of Mahmoud Darwish with a voice-over from Pink Floyd's bassist-turned-activist Roger Waters. In that same year, the Hakaya Festival hosted Raeda Taha's play *Where Can I Find Someone Like You, Ali*, written about Taha's father, who took part in a Black September plane hijacking in 1972. While the Baladk Festival was fielding objections regarding the visibility of identity politics, the al-Balad Music and Hakaya Festivals staged artistic interventions that confronted Jordanian-Palestinian identity politics head on. Putting the three festival scenarios in juxtaposition with one another is not about comparing content but more about pointing out the presence of political art in different contexts.

The differences in public response to the aforementioned festivals gesture at the complicated nature of the Jordanian public sphere: the proposed installation for the Baladk Festival is a large-scale potential provocation, while a band like Ayloul is too small for state censors to care; Trio Joubran is broadly legible as a traditional oud ensemble making use of popular Arab poetry;

and Raeda Taha's play was extremely popular among the elite Jordanian Palestinian community in Jordan (featuring a full house five nights in a row). Another significant reason might be that murals last for many years while music and theater performances are ephemeral and reach a niche audience. Toukan similarly notes from her meeting with the then minister of culture that the Jordanian state is interested in art that makes it look progressive in the eyes of the West, particularly if that art draws on traditional cultural tropes. It is also generally too underfunded to lean into repressive tactics (Toukan 2021, 189). One could make the argument that al-Balad Theater leverages this ambivalence to create space within the public sphere for commentary and intervention. While the sounds of al-Balad Music Festival or the stories of Hakaya are ephemeral compared to the lingering murals of the Baladk Festival, al-Balad Theater is proud of its role in bringing local and regional sounds to the Saḥa al-Hāshemīyya and its amphitheaters. If you stand on the street where Jofre Oliveras and Dalal Mitwally's mural is located in the right moment, you can see the lights and hear the sounds of al-Balad Music Festival and Hakaya down the slopes of the valley. In that instance, all three festivals overlap, creating a multisensory alternative experience of place conditioned by and resistant to authority.

The Possibilities of Festivity

Festivals and their "architecture, both social and physical," are instances of territorialization that open opportunities for challenging everyday spatial practices (MacDonald 2016, 64; Johansson and Kociatkiewicz 2011). Public gathering in Amman is subject to strict regulation, especially with regards to any form of political messaging. As discussed earlier, content of the public sphere has been increasingly constrained over the past two decades. Festival formats allow al-Balad Theater to organize and sustain deliberate collective appearance in public that interweaves entertainment and social commentary. On the one hand, cooperation with state power suggests that these festivals are "permissible ruptures of hegemony" (Eagleton 1981, 148); on the other, they are sites of intensive performative activity that offer "the ability to produce new relations and meanings" (Guss 2000).

Al-Balad Theater's festivals create space for possibility, visibility, and audibility: the visibility of the murals of the Baladk Festival, the audibility of al-Balad Music Festival, and the polyphony of sound and sight when a crowd gathers to listen to storytellers at the Hakaya Festival reorient public space.

Serene has discussed elsewhere that the distinguishing characteristic of festivals is the relationship between event and host community (Huleileh 1996). They hinge on participation and a shared sense of involvement that differentiates festivals from other forms of arts presentation. The involvement of volunteers and community organizations is paramount to the creation of festive experience as well as the management of logistics of a complex event. In this sense, the festivals of al-Balad Theater aim to be *jumāhīrīyya* and *sha'bīyya* at the same time, creating a *nukhba* (niche) of their own and distancing themselves from the commercial space while somehow always contesting it.

It is tempting to target the necessity of tickets and the niche nature of festival content as modalities of exclusion. David Guss reminds us not to mistake the bounded nature of festival space for a "hermetically sealed world" (Guss 2000, 9). Lubna Juqqa recalls: "When I was still working with [al-Balad] Music Festival, it was a policy of the theater to let as many kids and strangers in from the saḥa into the venue after the doors were closed. Some kids said that they just wanted to stay outside and listen while playing with their friends. Maybe they'll come back as volunteers." Indeed, affording the cost or possessing the social capital to feel comfortable within the space is a dimension of inclusion. However, two of the reasons behind locating the festival in an outdoor space downtown are permeability and openness.

The permeability of public space has, at the same time, led to issues. Mu'ath Iseed was proud of the fact that the theater was able to program the Baladk Festival in areas seldom visited by local Ammanis or tourists, such as the Hāshmi al-Shamālī neighborhood in East Amman. The murals painted there pay homage to a local artist (Suhaib Attar) who was the first to take the festival to his neighborhood, paving the way for an extensive series of murals addressing Syrian and Iraqi refugee communities and the right to education for women. In the wake of the Baladk Festival's success, Mu'ath Iseed explained that "every weekend now there are all kinds of Airbnb experiences and underground tours that go to Hashmi. Every weekend, there is at least one if not more of those big, massive buses carrying tourists to look at these murals. Don't forget that this is a former Palestinian camp; now it's a tourist destination. And now a café is opening there." The interventionist nature or impact of the Baladk Festival and any of al-Balad Theater's festivals is not absolute. In much the same way the original cinema space of al-Balad Theater eventually fell victim to the touristic reterritorialization of Waṣṭ al-Balad, each festival is vulnerable to the forces it pushes against. However, in each case, the festival organizers—the theater staff and volunteers—learn lessons in cultural activism, how to work with their communities, and the difficult realities of creating change.

Conclusions

The aim of this chapter has been to unpack the role that festivals play in the mission of al-Balad Theater and to understand the relationship between these festivals and the changing social and political dynamics of Amman and Jordan at large. Festivals are not the only events and projects al-Balad Theater works on, but the three festivals discussed here serve as flagship programs.

Al-Balad Theater's festivals draw on their discursive qualities as "fields of action in which both dominant and oppressed [actors] are able to dramatize competing claims" (Guss 2000, 10). As extensions of the theater, each festival constitutes a site of encounter and contestation with "the ways in which urban, national, and transnational identities overlap to create particular ways of belonging and/or alienation from public space" (Shami 2007, 209). Each festival is positioned as an intervention through different sensorial modes in some form of public space, whether the contested dynamics of Wasṭ al-Balad, the expanding urban sprawl of Amman at large, or the social terrain of education. These festivals have enabled al-Balad Theater to continue programming despite having to change its physical location. Beyond this, in the ritual cyclicality of festivals, recurring annually (the Baladk and Hakaya Festivals) or biannually (al-Balad Music Festival), there is an implied continuity through festival production, a parallel or alternative sense of social time. Whether promoting a feeling of collectivity rooted in audience experience or individual creative opportunity, the three festivals are marked spaces of possibility that, just like the workshop that preceded the first al-Balad Theater location, create alternative spaces in a changing city.

Notes

1. Translated by Serene Huleileh from an internal board document titled "Al-Balad Theater Strategic Plan 2020–2024."
2. Mohammad Amireh, interview by authors, August 24, 2023, Amman, Jordan.
3. Lubna Juqqa, interview by authors, February 16, 2022, video call.
4. Mu'ath Iseed, interview by authors, February 1, 2022, video call.
5. Yazan Mismar, interview by authors, September 19, 2023, Amman, Jordan.
6. Amman is popularly understood to be divided into western and eastern Amman: the western cosmopolitan areas of the city are rapidly being developed

while the eastern areas are working-class neighborhoods. Though this division is immediately problematic, the terminology is widespread.

7. The worker was based on the likeness of al-Balad Theater facilities handyman Waleed abu Na'ama.

8. "'The Column' New Mural by Jofre Oliveras and Dalal Mitwally in Amman Jordan," *Urbanite* online, October 14, 2021, https://www.urbanitewebzine.com/2021/10/14/the-column-new-mural-by-jofre-oliveras-and-dalal-mitwally-in-amman-jordan/.

9. "'The Column' New Mural."

10. Tareq Abu Kwaik, interview by authors, July 24, 2019, Amman, Jordan.

Bibliography

Ababsa, Myriam, ed. 2013. *Atlas of Jordan: History, Territories, and Society.* Beirut: IFPO Press.

Abu Hamdi, Eliana. 2016. "The Jordan Gate Towers of Amman: Surrendering Public Space to Build a Neoliberal Ruin." *International Journal of Islamic Architecture* 5(1): 73–101.

Abu Khafajah, Shatha, and Rama Al-Rabady. 2013. "The 'Jordanian' Roman Complex: Reinventing Urban Landscape to Accommodate Globalization." *Near Eastern Archaeology* 76(3): 186–92.

Abu Rumman, Muhammad. 2009. "Amman Valley Project Addresses the Challenges of Weak Commercial Traffic in the City Center." *Al-Ghad*, October 31, 2009. http://www.alghad.com/index.php/article/337697.html.

Al-Emam, Dana. 2016. "Murals Aimed at Launching Dialogue on Gender Equality." *Jordan Times*, March 24, 2016. https://jordantimes.com/news/local/murals-aimed-launching-social-dialogue-gender-equality.

Corbett, Elena. 2011. "Hashemite Antiquity and Modernity: Iconography in Neoliberal Jordan." *Studies in Ethnicity and Nationalism* 11(2): 163–93.

Corbett, Elena. 2013. *Competitive Archaeology in Jordan.* Austin: University of Texas Press.

Daher, Rami F. 1999. "Gentrification and the Politics of Power, Capital and Culture in an Emerging Jordanian Heritage Industry." *Traditional Dwellings and Settlements Review* 10(2): 33–45.

Daher, Rami F. 2013. "Neoliberal Urban Transformations in the Arab City Metanarratives, Urban Disparities and the Emergence of Consumerist Utopias and Geographies of Inequalities in Amman." *Urban Environment* 7: 99–115.

Delanty, Gerard, Liana Giorgi, and Monica Sassatelli, eds. 2011. *Festivals and the Cultural Public Sphere.* New York: Taylor & Francis.

Eagleton, Terry. 1981. *Walter Benjamin or towards a Revolutionary Criticism.* London: Verso.

Fasheh, Munir, ed. 2008. *Stone Polished by the Sea*. Amman: Arab Education Forum.
Guss, David. 2000. *The Festive State*. Berkeley: University of California Press.
Hashem, Reem, and Karen Starr. 2022. "Imported Policy Ideals and Distributed Leadership in Jordanian Schools." *Educational Management Administration & Leadership* 52(6): 1334–1351.
Hourani, Najib B. 2014. "Neoliberal Urbanism and the Arab Uprisings: A View from Amman." *Journal of Urban Affairs* 36(2): 650–62.
Huleileh, Serene. 1996. "Al-musīqa wa al-jumhūr." Paper presented at Mu'tamar al-musīqa fi Falastīn.
Johansson, Marjana, and Jerzy Kociatkiewicz. 2011. "City Festivals: Creativity and Control in Staged Urban Experiences." *European Urban and Regional Studies* 18(4): 392–405.
Karkabi, Nadeem. 2013. "Staging Particular Difference: Politics of Space in the Palestinian Alternative Music Scene." *Middle East Journal of Culture and Communication* 6(3): 308–28.
Katz, Kimberly. 2005. *Jordanian Jerusalem: Holy Places and National Spaces*. Gainesville: University of Florida Press.
Khamis, Lina E. 2018. *Cultural Policy in Jordan: System, Process, Policy*. Springer International.
Layne, Linda. 1994. *Home and Homeland: The Dialogics of Tribal and National Identities in Jordan*. Princeton: Princeton University Press.
MacDonald, Michael B. 2016. *Playing for Change: Music Festivals as Community Learning and Development*. New York: Peter Lang.
Malkawi, Fu'ad. 1996. *Hidden Structures: An Ethnographic Account of the Planning of Greater Amman*. Philadelphia: University of Pennsylvania Press.
Musa, Majd Abdallah Nemer. 2013. "Constructing Global Amman: Petrodollars, Identity, and the Built Environment in the Early Twenty-First Century." PhD diss., University of Illinois at Urbana-Champaign.
Parker, Christopher. 2009. "Tunnel Bypasses and Minarets of Capitalism: Amman as Neoliberal Assemblage." *Political Geography* 28(2): 110–20.
Schwedler, Jillian. 2003. "More Than a Mob: The Dynamic of Political Demonstration in Jordan." *Middle East Report* 226: 18–23
Schwedler, Jillian. 2010. "Amman Cosmopolitan: Space and Practices of Aspiration and Consumption." *Comparative Studies of South Asia, Africa, and the Middle East* 30(3): 547–62.
Schwedler, Jillian. 2012. "The Political Geography of Protest in Neoliberal Jordan." *Middle East Critique* 21(3): 259–70.
Shami, Seteney. 2007. "'Amman Is Not a City': Middle Eastern Cities in Question." In *Urban Imaginaries: Locating the Modern City*, edited by Alev Çinar and Thomas Bender, 208–35. Minneapolis: University of Minnesota Press.

Toukan, Hanan. 2021. *The Politics of Art: Dissent and Cultural Diplomacy in Lebanon, Palestine, and Jordan*. Stanford, CA: Stanford University Press.

Yaghi, Amro. 2019. "Performative Approaches to 'Reclaiming Public Spaces' in Amman." In *Reclaiming Public Space through Intercultural Dialogue*, edited by Christa Reicher, Fabio Bayro Kaiser, Maram Tawil, Katrin Bäumer, Janset Shawash, and Jan Polivka, 242–62. Münster: LIT Verlag.

SEVEN

Resignifying Traditional Festive Culture for Progressive Ends in Portugal from Dictatorship to Democracy

Associativism and the Production of Protest

MIGUEL MONIZ

The marchers paraded down Lisbon's Avenida da Liberdade, the central thoroughfare of Portugal's capital city. As is common in Portuguese folk processions, the parade included local brass, percussion, and wind bands; folklore dancers and singers; accordion music; and sundry interpretive floats representing elements of Portuguese traditional festive culture. Invited by the organizers to perform at the march was Farra Fanfarra, a community-based brass band and civil society organization from Sintra, located in the coastal countryside outside of Lisbon. As Farra Fanfarra played its arrangement of "Grândola, Vila Morena," a beloved Portuguese song from the Alentejo region associated with the country's Carnation Revolution, thousands lined the streets and marched, dancing and clapping to the music, waving Portuguese flags, and holding up banners as the procession followed its route toward Lisbon's largest and most recognized public square. Television programs, social media sites, and newspapers circulated sounds and images of the parade to the public. Such parades usually attract thousands of spectators who enjoy the pageantry, listen to the bands, and watch the creative displays. The qualities of performances are later hotly debated in cafés, bars, and internet discussion groups.[1]

Traditional social practices like the one described above are part of a ritual complex called *cultura popular,* or popular culture; they occur frequently during the year throughout Portugal as a ubiquitous element of annual ritual cycles central to sociocultural life. These parades processing through communities (called in different contexts *desfiles, cortejos, procissões,* and *marchas populares*), as well as related forms of festive behavior including social gatherings such as the *festa* (free festive events in public spaces), are ritualized manifestations of and spaces for the production of cultura popular. In the context of Portuguese traditional festive practices, cultura popular is distinguished from the Anglophone concept of popular culture—a mass-mediated phenomenon embedded in global marketing and capitalist production—and instead refers to local folkloric culture. Furthermore, in Portuguese sociocultural rituals, musical practices at the festa differ from those taking place at a *music festival*, especially as the term is used in English, generally referring to a series of performances or concerts that, in the context of what this book terms *festival activism*, can serve to promote a particular political view. In Portugal, the festa is a concept in which cultura popular, or traditional festive behavior, and locally produced festival practices are parts of longstanding, culturally embedded sociocultural processes of community gathering, belonging, and reinforcing of networks of reciprocity.

Moreover, cultura popular is not only defined by specific forms of ritualized cultural expression but is also related to how these forms are (re)produced. They are generated by community-based organizations of artists, musicians, performers and community members called *associações* (associations), often acting in the role of or serving as representatives of particular neighborhoods or communities at urban and translocal events. The elemental institutions for the broader social practice of *associativismo* (associativism), these non-profit voluntary associations are most frequently based in the local communities in which the marches take place, and they provide the structural capacities to organize such events. Around Portugal, multiple ritual cycles of celebration throughout the year involve processions down a city or village's central roadway, including spring/summer socioreligious and secular festival cycles, village patron saint days, municipal and national civic celebrations, and ambulatory concerts by Portuguese *filarmónica* (philharmonic) bands. This chapter shows how such organizations organize traditional cultural practices, resignifying them for progressive political ends.

Indeed, the ethnographic vignette of Portuguese cultura popular above depicts a particular marcha from 2011. It has elements that are similar to other traditional processions but stands apart, as the parade did not take place within the ritual space of a socioreligious or secularized annual life-cycle event. The parade was, instead, an activist protest, part of the massive public upheaval accompanying the Portuguese government's response to the global financial crisis. Adapting vocabularies of traditional folk performance, however, the protestors relied on ritual expressions of cultura popular as a common vocabulary for itinerant musical activism. Further, this protest action not only adapted performative modes typical to popular parades but also relied on a network of cultural and musical associations.

These state-chartered civic institutions have their origins in the nineteenth century and were heavily regulated during the Portuguese Estado Novo dictatorship (1933–1974), which used the organizations to promote cultura popular for right-wing propaganda. Following the Carnation Revolution on April 25, 1974, when a military coup ended the dictatorship and leftist political factions determined the outcome of Portugal's constitutional democracy, the institution of the association was revitalized. The organizations are now central vehicles for citizens to produce culture and engage socially and politically, with many participating in progressive causes and promoting alternative cultural practices.

Emerging from a twentieth-century right-wing, Christian-nationalist dictatorship, Portugal's integration into the European Union, beginning in 1986, has transformed over recent decades the country's political orientation and economic standing, broadly influencing cultural expressions, including those of the associations. Yet despite these new power reconfigurations, activist musical performance, protest festivals, and festive behavior continue to use older performative vocabularies. Further, festas, popular parades and processions, village celebrations, and other traditional ritualized cultural practices have become staples in political contexts, where they have been adapted by local populations to gain agency and negotiate the outcomes of state and municipal governmental policy within a paradigm of twenty-first-century EU integration.

Creative Adaptation of Cultural Forms as an Alternative to Creative Destruction

The semiotics of festival protest activism need not only rely on ruptures with and critiques of traditional forms. Tracing the historical evolution of musical and cultural association practices in different pre- and postrevolutionary contexts, this chapter explores adaptations of community-based music-making such as the popular parade and village festa. Emerging from socioreligious traditions, cultura popular was co-opted and in part invented by the reactionary right-wing dictatorship as a foil against progressive movements and liberal sociocultural transformation. Drawing on historical precedent and contemporary articulations of traditional cultural practices, the examples in this chapter demonstrate how ritual vocabularies and performative elements of traditional cultura popular and festive culture have been used by activists to create sonic and social spaces for political advocacy, local civic engagement, and democratic participation. Despite the progressive content of protests and alternative forms of music making frequently also on display, traditional festive culture provides a powerful semiotic frame effective at influencing political action and social behavior.

Vocabularies of political protest music and other artistic performances at social activist festivals are often analyzed in terms of "creative dissent" (Langdon, Jackson, and Kitcher 2020, 167), using activist pedagogies to change ideas or behaviors for progressive goals (Moro 2017; Galloway 2014; Campaign Choirs 2019). Unlike examples discussed in this chapter, progressive festival activism in these contexts is understood as rupturing, shocking, or "dislocating social norms," as Facchini (2011, 146) describes in a discussion of feminism in São Paulo's rock scene. This literature includes studies of progressive activism in which musical performances create utopic, idealized "emancipatory spaces for social change" (Lelea and Voiculesco 2017, 807; see also Davy 2010) for marginalized identities and, in a related context, "'sonic and social spaces'" that challenge norms and promote community transformation by providing a frame where "'disparate identity-formations, cultures and geographies historically kept and mapped separately are allowed to interact with each other'" (Moehn 2007, 183–84 citing Kun 2005, 23; see also Muna 2017). At the heart of such analyses is a presumption that progressive activist intent challenges and transforms mainstream norms and expectations for cultural production, social organization, and identity expression.

The progressive movements described in these and other studies point to important strategies of resistance for marginalized positions, organizations, and identities. Such approaches require challenging and transforming political hierarchies simultaneously with norms of behavior to confront power processes responsible for deprecation, oppression, and alienation. In these cases, progressive activism relies on creative and invented forms of performance that rupture traditional expectations of musical display while challenging a restrictive social order. I am sympathetic with these positions in my examination of vocabularies of protest. Indeed, these performative frames characterized some elements of festival activism in Portugal since prior to the dissolution of the dictatorship. Through the 1970s revolutionary period, for example, there occurred backlash against traditional cultural forms viewed as associated with the Estado Novo, including disparagement of the musical societies responsible for performances at state monitored and approved concerts and festivals. As discussed in this chapter, however, even among those who sought to rupture traditional expectations with their activism, traditional cultural forms were often integrated in protest activities.

Nonetheless, expressions of festival activism in present-day Portugal demonstrate that the aesthetic choices, communicative strategies, and organizational structure of these contemporary rearticulations of traditional forms belie oppositional antagonisms.[2] In this context, creative protest is undertaken not so much by tearing down social norms but rather by repurposing traditional folk performative frames to communicate progressive aims—strategies that can conciliate objections among the public at large. The performances link political activism expressed with expanding expectations of public music performance in twenty-first-century, EU-integrated Portugal with protest vocabularies, practices, and strategies established during the dictatorship and its aftermath.

Reviving traditional, folk-based cultural forms in the service of leftist social causes is not unique to Portugal; it characterizes aspects of Brazilian *música popular brasileira* (MPB), Latin American *nueva canción*, and Portuguese *música de intervenção* (protest song), among other folk-based protest musics of the twentieth century. What makes these Portuguese cases discussed in this chapter distinct is that they do not only meld folk-inspired music to leftist lyrics but rather adopt the frame of traditional ritualized festive practices and the local, community-based social context in which these cultural practices are embedded for protest purposes. By privileging and finding novel ways of performing using traditional cultural forms, postrevolution and contemporary associative music practices in Portugal that were controlled by the dictatorship continue to create norm-rupturing sonic and social spaces that challenge political hierarchies. However, they rely on and work within a performative frame that generally supports expectations of traditional folk cultural and musical practices.

Unfolding chronologically, this analysis of traditional, festive cultura popular and semiotics of protest performance in Portugal encompasses historical examples from the dictatorship era to the contemporary period. It elucidates how Portuguese cultura popular has been intertwined with activist protest in both subtle and confrontational ways; how associations that organize protests and provide music for activist causes creatively adapt cultura popular; and how contemporary protest activities have synthesized cultura popular and traditional performative frames to address political and economic pressures of twenty-first-century EU integration.

To summarize, this analysis advances several key arguments:

1. Closely associated for centuries with socioreligious festivals but now largely secularized, ritualized street parades and the village festa have been adapted for progressive political activist projects in Portugal. While not generally understood as music festivals, these manifestations of cultura popular are nonetheless part of the cultural complex of festas, a related element of traditional festive behavior. Cultura popular is defined beyond the expressive form and depends on the local, community-based institutions that produce them, and specific kinds of musical performances are always part of these events. Adapting these forms, activists use traditional festive culture to further progressive goals.
2. These kinds of protest performances have emerged through a decades-long reclamation of cultura popular from the Portuguese Estado Novo corporatist-fascist dictatorship and its efforts to control public performance. Indeed, contrary to the dictatorship's propaganda program, contemporary activists' progressive aims have bolstered older cultural forms to celebrate difference and forge creative adaptations of global musical styles.
3. Historically, state-chartered civil society organizations have been elemental to the structuring of social life in Portugal. Contemporary iterations of these cultural associations have taken on a critical organizational, discursive, and performative role in political activism. Historical precedents, such as local, community-based Portuguese filarmónica bands and folklore groups, have provided a basis for recent alternative iterations of cultural and musical associations, including community-based alternative brass and wind bands. Using the performative model accompanying traditional parades and village festas and the cultural complex in which these events are embedded allows activists to perform alternative repertoires where they can effectively teach, inform, and transform local communities and larger audiences—without rupturing expectations for the public display of cultura popular.
4. In this context, the role of music in activist causes involves more than musical styles, lyrics, and performances and is related to how presentations are situated in the traditional ritual complex of popular

parades and festas organized by community associations. Occupying a similar central community role as older (historically more conservative or reactionary) iterations, progressive cultural associations, by facilitating members' political activism, have helped to bring about social transformation. The structural role of these organizations, their close relationship to the public, and their centrality providing opportunities for members to participate in public life and democratic processes situate progressive associations in an influential position to advocate for political causes.
5. In considering festas in Portugal, this article expands notions of what constitutes festival activism by incorporating a broader complex of cultural production in the service of political aims, showing how, in a context of social rupture brought on by EU integration, traditional cultural forms and festive behavior can play a role in promoting activist causes.

Estado Novo Control and the Subtleties of Musical Protest

Musical and festival activism do not, of course, solely advocate progressive and liberal goals of expanding equality. Festivals can also advance reactionary adoptions of cultural practices intended to support state regimes or privileged social hierarchies within and "outside of the festival arena" (Gilman 2017; Stoeltje 1993, 135–56).

As part of its propaganda agenda, the Estado Novo developed programs and marshalled authoritarian state resources to adapt, control, promote, and even invent "traditional" popular cultural practices. Framing and promoting cultura popular as an expression of premodern, agrarian social life, the regime's propaganda apparatus attempted to thwart the use of music as a vehicle of protest. These efforts restricted various forms of musical production, including urban fado (the country's national genre), and were acutely directed at the musical associations that taught and performed traditional folk music, dance, and brass music (filarmónicas). Furthermore, requirements for musicians to limit their production to forms of expression deemed acceptable by the regime were policed by local officers, informants, and state violence through not only censorship of critical lyrics but also the repurposing of religious processions, which were channeled into state-sanctioned popular parades and exhibitions. To this end, the authoritarian state established rules for venues, festivals, uniforms, performance style, and set lists, monitoring and restricting the activities of folkloric music ensembles organized by the regime (*rancho folclóricos*) as well as local filarmónica associations (Holton 2005).

Yet the relationship between these reactionary efforts to limit artistic freedom, censor cultural production, and discourage protest against the regime were met with complex responses on the part of musicians, many of whom pushed past the boundaries of acceptable lyrics, venues, and repertoires. The members of musical and cultural associations were largely acquiescent to the state's limitations, but, in their negotiations over accepting or rejecting these restrictions, resistance occurred. Kimberly Holton (2005), citing João Vasconcellos (2001), points out that even research by ranchos folclóricos that uncovered earlier styles of dress and dance "considered less important than or potentially corrosive to the cannons of nationalistic rhetoric" were effectively a form of resistance (60). Familiarity with state rules and restrictions meant that conscious deviations from this frame, no matter how minor, could communicate opposition to state power. Musicians researching and favoring nonconformist performative choices point to intricacies in festival activist practices in which engaging in traditional practices need not be antithetical to pushing back against hierarchical systems of reactionary power. These forms of resistance continued in the postrevolutionary period when many rancho ethnographers researched, recuperated, and mounted festival presentations of styles banned by the Estado Novo censorship apparatus (Holton 2005, 59–87). Such precedents demonstrate how the recovery of what artists and communities considered to be traditional forms could serve progressive ends when expressed as part of well-understood ritual vocabularies.

Estado Novo–era ranchos folclóricos were not expressions of radical protest comparable to the movements of progressive musicians, some of whom directly challenged the regime in more confrontational ways. The singers of música de intervenção (protest song) during the final years of the Portuguese dictatorship undertook more direct critiques of the state and its oppressive practices. Indeed, many of the musicians who engaged in radical protest intended to create ruptures with the regime considered the ranchos to be antithetical to progressive and anti-authoritarian aims (Côrte-Real 1996). Nonetheless, activist musicians in Portugal needed to be cautious, often expressing contempt for the regime in subtle ways, as performers were forced to adhere to what could be safely put past state censors. Failing to do so resulted in the state's censorship apparatus banning artists' creative work and the state police harassing and attacking them. As a result, even among radical dissidents, traditional cultural practices were synthesized to communicate progressive goals.

Synthesizing Traditional Performative Forms with Global Protest Movements

Protest through musical performance was an intrinsic part of public expressions of popular activism and the uprising leading to the 1974 coup. The adaptation and mimesis of cultura popular tropes in activist musical festivals in contemporary Portugal were linked to folk musicians who had a prominent cultural role dissenting against the dictatorship. Like current protest practices in contemporary EU-integration Portugal, during the late dictatorship era a cultural protest vocabulary developed in dialogue with voices outside the country as international anticolonial discourse informed revolutionary political activism. When the country opened to formerly censored and outlawed forms of musical and artistic expression during the volatile postrevolutionary period, musical performance assisted efforts to reclaim institutions and grapple with the end of the regime, including musical genres developing from mass migration from former colonies.

Musical performance of traditional repertoires has been an indelible part of Portuguese political activist vocabularies. The most notable example is from the April 25, 1974 Carnation Revolution, when the radio broadcast of Zeca Afonso's "Grândola, Vila Morena," a well-known leftist protest song that had been performed at music festivals and public events, signaled officers and troops to put the coup into motion. Although the song is not itself a traditional tune, the structure of melodic lines and choral arrangement are related to polyphonic *cante alentejano*, an agricultural community musical expression of the Alentejo region.

Defining and constructing tradition through specific rural cultural practices were hallmarks of dictatorship propaganda used to advance an antimodernity narrative. This song, which has since been referred to as the national hymn of the revolution, was, however, the literal call to arms signaling the opposition's advance against the regime. Today, "Grândola" remains a national song of protest with a sacred place in Portuguese cultural memory, performed annually at revolutionary commemorations and intermittently in diverse public settings as a general political protest anthem. Public performances of the song were especially prevalent during leftist protests over the Portuguese government's response to the global financial crisis, including the protest marches described in this chapter.

Enjoying mythic stature in the public consciousness, this protest song was nonetheless only one element in an increasingly heated decade of protest music leading to the overthrow of Estado Novo rule. Reprisals in the form of state-sanctioned violence and imprisonment were common. Yet music festivals and public performances toward the end of the dictatorship provided popular activists with a microphone to protest policies—even as critiques were generally coded to defy censors and evade the state police (PIDE/DGS). Activist music festival performance in Portugal took inspiration from other Western anticolonial protests of the 1960s, notably in the US and France. Yet through the postrevolutionary period, even as dialogue with the music of international revolutionary anticolonial movements was of central influence, protest performances and festivals were nonetheless threaded with popular Portuguese musical forms.

Social scientist João Sarmento (2007) points out that summertime festivals before and after the revolution—including Vilar de Mouros, Paredes de Coura, and others—expanded dialogue between Portugal and the international community, assisting the country in its nascent democratization project. Founded in 1965 during the dictatorship, Vilar de Mouros was initially a regional folklore festival. As Sarmento points out, the festival took on an increasingly dissident character and became a site contesting the regime's authority. In 1968, for example, Vilar de Mouros included musicians who were outspoken against the Estado Novo, including Zeca Afonso, composer of "Grândola, Vila Morena." Later dictator-era editions of "the first modern music festival in Portugal" (Sarmento 2007, 13) attracted thirty thousand spectators and showcased international performers. The symbolism of Elton John's theatrical 1971 act, for example, flew in the face of the regime's rigidity and austerity. Moreover, the event was explicitly presented as a modern, countercultural festival. Indeed, state authorities perceived the festival as a protest event. An undercover secret police agent at the 1971 festival reported on what he described as illegal actions and moral transgressions, including widespread drug use, sexual openness (including homoeroticism), antigovernment attitudes, and anticolonial and antiregime rhetorical stances (some coming from the stage), with the band Manfred Mann called out as a subversive revolutionary influence (cited in Encarnação 2019, 100).

These events, despite providing clear examples of cultural dissidence expressed at the festival, took place in a protest frame that tried to harmonize modernism and more traditional musical forms. Of relevance to this analysis, the festival was not created explicitly to protest the regime and had, in fact, evolved from a showcase for traditional folk music. Earlier editions, for example, featured state-sanctioned performances of Portuguese folk artists including the world-renowned, regime-promoted fadista Amália Rodrigues; even the National Republican Guard's brass band performed. In the subtle game to evade state police censors, the foundation of the festival—not as a site of revolutionary social practice but as a celebration of state-approved regional and national folklife—established a performative frame to facilitate later activist musical performances.

Postrevolution activist critiques emerged as the population was politically unshackled from state restrictions and as traditional musicians opened repertoires to previously banned material. Transforming expectations for musical performance in democratic Portugal emerged as older, amateur-run festivals expanded their number of international acts. One major iteration of an activist music festival embodying how traditional forms could be adapted as part of an expressive vocabulary of protest is the Festa do Avante!, founded by the Portuguese Communist Party (PCP) in 1976. The PCP's primary fundraising festival today, Avante! remains the country's largest political activist festival. The first edition took place in the midst of the tense and dangerous postrevolutionary period, as different factions jockeyed for influence, and democratic control over Portugal's political, cultural, and economic institutions had not yet been secured.

Initiated by communist leaders of the revolutionary movement, Avante! included speeches, organizational activities, and the presence of key insurgents like Ary dos Santos. The acclaimed "poet of the revolution," Santos wrote song lyrics for Amália Rodrigues, Chico Buarque, and Simone de Oliveira, who sang his words in "Desfolhada Portuguesa" (Portuguese defoliation), Portugal's 1969 Eurovision song contest entry (Felix 2010, 1178). The song is another example of how musicians in Portugal used traditional language and imagery in veiled attacks on the regime. Dos Santos's use of agricultural imagery, for example, helped the song skirt censors even as it described Portugal as "burning in the sun." Despite hewing to conservative folk culture, the lyrics could be taken as a subversive expression of protest against colonialism, state power, and the patriarchal dictatorship-era legal system condoning and normalizing domestic violence.

In the turbulent period after the dictatorship's overthrow, the Festa do Avante! was a force harnessing revolutionary protest music to leftist political factions. Indeed, Ary dos Santos, Zeca Afonso, and other luminaries of the cultural left were frequent performers. As with other revolution-era music festivals, Festa do Avante! featured international acts including Max Roach, Chico Buarque, Kermit Ruffins, Dexy's Midnight Runner, Baden Powell, and Dixieland bands.[3] The number of international brass and wind bands is notable given the ubiquity and popular appeal of this kind of instrumentation in Portugal. The spotlight of the festival, however, has always been on Portuguese acts with diverse musical styles, including folk and cultura popular acts. Performances are part of a festival that sponsors workshops, hosts political speeches, and showcases informational booths with representatives from communist, progressive, and leftist party affiliations.

The festival is more than a gathering of the party faithful or rededication to first principles harkening back to the revolutionary generation. It is modeled on the form of a popular village festa or, more specifically, an *arraial*, a festive occupation of public space. As a fundraiser, Avante! takes place in a restricted concert space and charges an entry fee, unlike a festa popular, which is free and held in a public square. Nonetheless, the event evokes a village festa and shares many structural and performative elements with socioreligious or municipal festivals. For example, since 1981, a highlight of the Avante! festival has been a popular parade. Presented as political theater, the procession is modeled on socioreligious festive marches supported by civil society associations. Along with stages for international and national acts, there is a stage showcasing filarmónica bands, ranchos folclóricos, and community-based traditional music forms. Avante! presents an image of Portugal as a broad cross section of *camaradas* (comrades, as festivalgoers performatively call one another) represented by diverse contemporary acts mixed with traditional performances that participate in this adaptation of a traditional ritual complex using a performative vocabulary expressing political content.

Community Music Making, Alternative Associations, and Political Activism

Reliance on cultura popular elements goes beyond ritual performance, however, and is also expressed in the ways the performances are produced, adapted, and embedded in the cultural complex of the Portuguese communitarian civic associations. Historically, chartered cultural and civic organizations have been responsible for organizing and coordinating with state institutions and musical societies to mount cultura popular social events. Today, half of the population participates, directly or indirectly, in over thirty thousand associations (Monteiro 2018), providing members with a direct means of agency to engage civil society, while structuring society-wide funding for and organization of cultural production. Lahusen sees civil society organizations and associativism in general as a generative force for "institutionalizing related action forms, social roles, collective objectives, and identities" (2006, 121). Given the nature of their activities, musical, cultural, and arts societies are among the most prominent, visible, and, arguably, beloved of these organizations.

Contemporary iterations of these civil society associations are likewise key organizers of political activist protests, collaborating with other civic organizations, alternative brass bands, and folk ensembles. Activist music festivals are often organized by such associations, such as the annual Festa da Diversidade (Festa of Diversity) co-organized by the activist SOS Racismo association, and the Pride Lisboa Arraial and Marcha Orgulho LGBTI+ (Lisbon Pride March) organized by ILGA (Lesbian, Gay, Bisexual, Trans, and Intersex Intervention) and other progressive associations. Even referring to the latter event as an arraial signals the reappropriation of popular festa culture, and, indeed, the Pride Lisboa Arraial music festival has become a part of the Festas de Lisboa program of official events in the city's annual summertime festa cycle. Likewise, the Festa de Diversidade is co-organized by Lisbon City Hall as part of the Festas de Lisboa, with the *Lisbon Cultural Agenda* referring to the event as a festa for "marginalized associations and artists."[4] Adaptations of the association organizing model as venues for political protest facilitate activists' ability to speak for and to the communities represented. These progressive associations and bands make them structurally similar to older community-based cultural societies. This resemblance not only speaks to the adaptation of traditional performative forms as part of protest communication in festival activism but also reflects how organizers rely on popular sociocultural institutions that organize and structure community life as the medium to produce their activist performances.

For example, alternative community-based brass bands have been prominent participants in Portuguese protest marches in recent decades, and they are also organized as association. A Portuguese expression of the global alternative brass band movement (Snyder 2022; Snyder, Allen, and Garofalo 2020), these ensembles composed of woodwinds, brass, and percussion feature lively, innovative performance styles with eclectic global and national repertoires. On the one hand, their repertoire and performative styles may make the bands appear to have departed from the filarmónica tradition from which they emerged. Yet a consideration of the operations of the alternative band associations and their highly regarded roles within local communities shows that they in many ways build on traditional organizing forms of Portuguese associations (Moniz 2020; Moniz and Snyder forthcoming). The alternative bands' community-based roles are directly shaped by the filarmónica tradition, in which most alternative brass musicians were trained and enculturated in the community-based music ensembles. Like the filarmónica bands, alternative brass bands are, with few exceptions, coordinated as and supported by voluntary musical civil society organizations based in a particular village.

The articles of incorporation of both filarmónicas and alternative brass bands charge them with carrying out specified cultural, economic, and political activities. Founded to support the public good, their status allows the collectives to earn money and makes them eligible to compete for state-level funds. As of 2018, an estimated seven hundred filarmónica bands/societies in Portugal were spread throughout rural and urban areas (Pinto and Figueiras 2018, 119; Granjo 2020, 57), and are also prominent in Portuguese immigrant settlements (Brucher 2013; Niemesto 2020). Filarmónicas are essential sources of local musical instruction and have an amplified social and cultural role in their communities, where they are central to music performance at local socioreligious events, festas populares, and municipal events. The important local roles of community-based brass and wind bands have been examined extensively (Castelo-Branco and Lima 1998; Finnegan 1989; DuBois, Méon, and Pierru 2013; Reily and Brucher 2013; Pestana et al. 2020). Their associations are social and cultural hubs in rural and urban communities, sponsoring not only concerts but also dinners, fundraisers, and workshops. They often share a close relationship with other important community institutions including churches, *juntas de freguesia* (the smallest elected local administrative unit), the armed forces, and community centers. In some rural Portuguese villages, the filarmónica society is itself the primary public community center. Filarmónicas and other music associations encompass a cross section of ages and social classes, including individuals who have respected social roles within communities.

Alternative brass bands, first appearing in the mid-1990s and numbering around fifty today, are a small but growing number compared to the filarmónicas, yet they have come to occupy a similar social role in local communities as their more traditional counterparts. Considering the heightened role of community wind bands in structuring social transformation in local contexts, alternative brass bands and other bands supported by associative cultural organizations derive political influence and persuasive social cachet from this central community role. Alternative brass bands and other creative progressive cultural associations are deeply engaged in local community life, ensuring that their activities are part of broader social justice efforts, whether directly articulated through activist festival participation or in more subtle public performances throughout the year. The progressive associations of the alternative bands coordinate, launch, and collaborate in protest actions, including activist parades and popular festas.

The alternative bands' participation in activist musical protests during the contemporary period of EU integration show that musical performance has supported progressive social transformation while mobilizing rather than abandoning local popular cultural forms. A general revitalization of associativism has emerged since EU integration at the turn of the millennium, with a newer generation relying on associativism as a form of community civic engagement. In part, this revitalization has resulted from democratic Portugal's financial and logistical support of chartered civic and cultural societies by granting funding to the organizations to provide popular services as well as to design and carry out cultural policy initiatives. Associativist participation further increased as a result of the EU political and cultural integration project, notably the expansion of the Schengen area. EU integration has increased funds for cultural and musical associations to design and participate in international and local exchange projects and performances that promote European integration with progressive social agendas. Indeed, many alternative brass bands and their musicians have been ardent supporters of progressive social movements and causes and have participated in EU cultural integration programs that put them in collaboration with other progressive associations around Europe (Moniz 2020, 389–91; Moniz and Snyder forthcoming).

The reemergence of traditional forms like brass band associations in new guises has interestingly complicated many prognosticators of EU integration, which warned that integration would lead to a diminishment of local folkways in favor of broader, more homogenizing forms. A similar assumption underpins studies examining ruptures in cultural norms brought about by progressive political activism. These cultural and musical associations' activities challenge models that contemplate cultural circulation as part of an exported and hegemonic process by acting as a local manifestation of both resistance and transformation, in which new global styles converge with and support preexisting forms. Indeed, the influence of alternative brass bands' performances in protest festas and festivals—synthesizing normative and often conservative expectations of cultural production with progressive messaging—is directly related to the structural role of community-based music associativism from which the bands emerged.

Indeed, in the twenty-first-century EU-integration era, alternative brass bands have often supplanted the performative role of filarmónicas in popular parades and village festas. This development reflects changing musical tastes but also points to how these musical projects are able to synthesize expansive repertoires and nontraditional performative elements into traditional frames that provide space for cultural transformation without being perceived as a threat to local lifeways. The centrality of such bands at activist festivals adopting popular cultural frames likewise supports political activism, as the progressive aims of organizers can be effectively communicated without seeming minacious.

Francisco "Kiko" Amorim, founder of the alternative brass groups Farra Fanfarra and Kumpania Algazarra and himself trained in a local filarmónica, has stated that an impetus for creating the bands was to participate in political causes (Moniz 2020, 383). The bands have performed at Avante! and are a staple of Lusophone music festivals, which, in postcolonial contexts, argue for a multiculturally, racially, and geographically diverse vision of Portuguese citizenship. They have been key participants in locally organized activist festivals and have performed in Lisbon in popular marcha-style parades and street protests. These events have included the massive Lisbon anti-austerity marches arising from the global financial crisis, antiglobalism and anticapitalism protests, peace initiatives, bio- and eco-sustainable festivals, and others. The alternative brass bands' participation underlines tensions between local cultural production and broader economic and political considerations (Baumann 2010; Miguel et al. 2011; Moniz 2020; Moniz and Snyder forthcoming).

Responding to political and economic transformations wrought by recent decades of EU integration, the bands engage in local, national, pan-EU, and global political issues, bringing cosmopolitan repertoire and performance styles to traditional spaces as part of community-based protest. Yet despite these characteristics, it is the musical performances by alternative brass bands and other rearticulations of folk traditions that allow protest marches to mirror older cultural festivals. While marching in protests and activist commemorations along Lisbon's Avenida da Liberdade, for example, these bands walk the same route and occupy the same performative space as filarmónicas or other popular music and dance groups in secular and socioreligious popular processions. In such a performance context, alternative brass bands and folk groups add weight and legitimacy to the causes they support.

Contemporary protest movements involve musicians in ways that rely on the cultural power of these tropes to foment social change. Leftist representations of the symbols of the nation and nationalism, resulting from the prominence of left-wing revolutionaries in the coup that made democracy possible, make the expression of social protest a normalized part of civic participation. For example, the primary state celebration commemorating the fall of the dictatorship (the most relevant national celebration in contemporary Portugal) expresses nationalist patriotism in a protest march mimicking events of 1974. The Lisbon procession down the Avenida da Liberdade includes markers of state power like the military and police walking alongside progressive activist causes, unions, and groups supporting queer rights; social, racial, and economic justice causes; and other liberal civic aims. Filarmónica and alternative brass bands are ubiquitous at these commemorations in Lisbon and throughout Portugal. If one were to witness the parade without being aware of the date, one could easily think it was an activist protest march using popular culture forms rather than a state-sanctioned national commemoration.

Adapting Cultura Popular Performance and Political Action during Lisbon's Anti-austerity Movement

Contemporary ethnographic examples of protest activity in Portugal beginning in 2011 amid the global financial crisis demonstrate the prevalence and power of resignifying traditional frames for protest. The first local manifestations against governmental responses to the global financial crisis are often attributed to the Indignados and Movimiento 15-M (May 15) protests in Spain. Although not covered as widely in the international press, the massive Geração a Rasca (Generation at Risk) movement beginning on March 12, 2011, in Portugal, when marches in Lisbon, Porto, and other major cities brought the most people to a public protest since the 1974 revolution, preceded both protests in Spain. The movement also included an occupation of Lisbon's central Rossio Square well before the Occupy movement began in New York City. Progressive musical associations and alternative folk-traditional and brass musicians performed at all the Portuguese protests.

Protests and marches continued for several years in Lisbon with public protests down the Avenida da Liberdade, in front of the Portuguese Parliament, and in several key public *praças* (squares), as well as in cities throughout the country. The protests urged government action to solve high unemployment and other problems of inequality exacerbated by the crisis. Later protests dissented against the Portuguese government's acceptance of draconian anti-austerity measures raising taxes and cutting salaries to bring down debt required by the IMF (International Monetary Fund), the European Commission, and the European Central Bank, as conditions for the country to receive a financial bailout to avoid insolvency.

As mentioned in the opening vignette of this chapter, among the many alternative cultural associations and bands participating in the protests over these years was the Farra Fanfarra Associação Cultural. The band had for years collaborated with leaders of civil society associations organizing progressive activist causes—including performances at cultura popular parades and arraial-style protests like civic association-sponsored marijuana legalization marches, antigentrification efforts, anti-imperialism actions, pro-peace rallies, environmental causes, and HIV awareness/condom distribution drives. Aware of Farra Fanfarra Cultural Association's collaboration in previous protests, the citizens' committee organizing the anti-austerity action on March 12, 2013, asked association musicians to lead the march down the Avenida de Liberdade. During the parade, the association-assembled band repeatedly performed a Romani-rumba inspired version of Zeca Afonso's "Grândola, Vila Morena," a song performed by these musicians at numerous other political manifestations.[5] As the band marched, Stefano, Farra Fanfarra's *animador*,[6] crowed into his megaphone, leading the crowd in the chant "O povo unido jamais será vencido" (the people united will never be defeated). The phrase has been a *cri de coeur* in Portugal since the 1974 revolution, when it was popularized in a song by Luís Cília (based on the Chilean anthem by Quilapayún). As with other protest marches, images and videos of the band accompanied print and television news reports about the cause, also circulating virally on social media platforms.[7]

Protest vocabularies drawing on the revolutionary period went beyond the ubiquitous performances of the protest anthem "Grândola, Vila Morena" and included the repurposing of symbols of the earlier revolutionary generation to reach a broader audience. For example, the Homens da Luta, a popular satirical band emerging from performances at the protests, adopted the posture, dress, and musical style of mythical figures and archetypes from the 1974 revolution. Parodying Zeca Afonso and leftist protest singers, the Capitães de Abril (Captains of April), and *saloio* culture,[8] the representations conferred the band with the cultural wherewithal to speak with a popular voice in the exigency of the moment. As part of their shtick, the band chanted "Carvalhesa"—the ubiquitous earworm that plays constantly through loudspeakers during the Festa do Avante!. Homens da Luta was a key presence at protest marches, providing comic relief while launching a serious call to arms in the cause against the government response. Their song "A Luta é Alegria" (The struggle is joy) swept to victory in Portugal's national Festival da Canção (Festival of Song) contest, uniting generations in a revolutionary spirit and representing the country at the 2011 Eurovision Song Contest. The Homens da Luta performances, like those of alternative brass bands, repurposed traditional forms of cultural expression, reinventing them for contemporary contexts while relying on their power as markers of traditional Portuguese culture. These performative vocabularies transcend the traditional forms in which they are embedded and give significance and power to protesters.

Conclusions

In the face of economic rupture such as that of the 2011 financial crisis, traditional cultural forms are often activated by right-wing or reactionary populists. Yet, the cases presented in this chapter demonstrate how popular culture, or cultura popular in Portugal, can play a key role in the framing and achievement of progressive activists' political aims. These creative aesthetic and structural changes occur not by rejecting but by adapting older forms to meet progressive circumstances, refashioning ritualized cultural behavior and creating space for institutional practices to remain relevant. This development has become even more important given the political and cultural role of associations in broader EU-era integration efforts (Lahusen 2006).

This protest model demonstrates how effective political activism can rely on protest vocabularies that have evolved within existing cultural institutions to create sonic spaces that support rather than challenge long-standing popular culture ritual complexes and social institutions. This exploration of festive behavior and political resistance in Portugal has shown the following: (1) Popular parade, village festa/arraial forms, and other popular cultural performances have been adapted as part of progressive political activist projects. (2) They have served to celebrate difference and forge creative adaptations of global musical styles to support progressive causes. (3) They have enabled local communities to be persuaded in a frame that conciliates new cultural practices and political configurations without increasing tension over how older lifeways are threatened or diminished. (4) These performative protest vocabularies involve more than mere public presentations and are situated in traditional ritual complexes organized by community-based associative institutions. As a result, activism in the context of festive behavior undertaken by these respected local organizations provides a means to communicate progressive content effectively. (5) This overall argument expands notions of what constitutes festival activism to incorporate a broader complex of cultural production in the service of political aims.

The community-based roles and related social capital of older musical and cultural societies adopted by the newer associations have been central to engaging the public. Alternative brass bands' adherence to expectations of popular cultural expression, which adapt musical vocabularies and performative frames for progressive ends, magnifies their persuasive potential. The performances of alternative musical organizations help activist events advocate for social change, representing a traditional albeit subverted cultural form. This kind of syncretized and integrated performance has allowed contemporary performance groups in Portugal to reinvigorate and bolster older lifeways and festival practices with newer practices of social and political engagement.

Notes

1. I have conducted anthropological fieldwork with dozens of *fanfarras* (alternative brass bands) and Portuguese *filarmónica* bands over a period of almost twenty years as a member of the Farra Fanfarra Associação Cultural. I have played with brass bands at protest marches, activist festivals, and political events in Portugal and the EU.

2. Although Gilman (2017) relies on a more polysemous interpretation of Malawi's Umthetho Cultural Festival in her analysis of this theme, the overall point that festivals celebrating "traditional culture" can be useful in assisting marginalized or oppressed populations to negotiate power hierarchies is consistent with this analysis of Portuguese festivals (see Holton 2005; Futrell, Simi, and Gottschalk 2006; Borgonovo 2017).

3. A partial, undated list of performers: Os Artistas da Festa. Festa do Avante!, Partido Comunista Português (PCP), accessed March 23, 2025, https://www.pcp.pt/actpol/temas/f-avante/festa/artistas.htm.

4. Festa de Diversidade, *Lisbon Cultural Agenda*, 2022, accessed March 22, 2025, https://www.agendalx.pt/events/event/festa-da-diversidade/.

5. Bruno Massas, "manif.02/03/13," Facebook, March 2, 2013, https://www.facebook.com/bruno.massas/videos/4658274850012/.

6. An MC or front person in Portuguese *palhaçaria* (clown art presentation).

7. "Iedereen omhelst nu de 'wegwerpgeneratie'" [Everyone is now embracing the 'disposable generation'], *NRC Handelsblad* (Amsterdam), March 28, 2011: 11; "Portugal Protests against Austerity," *BBC News Europe*, March 2, 2013, http://www.bbc.com/news/world-europe-21644385; "Eurozone Crisis: Portugal Protests against Austerity," *BBC News World Europe*, March 2, 2013, https://www.bbc.com/news/world-europe-21643853; "Big Protest against Austerity in Lisbon, Portugal," *CNN* iReport, March 3, 2013.

8. The Captains of April were a group of military officers who broke ranks with the Estado Novo, responsible for carrying out the coup. *Saloio* culture is a style of dress, gastronomy, and lifeways associated with rural Portugal (often caricatured as backward).

Bibliography

Baumann, Max Peter. 2010. "Festivals, Musical Actors, and Mental Constructs in the Process of Globalization." *The World of Music: Readings in Ethnomusicology* 52(1/3): 294–313.

Borgonovo, John. 2017. "Political Percussions: Cork Brass Bands and the Irish Revolution, 1914–1922." In *Public Performances: Studies in the Carnivalesque and Ritualesque*, edited by Jack Santino, 93–112. Logan: Utah State University Press.

Brucher, Katherine. 2013. "Crossing the Longest Bridge: Portuguese Bands in the Diaspora." *The World of Music* (new series). Special Issue, *Transatlantic Musical Flows in the Lusophone World*. 2(2): 99–117.

Campaign Choirs Writing Collective. 2019. "'We Got the Power!': The Political Potential of Street Choirs." *Soundings: A Journal of Politics and Culture* 73: 129–43.

Castelo-Branco, Salwa, and Maria João Lima. 1998. "Práticas Musicais Locais: Alguns Indicadores Preliminares." *OBS* 4: 10–13.

Côrte-Real, Maria de S. José. 1996. "Sons de Abril: Estilos Musicais e Movimentos de Intervenção Político-Cultural na Revolução de 1974." *Revista Portuguesa de Musicologia* 6: 141–71.

Davy, Kate. 2011. *Lady Dicks and Lesbian Brothers: Staging the Unimaginable at the WOW Cafe Theatre*. Ann Arbor: University of Michigan Press.

DuBois, Vincent, Jean-Matthieu Méon, and Emanuel Pierru. 2013. *The Sociology of Wind Bands: Amateur Music between Cultural Domination and Autonomy*. Translated by Jean-Yves Bart. [First published as *Les Mondes de l'Harmonie*. Paris: La Dispute, 2009.] Surrey, England: Ashgate.

Encarnação. 2019. "Drogas, Festivais e Rock na Imprensa Brasileira e Portuguesa 1970/1975." *Revista Albuquerque* 11(21): 92–110.

Facchini, Regina. 2011. "'Não Faz Mal Pensar que Não se Está Só': Estilo, Produção Cultural e Feminismo Entre as Minas do Rock em São Paulo." *Cadernos Pagu* 36(1): 117–53.

Felix, Pedro. 2010. "Santos, José Carlos Perreira Ary dos." In *Enciclopédia da Música em Portugal*, edited by Salwa Castelo-Branco, 1178. Lisbon: Circulo de Leitores.

Finnegan, Ruth. 1989. *The Hidden Musicians Music-Making in an English Town*. Middletown, CT: Wesleyan University Press.

Futrell, Robert, Pete Simi, and Simon Gottschalk. 2006. "Understanding Music in Movements: The White Power Music Scene." *Sociological Quarterly* 47(2): 275–304.

Galloway, Kate. 2014. "Ecotopian Spaces: Soundscapes of Environmental Advocacy and Awareness." *Social Alternatives* 33(3): 71–79.

Gilman, Lisa. 2017. "The Politics of Cultural Promotion: The Umthetho Festival of Malawi's Northern Ngoni." In *Public Performances: Studies in the Carnivalesque and Ritualesque*, edited by Jack Santino, 93–112. Logan: Utah State University Press.

Granjo, André. 2020. In *Our Music/Our World: Wind Bands and Local Social Life*, edited by Maria do Rosário Pestana, André Granjo, Damien François Sagrillo, and Gloria Rodriguez Lorenzo, 57–82. Lisboa: Edições Colibri.

Holton, Kimberly. 2005. *Performing Folklore: Ranchos Folclóricos, from Lisbon to Newark*. Bloomington: Indiana University Press.

Kun, Josh. 2005. *Audiotopia: Music, Race, and America*. Los Angeles: University of California Press.

Lahusen, Christian. 2006. "European Integration and Civil Societies: Between Welfare Regimes and Service Markets." In *Europe in Motion: Social Dynamics and Political Institutions in an Enlarging Europe*, edited by Maurizio Bach, Christian Lahusen, and Georg Vobruba, 119–39. Berlin: Edition Sigma.

Langdon, Jonathan, Melissa Jackson, and Sophia Kitcher. 2020. "Pedagogy of Song and Restorying Hope: Stories and Songs as Social Movement Learning in Ada Songor Salt Movement." In *Doing Critical and Creative Research in Adult Education: Case Studies in Methodology and Theory*, edited by Bernie Grummell and Fergal Finnegan, 167–76. Leiden and Boston: Brill.

Lelea, Margareta Amy, and Sorina Voiculescu. 2017. "The Production of Emancipatory Feminist Spaces in a Post-socialist Context: Organization of Ladyfest in Romania." *Gender, Place & Culture* 24(6): 794–811.

Miguel, Ana Flávia, Isabel Castro, Flávia Duarte Lanna, and Alexsander Duarte. 2011. "Quatro Estudos de Caso Sobre a Música e a Identidade em Portugal, Cabo Verde, Moçambique e Brazil." Special Issue, *II Jornadas de Estudiantes de Musicología y Jóvenes Musicólogos. Cuadernos de Etnomusicología*, 1: 130–50.

Moehn, Frederick. 2007. "Music, Citizenship, and Violence in Postdictatorship Brazil." *Latin American Music Review* 28(2): 181–219.

Moniz, Miguel. 2020. "The Emergence of Fanfarra Brass Bands in Portugal (1990s to Present): Associativism, Local Activism, and Trans-local Cultural Production."

In *Our Music/Our World: Wind Bands and Local Social Life*, edited by Maria do Rosário Pestana, André Granjo, Damien François Sagrillo, and Gloria Rodriguez Lorenzo, 349–400. Lisboa: Edições Colibri.

Monteiro, Emília. 2018. "Associativismo: Metade dos Portugueses está Legada a Associações." *Jornal das Notícias* (Porto), January 21, 2018.

Moro, Pamela. 2017. "Music as Activist Spectacle: AIDS, Breast Cancer, and LGBT Choral Singing." In *Public Performances: Studies in the Carnivalesque and Ritualesque*, edited by Jack Santino, 189–204. Logan: Utah State University Press.

Muna, Ali. 2017. "'Art Is Not Just about Entertainment': The Social Activism and Cultural Production of Chicago's Inner-City Muslim Action Network (IMAN)." *Culture and Religion* 18(4): 353–70.

Niemesto, Paul. 2020. "North American Portuguese Filarmónicas—an Update and Summary." In *Our Music/Our World: Wind Bands and Local Social Life*, edited by Maria do Rosário Pestana, André Granjo, Damien François Sagrillo, and Gloria Rodriguez Lorenzo, 175–202. Lisboa: Edições Colibri.

Pestana, Maria do Rosário, André Granjo, Damien François Sagrillo, and Gloria Rodriguez Lorenzo, eds. 2020. *Our Music/Our World: Wind Bands and Local Social Life*. Lisboa: Edições Colibri.

Pinto, Diogo Miguel, and Célia Figueiras. 2018. "O Contributo das Bandas Filarmónicas para a Construção/Preservação da Identidade Local: O Caso de Baião." In *Overarching Issues of the European Space/Grandes Problemáticas do Espaço Europeu*, edited by Helena Pina, Conceição Ramos, Paula Remoaldo, 119–38. Porto: Faculdade de Letras, Universidade de Porto.

Reily, Suzel Ana, and Katherine Brucher. 2013. *Brass Bands of the World: Militarism Colonial Legacies, and Local Music Making*. Burlington, VT: Ashgate.

Sarmento, João. 2007. "Festivais de Música de Verão: Artes Performativas, Turismo e Território." In *GEO-Working Papers: Núcleo de Investigação em Geografia e Planeamento Universidade do Minho-Instituto de Ciências Sociais*, edited by João Sarmento and António Vieira. *Série Investigação* 13: 5–23.

Snyder, Andrew. 2022. *Critical Brass: Street Carnival and Musical Activism in Olympic Rio de Janeiro*. Middleton, CT: Wesleyan University Press.

Snyder, Andrew, Erin Allen, and Reebee Garofalo, eds. 2020. *HONK! A Street Band Renaissance of Music and Activism*. New York: Routledge.

Stoeltje, Beverly J. 1993. "Power and the Ritual Genres: American Rodeo." *Western Folklore* 52(2/4): 135–56.

Vasconcellos, João. 2001. "Estéticas e Políticas do Folklore." *Analíse Social* 36(158–159): 399–433.

DELIBERATION

EIGHT

Another Possible World
Transnational Activism at WOMAD

JAMES NISSEN

Rebellious birds of paradise circled around hourglass extinction symbols as the assembly danced, sang, shouted, jumped, laughed, cried in defiance. Towering floats held up a mirror and portended a world to come: bees, butterflies, sun, moon, stars, oil spills, bones, robes drenched in blood, water, drought, druids, fairies, a boat to liberty, a bus to safety, a globe, a globe on fire. These scrap creations, pieced together by festival children, ran on rhythm: *djembes* calling out to Casamance, *dhols* bouncing *bhangra*, choirs lamenting with a Gaelic hymn, brass bands skanking to a reggae beat. Sounds bled into one another and the chants and banners too: "Time is running out to save the Planet / Round the Earth to safety / Indigenous activists killed for protecting their lands / Open your arms to refugees / Time for rebellion / Declare a climate emergency!" The march snaked its way through the festival site, then whistle blasts, drum slaps, and shouts brought it to a halt in the center of the main arena. A speaker announced: "We are Extinction Rebellion. We are here at WOMAD, the world's festival, as the world's rebellion." After exchanges of "What do we want? Climate justice! When do we want it? Now!" the speaker called on members of the crowd to raise their voices together to give a "rebel roar" in defense of the planet. A mighty "ROAR," silence, then cheers erupted as the rhythms resumed and the ecstatic juggernaut of dissent took off. But the moment of silence left a lingering question: was this speaking truth to power or screaming into the abyss?

Since the 1980s, there has been a sea change in the strategies of leftist activism as activists have started to participate more profoundly in struggle and protest at a transnational level. Although the history of transnational activism is longer than often assumed, with social movements such as abolitionism and communism having clear transnational aspects prior to the 1980s, transnational collective action grew in response to the rise of neoliberalism (Berger and Scalmer 2018). This macroeconomic and political system involved globalization of capitalist production and market competition, erosion of workers' rights, and upward redistribution of public resources to private corporations. It also intensified state securitization measures, such as visas and public order laws, designed to control the movement of ordinary people and restrict their capacity to assemble and protest. Neoliberalism was rooted in postwar international economic institutions such as the World Bank, International Monetary Fund (IMF), and World Trade Organization (WTO); it took hold in the United States and Europe after the economic recession and debt crisis of the 1970s and became the dominant global political order following the collapse of the Soviet Union in 1991.

Transnational activism is a complex concept, and the aims and methods used by transnational social movements vary greatly (Clark 2009). At its most basic, the term refers to collective social action across national borders, combining the oppositional nature of activism, which challenges political structures and advocates for social change, with the multiple spatialities of transnationalism. Activism may be considered transnational if it addresses global causes, such as environmentalism or world peace; if its activists or targets include citizens of more than one state or multinational organizations; if its strategies of mobilization involve crossing national boundaries; or if its activists hold cosmopolitan worldviews or seek to disrupt the global political order (Piper and Uhlin 2004). As neoliberal globalization eroded the nation-state, transnational activist movements such as the alter-globalization movement and the global justice movement emerged to oppose the new political order and contest its destructive social, economic, cultural, and environmental impacts (Reitan 2007).

While transnational activists have used traditional action repertoires such as strikes and demonstrations, they have also employed performative strategies such as song, dance, poetry, and festival to nurture creative ways of engaging politically with the world and demanding social justice (McGarry et al. 2019). Music is an established tool for political communication in many cultures, and musicians often use songs to comment on social injustice, mobilize opposition, express solidarity, and support social change (Rosenthal and Flacks 2016; Garratt 2018). Musicians became active contributors to transnational political practices during the 1980s, as shown by campaigns such as Artists United Against Apartheid and mega-events like Live Aid (1985). Activists often draw on an eclectic canon of protest songs, such as "Bella Ciao," "We Shall Overcome," and "El Pueblo Unido Jamás Será Vencido," to strengthen senses of belonging to imagined transnational social formations. Recent transnational movements have developed their own musical repertoires, with a host of musicians releasing songs about police brutality and systemic racism as part of the Black Lives Matter movement (Orejuela and Shonekan 2018).

As public gatherings where antihegemonic behavior and alternative forms of identity can be articulated, festivals have also long held sociopolitical associations (Bakhtin 1984). During the 1960s, pop festivals became a "nodal point" for countercultural social movements such as the "hippie" movement in the United States (Bennett and Woodward 2014, 13). Manuel discusses how this period is often characterized as the heyday of political music because protest musics blossomed around the world, driven by social movements that shared "modernist ideals of secular, liberal, egalitarian justice and universal human rights" (2017, 3). Festivals such as Woodstock (1969) and Glastonbury (1970) offered liminal arenas for alternative lifestyles and ideological standpoints, and their legacy still determines the meanings of pop festivals for many attendees (McKay 2000, 2015; Anderton 2019). Alter-globalization activists have also used festivals as part of their political toolbox, organizing "protestivals" to mobilize carnivalesque opposition to the regimes of neoliberalism (St John 2015; Martin 2016).

In addition to use in overtly political social movements, music festivals can be understood as potential sites for activism and political opposition in themselves. While festivals may sometimes reproduce dominant social relations (Sharpe 2008), they can also provide a context for a countercultural politics based on creativity, interaction, dialogue, and imagination (Robinson 2016). Although this notion is reasonably well established in relation to pop festivals, there is more scope for considering these issues with regards to international music festivals. Snyder's work on alternative carnival practices in Rio de Janeiro shows the potential for festive practices to act not only as a "resource" for existing movements but also as "socio-musical movements" with their own "critical agency and political power" (2018, 3–5).

The interplay of music, politics, and festival raises questions about the significance of music festivals for transnational activism: What does it mean to engage with transnational activism musically? How do festivals engender transnational activist sensibilities? And how might festival activism shed light on transnational activism as a whole?

In this chapter, I consider how transnational activism is performed within international music festivals, using World of Music, Arts, and Dance (WOMAD), the UK's largest event of this kind, as a case study. Based on participant observation and interviews conducted with musicians, organizers, and attendees at WOMAD festivals between 2014 and 2019, I discuss the politics of WOMAD as an organization and the activism performed at its festivals. I show that WOMAD's participants undertake various aesthetic strategies to attribute political meaning to festival experiences and engage with transnational politics. Focusing on this process, I suggest that international music festivals can provide spaces for music-oriented styles of activism that extend the possibilities of transnational activism beyond overtly political social contexts.

WOMAD offers an interesting case study for exploring these issues because the festival captures the dilemmas of transnational politics. These problems include the challenges of facilitating activism without imposing an ethnocentric or nationalist agenda and enacting antihegemonic politics within societies so saturated by neoliberalism that it is increasingly difficult to oppose its effects without becoming entangled in its power (Olesen 2011; Dauvergne and LeBaron 2014). WOMAD was a product of radical activist movements in the early 1980s, and these political sensibilities continue to inform its organizational practices and underpin the ways in which many musicians and festivalgoers value the event. However, by the late 1980s, WOMAD had become one of Europe's most established "world music" stages, and it now acts as an influential tastemaker in the industry. This chapter thus concerns not only the strategies of transnational activism at WOMAD itself but also the potential paradoxes of performing activism within the commercial context of the global popular music industry.

My research at WOMAD was not explicitly aligned with any organization, activist group, or social movement, but all research is inherently political; this account may be considered a "politically engaged form of ethnographic research" (Juris and Khasnabish 2013, 8–9) given its special attention to musico-political logics. My critique is inevitably partial, as I write from an embedded position as a long-term festivalgoer, musician, and activist, and, although I made a conscious effort to allow myself to be transformed by the epistemological encounters of the research process, the perspectives and experiences that inform this account are always already filtered through my own positionality, unconscious biases, and individual worldview. With this in mind, I nevertheless seek to present a balanced, critical interpretation and believe my research is relevant for other festivalgoers and could enrich understandings of music-oriented forms of transnational activism.

The Politics of WOMAD

WOMAD is the largest international music festival in the UK. The annual destination festival in Malmesbury, Wiltshire, hosts more than one hundred musicians and attracts around thirty-five thousand attendees. WOMAD's program is remarkably diverse, featuring musicians from a vast array of places and cultural backgrounds performing a range of traditional, popular, and fusion musics. Festival artists present music across six main stages, and many facilitate masterclasses and participatory musicking in workshop spaces and take part in talks, interviews, and discussions on the World of Words stage. Along with its record label, Real World, and outreach organization, the WOMAD Foundation, WOMAD has provided a platform for hundreds of international artists and helped advance multicultural music education in England.

WOMAD's founders were active participants in the antiracism movements of the 1970s. It was a turbulent time for British multiculturalism, with mounting racial strife marked by the rise of the neofascist National Front. Multicultural politics was nevertheless making significant gains: the Labour government established the Commission for Racial Equality, the Commonwealth Institute sponsored musicians from around the world to travel and perform in the UK, and grassroots social movements developed to support cultural diversity and resist racial division. Rock Against Racism (RAR) combined antiracist politics with popular culture by staging carnivals of celebratory protest that brought together reggae and punk bands, the musics most associated with Black and White working-class youths (Goodyer 2009). The antiapartheid struggle grew into a mass transnational movement, with Western pop stars releasing songs to raise consciousness and generate international solidarity (Gilbert 2007). WOMAD's prime mover, Peter Gabriel, was a key player in this movement; his musical eulogy for activist Steve Biko, "Biko" (1980), became a well-known anti-apartheid protest song, and Gabriel took part in various solidarity campaigns, including Artists United Against Apartheid (Byerly 2010).

These dynamic political currents underpinned Gabriel's idea in 1980 for a "cross-cultural" festival that could challenge "the stupidity of racism" and show "the worth and potential of a multicultural society" (WOMAD Festival Programme 1982), but WOMAD's first festival in Shepton Mallet in 1982 represented its own emergent form of transnational festival politics. While many pop festivals such as Woodstock and Glastonbury had espoused the cause of transnationalism as an ideal, WOMAD was the first major event to put this ideal into practice through programming, in terms of both musical diversity and emphasis on cultural education. It not only signified the birth of a new era for British music festivals but also made a statement about the possibility of challenging social inequalities by widening musical horizons.

Although WOMAD was aligned with left-wing social movements, WOMAD's organizers chose not to affiliate the festival with any particular political party. This choice was perhaps an attempt to learn lessons from RAR, which had faced criticism for allowing its antiracist values to become sidelined by an ethnocentric nationalist agenda. Gilroy (1987) suggests that, while RAR carnivals in 1976 and 1977 exemplified what a transgressive antiracist subculture might look and sound like, the movement lost its radical inclusivity after its union with the Anti-Nazi League in 1978 because their appeal to reclaim British patriotism from the neofascist right did not sit well with immigrant and minority groups on the margins.

WOMAD's ethos was thus implicit within organizational practices rather than an explicit political affiliation. This move was evident in the design of its festivals, which promoted politically conscious musicians and encouraged festivalgoers to engage with activism through workshops, debates, and carnivalesque parade. It was also symbolized by its rejection of corporate sponsorship, its partnerships with NGOs such as Amnesty International, and its appeals to leftist causes such as racial equality and state multiculturalism. WOMAD's political function could thus be understood as providing the conditions for expressing opposition and engaging with activism within the festival without imposing its own specific agenda.

Despite its resistance to nationalism, WOMAD's relationship with neoliberalism has been less clearly oppositional. With the growth of the world music industry in the late 1980s, WOMAD became one of the industry's leading institutions and thus inadvertently a relatively powerful gatekeeper. The term *world music* was coined by ethnomusicologists in the United States in the 1960s to refer to the diversification of music curricula, but it was popularized as an industry marketing label after a media campaign led by international pop promoters in London in 1987 (Jackson 2013). *World music* has divided critics over whether it was a purely commercial label that accelerated the commodification of the world's music and reified inequitable power relations between producers in the West and artists in the rest of the world or whether it represented a movement for disrupting the dominance of Western pop and opening new avenues for musicians to interact with musical cosmopolitanism, share their political voices, and resist state control and corporate power (White 2012; Negus 2019; Sterling 2019; Nissen 2022). Although WOMAD's organizers have publicly disavowed the label in recent years, the festival's power and influence are inevitably tied to the world music industry and, perhaps by extension, the global inequalities perpetuated by neoliberal globalization.

Nevertheless, WOMAD was certainly oppositional to the Thatcherite brand of neoliberalism that came to dominate UK politics during the 1980s. WOMAD's antiracist, multiculturalist ethos denoted a struggle against the racist nationalism of this regime (Gifford 2021). Its spaces for musicians to engage with activism stood against criminal legislation such as the Public Order Act (1986), which was introduced by successive governments to clamp down on public gathering and assemblages of resistance (McKay 1996).

WOMAD's positionality was reinforced by its partnership with the Labour-dominated Reading Borough Council after the festival moved to the Rivermead Leisure Complex (1990–2006). In a time of rampant privatization, this move brought WOMAD into a local government partnership and expanded its provision for political activism. The One World stage, introduced in 1994, was curated by a local transnational activist group, Reading International Forum, to coordinate solidarity activities at the festival in relation to global issues including human rights, environmentalism, war and conflict, and neoliberal domination. WOMAD also hosted performances and workshops dedicated to Witness, an NGO set up by Peter Gabriel in 1992 to support the documentation of police brutality and other human rights violations. Local councilors recognized the value of welcoming musical "comrades from overseas . . . fighting against racist and oppressive regimes in their own countries" (WOMAD Festival Programme 1990). Although WOMAD's organizers did not hesitate to "celebrate" their "first festival under a Labour government" in 1997, they still distanced WOMAD from overt political affiliation, jesting that they would not feature "Peter Mandelson rapping over some trance-inducing vibes from Gordon Brown" after Labour politicians had been invited to speak at Glastonbury (WOMAD Festival Programme 1997). Instead, WOMAD nurtured a music-oriented politics of transnationalism that sought to transcend national party politics.

WOMAD's partnership with Reading Borough Council ended after it moved to Charlton Park (2007–present) to expand its site capacity and return to the more rural "global village" vibe of its early festivals. It remains an independent festival, making it unusual in the UK scene, where most festivals rely on corporate sponsorship for survival (Anderton 2019). WOMAD has struggled through recurrent financial crises to retain this status, relying mainly on patronage-style support from Peter Gabriel alongside public funds for outreach activities. Its resistance to corporatization seems ideological rather than pragmatic, although creeping commercialization at the festival, such as rising ticket prices and "glamping" services, might signal the mounting challenges faced by WOMAD in upholding this position.

Within its festivals, WOMAD still prioritizes the political voices of musicians rather than imposing its own political agenda. The One World stage became the World of Words, focused on exploring global issues through dialogue with festival musicians. It has built on WOMAD's long-standing efforts to provide platforms where artists can "raise public awareness" of political issues without being reduced to "poster campaigns" depicting them as "poor, hopeless people" in need of "rescue" (WOMAD Festival Programme 1990). This new stage shows the festival's ongoing commitment to decolonizing cross-cultural advocacy and avoiding the "white savior" narratives that remain prevalent in a great deal of transnational activism (Scott 2011).

However, beyond the festival, WOMAD has become more overtly oppositional with regards to institutionalized national politics. Organizers have been increasingly vocal in criticizing government visa policies that adversely affect its ability to deliver an international program of music, culture, and politics. In the late 2000s, they spoke against immigration bureaucracy introduced by the New Labour government that led to several artists being barred entry to perform at the festival. The scale of this problem was severely exacerbated by the "Hostile Environment" policy (2012) of the Conservative–Liberal Democrat coalition. WOMAD's organizers publicly denounced the new visa system for making it intentionally difficult, costly, and humiliating to apply, criticizing not only the impact on artists who were being denied visas but also the racist message it projected to the world. Through media interviews, organizers suggested that "culture is being crushed as politicians lurch to the right" (O'Hagan 2018) and called out the "growing anti-foreigner tide" (Snapes 2018) beneath the policy. With these statements, organizers made explicit WOMAD's resistance to the nationalist conservatism and xenophobic populism marked by Brexit and the new "culture wars." WOMAD reinforced this opposition by supporting certain transnational activist movements: in 2019, WOMAD formed a partnership with the climate and ecological justice group Extinction Rebellion to curate the Rebel Rebel stage and coordinate consciousness-raising activities across the festival site; in 2020, WOMAD endorsed Black Lives Matter by participating in the Black Out Tuesday protest and releasing a statement of solidarity with "black artists all over the world and black colleagues in the music industry" on its website and social media channels.

WOMAD faces growing challenges in resisting neoliberalism as it becomes a larger and more influential institution in the music industry, with tensions arising between political idealism and economic survival. However, its organizational practices, particularly its diverse programming, rejection of corporatization, and promotion of political activism, affirm that WOMAD remains a force for transnational politics that stands against rising nationalism, racism, securitization, and separatism in the UK and around the world.

Transnational Activism at WOMAD

Transnational activism at WOMAD festivals is notably diverse, which is perhaps unsurprising given that WOMAD creates the conditions for artists to engage with activism without conforming to a specific agenda. Activism at WOMAD involves many different strategies of music, festivity, politics, and various approaches to negotiating the relationship between politics and aesthetics. There are countless small acts of resistance on WOMAD's stages and across its site and numerous ways these acts could be conceptualized. I consider three main strategies employed by musicians to engage with transnational politics: protest music, intercultural interactions, and activist coordination. Then, I discuss illustrative examples that show how these strategies attribute political meanings to festival experiences.

The term *protest music* has sometimes been applied to refer exclusively to songs that use lyrics to deliver a political message. However, this limited definition has been refuted and expanded by many critics who have shown that protest music is rarely so straightforward: music has sonic and visual content that can convey political meaning without language, and performance often involves "semantically unfixed" forms of communication that are contextual and relational (Way 2016; Jensen et al. 2020, 215). Transnational protest music is even more complex because different cultures have different methods of politicizing musical aesthetics and aestheticizing political discourses.

At WOMAD, protest music is everywhere, which is itself a political statement given that protest music usually makes up a tiny percentage of festival performances due to commercial censorship (Manabe 2015). Some artists perform songs with direct activist messages, offer social commentary between songs during their sets, and engage with transnational politics through workshops, talks, and interviews at the festival. Many of the musicians I interviewed suggested that WOMAD was the first music festival where they had so much freedom to not only perform their music but also have their voices heard and promote their political message.

In 2016, Ana Tijoux, a Chilean rapper raised in France in exile from the Pinochet regime, set her megaphone against neoliberal colonialism. She denounced, "todo lo quitan, todo lo venden" (everything is stolen, everything is sold) and promised that the time will come when "la toma se toma la maquina rota" (the occupation consumes the broken machine). She also celebrated the political agency of the "mujer fuerte insurgente" (strong rebel woman) and led the audience in a display of collective resistance with chants of "basta de robo" (down with theft) and "la calle no calla" (the street won't shut up). The same year, Asian Dub Foundation, a British electronic band known for its antiracist, anticapitalist activism and support for community-building projects in London, challenged audiences to "fight for justice" against neoliberalism. The band called out neoliberalism's "racism," "media contamination," and "bankers who think they're above the law" and inverted pejorative depictions of migrants by celebrating their "power together," punctuated musically by Nathan Lee's virtuosic fluteboxing.

Some messages voiced by festival artists at WOMAD specifically express resistance to the neoliberal order, as shown by these two examples, while others address its manifestations in social problems that have impacted artists' personal lives. As such, the topics are wide-ranging, touching on both specific issues within local contexts and global problems such as environmental destruction and racial inequality. Performances and workshops include discussion of issues that might be considered taboo in wider British society, such as polygamy, drug use, and pagan religious rituals. However, some topics and forms of activism, particularly those associated with the far right, appear off limits. For example, artists who have expressed homophobic views have not received a welcome response at the festival: Jamaican dancehall musician Buju Banton was apparently dropped from WOMAD's lineup in the early 1990s after releasing the song "Boom Boom Bye," which seems to advocate for violence against the LGBTQ+ community. This example shows that there are boundaries for activism at WOMAD and that, even without imposing a specific agenda, its values of antiracism and inclusivity serve as a regulative framework, alluding to tensions that can arise between diversity and inclusion in contexts of transnational activism (Anderl 2022).

In addition to explanatory or oppositional lyrics, some artists engage with transnational protest at WOMAD through "embodied practice" (Merson 2020). Embodied practice means performing politics through implicit actions rather than explicit words, for example by defying social division or symbolizing peace through group membership. In 2014, the Good Ones brought together Tutsi, Hutu, and Abatwa musicians to personify the reconciliation process after the Rwandan genocide against the Tutsi minority. The group from Kigali sang about survival, and the interplay of the sounds of their self-made instruments and the soft textures of their lilting voices produced a soothing affect that merged sonic and social peace. Heartbeat, a collective of young Israeli and Palestinian artists, redirected the anger that often divides their communities at the authorities who sustain violence and inequality in Israel/Palestine. Their performance in 2016 was the result of years of music-based alliance-building work, which received support from the WOMAD Foundation. The funky "Make Hummus Not War" showed how its musicians use comedy as much as rage to subvert the devastating conflict that dominates their lives. WOMAD's programming might be viewed as supporting this subversion process by including a spectrum of Israeli/Palestinian musicians, such as leftist Jewish-Israeli indie singer Noga Erez, Ethiopian Israeli musician Gili Yalo, Palestinian singer-songwriter Maysa Daw, and "anticolonial" Palestinian Jordanian shamstep activists 47SOUL.

The Hanoi Masters showed in 2017 how performance practices can also be used to resist dominant political discourses. They contested hegemonic narratives about the Vietnam conflict in the Western media, reframing it as "the resistance war against America" and sharing collective memories of the harrowing experiences their parents faced during the invasion. In 2017, when I interviewed their musical director, Vân Ánh Võ, she explained that one of their songs, "Taking Your Spirit to the Next World," was a death rite dedicated to honor the spirits of *"all* who die in conflict," challenging nationalist discourses that maintain conflict to uphold the global order. These cases illustrate diverse ways in which musicians at WOMAD engage with transnational politics through musical protest—offering testimonies against injustice, voicing demands for social change, embodying opposition and resistance, and expressing solidarity with other musicians and activists in the struggle across borders.

Intercultural interactions can give rise to indirect forms of transnational activism at WOMAD. This strategy is predicated on the notion that music has its own sonic agency that can inspire and mobilize through collective experiences (LaBelle 2018) and challenge and resignify racially marked sounds and identities (Roberts 2016). Intercultural interactions can be particularly relevant for transnational politics when they enable people from different places to encounter one another, communicate political worldviews, and participate in coalition building.

Many festival artists use WOMAD to advance a politics of transnationalism that opposes local and global regimes of chauvinism. In 2017, Taru "Delhi Sultanate" Dalmia of the Ska Vengers, a New Delhi–based ska/dub/punk band recognized for its activism against Hindu nationalism and Western colonialism, praised the festival onstage for making "international solidarity—no borders, no nations, just people—a reality." During a workshop in the same year, Denise Carlos of Las Cafeteras, a Chicano band from Los Angeles, suggested that WOMAD was "building bridges which can go over the wall," placing its intercultural interactions in opposition to US president Donald Trump's nationalist campaign to expand the border wall with Mexico. In 2018, Melissa Laveaux, a Canadian Haitian singer-songwriter, alluded to how festival interactions can challenge global cultural hierarchies more broadly when she shouted to audiences that the festival was an "international protest" against "people like Trump who say shit like shithole country." She was referring to a meeting in which the president infamously labeled Haiti, El Salvador, and several African nations "shithole countries." Laveaux's statement positions WOMAD as a site for discourse that, by valuing global musical cultures and particularly by placing African musical creativity and diversity at the heart of its world festival, rejects racism and celebrates a transnational ethico-politics of "Afropolitanism" (Mbembe 2017).

Given WOMAD's location, some artists view their interactions with UK audiences as embodied acts of reconciliation after the wounds inflicted by European colonialism. In 2016, Diabel Cissokho, a griot from Senegal renowned for his traditional storytelling and pan-African grooves, dedicated his performance to the "slaves taken from West Africa." In the song "Gore," he told harrowing stories of the suffering endured by people taken from across Africa to Gorée Island to be transported as slaves to the Americas. When I interviewed Cissokho, he described WOMAD as a form of "reparation," empowering musicians who have been disadvantaged by colonialism's global inequalities and restoring respect for their traditional music and culture. He suggested that WOMAD offered a starting point for musicians and audiences across the geopolitical divide to "come together in love and harmony," learn to "trust each other," and start to "move past the past." In 2017, Msafiri Zawose, a contemporary Gogo musician from Tanzania, affirmed: "There's a lot of history in the UK of colonialization, but, through music, we can break through all that. At WOMAD, people see we are together; we're all human beings. The UK has the good and the bad of the world coming together, but WOMAD shows the change." These statements serve as a powerful reminder that transnationalism is not by definition progressive, as some of the greatest social injustices in history, such as the Atlantic slave trade, were vast international endeavors. The portrayal of WOMAD as a form of reparation is of course unrealistic against the harsh material realities of the global order, as the festival's attempts to promote a handful of artists can do little to tackle the inequalities perpetrated by Western colonialism. Nevertheless, it speaks to the ways in which individual musicians value WOMAD and the symbolic spaces it offers for performers and audiences to come together in solidarity and condemn hatred and exploitation in the past and present.

Intercultural interactions can also forge intimate connections of empathy, which may offer emotional support for those struggling against social oppression and collective shelter for invisible and unheard marginalized voices. The Tanzanian Albinism Collective provided a striking example of this in performances, workshops, and interviews in 2017. The group, which is made up of musicians with albinism from Ukerewe, used these platforms to speak against the persecution of people with albinism, a genetic condition that results in little or no pigmentation in the skin, hair, and eyes. Through traumatic personal stories, musicians recounted how their community faces discrimination, persecution, ghettoization, and violence due to beliefs that associate them with witchcraft. They explained how people with albinism are forced to live separately, denied access to communal drinking water, forbidden from singing, banned from attending church, and killed and dismembered by witch doctor gangs that believe their body parts have magical properties. They also highlighted that women with albinism are systematically raped by people with AIDS due to myths that it will cure their condition.

When I interviewed the group, members suggested that, although there is direct protest in their songs such as "Never Forget the Killings," "White African Power (We Live in Danger)," and "Albino Brotherhood," it was being treated with dignity and respect by audiences that made performing at WOMAD a "life-changing" experience. The group agreed that the "dream" moment was when children in the audience jumped onstage to dance alongside the band, as social stigmas in the band's home context prohibit members from any contact with other people's children. This transgression of oppression and performance of solidarity, beyond its immediate emotional and psychological effects, also had a broader social and political impact. Ian Brennan, who promotes Tanzanian Albinism Collective and several other activist music groups including the Good Ones, Hanoi Masters, and Khmer Rouge Survivors, suggested that interactions at WOMAD have a "tremendous" capacity to empower because they can make artists feel safe while performing at the festival and mobilize international support beyond the event. As a direct result of Tanzanian Albinism Collective's WOMAD performance, major media outlets including the *BBC* and the *Guardian* ran articles about the group and the discrimination faced by people with albinism worldwide, and several transnational antiracism groups added this issue to their repertoire of global causes. The international attention sparked a conversation within Tanzania that put pressure on local authorities to address these problems and introduce safeguarding measures to protect the health and well-being of people with albinism. This example demonstrates how intercultural interactions at WOMAD can offer a "witnessing" power that gives musicians the confidence to voice their suffering against silence and gain new international allies who can both promise and threaten that the "eyes of the world are watching" (Byerly 2010, 123). By taking their struggle to the transnational level, musicians can reverse the roles of the powerful and the disempowered and cultivate solidarity against indifference.

What McGarry calls "activist coordination," referring to activities that "inspire and mobilize people to action" (McGarry et al. 2019, 17), is also undertaken

Figure 8.1. Tanzanian Albinism Collective performing at WOMAD 2017.

by musicians and festivalgoers at WOMAD. Beyond raising awareness, musicians sometimes ask audiences to take concrete political actions, such as signing petitions or joining social movements. Some artists promote community organizations and encourage listeners to support them, for example by donating in return for a free CD. NGOs use a range of advocacy methods at the festival, such as canvassing, talks, and demonstrations. While these actions involve a degree of institutional politics, for example asking attendees to send an email to their local MP, the majority of work is cause based, including raising awareness of global issues, getting attendees to take part in social media campaigns, and acquiring recruits for postfestival activism. Some NGOs also fundraise at WOMAD, although usually through soft methods such as selling food.

The festive high point of WOMAD is the Sunday carnival, which has a distinctly activist function. Driven by a loose collective of UK-based community music groups including samba schools, choirs, street bands, and West African percussion groups, adults and children march and chant through

Figure 8.2. Scenes from the WOMAD Sunday carnivals, 2017–2019.

the site, displaying placards, artwork, floats, and costumes made during the festival that relate to global causes. NGOs such as Amnesty International and Choose Love support the carnival by organizing workshops to raise awareness on certain issues, often selected based on relevance to particular musicians performing in that year, and mobilize festivalgoers to demonstrate about them during the march. Tapping into long-standing associations between carnival, protest, and DIY ethics creates a spectacular celebratory protest event, as evoked in the description at the start of this chapter, which canalizes the political sensibilities at play (Martin 2016). Interviews I conducted with festivalgoers suggest that the processes that underpin these protest events have the potential to festivalize activism by disrupting alienation and complacency, raising consciousness, and mobilizing participants to get involved in transnational activism beyond the festival.

The solidarity partnership between WOMAD and Extinction Rebellion in 2019 exemplified the power of activist coordination at the festival. Extinction Rebellion inaugurated the festival with a three-hundred-foot extinction symbol crop circle to signify ecocide and climate chaos. It organized workshops, talks, nonviolent direct-action training, and a series of protests and demonstrations across the festival site. Extinction Rebellion also curated the Rebel Rebel stage, which featured activist musicians from many different places, societies, and cultures. Artists performed protest music, spoke against ecological destruction and climate injustice, and called on festivalgoers to take action against governments and international organizations.

The irony of this partnership was not lost on some activists given the environmental impact of putting on a music festival. WOMAD powers some of its stages and most of its festival site using renewable energy through a partnership with Ecotricity and has a strong ecological reputation in terms of site impact. However, the festival inevitably has a significant carbon footprint, particularly considering the air miles involved in bringing artists from around the world to perform in the UK. This contradiction alludes to the dilemmas of environmental activism, which requires mass transnational mobilization and thus almost inevitably incurs further ecological costs. Yet it also affirms that, while individual activists and social movements should minimize such costs as much as they can, the voices of diverse activists should not be sacrificed in the process, as separation and alienation only increase the power and lack of responsibility of the multinational corporations fueling the climate emergency (Fiske et al. 2014).

Figure 8.3. Kurikindi performing a *limpia* for the Pachamama at WOMAD 2019 (*left*); author receiving a *limpia* near Misahualli, Ecuador (*right*). Photo by Eduardo López Santana.

Kurikindi, a shamanic healer of the Kichwa people from the Amazon Rainforest in Ecuador, demonstrated the powerful aesthetic modes adopted by musicians to perform environmentalism at the festival. He offered a *limpia* (spiritual cleansing), which involved the whistling of an ancestral song accompanied by percussion from an *escobita* (a small brush made from the leaves of one or more healing plants). This traditional ceremony closely resembled a limpia I received from a shaman in the Indigenous community of Ayllu Awarina near Misahualli in the Ecuadorean Amazon, but it was directed not at any individual at the festival, rather toward the Pachamama, the Mother Earth.

Kurikindi's performance created the arresting impression of many ethereal voices whistling together in solidarity, while the repetitive pattern of the escobita induced a trance-like state aimed at forging a connection between the activist and Pachamama. Extinction Rebellion's activities at WOMAD recruited new participants for their Autumn Rebellion, a major international protest that subsequently took place in cities across the globe. Kurikindi explained the wider significance of transnational festival activism for bringing the voices of those on the frontlines of climate change to the fore, demonstrating the strong fit between WOMAD and transnational activist movements such as Extinction Rebellion in working toward global solidarity and enabling activists from different cultures to build coalitions in a creative context:

> We Indigenous people are traveling around the world to give the message about how the climate is changing. In the rainforest, we don't need a newspaper or television to know what is happening because it is all around us.... It is very important to be conscious, we are talking about the Pachamama.... We have to fight together, so thank you to WOMAD for helping me to be here.... Now talk to your friends, talk to your families, talk to your governments. We have to be the warriors. Together, we are many.

Conclusions

Despite admirable literature on the politics of music festivals and world music (e.g., McKay 2015 and Manuel 2017), the ways in which these two intersect demands further examination. WOMAD shows that international music festivals can create spaces for music-oriented styles of transnational activism. It presents a politics of transnationalism in its organizational practices and programming and provides platforms where performers and audiences can engage with transnational politics through protest music, intercultural interaction, and activist coordination. Festivals can engender transnational activist sensibilities by bringing together activists from different places and cultures, raising awareness of global issues, and enabling activists to express solidarities and form alliances across national borders. While this politics may be distinct in context, style, and purpose from more "confrontational" politics of demand in mainstream party politics or overtly political social movements (Volk 2019, 113), it is not necessarily less significant for festival participants. Billy Bragg, one of England's best known activist singer-songwriters, told a crowd at WOMAD in 1999: "WOMAD is a very important festival. Here, we have the opportunity to come together and celebrate a multicultural society. It's just as much a part of the antiracist, antifascist movement in this country as marching against some terrible tragedy."[1]

However, WOMAD also offers insights into the dilemmas of transnational festival activism and, perhaps, transnational activism as a whole. It has increasingly been recognized that, despite their best efforts, transnational activist movements tend to reflect global inequalities (Berger and Scalmer 2018). Olesen (2011) highlights that transnational activist organizations often have questionable credentials in terms of representation, as recipients of solidarity are frequently spoken for without being actively included, and De Waal (2015) points out that the agendas of Western activists are often legitimized over the needs of affected populations. Snyder (2020) discusses how this problem can arise in musical social movements too, showing that predominantly White street bands may express cross-racial solidarities while inadvertently reinforcing White supremacy by participating in cultural appropriation.

WOMAD seems to avoid the usual trap of prioritizing the voices and aspirations of Western activists by creating the conditions for transnational activism without imposing a specific agenda and building platforms that make visible musical activists from all over the world, privileging their voices, bodies, and actions on its stages. WOMAD appears to follow De Waal's "key tenet" for "responsible advocacy": "people affected by conflict, rights abuses, and other injustices should play the leading role in movements that advocate on their behalf," often colloquially expressed through the slogan "Nothing about us without us" (2015, 1). In a time of increasing disenchantment with institutionalized politics, WOMAD perhaps represents a refuge for cosmopolitan worldviews that transgress everyday realpolitik to challenge racist nationalism and thus disrupt the global political order, offering a safe and welcoming space that maximizes cooperation and empathy and minimizes confrontation and harm. By empowering, transforming, questioning, and imagining, WOMAD discursively insists that another world is possible and experientially prefigures this other possible world.

Yet the influence that WOMAD wields to achieve this end shows the extent to which its festivals are entangled in the power of neoliberal globalization, which accelerates the commodification of the world's music, culture, and politics and reinforces paternalistic dependencies between the "West and the rest." A cynical reading might suggest that its utopian festivals are about selling the suffering of others and marketing feelings of empathy to Western audiences rather than actually forging cross-cultural solidarities or solving global problems. While for some, the beat of the carnival drums at WOMAD may sound out the dreamy parade of a more equitable and united global civil society, for others, it may conjure the nightmarish march of the relentless neoliberal machine and its seemingly limitless capacity to commodify any object, including opposition to neoliberalism itself.

However, even the latter hearing does not necessarily mean that resistance is not possible at WOMAD. Transnational activism is often complex and contradictory, and even the most radical activist groups are finding increasingly little room to operate without unintentionally playing into the hands of neoliberalism. Hoofd (2012, 11) suggests that "alter-globalist activism has increasingly no choice but to accelerate neoliberal production if it wants to keep responding to the humanist call," and Dauvergne and LeBaron affirm that the long-term strategies of activism now increasingly "conform with, rather than challenge, global capitalism" (2014, 3). Nevertheless, transnational activism can still attempt to use the master's tools to dismantle the master's house. Much like world music, international music festivals have the potential to both commercialize and radicalize, to sell out to the system and strike back from within it. The dissenting voices of festival participants could thus be understood as both genuine efforts to speak truth to power against the global (dis)order *and* alienated screams lost in the vast neoliberal abyss. While WOMAD may have a limited scope for revolution or liberation, it can still provide meaningful spaces for performing transnational activism and forging connections across diversity and difference, perhaps symbolizing the "widening of solidarity toward strangers" essential for mobilizing "geographical and political difference" against the global order (Anderl 2022, 16). Although potentially paradoxical, festivals like WOMAD might be viewed as part of the transnational "web of struggle" involved in "pull[ing] at the strings of globalization" and building "multi-pronged and multi-level resistance" to neoliberalism (Reitan 2007, 9).

Notes

1. "Artist Interview: Billy Bragg," July 25, 1999, audiocassette, British Library Sound Archive, WOMAD (World of Music, Arts and Dance) Collection, C203/807.

Bibliography

Anderl, Felix. 2022. "False Friends: Leftist Nationalism and the Project of Transnational Solidarity." *Journal of International Political Theory* 19(1): 1–20. DOI:17550882221079860.

Anderton, Chris. 2019. *Music Festivals in the UK: Beyond the Carnivalesque*. Abingdon: Routledge.

Bakhtin, Mikhail. 1984. *Rabelais and His World*. Translated by Hélène Iswolsky. Bloomington: Indiana University Press.

Bennett, Andy, and Ian Woodward. 2014. "Festival Spaces, Identity, Experience and Belonging." In *The Festivalization of Culture*, edited by Andy Bennett, Jodie Taylor, and Ian Woodward, 11–26. Farnham: Ashgate.

Berger, Stefan, and Sean Scalmer, eds. 2018. *The Transnational Activist: Transformations and Comparisons from the Anglo-World since the Nineteenth Century*. Cham: Palgrave Macmillan.

Byerly, Ingrid. 2010. "Musical Markers as Catalysts in Social Revolutions: The Case of Gabriel's 'Biko.'" In *Peter Gabriel, from Genesis to Growing Up*, edited by Michael Drewett, Sarah Hill, and Kimi Kärki, 113–30. Farnham: Ashgate.

Clark, Howard, ed. 2009. *People Power: Unarmed Resistance and Global Solidarity*. London: Pluto Press.

Dauvergne, Peter, and Genevieve LeBaron. 2014. *Protest Inc.: The Corporatization of Activism*. Cambridge: Polity Press.

De Waal, Alex, ed. 2015. *Advocacy in Conflict: Critical Perspectives on Transnational Activism*. London: Zed Books.

Fiske, Shirley, Susan Crate, Carole Crumley, Kathleen Galvin, Heather Lazarus, George Luber, et al. 2014. *Changing the Atmosphere: Anthropology and Climate Change*. Arlington: American Anthropological Association.

Garratt, James. 2018. *Music and Politics: A Critical Introduction*. Cambridge: Cambridge University Press.

Gifford, Chris. 2021. "Brexit and Trump: Contesting New Cleavage Formation." *Journal of Contemporary European Studies* 29(3): 309–21. DOI:10.1080/1478280 4.2020.1858762.

Gilbert, Shirli. 2007. "Singing against Apartheid: ANC Cultural Groups and the International Anti-apartheid Struggle." *Journal of Southern African Studies* 33(2): 421–41. DOI:10.1080/03057070701292848.

Gilroy, Paul. 1987. *There Ain't No Black in the Union Jack: The Cultural Politics of Race and Nation*. London: Unwin Hyman.

Goodyer, Ian. 2009. *Crisis Music: The Cultural Politics of Rock against Racism*. Manchester: Manchester University Press.

Hoofd, Ingrid M. 2012. *Ambiguities of Activism: Alter-Globalism and the Imperatives of Speed*. Abingdon: Routledge.

Jackson, Travis A. 2013. "Disseminating World Music." In *The Cambridge History of World Music*, edited by Philip V. Bohlman, 705–25. Cambridge: Cambridge University Press.

Jensen, Olu, Itir Erhart, Hande Eslen-Ziya, Derya Güçdemir, Umut Korkut, and Aidan McGarry. 2020. "Music Videos as Protest Communication: The Gezi Park Protest on YouTube." In *The Aesthetics of Global Protest: Visual Culture and Communication*, edited by Aidan McGarry, Itir Erhart, Hande Eslen-Ziya, Olu Jenzen, and Umut Korkut, 211–32. Amsterdam: Amsterdam University Press.

Juris, Jeffrey S., and Alex Khasnabish, eds. 2013. *Insurgent Encounters: Transnational Activism, Ethnography, and the Political*. Durham, NC: Duke University Press.

LaBelle, Brandon. 2018. *Sonic Agency: Sound and Emergent Forms of Resistance*. London: Goldsmiths Press.

Manabe, Noriko. 2015. *The Revolution Will Not Be Televised: Protest Music after Fukushima*. New York: Oxford University Press.

Manuel, Peter. 2017. "World Music and Activism since the End of History." *Music and Politics* XI(1): 1–16. DOI:10.3998/mp.9460447.0011.101.

Martin, Greg. 2016. "The Politics, Pleasure and Performance of New Age Travellers, Ravers and Anti-road Protestors: Connecting Festivals, Carnival and New Social Movements." In *The Festivalization of Culture*, edited by Andy Bennett, Jodie Taylor, and Ian Woodward, 87–108. Abingdon: Routledge.

Mbembe, Achille. 2017. "Afropolitanism." In *Cosmopolitanisms*, edited by Bruce Robbins and Paulo Lemos Horta, 102–107. New York: New York University Press.

McGarry, Aidan, Itir Erhart, Hande Eslen-Ziya, Olu Jenzen, and Umut Korkut, eds. 2019. *The Aesthetics of Global Protest: Visual Culture and Communication.* Amsterdam: Amsterdam University Press.

McKay, George. 1996. *Senseless Acts of Beauty: Cultures of Resistance since the Sixties.* London: Verso.

McKay, George. 2000. *Glastonbury: A Very English Fair.* London: Gollancz.

McKay, George, ed. 2015. *The Pop Festival: History, Music, Media, Culture.* New York: Bloomsbury.

Merson, Emily, ed. 2020. *The Art of Global Power: Artwork and Popular Cultures as World-Making Practices.* Abingdon: Routledge.

Negus, Keith. 2019. "Nation-States, Transnational Corporations and Cosmopolitans in the Global Popular Music Economy." *Global Media and China* 4(4): 403–18. DOI:10.1177/2059436419867738.

Nissen, James. 2022. "'Give Us a Voice!' Voice, Envoicement, and the Politics of 'World Music' at WOMAD." *Ethnomusicology Forum* 31(2): 236–59. DOI:10.1080/17411912.2022.2117226.

O'Hagan, Simon. 2018. "Entering Brexit Britain for Womad Festival Is 'So Difficult and Humiliating' That Performers Are Giving up, Says Organiser." *RadioTimes*, July 25, 2018. https://www.radiotimes.com/audio/radio/womad-2018-festival-brexit-britain-visas.

Olesen, Thomas, ed. 2011. *Power and Transnational Activism.* Abingdon: Routledge.

Orejuela, Fernando, and Stephanie Shonekan, eds. 2018. *Black Lives Matter and Music: Protest, Intervention, Reflection.* Bloomington: Indiana University Press.

Piper, Nicola, and Anders Uhlin, eds. 2004. *Transnational Activism in Asia: Problems of Power and Democracy.* London: Routledge.

Reitan, Ruth. 2007. *Global Activism.* Abingdon: Routledge.

Roberts, Tamara. 2016. *Resounding Afro Asia: Interracial Music and the Politics of Collaboration.* Oxford: Oxford University Press.

Robinson, Roxy. 2016. *Music Festivals and the Politics of Participation.* Abingdon: Routledge.

Rosenthal, Rob, and Richard Flacks. 2016. *Playing for Change: Music and Musicians in the Service of Social Movements.* Abingdon: Routledge.

Scott, Varihi. 2011. "Big Dog Celebrity Activists: Barking up the Wrong Tree." In *Transnational Celebrity Activism in Global Politics: Changing the World?*, edited by Liza Tsaliki, Christos A. Frangonikolopoulos, and Asteris Huliaras, 279–94. Bristol: Intellect.

Sharpe, Erin. 2008. "Festivals and Social Change: Intersections of Pleasure and Politics at a Community Music Festival." *Leisure Studies: An Interdisciplinary Journal* 30(3): 217–34. DOI:10.1080/01490400802017324.

Snapes, Laura. 2018. "'A Brexited Flatland': Peter Gabriel Hits out after Womad Stars Refused Entry to UK." *The Guardian*, July 31, 2018. https://www.theguardian.com/culture/2018/jul/31/brexited-flatland-peter-gabriel-womad-stars-refused-entry-uk-visa.

Snyder, Andrew. 2018. "Critical Brass: The Alternative Brass Movement and Street Carnival Revival of Olympic Rio de Janeiro." PhD diss., University of California.

Snyder, Andrew. 2020. "Musical Eclecticism, Cultural Appropriation, and Whiteness in Mission Delirium and HONK!" In *Honk! A Street Band Renaissance of Music and Activism*, edited by Reebee Garofalo, Erin T. Allen, and Andrew Snyder, 77–88. Abingdon: Routledge.

Sterling, Cheryl, ed. 2019. *Transnational Trills in the Africana World*. Newcastle upon Tyne: Cambridge Scholars.

St John, Graham. 2015. "Protestival: Global Days of Action and Carnivalized Politics at the Turn of the Millennium." In *The Pop Festival: History, Music, Media, Culture*, edited by George McKay, 129–47. New York: Bloomsbury.

Volk, Christian. 2019. "Enacting a Parallel World: Political Protest against the Transnational Constellation." *Journal of International Political Theory* 15(1): 100–18. DOI:10.1177/1755088218806920.

Way, Lyndon. 2016. "Protest Music, Populism, Politics and Authenticity: The Limits and Potential of Popular Music's Articulation of Subversive Politics." *Journal of Language and Politics* 15(4): 422–45. DOI:10.1075/jlp.15.4.03way.

White, Bob W., ed. 2012. *Music and Globalization: Critical Encounters*. Bloomington: Indiana University Press.

WOMAD Festival Programme. 1982. Bristol: WOMAD.

WOMAD Festival Programme. 1990. Box: WOMAD and Real World.

WOMAD Festival Programme. 1997. Box: WOMAD and Real World.

NINE

Babaláwo and *Bataleras*

Translocal Academic and Ritual Activism at the Festival of the Caribbean (Festival del Caribe) in Eastern Santiago de Cuba

RUTHIE MEADOWS

In 1982, a group of Cuban intellectuals, writers, artists, ritual practitioners, and researchers helmed by essayist and historian Joel James Figarola (1942–2006) cofounded the cultural research institute Casa del Caribe in the eastern city of Santiago de Cuba. Located on the nation's periphery, on the opposite side of the island from the intellectual hub and capital of western Havana, Santiago de Cuba forms the cultural and artistic epicenter of a region explicitly connected to and conscious of its Caribbean—and Black and Afro-diasporic—cultural and ritual identity. Dubbed the most "Caribbean" of Cuban cities (Wirtz 2014, 6; Bodenheimer 2015), Santiago de Cuba hosts the island's largest carnival celebrations in July, openly celebrating the city's geographical proximity to Haiti, Jamaica, and other Caribbean locales. Every year, Casa del Caribe hosts the city-wide Festival del Caribe (Festival of the Caribbean), also called the Fiesta de Fuego (Festival of Fire), a robust, international, and pan-Caribbean arts and academic festival held in the weeks preceding carnival.

In this chapter, I explore academic ritual engagement at the Festival del Caribe, arguing that festival participants collapse commonly held distinctions between the presumedly separate domains of festival (and ritual) practice and academic scholarship. Rather than examining festival practices and their social and activist potentialities as separate from academic epistemologies and analysis, in other words, this chapter excavates the rich, emergent histories of academic engagement and activism among festival participants themselves, including female ritual percussionists (*bataleras*) of Regla de Ocha-Ifá (Santería-Ifá) and male priests (*babaláwo*) who use the festival as a forum to reimagine translocal, African-inspired ritual potentialities.

Through ethnographic research on practitioners' ritually minded academic engagements at the Festival del Caribe, this chapter explores the complex histories of how ritual practitioners-turned-academics (and academics-turned-practitioners) in eastern Cuba harness scholarly engagement at the festival as a potent means to assert novel—and often controversial—forms of African-inspired ritual revisionism. In so doing, this chapter points to the imbrication of academic scholarship in festival intervention and activist practices. I first trace the history of the state-sponsored Festival del Caribe as it emerged in a political landscape of socialist and Marxist-inspired atheism in the early 1980s, using extensive interviews and essays published by festival cofounders in Casa del Caribe's academic journal, *Del Caribe*. In excavating this history, I draw attention to eastern Cuban academics, intellectuals, and writers who have received far less scholarly attention than their Havana-based peers despite decades of prolific scholarly output and institutional influence (Bodenheimer 2015, 100). Through this archival history, I point to the centrality of African-inspired ritual assertion and revaluation as a core vision for the founding of the Festival del Caribe, placing this history within the revolutionary landscape of state-linked and state-monitored academic and cultural institutes in the 1970s and 1980s. Ultimately, I trace how the spirit of ritual-academic intervention and revaluation that contributed to the birth of the Festival del Caribe continues to serve as a driving force in festival participation over thirty years later. Through contemporary ethnographic research at the 2015 and 2016 festivals, I engage how the festival continues to offer practitioner-academics and ritual musicians novel spaces of academic-ritual assertion in the post-atheist revolutionary era, drawing attention specifically to the controversial debates that erupted surrounding "Nigerian-style" Ifá-Òrìṣà ritual practice in Cuban Regla de Ocha-Ifá at the festival in 2015.

While festivals in and beyond the Caribbean are regularly envisioned and organized by or in consultation with academics (Edmondson 2009; Ali 2019), the role of academics and academically informed participation in forging novel forms of sociopolitical and cultural intervention through festival participation has received relatively little scholarly attention in Caribbean studies, carnival studies, and ethnomusicology more broadly.[1] With this in mind, this chapter underscores the central role of eastern Cuban academics in the development and vision of the Festival del Caribe in Santiago de Cuba, tracing the ways in which the historical interventions of academics and researchers through festival organizing instigated significant shifts in

Cuba's state-monitored religious and cultural spheres in the 1970s and 1980s. Bringing these histories into the present through contemporary ethnographic research in 2015–2016, this chapter underscores the study of academic scholarship and participation itself as a generative site for understanding the histories and potentialities of festival activism in Cuba, the Caribbean, and beyond.

Ritual Ethnography and Revolutionary Atheism: The Birth of the Festival del Caribe

The foundation of the Festival del Caribe in 1981 (originally under the title Caribbean Performing Arts Festival, or Festival de las Artes Escénicas del Caribe) marked a key step in the establishment of a series of state-sponsored cultural and academic institutes and events in Santiago de Cuba between 1981 and 1983. These included the festival in 1981 (after a failed attempt in 1980; see Alarcón 2007), the cultural research institute Casa del Caribe in 1982, and the institute's academic journal, *Del Caribe*, in 1983. Joel James Figarola, a celebrated and prolific essayist and researcher, spearheaded the foundation of these events and institutes, materializing the desires of a diverse collective of eastern Cuban intellectuals, artists, and researchers who envisioned the foundation of a festival, a state-sponsored cultural research institute, and an academic journal dedicated to the particularity of eastern Cuba's cultural ties to the Caribbean. Looking back at this era over thirty years later, the poet, essayist, and anthropologist José Millet (b. 1949) details the intellectual origins of the Festival del Caribe in 1981: "The group of intellectuals, of artists, and of collaborators who had common concerns, some of us being very young, when we were studying at the Universidad de Oriente [in Santiago de Cuba] at the end of the sixties . . . became interested in something that had hardly been addressed in our country: our own identity" (2003, 193).[2] Continuing, Millet states that this concern

> never [arose] in terms of questioning what *cubanía* ["Cubanness," also *Cubanidad*] referred to, but rather in its projection within a larger set of peoples within which we were inserted since being born in the heartbreaking fury of capitalism imposed on the Americas by the European conqueror, call it Spanish, Portuguese, English, French, Dutch, and that threw this question our way in the middle of the twentieth century: Were we Latin Americans, as we had been baptized? Or Hispano-Africans? as someone defined us at some point to vindicate, in an act of justice and again to underline in doing so, our genetic and cultural debt to Africa. (194)

Here, Millet revives key narratives of the Cuban revolution—i.e., anticapitalist critiques of European colonialism and pernicious US neocolonialialism on the island—while subtly revealing a key gap in official discourses surrounding Cuban identity in the first decades of the revolution: the question of eastern Cubans' African and Afro-Caribbean identity.

Over the next years, eastern Cuban artists and intellectuals increasingly turned to the question of their status as Cuban, Hispano-African, and Caribbean, searching for and articulating forms of self-understanding that transcended—yet simultaneously subsumed—nationalist, revolutionary narratives. Far from the intellectual epicenter and political hub of Havana, this collective of artists, writers, and researchers increasingly sought to institutionally legitimate alternate forms of self-understanding from those of western Havana, aiming especially to revive and restore aspects of eastern Cuban experience often elided in relation to the region's palpable sense of Afro-Caribbean cultural (and ritual) identity. As ethnomusicologist Rebecca Bodenheimer states, "the cultural events and academic work sponsored by the Casa del Caribe reveal a very different conception of Cubanidad as compared to the dominant one found across much of the island: santiagueros [those from Santiago de Cuba] define themselves not only as Cuban but also as Caribbean" (2015, 101). This "Caribbean consciousness," or *conciencia de caribeñidad* (James, Millet, and Alarcón [1992] 2007, 27), "is not found in other parts of Cuba," as Bodenheimer observes (2015, 101). It was also absent from revolutionary nationalist, cultural, and academic discourses, animating a central concern with Afro-Caribbean cultural identity that drove the founders of the Festival del Caribe, the Casa del Caribe, and the *Del Caribe* journal.

Notably, this heightened concern with Santiagueros' Afro-Caribbean identity was directly tied to ethnographic research on African-inspired ritual practices in eastern Cuba among young members of various arts collectives and theater troupes beginning in the mid-1970s. At a roundtable with other festival and Casa del Caribe founders in 1996, for example, Figarola described how several members of the theater troupe Cabildo Teatral Santiago (originally the Conjunto Dramático de Oriente, CDO, founded in 1961) and the Taller Cultural arts collective (directed by renowned visual artist and cultural promoter Luís Díaz Oduardo), in a "certain competitive spirit" to outshine their peers (Figarola [1996] 2007, 109), began conducting research on African-inspired ritual practices. They portrayed this undertaking as part of an effort to "go to the streets" in "search of signs and symbols of our national culture" to integrate into their art and theater productions (Figarola [1996] 2007, 108). Figarola emphasizes that the very impetus behind the Caribbean origin of the first Caribbean Performing Arts Festival in 1981 arose specifically from research with Haitian *vodú* ritual groups in eastern Cuba beginning around 1975.

Significant waves of Haitian migration to Cuba left an indelible cultural and ritual mark on the eastern region (Viddal 2012). The slave rebellions that instigated the Haitian revolution in the French colony of Saint-Domingue in the 1790s brought some ten to thirty thousand migrants (according to estimates), impacting ritual, music, and dance practices of the region (Washburne 1997, 64). In the early twentieth century, a second wave of Haitian migrants via an influx of hundreds of thousands of agricultural laborers (*braceros*) further expanded the ritual and cultural impact of Haitian migration on eastern Cuba (Viddal 2012, 207). Haitian migration informed the renowned *tumba francesa* societies founded in Santiago de Cuba by Black Haitian immigrants (Washburne 1997); the prominence of vodú ritual and musical practices in the eastern region (Viddal 2012); and the ubiquity of musical rhythmic cells such as the *tresillo* and *cinquillo*, both abundant in Haitian styles, on styles ranging from eastern, Haitian-inspired *gagá* (a secular processional dance, or *comparsa*) to the ubiquitous *danzón* popularized in Cuba and beyond in the nineteenth and twentieth centuries (Washburne 1997, 68; Madrid and Moore 2013). As Figarola notes, members of the Cabildo Teatral Santiago, the Taller Cultural, and others (including Millet, Cabildo Teatral Santiago theater director Ramiero Herrero Beatón, actor Raúl Ramón Pomares Bory, and Regla de Ocha *batá* ritual drummer and Cabildo Teatral percussionist Milián Galí Riverí) made repeated trips to conduct research with Haitian migrant communities and attend vodú ceremonies in towns throughout the greater Santiago de Cuba regional province, including La Torcaza and Barrancas (Figarola [1996] 2007). "Before the idea to create a Caribbean Performing Arts Festival," Figarola states, "there was a five-year period of work with these [Haitian] groups" (109).

The centrality of research on Afro-Caribbean ritual music and dance—including Haitian-inspired vodú ceremonies—to understandings of eastern Cuban culture and art within state-sponsored arts and theater troupes in the 1970s and 1980s points to the broader, contradictory nature of the Cuban revolutionary government's position on African-inspired religion during this era (Delgado 2009; Moore 2004). From the mid-1960s to the Fourth Congress of the Communist Party in Havana in 1991, the revolutionary state promoted Afro-Cuban religious music and dance as emblematic of national folklore and popular culture while simultaneously denigrating those aspects deemed ritual or religious in nature (Castro Figueroa 2012). When the revolutionary government transitioned toward a stance of state-enforced, militant socialist atheism based on its alignment with the Soviet Union and espousal of Marxist-inspired socialist principles in the 1960s, the state effectively banned open religious practice and affiliation (Ayorinde 2004). All the same, the revolutionary state embraced popular culture (and Afro-Cuban popular culture specifically) as a key site of working-class, socialist solidarity, leading to a paradoxical celebration of Afro-Cuban music and dance in conjunction with a call for the elimination of associated ritual and religious "atavisms" (Moore 2004; Palmié 2002). In 1975, for example, the same year that Figarola and members of the Cabildo Teatral Santiago and Taller Cultural initiated research with Haitian vodú communities, attendees at the First Congress of the Communist Party in Havana urged artists to "assimilate" Afro-Cuban instruments, music, and dance into the socialist revolution under the condition that the "mystical" aspects of these practices be purged (Partido Comunista de Cuba 1976 [in Castro Figueroa 2012, 90]).[3]

The logic by which the revolutionary state encouraged state-sponsored arts and dance troupes to incorporate Afro-Cuban music and dance as emblematic of working-class culture while stripping these forms of their ritual functions and meanings points to Cuban—and broader American—postcolonialist and settler-colonialist histories of folklorization in service of the nation (Chasteen 2004; Ochoa Gautier 2006; Robinson 2020). Indigenous xwélmexw scholar Dylan Robinson (2020), drawing on Anishinaabe scholar Leanne Betasamosake Simpson and Naomi Klein, points to this colonialist impetus as a form of aesthetic "extractivism," a logic by which specific "operations ... extract cultural practices and restate them as contributions to defining exceptionalist narratives" through nationalistic or multicultural framings of "music, visual art, or performance" (14). Speaking to the "inclusionary" politics of Indigenous music in Canada, Robinson states: "a visual and kinetic intermingling of bodies on stage, an acoustic blending of musics, or a mixed use of languages ... remains premised on finding a way to 'fit' Indigenous musicians into Western paradigms of performance" (8). In such cases, "the fundamental tenets of Western musical genres and form remain intact ... without unsettling the worldview it supports" (8). In Cuba, likewise, the revolutionary mandate of extracting Black-associated ritual forms as emblematic of working-class popular culture while stripping these practices of their ritual resonance and function aimed to uphold a revolutionary worldview premised on largely White, middle-class, Marxist-inspired atheism as well as colonialist histories of Western musical aesthetic and perceptive frames more broadly. In Cuba, furthermore, this revolutionary impetus built on a long history of White and non-Black folklorization of African-inspired and Black-associated ritual practices as part of nationalistic understandings and artistic assertions of Cuban culture, including the *afrocubanismo* arts movement of the 1920s to 1940s (Moore 1997).

Rather than encouraging young artists and intellectuals to merely strip African-inspired ritual practices of their "mystical elements" in favor of Western aesthetic and folkloric frames, however, research with Haitian vodú communities and other African-inspired ritual groups in the 1970s consolidated a vision of African-inspired ritual as integral to eastern culture and arts and Cuban national culture more broadly. Ultimately, this vision inspired a palpable sense of resistance in eastern Cuba to framings of African-inspired ritual as antithetical to Cuban revolutionary socialism (Herrero Beatón 2003; Figarola [1996] 2007). Into the 1980s, Figarola, Herrero Beatón, Millet, and other festival founders increasingly perceived African-inspired ritual practices as indispensable to national revolutionary culture, contributing to a historic collapse of the revolutionary state's ontological split between elements of Afro-Cuban culture framed as "within the Revolution" (to use Fidel Castro's famous phrase from *Words to Intellectuals*; see Castro 1961) and those perceived as antithetical to socialist-inspired scientific atheism. Additionally, many artists' and researchers' personal ties to African-inspired ritual practices in eastern Cuba—as in the case of Casa del Caribe cofounder, Santería priest (*santero*), and palo priest (*palero*) Abelardo Larduet Luaces—further contributed to the collapse of this oppositional logic among festival organizers.

Alexis Alarcón, a researcher who copublished a seminal study on Haitian vodú ritual in eastern Cuba with Figarola and Millet (James, Millet, and Alarcón [1992] 2007), notes that this emergent, novel logic of ritual-as-culture centrally drove the foundation of both the Festival del Caribe and the Casa del Caribe (2007). Alarcón states:

> The creation of the festival first, and the Casa del Caribe later, were two conscious actions by Joel [James Figarola] as part of an interpretation of culture. First, because Joel realized that these [ritual] cultures were being marginalized, they were being forgotten, which he did not agree with, because he understood that they were part of the diversity of expressions

of Cuban identity. He dealt with this in a very clever way, opening up the space of the Festival and creating the Casa as a home for all these bearers of traditional popular culture. He opened the space not only to vodú but also to santería, la regla de palo, el espiritismo de cordón, el espiritismo cruzado.... These steps were very important, because Joel believed that, by strengthening local popular culture, national culture was strengthened. (Alarcón 2007, 103–104)

Here, Alarcón points to a profound desire to validate African-inspired ritual and ritual practitioners as authentic, nonatavistic "bearers of traditional popular culture" as a core drive in the foundation of the festival and the Casa del Caribe in eastern Cuba. As Alarcón describes, the "[re]interpretation of culture" espoused by Figarola and other festival and Casa del Caribe founders employed a radical conjunction of ritual practice and state-sponsored Cuban popular culture, one that would ultimately contribute to the revaluation of Afro-Cuban ritual forms in eastern Cuba in the 1980s (Trincado Fontán 2007; Viddal 2012).

This disruptive conjunction of ritual and national culture did, however, come with a degree of risk and potential backlash. Alarcón recalls:

> There was some tension with the authorities because of the difficulty they had in understanding Joel's [Figarola's] intentions. He had to be very firm and very brave to be able to walk that path and for these expressions of popular culture to be appreciated and seen without prejudice. I remember that whenever tensions arose between the Government and Party [Communist Party of Cuba] authorities because of what was being done, he asked that they allow him to do his job. He even asked the authorities if they preferred that those drums play for or against the revolution. From the work carried out by Joel and the team he led, there was another understanding of the issue. (Alarcón 2007, 104)

In this anecdote, Alarcón repeats a commonly told story among festival and Casa del Caribe founders: that Figarola brazenly asked party authorities in the 1980s whether they preferred ritual drums be played "for the revolution and Fidel or against the revolution and Fidel" (see Trincado Fontán 2007, 98). Figarola's question plays on Castro's famous 1961 *Words to Intellectuals*, in which Castro stated, "Within the revolution, everything; against the revolution, nothing" (Castro 1961). This statement influentially delimited revolutionary cultural policy and the limits of critique within a context rife with censorship and, increasingly, fear of repercussion (Routon 2010; Saunders 2015).

As Figarola relates, this brazenness was made possible by the fact that several key artists and intellectuals in the Cabildo Teatral Santiago and the Taller Cultural maintained a sense of camaraderie with members of the National Union of Writers and Artists of Cuba (Unión Nacional de Escritores y Artistas de Cuba, UNEAC), the influential revolutionary cultural body established by poet Nicolás Guillén in 1961, as well with members of the Cuban Ministry of Culture. These institutional connections helped garner the state support necessary for the establishment of the festival. Figarola states that "the UNEAC was a zone of creation and ideas were generated. Sometimes you'll see a group of people drinking rum, and what they're doing, really, is producing things, and that's where great ideas, great things come out.... These confluences allowed for the institutional support, the official backing, and the existence of a group of people with the volition to make things happen" (Figarola [1996] 2007, 108). Through advantageous connections with members of the UNEAC and the Cuban Ministry of Culture, Figarola and others succeeded in establishing the first festival in 1981. Over the course of the coming years, festival organizers would increasingly and explicitly use the spaces of the festival to revalorize the African-inspired and Afro-Caribbean ritual foundations of eastern Cuban culture, leading to a profound shift in Afro-Cuban ritual visibility in the region.

In 1985, for example, a key breach occurred at the Festival del Caribe when Ramiro Herrero Beatón (director of the Cabildo Teatral Santiago and president of the Santiago de Cuba delegation of UNEAC), members of the Cabildo Teatral Santiago, and members of the Casa del Caribe successfully advocated to include explicitly ritual ceremonies and performances as part of the cultural celebrations of the Festival del Caribe. In the first two years of the festival (1981 and 1982), the Cabildo Teatral Santiago, where Herrero Beatón was director, hosted the original Caribbean Performing Arts Festival (as it was then called) before the foundation of the Casa del Caribe and its subsequent hosting of the festival. As Herrero Beatón describes, by 1985, members of both the Cabildo Teatral Santiago and the Casa del Caribe "realized that it was necessary to include not only theatrical activities but all cultural manifestations"—actual ritual ceremonies—as part of the newly named Festival of Culture of Caribbean Origin (Festival de la Culture de Origen Caribeño) (Herrero Beatón 2003, 113). Outlining how organizers of the festival were able to accomplish this historic integration of ritual ceremonies within a wider context of state-sponsored atheism and vigilance, Herrero Beatón states: "We must remember a date of historical reference, which is when Julio Camacho Aguilera comes to Santiago de Cuba as first secretary [of the Communist Party of Cuba, Partido Comunista de Cuba, PCC]. The comrades who attended to the culture sector both in the Poder Popular [the Cuban National Assembly of People's Power, Asamblea Nacional del Poder Popular] and in the party had reservations—then natural—about presenting the magical-religious ceremonies in the festival. There was no openness regarding Afro-Cuban religions [at the time]" (2003, 113). When Camacho Aguilera, esteemed revolutionary fighter and subsequent first secretary of the Communist Party of Cuba, visited Santiago de Cuba preceding the 1985 festival, members of the Cabildo, the Casa del Caribe (including Figarola), and others held an *encontronazo*, what Herrero Beatón describes as "a moment of strong debate, a historic moment" (2003, 113). "There was fear of including these Afro-Cuban ceremonies" among organizers, as Herrero Beatón notes. "And I said: why? Let's do it, it's a cultural need." Ultimately, "They let us do it." That year, "the full participation of Afro-Cuban religions begins" (2003, 113).

The first ritual ceremonies held at the Cabildo Teatral Santiago and the Casa del Caribe as part of the Festival del Caribe included *palo monte* (a central African, Kongo-inspired, Afrodiasporic ritual practice; see Ochoa 2010) and West African, Yorùbá-inspired Regla de Ocha (Santería). *Espiritismo* (mediumship) rituals and Haitian-inspired vodú ceremonies also featured prominently in subsequent years. Renowned santero, palero, musical composer, researcher, and cofounder of the Casa del Caribe Abelardo Larduet Luaces officiated the first ritual ceremonies (in addition to santero Ibrahim Hechavarría), representing a strengthening contingent of institutionally linked practitioner-researchers dedicated to incorporating African-inspired ritual ceremonies into the official spaces of the festival. The renowned *houngán* (vodú priest) Nicolás Casals of nearby La Caridad (some twenty kilometers from Santiago de Cuba) also presided over vodú ceremonies, with numerous other paleros and santeros contributing to and officiating ceremonies (Herrero Beatón 2003).

These rituals—which occurred in the state-sponsored institutional spaces of the festival—"were real rituals," as Herrero Beatón describes, replete with ritual drumming (helmed by Galí Riverí), mediumship, *oricha* (deity) dance, ritual animal sacrifice (including the sacrifice of goats, black roosters, and other animals), and spirit possession (Herrero Beatón 2003, 114). Describing how theatrical-folkloric performances transmuted into "true" ceremony (114), Herrero Beatón states, "We turned the theatrical bembé [ritual party for the oricha and ancestors] into a real bembé. We waited for the priests' mass to end at twelve o'clock at night. There were about five thousand people there, and around thirteen people were mounted [by spirits]. They jumped and leapt and thrashed about" (114). Herrero Beatón adds, "We also did a *mesa espiritual* [espiritismo ceremony] that we dedicated to Ana Guerrero, and she appeared in a medium's trance with the gestures and the speech exactly like Ana: *Ramiro! Ramiro!* she said to me" (113). In this instance, the presence of Ana Guerrero—an actress and singer who had performed with the troupe but had subsequently passed away—marked the ceremony as "true ritual" (114). In this and other festival ritual ceremonies, oricha, ancestors, and the dead descended into and mounted the bodies of those gathered to offer advice and healing, transmuting festival space into ritual space (Hagedorn 2001; Vaughan and Aldama 2012).

Despite the tacit acceptance of ritual ceremonies as part of the festival by key figures in the PCC, the Ministry of Culture, and other state entities that oversaw festival activities in eastern Cuba in the mid-1980s, Herrero Beatón notes that organizers and practitioners (in some cases, organizers-practitioners) remained fearful of repercussion from revolutionary state governmental bodies and local police (2003). After the first Regla de Ocha ceremony at the Cabildo in 1985, for example, Herrero Beatón describes one such ominous interaction:

> In the first ceremony in the Cabildo, the center [officiant] was Ibrahim Hechavarría, because he was one of the most important santeros in the city. After the ceremony, Ibrahim gave me a sack with the viscera of the sacrificed animals and told me that I should take them to a crossroads outside and throw them away. When I was doing it, over there by the screw factory on the Mar Verde highway, very late at night, a police patrol car arrived, and they shouted at me from a distance, what was I doing. I replied: "This is a mandate from the dead, the product of a sacrifice." The patrolman said, "This is santería," quickly backed away, and left.

In this anecdote, Herrero Beatón evokes the specter of repercussion for open ritual practice in Cuba in the mid-1980s, pointing to a precarious and even potentially violent encounter with police (Routon 2010). In this particular interaction, however, the police somewhat mysteriously acknowledge the ritual nature of the action—describing the placement of sacrificial ritual animal remains at the crossroads as "santería"—and yet, without explanation, turn away. Despite the dissipation of a tense moment, many organizers and practitioners in the festival continued to articulate a palpable sense of fear, as Herrero Beatón notes. "Where fear was most felt was in those who had to show their faces when doing the ritual" (2003, 115), Herrero Beatón recalls, indexing especially the rituals' often Black officiants.[4]

Despite these fears, organizers and ritual officiants continued to include ritual ceremonies as part of the festival throughout the 1980s. In harnessing ritual ceremony as culture, these artists, organizers, and research-practitioners succeeded in collapsing the distinction between state-sponsored, folkorized cultural performance and ritual ceremony, radically reconfiguring the conceptualization and valence of African-inspired ritual practices in the eastern Cuban public sphere. In so doing, these artists and organizers also transmuted institutional space into ritual space, dismantling and repurposing the extractivist logics of Western and revolutionary aesthetic and folkloric frames. Additionally, these organizers, artists, and ritual practitioners created (and then redeployed) the institutional spaces of the festival as sites of ritual-cultural assertion, transforming academic-cultural institutions and events into conduits of African-inspired ritual manifestation. In and beyond Cuba, these actions mark a notable instance in which ritual musicians disrupted the "inclusionary" logics of aesthetic representation in nationalistic folkloric and multicultural projects across the Americas (Robinson 2020; Chasteen 2004). In Cuba specifically, the origins of the festival served as an early and crucial site of sociopolitical and ritual intervention within the larger institutional and cultural landscape of the nation. As I explore below, this festival potentiality continues through ongoing ritual and social interventions at the Festival del Caribe over thirty years later.

Nigerian-Style Ifá: The Festival Del Caribe and Contemporary Ritual-Academic Intervention

In 2015, when I first conducted research at the Festival del Caribe and Fiesta de Fuego as a foreign ethnomusicology researcher affiliated with the Cuban Ministry of Culture's Juan Marinello Cuban Cultural Research Institute (El Instituto Cubano de Investigaciones Culturales Juan Marinello), the Festival of Fire had grown into a robust, far-reaching event constituting one of the largest sponsored by the Cuban Ministry of Culture. Held July 3 to 9, in the weeks preceding carnival, the festival features regional, national, and international visiting artists and academics; artistic and ceremonial ritual group performances; and honored invitees from Caribbean countries and sites of honor. Representing a momentous effort to break the significant "linguistic silos" that hinder cross-Caribbean encounter and exchange (Torres-Saillant 2016, 34), the festival offers a powerful vision of pan-Caribbean solidarity. Each year, the festival is dedicated to a different Caribbean site or subregion, bringing artists, musicians, scholars, and literary figures from those sites to the island. Since the festival's foundation, countries of honor have included Granada (1984), Haiti (1985), Guyana (1987), Aruba and Surinam (2002), Curaçao (2010), Trinidad and Tobago (2011), Martinique (2012), and the Bahamas (2015), among numerous others. Likewise, the festival has hosted a variety of renowned francophone, anglophone, Dutch, and hispanophone Caribbean figures including Haitian activist, writer, and composer Marta Jean-Claude, Jamaican anthropologist and songwriter Barry Chevannes, Bajan novelist and poet George Lamming, Dominican poet Víctor Villegas, Brazilian poet Thiago de Mello, and Colombian author Gabriel García Márquez, among others (EcuRed 2022). Over the course of six days, the festival also hosts a wide-ranging series of academic and cultural panels. In 2015, these included the Network of Caribbean Carnivals symposium, featuring representatives and state cultural promoters from Aruba, the Bahamas, Colombia (Barranquilla), Granada, Guatemala, Guadalupe, Guyana, Mexico, Nicaragua, Haiti, Panama, Dominican Republic, St. Martin, Trinidad and Tobago, and Uruguay. Other yearly panels include the Encounter of Caribbean Poets (named after Afro-Cuban Santiago de Cuba poet, playwright, and journalist Jesús Cos Causse) and workshops in communication, theater, music, and fine arts. Most pertinent to the present discussion, the festival features a five-day academic conference and workshop on popular religion, titled the International Course-Workshop on Popular Religiosity (Curso Taller Internacional de Religiosidad Popular). In 2015, this course-workshop was coordinated by festival cofounder, santero, palero, and academic researcher Larduet Luaces.

Notably, each day of the five-day ritual-academic conference is dedicated to a salient African-inspired ritual tradition or aspect of ritual tradition in eastern Cuba: "Espiritismo," "Regla de Palo," "Vodú," "Santería-Ifá," and "Plant Medicine [*Medicina Verde*]" (July 4–8, 2015 festival). Additionally, each day of the Curso Taller Internacional de Religiosidad Popular's academic panels culminates with afternoon and evening ritual ceremonies—at times, multiple simultaneously—held in the private home-temples (*casa-templos*) of prominent local religious leaders or in public sites. In 2015, for example, festival attendees could attend cajón para al muerto, espiritismo, palo monte, and Regla de Ocha ceremonies at the venues Patio Palenque and Casa de los Espíritus, in the private casa-templo residences of ritual leaders (with their addresses listed in the official program), or, in the case of the closing Festival to Yemayá, at an enormous, culminating ritual ceremony held on the Playa Juan González beach and dedicated to the prominent oricha of the oceans in Regla de Ocha. In 2015, this large, public beach ritual to Yemayá featured batá ritual drumming on the consecrated Añá drums of local santero José Luis "Pipo" Guzmán Pérez, oricha drumming and dance, spirit possession, and animal ritual sacrifice, with hundreds in attendance. Through the incorporation of explicitly ritual ceremonies as part of the academic and cultural festival, practitioner-academics and organizers continue the tradition established in the 1980s of harnessing "true" African-inspired ritual as a key manifestation of eastern Cuban (and, more broadly, Afro-Caribbean) culture, though within a decidedly more open, postatheist revolutionary environment that is largely—though not universally—tolerant of open religious practice (Delgado 2009; Hagedorn 2001; Meadows 2023).

The festival also continues to serve as a key site for ritual and sociopolitical intervention for Cuban ritual practitioner-academics decades after its establishment in 1981. In 2015, for example, numerous panels of the five-day International Course-Workshop on Popular Religiosity centered on contentious national debates concerning the emergence of Nigerian-style Ifá in Regla de Ocha (Santería) and Ifá divination, with practitioners utilizing the academic spaces of the festival to assert and validate controversial forms of ritual and gendered revisionism. Beginning in the 1990s and gaining force in the 2000s and 2010s, purveyors of Nigerian-style Ifá pushed forward Yorùbá-centric ritual ideologies drawn from contemporary ritual practices in Yorùbáland, Nigeria (the original site of the oricha/òrìṣà and Ifá worship brought to Cuba via transatlantic slavery). These, in turn, controversially upended gendered and ritual mores in Cuban Regla de Ocha-Ifá on the island itself (Beliso-De Jesús 2015; Meadows 2023; Palmié 2013).[5] After an important series of reconnections with Nigerian priests (*babaláwo*) who traveled to Cuba and across the Americas to instigate novel forms of Yorùbá-inspired ritual revisionism (Meadows 2023; Palmié 2013; Villepastour 2015), numerous practitioners in Cuba now look toward the gender norms and ritual practices of Ifá and òrìṣà (oricha in Cuba) worship in contemporary Yorùbáland as the originary homeland for Regla de Ocha-Ifá. Controversially, this turn has opened novel spaces of possibility unthinkable for practitioners within the landscape of Cuban

Figure 9.1. Closing festival to Yemayá at Playa Juan González beach featuring *batá* ritual drumming on the consecrated Añá drum set of José Luis "Pipo" Guzmán Pérez. Festival del Caribe (Festival of the Caribbean), Santiago de Cuba (June 8, 2015). Photo by author.

ritual practice, particularly in the domain of gendered participation. These possibilities include the capacity of women to be priestesses (ìyánífá) and, additionally, to be òrìṣà ritual drummers, drawing on the gendered norms of Yorùbáland itself (Beliso-De Jesús 2015; Meadows 2021).

At the Festival del Caribe, Nigerian-style ritual practitioners use the academic panels of the conference as key sites of revisionist ritual assertion within the contentious landscape of the national religious debate on Nigerian-style Ifá-Òrìṣà. In the context of postatheist, post-1991 Cuba, for example, these Nigerian-style reevaluations are seen as disrupting Cuban-style *babalaos'* (priests) claims to ritual authority and more broadly as threatening the Cuban state's elevation of Santería as emblematic of national culture and central to religious tourism to the island. In 1991, the Fourth Congress of the Communist Party in Havana announced a new era of postatheist, open religious freedom in Cuba (Ayorinde 2004). Since then, Afro-Cuban religion (and particularly Santería) has formed a notable aspect of revolutionary efforts to elevate Afro-Cuban religion as national culture and draw foreign religious tourists to the island (Delgado 2009; Hagedorn 2014), particularly following the collapse of the Soviet Union and subsequent exigencies of shifting toward a tourist-oriented economy (Ayorinde 2004; Palmié 2013). This reversal in revolutionary views toward African-inspired religion, for example, inspired the establishment of the Yoruba Cultural Association of Cuba (ACYC), a state-sponsored institute that promotes Cuba as the homeland for orisha and Ifá ritual practice globally and, to a degree, polices the boundaries of Regla de Ocha and Ifá practice on the island (Palmié 2013). Within this shifting state and institutional religious landscape, the Nigerian-style ritual movement has led to contentious divides between Nigerian-style practitioners, Cuban-style babalaos, and state-sponsored religious institutions concerning the turn to contemporary Yorùbáland as a model (Beliso-De Jesús 2015; Palmié 2013).

Notably, practitioner-academics at the Festival del Caribe (including women and men actively affiliated with and unaffiliated with Cuban universities) intentionally harness the spaces and audiences of the festival to assert and validate novel forms of gendered and ritual intervention through academic engagement. These practitioner-academics directly intervene into Cuban ritual practice through the presentation of research and academic argumentation, collapsing purported boundaries between ritual praxis and academic study in Afro-Cuban religion (Meadows 2021; Palmié 2013). In 2015, for example, numerous presenters and ritual musicians used the academic spaces of the festival to make explicitly ritual arguments about Nigerian-style practice, mobilizing wide-reaching scholarship in religious studies, Africana studies, and the long history of Afro-Cuban ritual ethnography on the island (i.e., the twentieth-century publications of Fernando Ortiz, Lydia Cabrera, and others) to make revisionist arguments about gendered roles and musical instrumentation in òrìṣà and Ifá ritual. On the third and fourth days of the International Course-Workshop on Popular Religiosity especially, numerous panels and presentations centered on the issue of Nigerian-style Ifá. Nigerian-style babaláwo and University of Havana–affiliated ethnobotanist Julio Martínez Betancourt, for example, presented academic research tracing the efforts of Nigerian-style priests to "rescue" Yorùbá-language phytonyms (plant names) as potential sources of "magical-medicinal" knowledge regarding potential uses and properties of ritual plants (Martínez Betancourt 2015). Betancourt's research underscores the importance of plant materiality to African-inspired ritual practice in Cuba (Martínez Betancourt 2013) while also tracing the ways that Nigerian-style priests increasingly turn to the ritual-linguistic knowledge of Nigerian babaláwo in Yorùbáland as a source of ritual revisionism. Havana-based sociologists and religious studies scholars Ileana Hodge Limonta and Bentia Expósito Álvarez likewise presented academically minded research on the emergence of "Two Ifás in Contemporary Cuba" (*Dos Ifá en la Cuba actual*), or the history and characteristics marking the emergence of two "styles" of Ifá in Cuba—Cuban-style and Nigerian-style—since the 1990s (Limonta and Expósito Álvarez 2015). Notably, this presentation was met with immediate resistance from the subsequent academic presenter, Pinar del Río–based babalao (Cuban-style Ifá priest) Enrique Machín Hernández, who emphasized that the notion of "two Ifás" constituted "a concept[ual] problem" (Machín Hernández 2015). "Ifá is only one, in Cuba, in Japan, in China, or wherever," Machín Hernández responded (2015). This negation of the notion of so-called Nigerian-style Ifá as ontologically distinct from the divinatory ritual power of Cuban-style Ifá constitutes a regular point of assertion for Cuban-style practitioner-academics, many of whom refute the claim that Nigerian-style Ifá constitutes a truer, closer-to-the-root form of ritual practice in comparison with its Cuban counterpart (Meadows 2023).

Notably, Machín Hernández and other ritual practitioners and practitioner-academics at the festival regularly insert explicitly ritual argumentation into their academic presentations, drawing on the sacred oral "signs" (*odú*) of the divinatory practice of Ifá in addition to academic scholarship to make ritual arguments for or against Nigerian-style revisionism. Two of the most salient research papers presented in this regard included those of Santiago de Cuba–based, Nigerian-style babaláwo, *olubatá* (owner of a consecrated batá set), and *omo Añá* (initiated ritual drummer) Enrique Orozco Rubio and female batá percussionist (batalera) and Nigerian-style ritual practitioner Nagybe Madariaga Pouymiró. Orozco Rubio's presentation, for its part, employed research on the contemporary Yorùbá ritual practices of Ìyámi Òṣòròngá in Nigeria, a closed, women's ritual society in Yorùbáland, to explicitly debunk what he framed as "scams" in contemporary Cuban ritual practice. Titled "Ìyámi Òṣòròngá: Myth and Reality" (*Ìyámi Òṣòròngá: Mito y Realiad*), the presentation began with Orozco Rubio stating: "There are many [priests] who, based on these debates that are taking place in this new confluence between these two Nigerian and Afro-Cuban trends, and in the face of the lack of knowledge and uncertainty of the population, take advantage of this to start implementing new, very subtle forms of scams justified with knowledge that no one can prove" (Orozco Rubio 2015). Continuing, Orozco Rubio drew on his knowledge as a Nigerian-style babaláwo and his own ritual readings of the sacred *odú* (oral poetic verses) of Ifá to warn practitioners against "these possible scams." Notably, Orozco Rubio employed explicitly ritual argumentation regarding the sacred verses of Ifá in addition to academically framed research claims. Through recourse to academic epistemologies transmuted as ritual truth, Orozco Rubio and others harness the academic legitimacy of the state-sponsored festival to make explicitly ritual arguments about African-inspired ritual practice. In turn, these practitioner-academics legitimate both Nigerian-style forms of knowledge and their own authority as babaláwo in and outside of the spaces of the festival.

In 2015, likewise, professional female percussionist Nagybe Madariaga Pouymiró used the academic spaces of the festival to assert the right of women to play the consecrated batá set of Regla de Ocha through the tenets of Nigerian-style Ifá in her academic presentation, titled "Menstruation: Blessing or Curse of Enrique Orozco Rubio" (Pouymiró 2015; Jassey 2019; Meadows 2021). In the presentation, Pouymiró drew on the authority of her authorizing Nigerian-style priest and olubatá Orozco Rubio, including his academically framed knowledge of ritual practice in Nigeria (where there is no explicit ban on women playing the Nigerian bàtá, unlike in Cuba) to make a case for women's right to play these sacred instruments on the island.

Pouymiró, like Orozco Rubio, is a university-trained ritual practitioner, musician, and physicist who regularly uses the academic space of the festival to advocate for Nigerian-style gendered and ritual interventions—in this case, regarding women's right to play the ritual batá instruments (Jassey 2019; Meadows 2021). In her presentation, Pouymiró heavily incorporated

Figure 9.2. Percussionist Nagybe Madariaga Pouymiró argues for women's right to play the consecrated *batá* ritual instruments of Regla de Ocha Ifá. Festival del Caribe (Festival of the Caribbean), Santiago de Cuba (June 6, 2015). Photo by author.

ritual argumentation rooted in readings of the odú of Ifá, mirroring the ritual-as-academic argumentation of her male babalao/babaláwo counterparts Machín Hernández and Orozco Rubio. Drawing on the odú of Ifá, Pouymiró emphatically critiqued the prevailing argument that women's menstruation makes them "incompatible with the Añá deity" that resides within the consecrated instruments, arguing instead for an "opening of the mind." Pouymiró then boldly declared, "In the religious system [in Cuba], it is not the *orichas* who discriminate against women; those who do it are its practitioners, permeated by their patriarchal cultural patterns" (Pouymiró 2015). Reframing female exclusion from batá ritual drumming as a consequence of patriarchal human discriminatory systems rather than the will of the deities, Pouymiró harnessed the academic spaces of the festival to assert novel gendered potentialities in and through the arrival of Nigerian-style Ifá on the island. Noting that Nigerian-style Ifá had opened the possibility for women to play the previously prohibited batá ceremonial drums in Cuba, Pouymiró also revealed in the presentation that a group of women led by Orozco Rubio had in fact already accessed and played the instruments in Santiago de Cuba, following the controversial gendered tenets of Nigerian-style Ifá (Jassey 2019; Meadows 2021).

For Pouymiró and other women batá percussionists in Cuba and internationally, the academic religious conference and cultural spaces of the Festival del Caribe offer a means to announce and validate gendered interventions in Cuba and pave the way for other women to access prohibited instruments in the future (personal communication, Pouymiró 2015). Two years before her presentation in 2015, for example, Pouymiró helped organize the First Encounter of Women Batá Percussionists and Female Percussion at the 2013 Festival del Caribe, which included the participation of women batá players from cities across the island (Havana, Santiago de Cuba, and Cienfuegos) as well as from the United States (Meadows 2021). In this and other years, Pouymiró has participated in the festival as both a musician playing the unconsecrated batá set at ritual-cultural venues (i.e., the Casa de las Tradiciones) and as a practitioner-academic utilizing the academic spaces of the festival to make explicitly ritual-academic argumentation concerning women's right to access the consecrated instruments—assertions that have been met with both praise and refutation (Jassey 2019, 121).[6] Pouymiró's and other ritual practitioners' multifaceted participation at the Festival del Caribe speaks to the ongoing ways in which ritual practitioners harness the cultural and academic spaces of the festival to revalorize and intervene into African-inspired ritual practice in Cuba, particularly within the larger and ever-shifting religious, political, and institutional landscapes of the nation.

Conclusions

From its earliest years in the 1980s, the Festival del Caribe emerged from a foundational desire among academics, intellectuals, artists, and ritual practitioners to acknowledge and openly celebrate the African-inspired, Caribbean roots and manifestations of eastern Cuban culture. Within the state-sponsored atheism of the 1970s and 1980s, the festival also served as a crucial vehicle to legitimate African-inspired ritual practices and practitioners through public visibility in state-sponsored and state-legitimated events and institutions. From the start, this desire was intimately bound with arts-driven yet academically minded research: first with Haitian immigrant ritual vodú communities and, later, with other African-inspired ritual practices (i.e., palo monte, espiritismo, cajón al muerto, and Regla de Ocha) (James, Millet, and Alarcón [1992] 2007; Figarola [1996] 2007). From 1985 onward, the festival radically centered "true" African-inspired ritual ceremonies as sites of cultural, institutional, and sociopolitical manifestation and assertion. This centering, in turn, significantly impacted the reception and visibility of these practices in eastern Cuba in the 1980s.

As the festival expands in the postatheist revolutionary era, it continues to constitute a vital site of ritual-academic assertion and potentiality for attendees and audiences. Practitioners use the academic spaces of the festival to argue for gendered, ritual, and other forms of rupture, revaluation, and visibility, as evidenced by the prevalence of Nigerian-style ritual-academic presentations at the festival in 2015. Additionally, the festival holds ritual ceremonies as authentic manifestations of eastern Cuban culture in its official programming, continuing a decades-long tradition established in the 1980s. In collapsing the myriad boundaries between academic practice and ritual praxis; academic space and ceremonial space; and academic epistemologies and ritual forms of knowledge and knowledge making, practitioners (and practitioner-academics) use the Festival del Caribe to disrupt state logics surrounding the entextualization of African-inspired ritual within Western aesthetic and folkloric frames (Robinson 2020; Ochoa Gautier 2006). In repurposing the academic spaces of the festival as sites of "true" ritual-cultural manifestation, festival participants also provide an important historical instance of disrupting the extractivist logics that continue to afflict multicultural and inclusionary projects throughout the Americas (Robinson 2020). Ultimately, the interventions of Festival del Fuego organizers and attendees underscore academic participation and agency as a key component of festival activism in the Caribbean and the Americas, contributing to our understandings of the histories and potentialities of festival activism within Caribbean and Latin American studies, festival studies, and ethnomusicology more broadly.

Notes

1. For an example of scholarship that draws attention to the relation of Caribbean festivals to academic participation, see, for example, Edmondson (2009). Edmondson generatively explores the multitudinous links between governmental bodies, cultural brokers, and academic scholars in the festivalization of Caribbean culture, including the push toward "festival tourism" beginning in the later half of the twentieth century (126). In Jamaica, for example, the Calabash Literary Festival, first directed by Jamaican academic and literary critic Carolyn Cooper, includes music, poetry, and other oral/aural performances (144). Jonathan Ali likewise points to how the Kairi Film Festival in Trinidad, established in 2002, was created by academic and filmmaker

Bruce Paddington (2019). In the realm of Caribbean carnival, the Trinidadian government's National Carnival Commission (NCC) has also actively "encouraged carnival's academicization by sponsoring conferences and journals on the festival" (Edmondson 2009, 133).

2. All English-language translations of Spanish sources in this chapter are my own (Alarcón 2007; Figarola [1996] 2007; James, Millet, and Alarcón [1992] 2007; Herrero Beatón 2003; Limonta and Expósito Álvarez 2015; Martínez Betancourt 2015; Millet 2003; Orozco Rubio 2015; and Pouymiró 2015).

3. For the original text, see Partido Comunista de Cuba 1976 (Castro Figueroa 2012, 90).

4. Literally "where fear was most breathed" (*Donde más se respiraba*) (Herrero Beatón 2007, 115).

5. For more on the use of the term *estilos* (styles) to refer to "African-style" versus "Cuban-style" Ifá in Cuba and across the hispanophone Americas, see Beliso-De Jesús 2015, 817.

6. In Cuba, a distinction developed between consecrated batá sets (tambores de Añá) used for ritual ceremonies and unconsecrated batá sets (*aberinkulá*) used for folkloric, nonritual, or popular music settings (see Vaughan 2012; Villepastour 2015a). Since the 1990s, women in Cuba have been able to play and access unconsecrated sets, not consecrated ritual ones.

Bibliography

Alarcón, Alexis. 2007. "Joel James y el camino de los loas." *Del Caribe* 48–49: 101–104.

Ali, Jonathan. 2019. "'Our Voices, Our Stories, Our Films': Programming the Trinidad and Tobago Film Festival." *Black Camera* 11(1): 242–64.

Ayorinde, Christine. 2004. *Afro-Cuban Religiosity, Revolution, and National Identity*. Gainesville: University Press of Florida.

Beliso-De Jesús, Aisha M. 2015. "Contentious Diasporas: Gender, Sexuality, and Heteronationalisms in the Cuban Iyanifa Debate." *Signs: Journal of Women in Culture and Society* 40(4): 817–40.

Bodenheimer, Rebecca M. 2015. *Geographies of Cubanidad: Place, Race, and Musical Performance in Contemporary Cuba*. Jackson: University Press of Mississippi.

Castro, Fidel. 1961. *Palabras a los Intelectuales* [Words to Intellectuals]. Havana, National Cultural Council. http://lanic.utexas.edu/project/castro/db/1961/19610630.html.

Castro Figueroa, Abel R. 2012. *Quo Vadis, Cuba? Religión y revolución*. Bloomington, IN: Palibrio.

Chasteen, John Charles. 2004. *National Rhythms, African Roots: The Deep History of Latin American Popular Dance*. Albuquerque: University of New Mexico Press.

Delgado, Kevin M. 2009. "Spiritual Capital: Foreign Patronage and the Trafficking of Santería." In *Cuban in the Special Period: Culture and Ideology in the 1990s*, edited by Ariana Hernandez-Reguant, 51–66. New York: Palgrave Macmillan.

EcuRed. n.d. "Festival del Caribe." Accessed April 21, 2022. https://www.ecured.cu/Festival_del_Caribe.

Edmondson, Belinda. 2009. *Caribbean Middlebrow: Leisure Culture and the Middle Class*. Ithaca: Cornell University Press.

Figarola, Joel James. (1996) 2007. "Intervención de Joel en la mesa redonda con fundadores de la Casa y el Festival, febrero de 1996 (Joel James Figuerola)." *Del Caribe* 48–49: 108–116.

Hagedorn, Katherine J. 2001. *Divine Utterances: The Performance of Afro-Cuban Santeria*. Washington, DC: Smithsonian Institution Press.

Hagedorn, Katherine J. 2014. "Resorting to Spiritual Tourism: Sacred Spectacle in Afro-Cuban Regla de Ocha." In *Sun, Sound, and Sand: Music Tourism in the Circum-Caribbean*, edited by Timothy Rommen and Daniel Neely, 289–305. Oxford: Oxford University Press.

Herrero Beatón, Ramiro. 2003. "El Festival del Caribe, el Cabildo Teatral Santiago y las religiones afrocubanas." *Del Caribe* 42: 113–14.

James, Joel, José Millet, and Alexis Alarcón. (1992) 2007. *El vodú en Cuba*. Santiago de Cuba: Editorial Oriente.

Jassey, Victoria Rosemary. 2019. "Tambor Reverberations: Gender, Sexuality and Change in Cuban Batá Performance." PhD diss., Cardiff University.

Larduet Luaces, Abelardo. 2014. *Hacia una historia de la santería santiaguera y otras consideraciones*. Santiago de Cuba: Editorial del Caribe.

Limonta, Ileana Hodge, and Bentia Expósito Álvarez. 2015. "Dos Ifá en la Cuba actual." Paper presented at the Curso Taller Internacional de Religiosidad Popular, Festival del Caribe, Santiago de Cuba, Cuba, July 7, 2015.

Machín Hernández, Enrique. 2015. "Del circulo vital yoruba a la maternidad ancestral." Paper presented at the Curso Taller Internacional de Religiosidad Popular, Festival del Caribe, Santiago de Cuba, Cuba, July 7, 2015.

Madrid, Alejandro L., and Robin D. Moore. 2013. *Danzón: Circum-Caribbean Dialogues in Music and Dance*. New York: Oxford University Press.

Martínez Betancourt, Julio Ismael. 2013. *Yerberos en La Habana*. Colección La Fuente Viva, no. 40. La Habana: Fundación Fernando Ortiz.

Martínez Betancourt, Julio Ismael. 2015. "Sitonimia yoruba y aplicación en Cuba." Paper presented at the Curso Taller Internacional de Religiosidad Popular, Festival del Caribe, Santiago de Cuba, Cuba, July 6, 2015.

Meadows, Ruthie. 2023. *Efficacy of Sound: Power, Potency, and Promise in the Translocal Ritual Music of Cuban Ifá-Òrìṣà*. Chicago: University of Chicago Press, 2023.

Meadows, Ruthie. 2021. "*El Tradicionalismo Africano*: Women, Consecrated Batá, and the Polemics of 'Re-Yorubization' in Cuban Ritual Music." *Ethnomusicology* 65(1): 86–111.

Millet, José. 2003. "El Caribe a la hora de Santiago de Cuba (Hablo del Festival Fiesta del Fuego)." Revista del CESLA. No. 5: 193-6.

Moore, Robin D. 1997. *Nationalizing Blackness: Afrocubanismo and Artistic Revolution in Havana, 1920–1940*. Pittsburgh: University of Pittsburgh Press.

Moore, Robin D. 2004. "Revolution and Religion: Yoruba Sacred Music in Socialist Cuba." In *The Yoruba Diaspora in the Atlantic World*, edited by Matt D. Childs and Toyin Falola, 260–90. Bloomington: Indiana University Press.

Ochoa, Todd. 2010. *Society of the Dead: Quita Manaquita and Palo Praise in Cuba*. Berkeley: University of California Press.

Ochoa Gautier, Ana María. 2006. "Sonic Transculturation, Epistemologies of Purification and the Aural Public Sphere in Latin America." *Social Identities* 12(6): 803–25.

Orozco Rubio, Enrique. 2015. "Ìyámi Òsòròngá: Mito y Realiad." Paper presented at the Curso Taller Internacional de Religiosidad Popular, Festival del Caribe, Santiago de Cuba, Cuba, July 7, 2015.

Palmié, Stephan. 2002. *Wizards and Scientists: Explorations in Afro-Cuban Modernity and Tradition*. Durham, NC: Duke University Press.

Palmié, Stephan. 2013. *The Cooking of History: How Not to Study Afro-Cuban Religion*. Chicago: University of Chicago Press.

Pouymiró, Nagybe Madariaga. 2015. "La menstruación, bendición o maldición de Enrique Orozco Rubio." Paper presented at the Curso Taller Internacional de Religiosidad Popular, Festival del Caribe, Santiago de Cuba, Cuba, July 6, 2015.

Robinson, Dylan. 2020. *Hungry Listening: Resonant Theory for Indigenous Sound Studies*. Minneapolis, MN: University of Minnesota Press.

Routon, Kenneth. 2010. *Hidden Powers of the State in the Cuban Imagination*. Gainesville: University of Florida Press.

Saunders, Tanya L. 2015. *Cuban Underground Hip Hop: Black Thoughts, Black Revolution, Black Modernity*. Austin: University of Texas Press.

Torres-Saillant, Silvio. 2016. "The Hispanic Caribbean Question: On Geographies of Knowledge and Interlaced Human Landscapes." *Small Axe: A Caribbean Journal of Criticism* 20(3): 32–48.

Trincado Fontán, María Nelsa. 2007. "La obsesión de Joel fue la Historia de Cuba." *Del Caribe* 48–49: 93–100.

Vaughan, Umi, and Carlos Aldama. 2012. *Carlos Aldama's Life in Batá: Cuba, Diaspora, and the Drum*. Bloomington: Indiana University Press.

Viddal, Grete. 2012. "Vodú Chic: Haitian Religion and the Folkloric Imaginary in Socialist Cuba." *New West Indian Guide/Nieuwe West-Indische Gids* 86(3–4): 205–36.

Villepastour, Amanda. 2015. "Anthropomorphizing Ayan in Transatlantic Gender Narratives." In *The Yorùbá God of Drumming: Transatlantic Perspectives on the Wood That Talks*, edited by Amanda Villepastour, 125–46. Jackson: University Press of Mississippi.

Washburne, Christopher. 1997. "The Clave of Jazz: A Caribbean Contribution to the Rhythmic Foundation of an African-American Music." *Black Music Research Journal* 17(1): 59–80.

Wirtz, Kristina. 2014. *Performing Afro-Cuba: Image, Voice, Spectacle in the Making of Race and History*. Chicago: University of Chicago Press.

TEN

Festival Study as a Framework for Dialogic Social Justice

A Perspective from Johannesburg

OLADELE AYORINDE

> Without the Cosmology Festival, I will never be able to step my feet on the Wits University campus. I will never have the opportunity to experience the Wits Theatre. The opportunity you have created for us is not only for us; our young ones in the township will be proud of us and they will be inspired also to go to Wits.

The statement above is a reflection by Jennifer Mahlangu, jazz appreciator and dancer, at the inaugural meeting of the Cosmopolitan Collective, a group of community jazz *stokvels* (clubs), on Saturday, November 7, 2020. Jazz clubs are networks of micro socioeconomic organizations, and members of these clubs are locally known as jazz appreciators. Mahlangu is a member of the Cosmopolitan Collective, a new group comprising many jazz clubs in townships within and outside Johannesburg and Pretoria.[1] Mahlangu's reflection alludes to dynamics and politics of inclusion and exclusion that have kept the activities of jazz clubs invisible in contemporary South Africa's public sphere, particularly the jazz festival sphere. Members of jazz clubs are mostly musicians, dancers, and cultural activists who operate within the lowest social and economic class in South Africa. Many of them are domestic workers, factory workers, and people without formal employment. In other words, they belong to the economically marginalized and historically disadvantaged Black demographic. But jazz occupies a significant place in their lives.

Over the years, these appreciators have kept their jazz-centered sociality alive in the shadows of the mainstream jazz industry. They have done so through regular, rotational weekly meetings of jazz sessions. In the apartheid era, when public gatherings and jazz festivals were banned among Black people, jazz appreciators sustained a distinct culture at grassroots levels. However, the jazz appreciators and their jazz-centered social organizations remain elusive. Their social and economic conditions remain marginalized, and they have no access to mainstream jazz scenes and stages. This was the context in which Mahlangu reflected on the Cosmology Festival's capacity for social inclusion. Therefore, central to Mahlangu's reflection is the question of access for historically disadvantaged Black South Africans.

The social and economic conditions of jazz appreciators provide insight into how, almost thirty years after the demise of apartheid, many South Africans like Mahlangu are still confined by apartheid's infrastructure. Characteristics of this infrastructure—including class stratification, inequality, and economic exclusion—are also visible in contemporary South Africa's jazz festival public. Strategic exclusion in the jazz festival sphere contradicts the essence of freedom for which 1994, the year apartheid ended, stands in South Africa's history. Thus, the event Mahlangu references provides insight into how festivals can constitute a site of activism and inclusion and how festival activism can engage issues around social justice in contemporary South Africa.

In this chapter, I make a case for festivals and their study as providing frameworks for advancing dialogical social justice. By this, I mean ways in which festival creation and studies can provide pragmatic approaches to mediate forms of exclusion and inclusion that inherently shape public festivals (music, art, dance, religion, and others), especially by directly involving communities in their realization. I draw on cases from an ongoing applied/practice-led research initiative, the Wits Festival Study Group in Johannesburg and its Cosmology Project. I also explain how its pragmatic approach, applied research, and public work in ethnomusicology provide a framework for understanding festival planning and organization as forms of social activism and political intervention.

The Wits Festival Study Group is an extracurricular academic initiative for registered students at the University of the Witwatersrand and professionals in the arts and culture sectors in South Africa. The group is premised on blurring the gaps between theory (academia and scholarship) and practice (professional and policy-oriented practical knowledge) in arts, culture, and heritage event planning, organization, and management (broadly conceived as *festival*). The group's conceptualization of festival builds on members' practical and industry experiences and theoretical ideas from scholarly works. These scholarly works include seminal texts like Donald Getz's (2010) exploration of the nature and scope of festival studies and Alessandro Falassi's (1987) edited volume *Time Out of Time*, where the etymology, histories, and practices of festivals across cultures are detailed through an interdisciplinary perspective. Contemporary perspectives have also provided nuanced explanations of festivals, mainly in European contexts (i.e., Nita and Kidwell 2021; Woodward, Taylor, and Bennett 2014; Delanty, Giorgi, and Sassatelli 2011). These scholarly works are useful for understanding the nature and manifestations of festivals, as they provide insightful perspectives from across European societies. However, their perspectives share little cultural or social resemblance with the festival ecosystem in contemporary Africa. The divide between the academic understanding of festivals and industry ideas and practice of festivals was one factor that motivated the creation of the Wits Festival Study Group.

The group was created not as a mere extracurricular activity but as a scholarly initiative aimed at responding to social and economic needs. As such, the group reconceptualized festival and its study as tools for social and economic mediation in contemporary Africa. Drawing on relevant academic theory, contemporary professional business practice, and event management practice, the group's understanding of festivals is rooted in the political economy of the everyday life of marginalized communities in contemporary Africa. Apart from the established knowledge of heritage and arts festivals, cyclical religious and social events—like the emerging charismatic conferences among Christians and Muslims and wedding and burial ceremonies—belong to new categories of festivals. The group has also examined political rallies, academic conferences, protests, music concerts, and art exhibitions as forms of festivals. Rather than relying on academic definitions, the group approaches festival as a public sphere where all manners of social, political, and economic relations, subjectivities, and expression converge. While festivals serve social spaces across Africa, I argue that they are also public spheres where personal and collective political agendas are nurtured and performed.

My notion of the public sphere in festivals follows Jürgen Habermas's view that events and "occasions are public when they are open to all, in contrast to closed or exclusive affairs" (1989, 1). For Habermas, the public is the carrier of public opinion because "its function as a critical judge is precisely what makes the public" (1989, 2). This can also be true in social spaces like festivals in contemporary Africa. The Wits Festival Study Group conceptualizes festival as a public sphere not only because festivals enable sociality but also because, in certain conditions like those of post-apartheid South Africa, festivals can animate people's agency (individually and collectively) within spaces that "could appropriate and transform affairs of state" (Habermas 1989, 29–30). In this sense, the study group approaches festivals and their planning, organization, and management as critical approaches to dialogic social justice, viewing festival studies as a site of critical social activism and as providing frameworks for promoting social and economic inclusion and empowerment of historically disempowered people in contemporary South Africa.

My idea of dialogic social justice builds on Samuel Araújo's work in ethnomusicology with the community of the Maré favela of Rio de Janeiro, which directly involves the community in the study of its musical practices. Drawing on Paulo Freire's ideas on dialogic knowledge building, Araújo advances an advocacy and activist scholarly agenda that brings to bear the expectations of communities from academics (2008). Of particular importance is how Araújo's approach seeks to empower people from the favela not as research subjects but as co-researchers, providing them with access to institutional infrastructure. Therefore, by dialogic social justice, I mean a people-centered approach to mitigating social injustice and economic inequality. I view this concept as premised on negotiation and conversation between scholars and communities, creating an inclusive festival model that could ideally transform participants' social, economic, and political conditions. Through this framework, we aim to empower people and relocate social justice and decolonization out of the ivory towers and into the community. The festival discussed below adopts a dialogic social justice framework premised on providing access to historically disempowered people in South Africa.

Jazz Festival Spheres and Elusive Social Justice in Post-1994 South Africa

Dennis Davis, a judge at the High Court of Cape Town, gave the inaugural social justice lecture on Thursday, February 20, 2020, to mark World Social Justice Day at Stellenbosch University, Cape Town. Davis's lecture, titled "Social Justice and Economic Inclusion: Where to, South Africa?," instantly got attention. It garnered relevance among scholars and students in South Africa's higher learning institutions and in the media. Quickly exploding in popularity, the lecture provided insight into the elusive nature of social justice in contemporary South Africa. Davis argued that the current social and economic landscape reflects an unjust political economy rooted in the country's complicated history, as apartheid stripped Black people's participation rights in all spheres of society. For him, current Black South African social conditions stand in stark contrast to the constitutional ambition of the nation at its transition to democracy in 1994. Davis understood social justice as "the ability of all South Africans to live a dignified life through fair and reasonable participation in the economic intercourse of the country; because the issue of social justice is coupled to that of economic exclusion" (Davis 2020).

An interesting dynamic at the intersection of Mahlangu's reflection and Davis's argument about the politics of social justice in post-1994 South Africa shows how jazz festivals can continually reinvent inequality, class, exclusion, and economic and social binaries. Indeed, more than twenty years into post-apartheid, music festivals, particularly jazz festivals, have become problematic in many ways. On the one hand, jazz music and festivals have facilitated social cohesion and encouraged a multiracial public sphere by valorizing Afro-diasporic music. On the other hand, jazz festivals can constitute a tool of strategic exclusion and ordering, reinventing the socially and racially stratified South Africa that 1994 had symbolically laid to rest.

This fact is antithetical to the significant role of jazz in the anti-apartheid struggle and the envisaged mediative roles of the genre in the discourse of transformation. The term *transformation* was adopted by the new government and became a signifier of "improvement" and a promise of better living conditions (Ayorinde 2019, 40). This promise and the disappointment that accompanied it are central to Mahlangu's reflection at the beginning of this chapter. On the eve of President Nelson Mandela's inauguration in 1994, many historically disadvantaged South Africans like Mahlangu did not expect to still be waiting for transformation after twenty-five years of democratic rule.

One social reorganization initiative after Mandela's inauguration was the emergence of multiracial public spheres such as music festivals. These 1994 democratic reorganizational initiatives facilitated forms of public culture that had been rarely experienced by many Black people during the apartheid era. Jazz music and festivals were essential to artistic activism during the apartheid era. This artistic activism is evident in the careers of South African jazz musicians like Hugh Masekela, Miriam Makeba, and Abdullah Ibrahim, who gave the genre new prominence as a social and economic tool. The roles of jazz and jazz festival activism in the fight against the apartheid regime have been well documented (Coplan [1985] 2008; Ballantine [1993] 2012; Ansell 2004; Pyper

2014). Scholars have detailed the many ways jazz and jazz festivals facilitated spaces of conviviality in Black communities despite the draconian laws of the apartheid regime between the 1960s and 1980s. For example, in *In Township Tonight!*, David Coplan ([1985] 2008, 246) explains how constant police harassment rendered self-supporting Black musical events impossible and created social conditions in which violence was commonplace in performance spaces. Despite the disruptive acts of the apartheid police, Coplan explains, "the festival format remained the only workable commercial setting for live jazz and its various popular hybrids"; thus, "festivals were held in townships near various cities every year" ([1985] 2008, 246).

Brett Pyper (2016, 112) explains that despite apartheid legislation, festivals persisted at the grassroots level through the activities of jazz clubs in the township. Pyper argues that the activities of jazz appreciation societies and the agency of their members "played a crucial if largely undocumented role in keeping a certain kind of jazz-oriented public culture alive" (2016, 112). South African jazz culture and festivals have been preserved and sustained by jazz-oriented publics and social agents like Mahlangu. Thus, festival cultures, particularly jazz festivals, were rekindled following South Africa's transition to democratic government in 1994; jazz became crucial in the nation's social justice project and transformation agendas, seeking to inspire people of color at the grassroots level.

However, the dream of making jazz and jazz festivals into sites of the nation's social justice project was short lived. By 2014, many promising jazz festivals had changed their focus and moved to a more "sophisticated" space for high-end profiting, a pattern of bourgeoisification seen in many moments in jazz history. For example, the Joy of Jazz festival, one of the most popular and influential festivals in post-1994 South Africa, was conceived in reference to social cohesion at the grassroots level but became a corporate festival servicing the interests of the privileged and elite class. According to Pyper (2016, 117), the Joy of Jazz Festival emerged in Pretoria in 1998 from conversations between a Black entrepreneur, Peter Tladi, and members of jazz clubs in the township communities. However, by 2014, the festival's ideal had drifted away from its essence: the revival of "the collective experience and sensibilities of the cross-class alliances that incubated jazz in South Africa for much of the previous century" (Pyper 2016, 117). The festival was also relocated out of downtown Johannesburg to the Sandton Convention Centre, one of the most sophisticated high-end event centers in South Africa.

The equivalent of the Joy of Jazz Festival in the Western Cape province, the Cape Town International Jazz Festival (CTIJF), followed almost the same trajectory. The CTIJF emerged in 1998 in Cape Town; it moved out of its initial venue, the Good Hope Centre, after three years and into the Cape Town International Convention Centre (CTICC). Like the CTIJF in Cape Town, the Joy of Jazz Festival is also sponsored by Standard Bank, one of South Africa's multinational banks. This type of sponsorship and network provided the two festivals with certain forms of social capital, which ultimately facilitated visibility and attracted globally renowned jazz musicians like George Duke, Herbie Hancock, and Wynton Marsalis.

Interestingly, political elites and the state also validated these festivals as offshoots of their neoliberal agenda and commodified political and economic tools to boost South Africa's tourism industry. This commodification gave political elites the privilege of using jazz festival spaces to display their conspicuous consumption. As Gwen Ansell, one of the famous jazz commentators in South Africa, noted, the relocation of these festivals to convention centers in the wealthiest and most fortified part of town has necessarily placed them "on the far right of corporate festivals" (Pyper 2016, 117).

The exorbitant characteristics of the festivals, which include tickets at R750 for one night or R1,200 for both (as of 2015), plus travel costs, parking, food, and drink, constitute an insurmountable economic barrier for South Africans who rely on weekly wages for subsistence. This dynamic has reproduced and maintained the apartheid logic of exclusion and complicated the state's 1994 commitment to social justice and inclusive social, economic, and public spheres, of which jazz was an important symbol. Rather than challenging these conspicuous elements, the state has embraced them as a strategic avenue in its quest for economic development, leveraging them as a crucial component of its tourism market. This quest for economic development through jazz festivals is supported not only by endorsement but also by this aggressive press release: "Johannesburg is expected to reap substantial economic benefits thanks to the upcoming Standard Bank Joy of Jazz. Standard Bank Joy of Jazz—which will attract more than 30,000 fans when it takes place at the Sandton Convention Centre from September 25 to 27—injects approximately R600 million annually into the Gauteng economy. Building up to the weekend of the Standard Bank Joy of Jazz Festival, the 'City of Gold' becomes the centre of the jazz universe attracting a cross-spectrum of individuals and corporates, including top-level executives from a variety of companies operating in music, film, TV and digital distribution" (quoted in Pyper 2016, 117).

As Pyper explains, the reference to the "City of Gold" resonates with the strategic focus of the South African government, which since 2011 has highlighted the economic value of the arts. This initiative in itself is novel. However, the touristification and commodification of jazz festivals for financial gain—for and from a specific privileged public—contradicts its supposed commitment to social justice and transformation. This is what Davis means when he argues that various forms of rhetoric and practices have emerged to promote new forms of exclusion, all of which are at war with the constitutional commitment to construct a contemporary nonracist, nonsexist society. It might not be an overstatement to argue that social justice is an elusive reality in post-1994 South Africa. The elusiveness of social transformation and the politics of social justice among elites who only pay lip service to it have frustrated the hope for good living conditions among many South Africans, particularly historically disadvantaged people of color. This seems to be the case with Mahlangu's reflection: she feels that she might not have experienced the Wits Theatre and Wits University campus without the Cosmology festival.

The Wits Festival Study and Its Socially Inclusive Festival Model

The Wits Festival Study Group was born out of shared interest between Professor Brett Pyper and me in 2019. Pyper, who at the time was head of the Wits School of Arts (WSOA) at the University of the Witwatersrand, had worked in South Africa's festival spheres in one capacity or another since the 1990s. His research emerged from this experience, particularly his doctoral study focusing on jazz appreciators' activities in Mamelodi, Pretoria. My interest in festival culture is rooted in my childhood experiences with Yoruba festivals from southwest Nigeria and my research on Nigeria's contemporary festivals, specifically the transformation of the *Eyo* Festival of Lagos Island.

Recently, a new focus in festival studies that engages problems around identity, community, and place making has emerged in Africanist ethnomusicology, of which Sylvia Bruinders's (2017) *Parading Respectability* and Pyper's (2014) doctoral thesis are examples. Nonetheless, contemporary African festival landscapes foreshadow a new frontier, an ecology that profoundly reflects the political economy of everyday life. An aspect of this unique ecology contrasts with festivals of the 1960s and 1970s in Africa, which, particularly in the fields of music and theater, were staged as acts of resistance and part of anti-apartheid movements.

In post-1994 South Africa, Black ruling elites have promoted and sponsored music, art, dance, and cultural festivals for their own political agendas. Likewise, in Lagos, old ritual festivals like the Adamu-Orisa Festival are reimagined and staged to legitimize state agendas. An African cultural icon like Fela Anikulapo-Kuti, who challenged the extravagant lifestyle of Nigerian political elites, is now memorialized through a state-sponsored festival, the Felabration. Some festivals that initially emerged as spaces of sociality for ordinary people have been transformed and relocated into sophisticated areas and commodified for high-end gain, such as the Joy of Jazz Festival in South Africa, discussed earlier. These are some of the developments I noticed as of 2018 that motivated my proposal for a festival study concerned with negotiating a new path—bringing to the fore contemporary issues and seeking ways to engage the problems of social justice and transformation through a festival model.

The Wits Festival Study Group was initiated in 2019 to raise awareness, exchange scholarly ideas about facilitating change in the arts, and develop new and more inclusive models of festival practice in Africa. The group rigorously engages theoretical concepts and policy-oriented knowledge informed by well-researched data. Through Pyper's network with the Festival Academy, the group grew from its founding nine members in 2019 to sixty-five members in the second quarter of 2020.[2] Through readings, discussions, and management initiatives, the group launched a practice-led research project to organize an inclusive festival template in South Africa. Titled "Jazz Cosmology (Not Another Jazz Festival) NAJF" (hereafter Cosmology), it is a social justice project concerned with diversity, equity, and inclusion.

Cosmology Planning and Organization

The planning process of the residency began in late 2019 and developed in February 2020. Cosmology was conceived as a practice-led action research project and artist residency. The project was based on two of Pyper's initial research relationships, first with anthropologist/ethnomusicologist Steven Feld and the Anyaa Arts Quartet in Accra, Ghana. The Anyaa Arts Quartet comprises sculptor, community arts archivist, activist, musician, and instrument inventor Nii Noi Nortey; master percussionist and bass player Nii Otoo Annan; and Amsterdam-based flutist Alex Coke. The story of these Ghanaian musicians and network is the subject of Feld's (2012) book, *Jazz Cosmopolitanism in Accra.* Feld uses the term *jazz cosmopolitanism* to refer to different ways in which jazz has articulated modernity and enabled Afro-diasporic music aesthetics, creativity, and artistic dialogues in Africa. The concept eventually became a core component of our festival.

The second contact was based on Pyper's long-standing relationship with members of the Tshwane Jazz Veterans Club and the broader jazz appreciator community in Mamelodi, Pretoria. Engaging the decolonial turn and issues around transformation, social partnership with community-based jazz appreciators and cultural organizers involves introducing local curatorial practices in ways that question established scholarly ideas of festival organization. The musical aim of the residency was to establish a proverbial pan-African call-and-response between Johannesburg and Accra by exploring how jazz has articulated notions of cosmopolitanism in the two African cities. The intention was to develop collaborative performances over a five-day residency both on campus and with community venues in Johannesburg, Mamelodi, and Soweto.

The planning process developed rapidly during the first two weeks of February 2020. We had been able to attract more members from the art scene in Johannesburg, some of whom were established as promoters and managers. These members of the Festival Study Group were instrumental in kickstarting the planning process across Johannesburg and Pretoria. We arrived at the festival title, Cosmology NAJF, in mid-February 2020 at a meeting with members of the Tshwane Jazz Veterans Club, the jazz appreciators, and the Festival Study Group. We agreed on and adopted *Cosmology* because we felt that it spoke to the social, cultural, and religious lives in the community and that people would easily connect with the concept. Following the collective adoption of the festival theme, a new planning phase was unveiled.

The first step of this planning phase was to identify musicians who would listen to the recorded music of the Anyaa Arts Quartet and respond musically from an artistic research perspective. This phase was achieved without delay, as the Music Unit of the Wits School of Arts has a formidable jazz section, comprising both music faculty and students. Through established scholarly networks, we also invited two prominent jazz musicians and scholars from other institutions to work with the ensemble: Nduduzo Makhathini from the Music Department of the University of Fort Hare and Salim Washington from the School of Arts at the University of KwaZulu-Natal. We decided to hold a five-day event—Wednesday, March 18, to Sunday, March 22—spreading across specific communities in Johannesburg and Pretoria. Based on recommendations from the jazz appreciators, we engaged five community-based musicians and bands. These musicians were members of jazz clubs and had little or no space on mainstream South African jazz platforms.

The second step of the new planning phase concerned defining the event's structure, making contacts with venues, and designing publicity posters. Because of the educational benefit to students, we decided to begin the first two days of the event with an academic discussion. It would be followed by a jazz concert at the Wits Theatre. Members of the group and our community partners, the jazz appreciators, committed time to this planning process. The role of one of our members, Christine Msibi, is worth mentioning. A member who joined the Festival Study Group from Johannesburg, Christine, was already running an art outlet called Jozi Unsigned before joining our group. She helped design the Cosmology logo and facilitated the printing of posters and programming for the event. She also helped with contacts and securing a collaboration with many community venues in Johannesburg, where we planned to stage some of the concerts as part of our community engagement and collaborations.

Reimagining Cosmology as a Hybrid Online Festival

By the week of March 15, 2020, we were set to stage the first Cosmology Festival. Some of our guests from Ghana had received their visas, while others were still waiting. One member of the Anyaa Arts Quartet, mural artist Nicolas Wayo, was already in Johannesburg to forge the visual aspect of the residency. We had paid for flights and booked accommodation and were awaiting the arrival of Steven Feld and the remaining members of the Anyaa Arts Quartet. Our community partner, the jazz appreciation community in Mamelodi, Pretoria, was already set. However, President Cyril Ramaphosa of South Africa announced a nationwide lockdown to contain the COVID-19 outbreak in the country. We had no choice but to indefinitely suspend and postpone the festival on March 17, a day before the event was set to start. We eventually resumed the planning process and reimagined the festival with a hybrid model for pandemic conditions, which was a learning process for our members. We launched into the process and scheduled the new festival for October 29 and 30, 2020—only two days instead of the original five.

The new planning was shaped by continuing dialogic engagement with the jazz appreciators community. This form of dialogic negotiation was characterized by "incomplete" thinking and a people-centered collaborative approach, a process Francis Nyanmjoh terms "conviviality," which "encourages us to reach out, encounter, and explore ways of enhancing or complementing ourselves with the added possibilities of potency brought our way by the incompleteness of others (human, natural, superhuman and supernatural alike), never as a ploy to becoming complete (an extravagant illusion ultimately), but to make us more efficacious in our relationships and sociality" (Nyamnjoh 2017, 262). The notions Nyamnjoh mentions of reaching out, encountering, and exploring formed the core agenda of the Wits Festival Study Group, facilitating knowledge production, transformation, and decolonization beyond the walls of academic institutions. We aimed to reimagine the jazz festival as a convivial space that would collapse social, economic, and class boundaries through its organizational model. Thus, the Cosmology Festival was conceptualized and organized based on the framework of the study group, the three components of which were theorizing, organizing, and music making.

From Theory to Practice

The theoretical underpinning was based on critical engagement and practice-informed ideas and experiences from the community, business, and festival spheres. Two critical texts in particular shaped the theorization of the festival. First, Feld's work (2012) provided theoretical grounding for our ideas around jazz cosmopolitanism. Feld's notion of jazz cosmopolitanism argues for "jazz as diasporic dialogue in an African urban modernity" (2012, 2). On the one hand, jazz cosmopolitanism points to the many ways jazz facilitates creative, artistic, and aesthetic dialogues between musicians and aficionados in Africa and their African American jazz heroes in the US. On the other hand, the concept alludes to how these dialogues (listening, dressing, sociality, and others) spread across world cities. As mentioned earlier, jazz has articulated notions of cosmopolitanism as both aesthetic phenomenon and cultural practice in Johannesburg and other African societies. It is important to note that in Feld's view, manifestations of jazz cosmopolitanism across Africa follow a distinct direction. Jazz cosmopolitanism in Johannesburg and other African cities does not align strictly with the notion of cosmopolitanism or globalization that references top-down power relations between Africa and the West. Approaches to jazz and its culture in Africa follow processes of reinterpretation and recontextualization to fit and respond to local social and economic conditions of cities like Lagos, Johannesburg, Cape Town, Accra, Kinshasa, Nairobi, and Cairo. Second, Samuel Araújo's (2008) not only provides a working framework for the Cosmology planning process but also encapsulates the study group's core premise of working in partnership with the community to produce the festival.

The organizing process took a somewhat different dimension. Nonstudent members of the group who were already managing and planning events in various South African communities volunteered to serve. The group empowered them to operate and bring their knowledge and experience in conversation with scholars despite not being students, enabling synergy and collaborative learning between community art managers and us at the university. This process provided a dialogic exchange, and the organization of the festival emerged from it.

The music making itself comprised the music staff and students of the Wits School of Arts, Salim Washington, and a veteran South African jazz musician, Prince Lengoasa. Andre and Chantal Petersen, lecturers in jazz, took a lead role and provided musical direction. They studied the music of the Anyaa Arts Quartet and devised a South African musical response to the musical materials from Ghana through jazz arrangements and reinterpretations. Importantly, this music-making component facilitated intergenerational dialogues between young and emerging jazz musicians and much older, established jazz musicians.

The two-day festival started with a symposium in homage to Feld titled "African Jazz Cosmopolitanisms," which established a dialogue between Johannesburg, Accra, and other African societies. The symposium provided a context for the second day's jazz concert, "Cosmology," which was shaped by Africa's cultural and political history and collective musical cosmopolitanisms across postcolonial Africa and beyond.

Sanibonani!: Diga Activism on the Wits Theatre Stage

It was already 6:55 p.m. on the long-awaited day of the jazz Cosmology concert, the festival finale. As is tradition in many concert halls in South Africa, the Wits Theatre had made its final call, and the door might shut anytime. In spite of the South African COVID-19 level 5 regulation of 50 percent capacity for indoor concerts and gatherings, some thirty minutes before the concert, the area surrounding the Wits Theatre had been full of conviviality. Everyone was putting on face masks. It was the first time the Wits Theatre was reopening and the first concert since the lockdown in March. The bar and cafeteria at the foyer were busy as people hung around and exchanged words and drinks. "Sanibonani! Sanibonani!!" (Hello, good evening! [in the Zulu language]) echoed with differing registers as people waved their hands in excitement to one another from afar. "Ufuna ukuhlala kuphi" (Where do you want to sit?), asked one of the two ladies who had just passed by me at the entrance. A few seconds later, another lady gestured with excitement to a group of elderly women, "nansi indlela eya esihlalweni!" (This is the road to the chair!). "Aibo! le ndawo yinhle kakhulu!" (Oh! This place is so beautiful!), exclaimed one of the older women in their late fifties or early sixties. Another member of the group, who was amazed at the design and interior of the hall, responded, "laba abamhlophe benza izinto lapha mngani wami" (These white people are making things happen here, my friend). As they were about to sit, just a few rows before the stage, they turned around and shared greetings with those already seated in the hall: "Sanibonani non ke!" (Hello, everyone!).

The ambiance across the hall was somewhat different from that of the usual Eurocentric, "cultured" audience often encountered at the Wits Theatre. It was apparent that many people in the hall were not usual concert attendants. People greeting each other from afar, moving from one row or seat to another, and exchanging pleasantries are not necessarily part of the concert culture of canonical halls like Wits Theatre. A significant percentage of the people at this particular concert come from townships around Johannesburg and Pretoria—a distance of approximately 81.6 kilometers (1.5 hour drive) from Witwatersrand University. This particular public consisted of members of the South African jazz appreciation society, community-based jazz clubs, and *stokvel* (social clubs) in and around Pretoria. It was the first time some of them were experiencing the Wits Theatre or a European-model concert hall. As stated earlier, they have weekly concert-like socio-musical gatherings across the township communities called jazz sessions, where audiences not only listen and dance to jazz but also operate *Magodisano* (a financial contribution and mutual rotating credit often used by jazz appreciation societies to organize sessions and pay for burials of their members). These communities were invited by jazz appreciator clubs that worked and planned the festival with us. We made arrangements for buses to collect them across communities and bring them to the festival, and the buses took them back to their communities after the event.

The concert began at 7 p.m. The musicians on stage, comprising staff and students, started in a promising mood, with sounds deeply located in South

African music. A few minutes in, the group of people from the townships started mounting the stage on a rotational basis to perform the *Diga* jazz dance, a solo improvised dance associated with South African jazz appreciation communities and an urban popular culture form from the communities in and around Pretoria and Johannesburg. The Diga draws on and mixes aesthetic resources from different global popular music dances and indigenous South African dances, particularly from the Zulu, Basotho, Bapedi, Venda, and Xhosa traditions. Central to the Diga spectacle are its comical, kinetic characters, which took center stage, not only constituting a visual representation of the music but also distilling an important social and political message to older and younger generations of South Africans who had never witnessed it before. As displayed throughout the concert, the Diga jazz dance does not align with common understandings of dance, where music provides direction for bodily gestures, movements, and coordination within a specific space. Rather than following or responding to the rhythms of music, Diga dancers provide a counterpoint through dance steps and body gestures, contributing a new, superimposed visual aesthetic layer to the ensemble's music.

There is more than meets the eye in the Diga jazz dance. In its comic sense, the Diga elicits some levels of humor, as people think the dancers are offbeat. Per its kinetic character, Diga provides the audience with images of sports activities like dribbling, passing, and shooting a ball. Diga provides a counterculture to stereotypical renderings of jazz and jazz dance within established canons of jazz festivals and concert culture in South Africa. I read Diga's eccentric character as a spectra-like visual phenomenon that transports its audience into an imaginary world where it is possible to experience global dance cultures including ballet from Italy, hip-hop from the US, salsa from Cuba, ballroom from France, *Ngoma* from South Africa, *Bata* from Nigeria, and *Paklongo* from Ghana. The Diga provided an imaginary world for the audience and elicited a perplexing visual and aesthetic gaze at the Wits Theatre. The dancers brilliantly displayed the Diga spectacle and, in the process, challenged established jazz ideals and their listening and dance cultures.

Diga dancers present a form of jazz culture that draws aesthetic references from South African cultures and beyond. Here, Diga offers historical details about South African jazz cultures and, at the same time, comments on township life in contemporary South Africa through the invocation of the township's everyday logic of "modernity from below"—language, dance steps, dress, and respectability. At play in this eccentric character of Diga, what I call Diga activism, is a deconstruction of the long-standing European concert tradition the Wits Theatre's stage embodies. It is, in other words, a decanonization of the Wits stage drawing on jazz cosmopolitanism and its pan-Africanist approaches. The Diga jazz spectacle became a form of resistance that brought to the fore ways in which festival initiatives like Cosmology can constitute a framework for understanding festival activism—bringing to bear issues around social justice, decolonization, transformation, and equality as well as socioeconomic inclusion in post-1994 South Africa.

Concluding Notes: Dialogic Social Justice as Access

The Cosmology Festival's initiative emerged as an ethnomusicological response to stalled transformation in post-1994 South Africa. Cosmology advanced from a practice-led research initiative, somewhat of an experiment, that aimed at providing an alternative model for social inclusion through a different kind of jazz festival. As the case above shows, people from the townships were invited to the Cosmology Festival not as performers but as an audience, yet they mounted the stage on their own and contributed their jazz practice to the ongoing performance. This unplanned performance on one of the most sophisticated concert stages in South Africa became the highlight of the Cosmology concert. It is important to note that the presence of Diga on the stage was not an attempt by dancers to elicit their practice. For them, it was Diga in the same way it is performed casually in township meetings with food and drinks. The Cosmology Festival provided them access to the space, and they engaged and made sense of the space on their own terms.

The Wits Festival Study's model is a critical approach to dialogic social justice, and it provides a framework for studying festivals in a troubled society like post-1994 South Africa. The Cosmology initiative is a dialogic social justice project because it emerged from an academic agenda that questions the normative idea of research and knowledge production in the university system. Critical reflections shaped the process as we (the conveners) had to constantly negotiate our positionality as scholars from the university and people engaged in social and activist work in the community.

The project's organizing and performance components are also means through which we explored deep-rooted social issues in contemporary South Africa. Taking a cue from Araújo's (2008) practice-led action research in ethnomusicology, we conceptualize festivals and their studies as providing critical tools to interrogate existing social and economic structures; doing so, we negotiate an alternative model for an inclusive festival sphere. The initiative doubles as a tool for empowering historically disadvantaged people in the community, evident in the academic component of the festival, such as the October 29, 2020, colloquium, which featured community art practitioners, musicians, and scholarly presentations. This critical aspect of the festival constituted a form of academic activism, an example of a decolonized process of knowledge production—including teaching, research, and methodologies—as scholars engaged in dialogue with community art managers, practitioners, and musicians on equal terms.

The Cosmology Festival initiative is ongoing, and further research is needed, particularly exploring the economic impacts of festivals and applied knowledge like sustainable marketing, finance, and fundraising models. It is difficult to conclude or suggest that we have achieved our research aims at this initial stage. But what is essential is that the initiative has promoted social justice as access, as the initiative enabled community partners to access institutional support for their projects and scholarly support from the university for initiatives like oral history projects that aim to honor community members. Cosmology facilitates access, and what this access means in the context of post-apartheid South Africa is evident in Mahlangu's reflection at the beginning of this chapter: without the Cosmology Festival, she would never have been able to set foot on the Wits University campus. Mahlangu's position points us to what a festival initiative like Cosmology means for our understanding of festivals as tools of activism.

The Wits Festival Study Group's conception of dialogic social justice as access is relevant to the ongoing discourse around transformation in South Africa and to issues around social justice and decolonization. This notion of access is equally helpful for rethinking social justice and issues around decolonization in ethnomusicological research. As the Cosmology case shows, access needs to be dialogically negotiated based on people's needs and social context. Thus, access is not just about inclusion but also about empowering disempowered people to renegotiate their social, economic, and political conditions on their own terms.

Notes

1. In the South African context, townships are underdeveloped urban settlements for people of color. Following the apartheid Population Registration and Group Acts of 1950, Black people were forcefully evicted from many parts of South

Africa—which were designated "white only"—and moved into segregated townships, often located at the fringes of cities.

2. For more details about the initiative of the European Festivals Association, see "The Festival Academy," accessed September 25, 2023, https://www.thefestivalacademy.eu/en/home/.

Bibliography

Ansell, Gwen. 2004. *Soweto Blues: Jazz, Popular Music, and Politics in South Africa*. New York: Continuum.

Araújo, Samuel. 2008. "From Neutrality to Praxis: The Shifting Politics of Ethnomusicology in the Contemporary World." *Musicological Annual* 44: 13–30.

Ayorinde, Oladele. 2019. "'Unholy Trinity' and 'Transformation' in Post-1994 South Africa: Re-focusing Transformation in Higher Education for Social and Economic Empowerment." *Leeds African Studies Bulletin* 80: 68–98.

Ballantine, Christopher. (1993) 2012. *Marabi Nights: Jazz, "Race" and Society in Early Apartheid South Africa*. Pietermaritzburg: University of KwaZulu-Natal Press.

Bruinders, Sylvia. 2017. *Parading Respectability: The Cultural and Moral Aesthetics of the Christmas Bands Movement in the Western Cape, South Africa*. Grahamstown: African Humanities Program.

Coplan, David. (1985) 2008. *In Township Tonight! Three Centuries of South African Black City Music and Theatre*. Johannesburg: Jacana.

Davis, Dennis. 2020. "Social Justice and Economic Inclusion: Where to South Africa?" *Daily Maverick*, February 23, 2020. https://www.dailymaverick.co.za/article/2020-02-23-social-justice-and-economic-inclusion-where-to-south-africa/.

Delanty, Gerard, Liana Giorgi, and Monica Sassatelli, eds. 2011. *Festivals and the Cultural Public Sphere*. London: Routledge.

Falassi, Alessandro, ed. 1987. *Time Out of Time: Essays on the Festival*. Albuquerque: University of New Mexico Press.

Feld, Steven. 2012. *Jazz Cosmopolitanism in Accra: Five Musical Years in Ghana*. Durham, NC: Duke University Press.

Getz, Donald. 2010. "The Nature and Scope of Festival Studies." *International Journal of Event Management Research* 5(1): 1–47.

Habermas, Jürgen. 1989. *The Structural Transformation of the Public Sphere: An Inquiry into a Category of Bourgeois Society*. Cambridge: MIT Press.

Nita, Maria, and Jeremy Kidwell, ed. 2021. *Festival Cultures: Mapping New Fields in the Arts and Social Sciences*. London: Palgrave Macmillan.

Nyamnjoh, Francis B. 2017. "Incompleteness: Frontier Africa and the Currency of Conviviality." *Journal of Asian and African Studies* 52(3): 253–70.

Pyper, Brett. 2014. "'You Can't Listen Alone': Jazz, Listening and Sociality in a Transitioning South Africa." PhD diss., New York University.

Pyper, Brett. 2016. "Jazz Festivals and the Post-apartheid Public Sphere." *World of Music* 5(2): 107–23.

Woodward, Ian, Jodie Taylor, and Andy Bennett, eds. 2014. *The Festivalization of Culture*. Farnham: Ashgate.

FUTURITY

ELEVEN

Festival Futurity at the Palestine Music Expo

DAVID A. MCDONALD

"I'm Not Crazy!"

Bashar Murad stands pensively backstage at the Palestine Music Expo (PMX) in April 2019. The sound engineer hands him a microphone, positions his earpiece, and checks sound levels. But Bashar barely notices. His mind is elsewhere. Festival cofounder Martin Goldschmidt approaches with smiles and words of encouragement. Bashar nods with appreciation but maneuvers stage right, where two assistants place a large, layered wedding veil atop his platinum blond head. The veil cascades over a beautifully tailored white suit with gold-feathered wings on each shoulder. The suit and wedding veil were commissioned from a fashion designer featured on the US TV show *Rupaul's Drag Race*. Bashar repositions and fluffs the veil several times. It must be perfect. There is too much riding on this performance to leave anything to chance.[1]

Two years had passed since Bashar last performed on this stage. His set list had been a mix of English-language pop covers performed with modest guitar accompaniment. And while the 2017 crowd had seemed to love the performance, Bashar spent the next two years planning his return: writing Arabic-language songs, crafting a gender-bending stage persona, and devising new ways of breaking down stereotypes in sound, fashion, and image. PMX 2017 had given Bashar the confidence to really explore his artistry—to step outside the shadow of his family's musical legacy and push the limits of Palestinian pop music.[2] At PMX 2019, in front of an enthusiastic audience of locals and international music industry delegates, Bashar planned his reemergence into the pop music world.

Bashar waits silently as the festival emcees announce his name. The crowd quiets, and tension mounts. A montage of carefully curated images streams as a drummer plays a march-like pattern on the snare. Bass and violin join with repeated fourths reminiscent of a wedding march. Deliberately, elegantly, Bashar ascends the stage, the long wedding veil flowing behind him. Waving the microphone, he begins to sing his recently released song "al-kul 'am bitjawwaz" (Everyone is getting married).

> Everyone around me is getting married
> And I don't know my head from my toes
> It's not that I don't want to
> But my house fits only me

For many in the audience, this song and its gender-bending themes are already familiar. Bashar released the music video only a few weeks prior. In it, he wanders aimlessly through various wedding scenes as a disinterested interloper, never quite fitting in, never knowing why. Later, when his own wedding is imagined, Bashar surprisingly assumes the role of bride, groom, and clergy. Ridiculous and satirical, each role further reflects and amplifies his queer subjectivity. On this stage too, he uncomfortably inhabits multiple gendered personas. "My house fits only me," he sings.

> So let whatever happens happen
> I'll accept my destiny
> And let what may be, be
> Even if they say that I am crazy
> I'm not crazy, I'm not crazy, I'm not crazy!

It is on this particular line, repeated three times as the bridge to the third chorus, that Bashar spins, shouts, and releases the veil to thundering cheers. His message lands. It all makes sense. Conjuring Arab Israeli transsexual pop sensation Dana International's 1996 hit "Majnūna" (Crazy), which features the same line, this cross-dressing performance directs ridicule not at the image of Bashar acting the bride but rather at the system of cultural values and expectations that demands he choose. He's not crazy. His house fits only him. He accepts his destiny. Let what may be, be. Standing in front of the stage, I am overcome by what I've just witnessed. Here in downtown Ramallah, before approximately two thousand fans, Bashar Murad has playfully, skillfully, and beautifully reimagined his masculinity. Using one of the most important cultural tropes in Palestinian folklore (grooms/weddings) amid a political field

Figure 11.1. Bashar Murad performing at PMX 2019. Used with permission, Palestine Music Expo.

where expressions of queer subjectivity can be met with significant threat and violence, Bashar asserts a transgressive positioning of himself and his world (McDonald 2010). And while it is impossible to quantify the audience's varied reactions, it seems to me that the crowd is moved by the message.[3]

It is in these brief performative spaces that the affective power of music to shape bodies and the body politic becomes most obvious. Indeed, music is powerful in its capacity to not merely engage but also transform communities—to guide them through a multilayered process of confrontational, deliberative, and pragmatic social action (Mattern 1998). In this moment, familiar sounds, tropes, and images drawn from cultural tradition prove to be affective tools for demanding recognition, asserting presence, and rewriting normative codes of legibility. At first confrontational (the wedding veil/march), Bashar's crossdressing performance takes on a deliberative character ("my house fits only me"), moving toward pragmatic social transformation ("I'll accept my destiny, I'm not crazy"). His body, moving in coordinated action, disrupts the gendered contours of the body politic. Transgressive notions of masculinity, culture, and citizenship are performed for public deliberation. On stage, Bashar Murad plays with the status quo, making explicit demands for queer recognition and acceptance. And from these demands, the community may venture forward in new ways.

I focus on this moment, brief as it was, to begin a conversation on the activist potential of festival practice. This was not a typical performance or protest. Bashar's intervention was explicitly enabled by and protected within the boundaries of festival. PMX gave Bashar the confidence to explore and experiment. It was a "safe space," he tells me in our interview in June 2023, a place where he could take refuge. PMX provided the safety to confront stereotypes and seek recognition. Refuge in this sense is a nested concept, providing protection from immediate audiences, local Islamist authoritarians, and a brutal Israeli occupation. Moreso than a singular concert or performance, in festival, refuge enhances political impact: first, through exposure to larger, more diverse audiences; and second, by situating a singular message within a broader political field. In providing a platform for disruptive, transgressive performance within a political field defined by intense vulnerability, PMX manifests the activist potential of festival practice. In both form and content, PMX disrupts the status quo and offers refuge to performers and participants. In each of these maneuvers, festival organizers, performers, and participants collectively imagine and enact (im)possible interventions and future aspirations. There is world-making potential in festival practice. Disruption opens spaces of refuge, which in turn facilitate transgressive aspirational imaginings of self and other. Such collective imagining articulates a form of possibility that, while ephemeral, nevertheless envisions a desired future beyond violence, intolerance, and hopelessness. Bashar and his PMX interlocutors collectively perform the unimaginable as a possible, even inevitable, reality.

This is what I mean by *festival futurity*. In varying ways, PMX performances collectively point to a desired political alternative. They maintain an enthusiasm for the act of imagining and give experimental, disruptive, and transgressive ideas of the yet to come a space in the here and now. Festival futurity describes the mechanics of using festival to create a desired future the present has yet to acknowledge, as well as the spatial, logistical, and material resources required to experience that future in the present. It is both imagining and enacting. Bashar Murad's PMX 2019 performance informs this discussion of festival futurity in two ways: first, it demonstrates how festival participants imagine and project themselves into an unrealized future; and second, it reminds us that festival futurity emerges as the result of the intrinsic yet ephemeral festival condition of assembly. Disruption and refuge are two such elements through which the possibility for imagining and enacting desired political alternatives emerges. Festivals are unique spaces wherein these conditions can be strategically mobilized for maximum effect in both time and space. Moreso than political protests or singular concerts, festivals aggregate political impact by marshaling the forces of political desire, participatory assembly, and festive celebration. The political effects of assembly and appearance are enhanced through festivity, and the organizational structure and size of festivals increase exposure to, and impact of, political messaging.

This exploration of festival futurity is inspired by myriad political projects, in Palestine and elsewhere, that explicitly defy the limits of the present in pursuit of a desired alternative. I argue that PMX, viewed through the lens of Palestinian dispossession and "social death," opens crucial spaces for imagining beyond the limits of the present moment (Cacho 2021). In that imagining, PMX embodies an important form of festival activism. I demonstrate how festivals like PMX embody forms of direct action and sociopolitical intervention distinct from traditional concerts and street protests. Such festivals hold significant potential for advancing Palestinian demands for self-determination—by attending to festival futurity as a strategic form of direct action and anticolonial politics, we come to understand the way festival organizers, performers, and other participants encounter and challenge the myriad forms of violence that frame their worlds.

Palestine Music Expo 2019

The Palestine Music Expo (PMX) was conceived in 2016 by Rami Younis, Martin Goldschmidt, Mahmoud Jrere, and Abed Hathout as a means of providing valuable performance opportunities to Palestinian musicians. Their idea was to bring leading music industry professionals to Ramallah for a three-day festival where they would interact with local musicians in a variety of contexts: panels, workshops, and performances. International delegates were invited to lead professional development sessions, provide feedback, and work with musicians on cultivating their craft. In his interview with PBS News Hour, PMX cofounder Rami Younis explained: "We are connecting Palestine to the rest of the world using music. That is [how] I would describe PMX with one sentence. That is what we do. This is us, trying to tell the world that Palestine isn't just Gaza, occupation, soldiers, checkpoints, and that. Palestine is also music. Palestine is also cinema. Palestine is all of this stuff. People don't see that. And we are not victims. We're not victimizing ourselves."[4] In a meeting with artists prior to the 2017 festival, PMX cofounder Martin Goldschmidt stated:

Basically, as you all know, it is not easy being a musician anywhere. It is more than doubly not easy being a musician in the West Bank. So we are trying to find ways to help. The first thing we are going to do is bring people from international festivals.... We are going to bring booking agents [who] book tours in Europe and America to Ramallah... and you'll have a chance to ask their advice, see what they are looking for... and you can learn a lot about what to do and what not to do.... You will realize that they are real people.

The other side of it is *they will realize that you are not a bunch of terrorists [laughter]*; you are stable musicians. It's quite frightening to come here. *We will create that sort of one-to-one opportunity. And the ways to learn how it works. But we want to do more than that. We want to do things that [create] long-term, healthy infrastructure.* We are not sure what they are, what we need. We also need to raise a lot of money to do it. Maybe. Hopefully this event is something that grows bigger. *Ways of connecting you with each other, so you learn from other Palestinian musicians what works and what doesn't work. Ways of connecting you with the international community. And to connect the international community with you.* (Emphasis added)[5]

Each of these comments articulates a sincere desire to build infrastructure, develop musical acts, and connect Palestine to international audiences. However, it is important to point out a parallel desire to change the ways in which international audiences view or otherwise interpret Palestine. Both Goldschmidt and Younis express a desire to humanize Palestinians through popular music and culture. Insofar as the festival provides essential performance opportunities for young musicians, it also provides the outside, cosmopolitan world with a new lens through which to see and hear Palestine.

The overall production of the festival reflects these goals. The 2019 event was held in one of Ramallah's finest resort hotels, the Grand Park. Festival delegates and artists were provided catered meals, refreshments, and concierge services. Merchandise tables offered T-shirts, CDs, posters, and other pop-music paraphernalia. The stage, sound, and lighting were state of the art, akin to those at major music festivals in Europe and North America. Documentary film crews circulated among the crowd, interviewing performers and audience members, while nightly performances were live streamed. In my two decades of attending music festivals throughout the region, PMX was by far the most impressive in design, production, and execution.

In just its first three years, PMX drew over fifteen thousand visitors. Of those attendees, 60 percent were between the ages of eighteen and thirty-four. PMX 2019 featured seventy-five invited delegates from ten different countries with twenty-one bands performing for a crowd of over five thousand.[6] And all of this occurred amid an ongoing humanitarian crisis and military occupation. It goes without saying that an event of this size presents considerable logistical challenges. As Rami Younis pointed out to me, "the biggest challenge [for us] is always getting people to where they need to be. At times it's impossible. But that is the whole point, showing the world that the occupation can't prevent us from putting on a great show."[7] Indeed, the infrastructural and technological means of producing an event of this magnitude were themselves a kind of victory against the occupation. PMX performer Apo Sahagian noted, "It's definitely an escape to have fun. We enjoy, we see, we do, and it's great stuff, but alas I'm going to pass these checkpoints again. I'm going to have to talk to these soldiers so I [can] go back to my home. [It] doesn't feel good, but that is life."[8] Similarly, Hamada Nasrallah, lead singer of the Gaza-based Sol Band, said, "It was so difficult just to get here. We are just so happy to have made it here at all. . . . I don't want to think about [what will happen] tomorrow."[9]

These comments highlight the often-insurmountable obstacles of producing a music festival in occupied Palestine. Immobility, vulnerability, and escape were important touchstones for social meaning, each indexically pointing toward the violent carceral geographies Palestinians must navigate in their daily lives. Indeed, the occupation was the not-so-subtle context within and against which festival participants assembled. By this, I mean that the occupation was more than mere backdrop: it was a determining condition. And therefore, the occupation was central to PMX's signifying effect and activist potential.

The Matrix of Control

While Ramallah holds the trappings of any cosmopolitan city in the Arab world, it exists as an "enclave" of provisional life under military occupation (Peteet 2017). In this enclave, the local population lacks any form of nationally or internationally recognized citizenship or legal protection. Governed by the Israeli military, Palestinians in the West Bank and Gaza live under the ambiguously defined jurisdiction of the Israeli state, yet they are by no means citizens of that state. They are subjected to Israeli military law but refused the legal means to contest the law. Lisa Marie Cacho refers to such targeted groups as experiencing a form of "social death." "Ineligible for personhood," these populations "are excluded from the ostensibly democratic processes that legitimate law, yet they are expected to unambiguously accept and unequivocally uphold a legal and political system that depends on the unquestioned permanency of their rightlessness" (Cacho 2021, 6).[10]

The rightlessness Palestinians experience is rooted in a settler-colonial project that seeks to ensure the mobility and security of Israeli Jews at the expense of the Palestinian population (Wolfe 2006; Weizman 2012; Peteet 2017). Patrick Wolfe labels this a "logic of elimination," whereby Indigenous bodies, histories, and presence must be eliminated in the act of constructing a new colonial society (2006, 389). The fundamental premise of the settler colony, Wolfe argues, rests on an empty landscape—so goes the Zionist trope, "a land without a people, for a people without land."[11] The settler-colonial regime thus relies on and produces differential visibilities through which the settler colony is instantiated and legitimized while the native's presence is erased (Shalhoub-Kevorkian 2010, 10). This erasure is enforced through various forms of colonial governance that criminalize Palestinian presence as an existential threat to the Israeli state and its founding narrative. Where Israeli law presumes, requires, and enacts their erasure, Palestinians are denied the option to be law abiding. Simply being Palestinian is a criminal act of noncompliance against the Israeli state's demand of nonpresence and removal (Berda 2011, 45; Peteet 2017, 21).

The ongoing military occupation of the West Bank and Gaza is the most visible—though by no means only—mechanism of Israeli settler-colonialism. Justified by twin discourses of Israeli security and Palestinian criminality, the occupation exerts a "matrix of control" over Palestinian life (Halper 2006). Israel's spatial occupation seeks to control land through Jewish-only settler colonies and their constitutive bypass roads, military bases, surveillance towers, checkpoints, closed military areas, and aboveground airpower. To do this, the Israeli military oversees a complex network of laws, permits, architectural planning systems, and home demolitions designed to severely constrain Palestinian mobility (Weizman 2012). Both fields, spatial and legal, impose divisions that separate and transform Palestinian spaces and implement a hierarchy of access to natural resources. In addition, the occupation enforces temporal hardship, disrupting the rhythms of everyday life through forced closures, circuitous routes, bureaucratic delays, and long, debilitating lines. Routine closures, confinement, searches, and arrests constitute choreographed conditions of disorder and unpredictability, a kind of "calibrated chaos" that serves as a form of colonial governance and collective punishment (Peteet 2017, 18).

Within a settler-colonial discourse where millions of exiled and dispossessed Palestinians are not only unrecognized but profoundly unrecognizable—where simply being Palestinian is a transgressive, if not criminal, act—festivals like PMX not only provide a powerful means of being Palestinian but also create essential pathways of being heard and seen as such (McDonald 2020). Through the assembly and appearance of transgressive bodies, PMX reveals the incarcerating effects of the occupation; in denying and defying its precepts, PMX takes direct action against it. For example, PMX's international delegates experience Palestinian life firsthand through solidarity tours of Bethlehem, Hebron, and Jerusalem. These tours are both strategic and effective, educating delegates on the history of the crisis, providing firsthand experience of life under occupation, and soliciting empathy for Palestinian artists. Likewise, invited artists and ticket holders face hardship traveling to Ramallah. In their very appearance, Palestinian musicians and audiences transgress the demands for their nonpresence. And in that transgressive act, they make explicit demands for recognition. To refuse the underlying premises of the occupation is to take action against it.

But PMX also demonstrates the unique potential of festival activism. In greater degree than a traditional concert and with greater impact than an organized political protest, PMX collectively marshals the forces of political desire, participatory action, and festive celebration. PMX was conceived as a political instrument, to be sure. And while intervention is its goal, festive celebration is its methodology. The political effects of assembly and appearance are aggregated through festivity. As Nadeem Karkabi has eloquently demonstrated in the area of underground Palestinian raves, pleasurable experiences, such as those facilitated by PMX, generate enthusiasm for political action extending beyond the temporal and spatial boundaries of the event (Karkabi 2020, 2018). More than a political protest, PMX embeds desire for self-determination within a joyful celebration of Palestinian creativity. Likewise, PMX demonstrates the ways in which festivals hold more political potential than a singular performance, concert, or musical event. Every aspect of PMX is designed to maximize political impact. Stretched across a week of performances, solidarity tours, workshops, and other public events, PMX organizers can extend their message (temporally and spatially) in ways they could not through a traditional concert or event. The organizational structure and sheer size of the event amplify its potential political impact.

Disruption, Refuge, and Futurity

> [PMX 2019] was something that I was looking forward to. I was constantly thinking about every aspect of the show. *How can I shock people and entertain and do something that hasn't been done [before]?* And you know, I was also thinking of the audience, that it is mixed between Palestinians and the international

music industry professionals. I wanted to break the stereotype of what they expected to see on stage. And I think that's what I did. Because as soon as I walked on stage ... with that wedding dress—I was a little nervous, of course—but then I got on stage, and everyone was screaming and cheering for it. That was just the kickstart to that really special show for me. (Emphasis added)

In this recollection from June 2023, Bashar Murad describes to me his motivation for PMX 2019: to shock, to entertain, and to break Palestinian stereotypes on stage. Disruption was his underlying goal, and PMX was the space within which this disruption would have maximum effect: "My purpose always is to break stereotypes. Maybe back then I was even more adamant about it. I wanted to show a different side of Palestinians. But it's important to note that *I'm not trying to replace anything. Just to show another side to Palestinians. Because we are so diverse*, and the situations and circumstances that we are born into kind of direct where your life, how your life ends up, especially in this space" (emphasis added).

It is in disrupting essentialized images of Palestinian life and politics that Bashar finds inspiration. There are many different facets of Palestinian experience, he notes, and this performance pushed against lines of class, gender, sexuality, and vulnerability. Not at anyone's expense, Bashar endeavors to reveal Palestinian life in its diversity. Here, he proffers that one's uniquely situated experiences and circumstances determine "how your life ends up." His intervention aims to broaden notions of Palestine: first, by noting the incredible diversity of Palestinian experience in gender and sexuality; and second, by critiquing the cultural and political fields responsible for his precarity.

PMX was the ideal space to make these demands. It was, for him, a safe space, a refuge within which he felt empowered to experiment:

[PMX] was the first place where I experimented with gender bending performance. You know, even though it was just a veil on my head, that still has a certain connotation in every culture. And just crossing that line a little bit, you know, you never know how people will react. And you're in a public setting when you don't know who's there.... But you know, to me, I felt confident in what I was doing. *I felt safe*. At least because I knew the organizers had my back. And the people, the artists who were around me. So I don't think I would have ever ... done it anywhere else, in any other space. (Emphasis added)

In this brief exchange, Bashar points to several pathways through which festivals intervene in the social, political, and cultural worlds of their participants.

First, there is the drive to disrupt the status quo, to intervene into stereotypical articulations of Palestinian subjectivity across the public sphere. Just as cofounder Martin Goldschmidt created PMX to disrupt the way international audiences see and hear Palestine, Bashar made a similar gambit. Although locally directed, Bashar's disruption intervened across several fields. These transgressive moments, brief as they may be, nevertheless hold significant potential for long-term social and political change.

That disruption, however, was predicated on the refuge PMX provided its performers and participants. At no other venue would Bashar have ventured this kind of intervention. The support and safety afforded to him by festival organizers unlocked his creativity and inspiration. And yet, refuge was more than friendly support and encouragement. It was also forged in the logistical and material dynamics of the festival itself. Held at a four-star hotel with professional stage, sound, and lighting in the safety of the Ramallah "bubble" before an audience of progressive cosmopolitan Palestinians and international music industry delegates, Bashar's intervention was propelled by the refuge provided by and within festival spaces. In this sense, the activism of Bashar's performance was an aggregate of intentional transgressive action; the dispositions of his audiences and coparticipants; and the material conditions that enabled such action to occur. Disruption is a powerful means of social, cultural, and political intervention, but it was from a place of refuge that Bashar felt inspired, motivated, and empowered to act. And it was in the assembly of like-minded supportive audiences that this intervention held meaning.

Festival activism, in this sense, arises from a configuration of transgressive action and various enabling conditions. PMX provided refuge in ways that a traditional performance or underground event could not. In a larger, more elaborate event with a diverse assemblage of audience members, in juxtaposition with other artists, and framed within a politics of Palestinian emancipation, Bashar's transgressive performance was significantly enhanced—not merely by the increased exposure PMX provided but, much more importantly, by opening the idea of Palestinian self-determination to include gender and sexuality. Drag performance and cross-dressing is by no means a foreign concept in Arab popular culture (Menicucci 1998). So too has queer subjectivity increasingly found space for public articulation in Palestinian pop music and political activism (Atshan 2020; Munk 2021). Bashar's performance further indexed transsexual Arab Israeli pop star Dana International and her 1996 hit

"Majnūna" (Crazy). In both songs, queer subjectivity is valorized in the repeated line, "I'm not crazy!" Audience familiarity with these tropes certainly contextualized Bashar's favorable PMX reception. But in this festival setting, Bashar's political intervention took on additional importance. Framed within a larger field of Palestinian self-determination, Bashar's transgressive message evolved from queer recognition to intersectional emancipation. PMX enabled the performance through refuge, enhancing its message through juxtaposition with other emancipatory acts. Bashar directed his audience to view self-determination intersectionally, highlighting the forces of occupation within Palestinian society: "I see my music and my videos as a space, as a platform, to highlight *my version of Palestine*. . . . Which not everyone . . . might understand. But this is one version, whether it's working with fashion designers or working with amazing film crews [or] working with producers, collaborating with artists, just showing the diversity and the beauty [of Palestinian life]. Despite the ugliness of the occupation, that's what I want to highlight—*even with the occupation, to show the potential of what it could be*, if the occupation ever ends" (emphasis added).

Amid military occupation and humanitarian crisis, Bashar nevertheless finds great beauty in Palestine. Through music, image, gesture, and fashion, he shares his version of, and vision for, Palestine. Knowing full well that not all will understand, Bashar endeavors to show the potential of what Palestine could one day be: diverse, inclusive, beautiful. These sentiments reveal an attempt at artistic intervention—to not only imagine Palestine's potential but, more importantly, to actively participate in its becoming. Each performance offers the opportunity to embody something radically new. In a political reality dominated by chaos, carceral instability, and ubiquitous violence, Bashar performs from a position of possibility. Imagination is central to this process of becoming precisely because its temporality exceeds the inertia of past and present (Hochberg 2021). Bashar takes solace in Palestine's potential. It transcends the ugliness of the occupation not as mere escapism but as a form of engagement and direct political action.

Similarly, PMX endeavors to show the potential of what Palestine could one day become. As an example of festival futurity, PMX participates in Palestine's creative and aspirational imagining. It marshals conceptual, material, and logistical resources to enable and enact a desired political alternative. It gives experimental, disruptive, and transgressive ideas of the yet to come in the here and now. And, in its enactment, PMX presents the

Figure 11.2. PMX 2019 logo.

unimaginable as a possible, even inevitable, reality. In this way, PMX collectively points to (and advances toward) new political horizons—as Bashar alludes, to show the potential of what [Palestine] could be, if the occupation ever ends. But perhaps most importantly, PMX nurtures enthusiasm for the act of imagining. Through the cultivation of joy and profound feelings of communitas, festivals cloak politics. There is hope in imagining (im)possible futures. And where there is hope, there is greater possibility for long-term and sustained political action (Turino 2008). Both Bashar and PMX demonstrate the utility of collective imagining as a form of activist intervention.

Direct Action

Later in our conversation, Bashar Murad reiterates the politics of appearance discussed above.

> I think everything is political. Just because I'm not directly talking about politics, doesn't mean that my music isn't political.... Even in my fun dance songs I address politics, but in a satirical way.... I don't always have to be directly speaking about the occupation to be resisting. *Because anything I do, at the end of the day, is resistance.* ... There's a lot more angles that can be addressed. And that's what I care about doing. I tried to sum it up in my track 'Intifada on the Dance Floor.' It's a satirical song. It sounds like a fun dance song. But in my own way, *I'm saying that art and music are a form of resistance. They are not the only form of resistance. But they are a form of resistance.* (Emphasis added)

Where Palestinian presence is criminalized as an existential threat to the Israeli state, and where Israeli law therefore compels Palestinian erasure, any Palestinian act carries political potential. Even fun satirical dance songs are credible forms of political resistance in that they index the very real lifeways and experiences of those bodies denied the right to appear (Arendt 1958). To sing, to dance, to celebrate and imagine—all are politically charged acts of intervention against a field of appearance that denies or dismisses Palestinian presence. In similar fashion, PMX mobilizes festival practice as a mechanism of appearance and therefore a form of direct action against the occupation. The Midwest Academy Manual for Activists defines *direct action* as when "the people directly affected by the problem take action to solve it" in ways that alter power relationships and give those affected a sense of their own power, defined on their own terms (Bobo 2001, 11). David Graeber similarly defines direct action as a kind of "insistence, when faced with structures of unjust authority, on acting as if one is already free.... One does not solicit the state. One does not even necessarily make a grand gesture of defiance. Insofar as one is capable, one proceeds as if the state does not exist" (2009, 203). Graeber further explains that direct action is "a way of actively engaging with the world to bring about change, in which the form of the action—or at least the organization of the action—is itself a model for the change one wishes to bring about" (2009, 206).

At PMX 2019, we find all these elements. Festival organizers were clear in their desire to act against the occupation and its underlying logic of elimination. They did so by imagining and enacting a desired political alternative without regard or deference to the Israeli state. Festival organizers strategically crafted a pop-music experience intended to disrupt and displace the overdetermining effects of the occupation. PMX was more about staging Palestine and Palestinian music as it one day might be, as it one day should be. Akin to what Ghassan Hage conceives as "alter-politics," PMX offered a desire-based enactment of a political alternative rather than a demand-based performance of political opposition (Hage 2015, 2). Not a protest per se, PMX was an enactment of an alternative Palestine richly desired by its participants. It is here, in the enactment of alter-politics, that festivals and protests diverge.

As Graeber suggests, PMX actively endeavored to bring about change in a manner that modeled the change PMX wished to bring about. As both a means and ends, PMX imagined Palestinian sovereignty through its enactment. Andrew Snyder describes this as "pre-figurative politics, in which the action is a performative manifestation of new social and political relations, as well as an explicit and targeted petitioning of power" (Snyder 2022, 244). In my conversations with festival participants, it was common to hear exclamations like, "I can't believe we are sitting in Ramallah right now!" "Who knew we could do this?" or, "This festival is exactly what we are fighting for." Speaking about PMX in a televised interview with *al-Jazeera*, Palestinian activist and journalist Basem Tamimi explained: "What we can do now is *cultural* resistance. We have a new audience, not the political people, but music and others, poetry, sports. And this is a new way, not war but through culture. The idea is not just to scream against occupation but to show that this is a place of joy. *Joy is the best revenge.* You are supposed to be a repressed people. But if you show it's a place of life, it's a great thing" (emphasis added).[12]

Tamimi's reference to joy is particularly important as it further affirms the political potential of joyful affect (Jasper 2018). It is in the affective realm of alter-politics and festival futurity that PMX makes its greatest impact: by ignoring the logics of the occupation, assembling Palestinian bodies, and collectively imagining Palestine beyond the limits of the present sociopolitical moment.

Alter-politics is a form of direct action that resists occupation through pleasure and the desire for an alternative future (Hage 2015). The idea of resistance through creative participatory politics and its pleasures reorients our thinking away from activism based in anger and refusal. Celebratory forms of resistance such as these may not directly end the occupation, but they offer Palestinians an opportunity for dignity and self-fashioning. PMX performer Jasmine explains: "The beautiful thing is that we are not coming here [PMX] and going back and saying, 'Yeah it's so hard and everything.' I go back and say it was amazing. I met these amazing ladies, we had the best time ever, and it was just beautiful. *It brings beauty to me.* That is the magic that I experience."[13] Watching thousands of young Palestinian fans scream and dance without concern for the violence awaiting outside, I am reminded of the importance of pleasure, joy, and beauty in any political endeavor. Moments of joy such as these make possible the continued struggle against seemingly insurmountable odds.

PMX explicitly enacts a redistribution and reinvention of bodies, affects, and sensorial politics through disruption, refuge, and futurity. Even in the brief moment described above where Bashar Murad creatively espoused a queer masculine subjectivity, we witness a kind of experimental exercise of political freedom. Within Bashar's performance and the crowd's various reactions, participants learn how to move politically—how to activate, explore, or experiment with a kind of agency unavailable in everyday life. As a form of direct action, PMX actively counters the occupation by acting on the premise that the Israeli state has no legitimate authority to determine, sanction, or control modes of popular dissent and political action. And in these acts, a desired political alternative begins to take shape. Over time, as these pleasurable participatory experiences become sedimented into daily practice, new habits of thought and action, new dispositions and values, transform social and political life.

Conclusions

As an act of festival futurity, PMX creates important spaces for seeing and hearing Palestine beyond the logic of elimination. According to its creators, PMX seeks to mobilize Palestinians as visible, legible, knowable subjects for various internal and external audiences. Indeed, each panel, workshop, and performance might be considered a strategic act of intervention against the carceral mechanics of the occupation, against Israeli efforts to segregate Palestinians from each other, and against the colonial spheres of appearance through which Palestinians have been historically erased. In all these spaces, festival participants deploy festival futurity as a means of advancing emancipatory goals.

But what makes PMX unique is its use of festival as a form of direct action and anticolonial politics. For many of its participants, PMX is a coalitional performance of emancipation and sovereignty. And while it affords a kind of ephemeral escapism, I would argue that this type of direct action is not trivial.

Indeed, this work has both immediate and long-term effects. In making Palestinian life a bit more livable, PMX can be a crucial force in political transformation. As Turino reminds us, musical experiences such as these foreground "the crucial interplay between the possible and the actual" (2008, 16–17). PMX offers a multisensorial opportunity for the impossible, the nonexistent, the ideal to be imagined and enacted, leading to new lived realities. Performance experiences draw our attention to what is possible; they wake us from habit and provide "a temporary sense of a life more deeply lived" (Turino 2008, 18).

To this, I would add that in contexts of extreme precarity, attention to the possible takes on even greater activist potential. The stakes are different. The escalation of risk heightens the potential for political transformation. Although participants at PMX explicitly vocalize an opposition to Israeli occupation, they also, by virtue of their assembly, pose their challenge in corporeal terms. Simply in their appearance, these Palestinian bodies "signify" prior to and apart from any musical gesture. There is a profound sincerity in their demands. The intervention occurs in the very act of assembly, in the demand for appearance, and in the resulting exposure and vulnerability to state violence. To assert that Palestinians live, create, dance, and celebrate is already a politically significant form of countervisibility that implicitly challenges the underlying tenets of the occupation. Appearing together in a kind of coalitional performance where Palestine is reimagined, seen, heard, and felt through desire and joy, PMX participants enact a kind of activism that aggregates and extends conventional political demands. In this way, PMX offers a fascinating case study in festival activism, not merely in its presentation of politically engaged artists or its connecting of those artists to the outside world but as an act of festival futurity wherein Palestinians come together in embodied action and in that act collectively imagine the potential of what Palestine could be, if the occupation ever ends.

Notes

1. Portions of this chapter were previously published in "Affective Assembly and Participatory Politics at the Palestine Music Expo," in *Music Making Community*, ed. Tony Perman and Stefan Fiol (Urbana: University of Illinois Press, 2024).

2. Bashar Murad is the son of Said Murad, famed musician, activist, and founder of Sabreen, one of the most important Palestinian music ensembles throughout the 1980s and 1990s.

3. "MASKHARATV #1: Bashar Murad at Palestine Music Expo 2019, Ramallah," YouTube video, 2022, https://www.youtube.com/watch?v=nmCsXrpuztc.

4. Rami Younis, "PMX 2017," interview by John Yang, *PBS News Hour*, June 13, 2019, https://www.pbs.org/newshour/show/how-this-palestinian-music-festival-is-breaking-down-cultural-barriers.

5. Martin Goldschmidt, "What Is PMX," YouTube video, December 22, 2006, https://www.youtube.com/watch?v=HN8meomno_s.

6. For PMX statistics, see https://www.palestinemusicexpo.com/about.

7. Rami Younis, interview by author, April 5, 2019, Ramallah, Palestine.

8. Apo, "Palestine Music Expo Aims for International Attention," interview by Imran Khan, *Al-Jazeera*, April 8, 2017, https://www.aljazeera.com/videos/2017/4/8/palestine-music-expo-aims-for-international-attention.

9. Hamada Nasrallah, interview by author, April 5, 2019, Ramallah, Palestine.

10. While Cacho's research is directed at the United States, her argument is pertinent to other settler-colonial environments. For more on the concept of social death, see Orlando Patterson, *Slavery and Social Death: A Comparative Study* (Cambridge: Harvard University Press, 1982).

11. For an analysis of this common trope in Palestinian studies, see Said 1979, 9; Khalidi 1997, 101; Pappe 2017, 31–35.

12. Basem Tamimi, televised interview with *al-Jazeera*, April 8, 2017, Ramallah, Palestine

13. Jasmine, televised interview with *PBS News Hour*, June 13, 2019, Ramallah, Palestine.

Bibliography

Arendt, Hannah. 1958. *The Human Condition*. Chicago: University of Chicago Press.

Atshan, Sa'ed. 2020. *Queer Palestine and the Empire of Critique*. Palo Alto, CA: Stanford University Press.

Berda, Yael. 2011. "The Security Risk as a Security Risk: Notes on the Classification Practices of the Secret Service." In *Threat: Palestinian Prisoners in Israel*, edited by Abeer Baker and Anat Matar, 44–56. London: Pluto Press.

Bobo, Kimberley A. 2001. *Organizing for Social Change: Midwest Academy Manual for Activists*. Santa Ana, CA: Forum Press.

Cacho, Lisa Marie. 2021. *Social Death: Racialized Rightlessness and the Criminalization of the Unprotected*. Durham, NC: Duke University Press.

Graeber, David. 2009. *Direct Action: An Ethnography*. Edinburgh: AK Press.

Hage, Ghassan. 2015. *Alter-Politics: Critical Anthropology and the Radical Imagination*. Carlton: Melbourne University Press.

Halper, Jeff. 2006. "The 94% Solution: Israel's Matrix of Control." In *The Struggle for Sovereignty: Palestine and Israel, 1993–2005*, edited by Joel Beinin and Rebecca L. Stein, 62–74. Stanford: Stanford University Press.

Hochberg, Gil. 2021. *Becoming Palestine: Toward an Archival Imagination of the Future*. Durham, NC: Duke University Press.

Jasper, James M. 2018. *The Emotions of Protest*. Chicago: University of Chicago Press.

Karkabi, Nadeem. 2018. "Electro Dabke: Performing Cosmopolitan-Nationalism and Borderless Humanity." *Public Culture* 30(1): 173–96.

Karkabi, Nadeem. 2020. "Self-Liberated Citizens: Unproductive Pleasures, Loss of Self, and Playful Subjectivities in Palestinian Raves." *Anthropological Quarterly* 93(4): 679–708.

Khalidi, Rashid. 1997. *Palestinian Identity: The Construction of Modern National Consciousness*. New York: Columbia University Press.

Mattern, Mark. 1998. *Acting in Concert: Music, Community, and Political Action*. New Brunswick, NJ: Rutgers University Press.

McDonald, David A. 2010. "Geographies of the Body: Music, Violence and Manhood in Palestine." *Ethnomusicology Forum* 19(2): 191–214.

McDonald, David A. 2020. "Junction 48: Hip-Hop Activism, Gendered Violence, and Vulnerability in Palestine." *Journal of Popular Music Studies* 32(1): 26–43.

McDonald, David A. 2024. "Affective Assembly and Participatory Politics at the Palestine Music Expo." In *Music Making Community*, edited by Tony Perman and Stefan Fiol, 190–208. Urbana: University of Illinois Press.

Menicucci, Garay. 1998. "Unlocking the Arab Celluloid Closet: Homosexuality in Egyptian Film." *Middle East Report* 206(Spring): 32–36.

Munk, Liza. 2021. "Don't Tell Me Underground: The Politics of Joy and Melancholy in Jordan's Alternative Arabic Music" PhD diss., UC Santa Barbara.

Pappe, Ilan. 2017. *The Biggest Prison on Earth: A History of the Occupied Territories*. Oxford: One World.

Peteet, Julie Marie. 2017. *Space and Mobility in Palestine*. Bloomington: Indiana University Press.

Said, Edward. 1979. *The Question of Palestine*. New York: Times Books.

Shalhoub-Kevorkian, Nadera. 2010. "Palestinian Women and the Politics of Invisibility: Towards a Feminist Methodology." *Peace Prints: South Asian Journal of Peacebuilding* 3(1): 1–21.

Snyder, Andrew. 2022. "'Music Is Liberation': The Brass Liberation Orchestra and Direct Action." In *At the Crossroads of Music and Social Justice*, edited by Romero, Asai, McDonald, Snyder, and Best, 239–58. Bloomington: Indiana University Press.

Turino, Thomas. 2008. *Music as Social Life: The Politics of Participation*. Chicago: University of Chicago Press.

Weizman, Eyal. 2012. *Hollow Land: Israel's Architecture of Occupation*. London: Verso.

Wolfe, Patrick. 2006. "Settler Colonialism and the Elimination of the Native." *Journal of Genocide Research* 8(4): 387–409.

TWELVE

"The Many Ways We Are Alike"

The Perils of Multiculturalism in Boise's World Village Festival

KIMBERLY J. MARSHALL AND STEVEN HATCHER

Since 2015, Boise's World Village Festival has celebrated Idaho's multiculturalism through song, dance, and food at the steps of the State Capitol. Idaho is better known for its potatoes than its cultural diversity and is sometimes associated with multiculturalism's antithesis: white nationalism. But, in fact, the population of Idaho has always been a diverse mix of Native American, Asian, Hispanic, and various European cultures, and its diversity has increased over the past few decades through both explosive population growth and active refugee resettlement from Southeast Asia, central Europe, and central Africa. The arrival of these new Idahoans has set off some alt-right alarmism. Figures like Pamela Geller, Alex Jones, and Vincent James Foxx have argued that Idaho's increasing diversity is a threat to American values and safety (Mathias 2022).

The World Village Festival was created in response to the perilous, potentially violent consequences of this increasingly multicultural pressure cooker. As a strategic form of direct action, this festival was designed by organizers to connect "Old Boiseans" and "New Boiseans" through joyful sharing of cultural arts. The festival emphasizes multiculturalism—the celebration of cultural diversity—as a productive answer to rising alt-right extremism and declining feelings of social cohesion. As the festival mission statement asserts, "Growing together as a community requires understanding and validation of our unique experiences and backgrounds.... The collaborative nature of art, music, film, dance and culture create the environment needed to open doors between ethnic groups in a vibrant and welcoming way. Through discovery of differences in art and culture, we also discover *the many ways we are alike* in our human experiences and values" (emphasis added).[1]

As Idaho state folklorist, Hatcher recruits participants for the festival and provides a window into their artistic activism. In this chapter, he argues that the aim of the World Village Festival is to produce what Michel Foucault (1986) terms a *heterotopia*. The performers, vendors, audience, and geography of the festival combine to create a space—with the performance stage as its nourishing heart—that models an alternative to the politically divisive and antagonistic realities of Idaho.

And yet, while we agree that this festival does important activist-advocacy work in fostering multicultural heterotopia in Boise, we are also aware of the perils of a multicultural framework. At what point does the universalizing framework of the festival ("the many ways we are alike") erase or even perpetuate systematic inequalities? In the second part of this essay, Marshall focuses on the ways in which the multicultural frame can perpetuate social injustice. She argues that because of Boise's unresolved settler-colonial origins, the integration of Native people into festival programming is also perilous. It too easily fits into larger frameworks of settler-colonialism, erasing Native histories of dispossession, removal, and discrimination and replacing them with settler-generated ideas about Native people and their place in Boise's multicultural story.

In sum, we ask whether a broader awareness of the perils of the multicultural framework within a settler-colonial context can help us better meet the activist goals of the heterotopic festival: a celebration of the arts as direct action to build broad, multicultural coalitions in the face of rising divisiveness and hate. This perspective on festival expands beyond our received "social microcosm" frameworks (Singer 1972) and "communitas-activating" frameworks (Turner 1969). It brings folklore and ethnomusicology into conversation with cutting-edge work in visual arts scholarship, which has begun to take seriously artistic practice as direct action that attempts to make positive change in the social fabric (van den Berg, Jordan, and Kleinmichel 2019).

The World Village Festival

The World Village Festival is a three-day festival that takes place annually in Boise, Idaho, a mid-sized city in the Intermountain West. Bounded to the north by the impenetrable mountain ranges of central Idaho, the Boise Valley lies on the Snake River Plain and shares a high-altitude desert climate similar to that of northern Nevada or Utah. The Boise metropolitan area contains the bulk of Idaho's population—including the rapidly expanding cities of Meridian, Eagle, Nampa, and Caldwell—and its geographical isolation is part of its appeal, since isolation promotes the development of many cultural and economic resources a more connected city of its size would not typically contain. With easy access to outdoor recreation and generally sunny days to enjoy it, Boise has recently experienced explosive growth, especially among wealthy, conservative, white tech-sector workers out of California.[2]

While Boise has been marketed to Silicon Valley for its outdoor appeal, it has been growing in diversity as well. Agricultural labor communities from Mexico and Central America have made up southern Idaho's largest minority population for over a century, outpacing Asian (primarily Chinese) settlers who built the railroads and grew food for the mining boom towns of the gold rush era. Sheepherders from Basque country have long made Boise a center of Basque culture outside the homeland. Adding to this diversity, Idaho became involved in formal refugee resettlement in 1975 with the Indochinese Refugee Assistance Program, and settled large numbers of Bosnian refugees in the mid-1990s. Since the early 2000s, resettlement has largely involved refugees from central African countries like the Democratic Republic of Congo, Uganda, Burundi, and Sudan, as well as Afghanistan and Myanmar.

For the majority white population of Idaho, the most recent waves of immigration are marked, and not always in positive ways. Boise is more liberal than the rest of Idaho, but it is still very conservative. It is also the capital city, and the convening of the state legislature introduces many opportunities for white nationalist rhetoric. White nationalism itself is no stranger to Idaho, where the remote mountains of the northern panhandle have occasionally been home to an active Aryan Nations presence. This facet of Idaho got national attention during the 1992 Ruby Ridge standoff between white separatists and the FBI.[3] While Idahoans have been actively engaged in combatting white nationalist logics for years, the increasing diversity of southern Idaho and the America First rhetoric that came to the fore in the years leading up to 2016—combined with white flight out of California—have certainly contributed to a polarized and fractured climate around multicultural belonging in the state (Mathias 2022).[4] The World Village Festival was created in response to the perilous and potentially violent consequences of backlash against an increasingly diverse Idaho population.

Reflecting the geographic isolation of Boise, the World Village Festival stands alone, not only in the Boise Valley but within the whole state, as the singular event to curate and present so many ethnic and cultural communities. In fact, the closest similar festivals are over 350 miles away in all directions.[5] Set at the steps of the State Capitol Building among historic shade trees with both the Boise foothills and the heart of downtown as a backdrop, the World Village Festival is structured to highlight a maximum number of Boise Valley cultural communities. It features groups that celebrate their ethnicity (Laotian, Chinese, Mexican, Basque, Scandinavian, Indonesian, Japanese, Bosnian, etc.) but also their occupation (agricultural communities that occupy the Snake River Basin) and other oral, musical, and performance cultures throughout the valley (fiddlers from Weiser, Afro-rock from Boise, Gypsy Jazz). There are three days of free performances in about forty-five-minute blocks. Typically, about twenty-five local music, dance, and spoken word performers occupy the stage over the course of the weekend. Each person receives a small honorarium for their time—$100–200, depending on the length of performance. Friday and Saturday nights feature headlining national, tradition-based acts like the Preservation Hall Legacy Quintet or Ozomatli.[6]

In addition to constant performances, the festival grounds are filled with food vendors, artisans hosting craft and other expressive demonstrations, children's activities, a street soccer competition, and more. Food vendors mirror the ethnic diversity of performers: Mexican, Ethiopian, a range of Asian foodways, barbeque, and soul food, among others. Social service organizations from refugee resettlement agencies, community health organizations, and volunteer opportunities occupy informational booths. A community-based radio station, Radio Boise, broadcasts live from the festival.

Attendees at the festival reflect the larger demographic composition of the Boise Valley. Significantly, performers are often accompanied by large crowds from their corresponding cultural community, in attendance to support their own dance and music traditions. Thus, traditional Basque dancing will erupt spontaneously in the audience when the Basque folk-rock band Amuma Says No plays at the festival. Several generations of Mexican families will drive in from Nampa and Caldwell on a Sunday to spend the day at the park when the schedule prominently features Mexican and other Latino artists. Relatives, friends, and Indonesian community members will hover around the stage when Indo Idaho perform their ancient dances. White attendees filter in from the suburbs or affluent neighborhoods to witness cultural practices unavailable or inaccessible to the general public for most of the year.

The festival is produced by the umbrella organization Global Lounge, a Boise 501(c)(3) established in 2006. Funding is pieced together every year by small to medium-sized grants and donations, vendor fees, a percentage of food and drink sales, and other income generated through public programs throughout the year. A president, vice president, five-person board, and five-person advisory council assist the two founding and executive directors: Dayo Ayodele and Donna Kovaleski. All of these positions are unpaid volunteer positions.

Celebrating Diversity in Perilous Times

The World Village Festival was conceived by organizers as a strategic form of direct action: using art to connect "Old Boiseans" and "New Boiseans" through joyful sharing of cultural arts.[7] It grew out of the multicultural arts education work of Dayo Ayodele (from Nigeria, living in Boise since the 1980s) and Donna Kovaleski (from Minnesota, living in Boise since the 1990s). Ayodele and Kovaleski were working on a multicultural exchange program for the local YMCA, encouraging kids to learn about the different cultures that exist in Idaho—primarily through arts, crafts, music, and dance. This multicultural programming eventually grew into an organization called Global Lounge; starting in 2011, the organization began to have a yearly presence with a booth at a local street festival. The group's yearly programming grew until 2015, when it staged its first solo multiday multicultural arts festival downtown—where the festival returns annually.[8] Celebrating Idaho's multiculturalism remains at the festival's core.

The fact that the benefits of multiculturalism need to be highlighted is directly related to rising tensions around southern Idaho's growing racial, ethnic, and religious diversity. In 2016, Idaho gained national attention for an incident in Twin Falls (about an hour from Boise) that was picked up by well-known alt-right websites (including *Breitbart News*) and used to stoke fear and resentment toward refugees. The incident involved two young refugee boys who assaulted a five-year-old girl, but the details of the assault (and the police response to it) were spun into exaggeration and falsehood through the media attention of Pamela Geller, Alex Jones, and Brigette Gabirel (Hauser 2017).[9]

More recently, in 2022, Idaho's lieutenant governor Janice McGeachin delivered a prerecorded speech at the America First Political Action Conference hosted by white nationalist Nicholas Fuentes, encouraging attendees to "Keep up the good work fighting for our country" (Mathias 2022). During a campaign event for her bid for governor of Idaho in 2022 (she received nearly 25 percent of the vote in the Republican primary), McGeachin posed for a selfie with well-known white supremacist Vincent James Foxx, who claims to have deep connections to her. Hate crimes are increasing in Idaho, with an increase of 42 percent in 2020 over hate crimes in 2019 and an increase of 108 percent in 2019 over 2018 (Goodwin 2022). Boise has seen an increase in antisemitic crimes including the repeated spraying of antisemitic graffiti near Boise's Anne Frank Memorial Park (Anderson 2021). So powerful has the Far Right Insurgency become in Idaho that it was recently featured in a long-form investigation published in *HuffPost* (Mathias 2022). A month later, thirty-one members of the white supremacist Patriot Front were arrested on their way to disrupt a Pride parade in northern Idaho (Rose 2022).

This is the perilous context into which the World Village Festival is introducing arts-based direct action: a type of artistic practice aimed at enacting positive change (van den Berg, Jordan, and Kleinmichel 2019). Encouraging communication across the community, according to Kovaleski, is a major aim of all of its programming. In our interview, Kovaleski says:

> We have a really diverse community. But so many people stay in their pocket communities... so we wanted to figure out a way to allow each of these groups to open up and share who they are with the general public. And we also felt like that in a rural, farming community that Idaho has been... there hasn't always been a lot of exposure to global cultures and other parts of the world. And we really wanted to say, "How do we help the existing community to feel comfortable with the newcomers, and as the newcomers are coming in, how do they get to feel a part of this place?"

This is the context in which the Boise World Village Festival was founded, as direct action to cultivate heterotopia out of diversity.

Sheer Sincerity and Raw Beauty

Since the first festival, in 2015, I (Hatcher) have been responsible for finding, programming, and presenting all local performers. I have worked with many of the performers much longer. I am the state folklorist and director of the Folk and Traditional Arts Program at the Idaho Commission on the Arts. My job at the commission is to document, support, and celebrate the folklife of Idaho through public programs and grant funding. While my role at the World Village Festival is not in this official capacity, I volunteer many months of my time to energize the annual festival with new and returning performers, present performers to the audience with culturally contextual information, and keep the weekend's schedule flowing and on time.[10]

On average, roughly 80 percent of the performers at the festival are individuals or groups I work with throughout the year in my role as folk arts director, either through other public programs or funding. Most importantly, many of the performing groups participate in the Traditional Arts Apprenticeship Program, an annual grant program at the commission that supports a learning partnership between a recognized master artist and one or more qualified apprentices to continue artistic traditions of a shared cultural heritage. One requirement of the program is that the apprenticeship team must schedule at least one public performance or presentation at the end of the grant term. This performance not only allows the public to observe the work accomplished between the mentor and apprentice but also acts as a type of advertisement for the program, which has formed the backbone of the Folk and Traditional Arts Program since 1986.

In many cases, the World Village Festival serves as the public performance component for apprenticeship teams. For example, Mexican *folklórico* dancer Norma Pintar has presented students she apprenticed the prior year. A burgeoning drummer and flute player with Kawa Taiko, a Japanese taiko group, fulfilled her apprenticeship requirement in 2019. In these cases, my introduction includes information about the program before the mentor presents the apprentice and discusses the specific skills and techniques they have worked on for the year.

The relationships between me and the performers are vital to the health of the Folk Arts Program at the Idaho Commission on the Arts as well as that of the festival. These long-standing relationships contain trust and a shared sense of advocacy. Many of the performers come from marginalized groups whose performances, often defined by calendar rituals or customs, are primarily staged for their own communities. To bring them onstage in a public venue is to ask them to accept a certain amount of vulnerability. Others relish the opportunity to perform for a broader audience. Either way, as a civil servant, I feel it is my duty to honor performers' cultures, present them with respect, allow them cultural autonomy, and ensure that they enjoy themselves. These reciprocal relationships, cultivated in my work as State Folklorist and celebrated as a volunteer presenter at the World Village, contribute to the success of the festival.

Heterotopic Possibilities

If artistic activism aims to use art to remake the social fabric, the World Village Festival attempts to do so by creating what Foucault terms a heterotopia, or sites "that have the curious property of being in relation with all the other sites, but in such a way as to suspect, neutralize, or invent the set of relations that they happen to designate, mirror, or reflect" (Foucault and Miskowiec 1986). Heterotopias, Foucault argues, are not utopias. For him, a utopia is an ideal—an unreal fantasy. Utopias are idealized impossibilities because they invert rather than subvert the sites they mirror. Heterotopias, on the other hand, create an alternative social ordering based on the dominant order. They are real places made up of what is actually around us but jumbled up from the usual ordering. Because of this dijuncture, heterotopias have the potential to generate new orders, new possibilities, new futures. Folklife festivals have these characteristics. Limited, time-based, performative festivals capture and oppose the surrounding site(s) and reflect a potentially more productive, progressive, and proactive set of circumstances than those they mirror.

Scholars Linda Wilks and Bernadette Quinn (2016) argue that key to Foucault's 1967 idea of heterotopia are the concepts of variation, changeable function, juxtaposition, disruption, required performance or ritual, and relative relationship to others. But these characteristics could also define what it means to participate in a folk group or cultural community. Creating an alternative site to the established social order is what marks a folk group and its practitioners as unique, self-sustained, edified, and democratized (Toelken 1996).

Folk festivals build on these characteristics of the folk group, providing an actual site where social boundaries can be blurred. In an exhaustive 2010 report on outdoor arts festivals, the National Endowment for the Arts noted the changing nature of audiences at festivals—from spectators to active observers who interact and assume roles in the curation of the festival. Audiences crave new levels of interactivity, value personal creation and performance as part of the overall arts experience, and appear to prefer those activities in informal settings. As the case studies in this article illustrate, festival audiences derive special satisfaction from encounters with artists and art forms in an open space that reinforces choice, experimentation, and free movement (NEA Office of Research and Analysis 2010). The World Village Festival has typified this free-flowing, open-choice experience since its inception. With plenty of simultaneous activities happening throughout the park, there is no central focus. Even when a group is performing on stage, people freely wander, chatting, lounging, and enjoying the atmosphere. In this park, during this festival, Old Boiseans and New Boiseans share space together in ways they do not typically.

Another way folk festivals foster heterotopia is by allowing cultural communities to display their ethnic identity, troubling the dominant order by contributing to the cultural capital of marginalized ethnic identities. Boise's World Village acts as a microcosm of the greater Boise Valley, albeit with a set of fine filters. The arts and crafts, food, music, dance, customs, and rituals highlighted in the three-day festival are found, perpetuated, and even relatively common in Idaho. Through sheer size and volume of other, more dominant cultural communities, however, many smaller cultural communities often hide in plain sight. The World Village becomes a heterotopia by providing a venue for minority groups to highlight aspects of culture they value: worldviews, skills, knowledge, and traditional cultural expressions.

Likewise, an Oinkari dancer, Heart of Praise Choir percussionist, Indonesian master chef of *nasi goreng* (fried rice), and Norwegian *rosemåler* (traditional painting technique) all tend to have workaday routines as everyday citizens within the larger social order. They attend Boise State University or an eighth-grade public school in Caldwell. They work in hospital administration or an import retail store. They wear blue jeans and T-shirts. They eat hamburgers and breakfast cereal. A three-day folklife festival, however, strips away the pretense of a life lived in anything but a constant state of performance. The folklife festival is hyperfocused in its ability to do away with the filler of life— the hours spent on hold, the weekly chores, the obligatory maintenance—and concentrate for a short, intense time on what folklorists Tim Lloyd and Charley Camp call the "cultural metabolism of these communities" (Camp and Lloyd 1980). For a brief moment in time, a folklife festival allows a cultural community, a folk group, to express itself to the larger society and, consequently, see itself within the larger community.

Heterotopia as Artistic Activism

In the World Village Festival, the creation of heterotopia is a form of artistic direction action. In an era where movements against change and diversity have simmered to a volatile roil, the work of promoting communitas and feelings of goodwill is a powerful and profound antidote not to be dismissed as frivolous or unimportant. Audience members participate in the larger performance or ritual of the festival under the assumed condition that they, too, will contribute to the feeling of goodwill within the space. In her essay "Producing Festivals," Maribel Alvarez, folklorist at the University of Arizona and program director for the forty-eight-year-old Tucson Meet Yourself Folklife

Festival, writes that "people commit time and effort for the greater cause of art, culture, and traditions, certainly, but they choose to go the extra mile of devotion for the rewards of social lubrication that yield the pleasure of knowing one another and the community's needs with astounding degrees of specificity. . . . Folklife festivals are love affairs: they seduce you with their sheer sincerity and raw beauty" (Alvarez 2021). The common social purpose of the World Village is to allow residents of the Boise Valley to become more acquainted with one another "with astounding degrees of specificity." And through the festival framework, cultivated feelings of goodwill and communitas take an active, defiant stand against the dominant culture of divisiveness and antagonism.

The location of the festival itself speaks to its role as artistic direct action. Since 2015, the World Village Festival has been staged in Cecil Andrus Park (Capitol Park before 2018), a grassy area directly in front of the Idaho State Capitol. Recently, this park has served not only office workers from surrounding state government agencies at lunchtime but also numerous political and social protests from all sides of the spectrum, with many turning unruly and violent. Such scenes, associated more often with larger cities, were almost unheard of in Boise—or anywhere in Idaho—a decade ago. At this location, the World Village Festival stands in stark contrast to the protests, mob scenes, and police barricades that have accompanied the development and expansion of the Boise Valley. In fact, along with the Boise Pride Festival, the World Village Festival is one of the few large-scale public events in the park designed to celebrate, honor diversity, cultivate goodwill, and encourage communitas. According to my years of planning meetings with festival developers, this is precisely the point: to create a heterotopia in the same location where the state legislature wrestles with and often supplies the divisiveness of the current social climate.

In the face of this divisiveness, the World Village Festival is a celebration, transforming the grounds on which it takes place into a kind of sacred space rife with symbolic meaning. As Wilks and Quinn note, "at the centre of this sacred festival space is the celebration of something of particular import both to the people of the place and to those who visit specifically for the festival" (Wilks and Quinn 2016). Multiculturalism is the "something of particular import" around which people gather for the World Village Festival. As such, participation transforms festival attendance into a kind of peaceful protest, taking an active and deliberate step to counteract other heterotopias that have been curated through riot gear and neo-Nazi flags. Those thousands of Idahoans who participate in World Village—everyone from developers to vendors to performers to participant-audience—may not view and articulate the festival as an act of protest. But to perform or spend the day in the park is to participate in an "alternative social ordering" and to normalize this ordering. The festival is not a perfect heterotopia (and it is certainly not a utopia), but it is a temporary, curated space held on sacred ground where the opportunity is afforded to many communities within the Boise Valley to communicate through their expressive cultural traditions. And if productive and creative communication is the only result from three days of celebration, then the festival is a resounding success.

The message at the World Village is one of direct action: *this is our community, and we are here to celebrate its sincerity and raw beauty.* Intended or not, the curation of such a festival sends a powerful message of unity, cohesiveness, and communitas into a world where that vision of multiculturalism is under dire threat.

Settler-Colonialism and Trickster Activism

As shown above, the World Village Festival is a good example of the way in which folk festivals do activist work in fostering heterotopia in the perilous multicultural context of Boise. They celebrate diversity and promote positive multicultural exchange. But there are perils in the multicultural framework, too, and these dangers are thrown into sharp relief when it comes to the way the World Village Festival represents Native North Americans.

For example, the 2016 World Village Festival opened with what one news station called a "Lakota People Drum Circle" invited to represent Idaho's "Native American heritage," even though Idaho is not Lakota homelands. Meanwhile, unbeknownst to the Boiseans gathered at World Village, a gathering of the actual descendants of the Boise Valley People was happening just two miles down the road.

In my (Marshall) research, I investigate the ways in which patterns of erasure are produced in cultural form: in Boise's contemporary folklore, visual arts, public artwork, musical culture, museum exhibits, placenames, and dance. Folklife festivals like the World Village Festival make up one part of what I call Boise's expressive culture of erasure. For this research, I have occupied many roles at the World Village Festival over the past half-dozen years: emcee, setup and teardown crew, program hawker, and seller of beer tokens. While volunteering at the festival, I have also listened and learned, observed, and taken notes.

I combine this research on the ground with over a decade of research and teaching about the politics and poetics of expressive culture in Native North America (Marshall 2016). So while I care deeply about the promotion of inclusion and multicultural acceptance in Boise, I recognize that the multicultural framework within a fraught settler-colonial context can produce a kind of representational erasure where the specific and still-consequential histories of Boise's Native story can be erased and replaced with a "Lakota people drum circle" and no one knows the difference.

Representational erasure is one of the perils of the multicultural framework within settler-colonial contexts. Scholars have well established that settler-colonialism is not just the occupation of land but also the control of narratives about occupation (Wolfe 2006; Tuck and Yang 2012; O'Brien 2010). And the multicultural framework is very much part of the liberal image of the modern state, thrown recently into sharp relief against white Christian nationalism. But as Elizabeth Povinelli has argued (2002), if these are the only two options, the multicultural framework is not entirely beneficial for Indigenous people either. It produces a politics of recognition that forces Indigenous people into high stakes games of authenticity.[11] Settler-colonial narratives place authentic Indigeneity as the "past" along a timeline where American multicultural modernity represents the "present" (Tuck and Yang 2012; O'Brien 2010). So within the multicultural framework, Indigenous people must act premodern enough to be recognized as a constituent part of the modern multicultural state yet be excluded from full participation in the state by that very premodern association. It is a self-serving catch-22 for the settler state—what Tuck and Yang call a "settler move to innocence" (2012, 10).[12]

At the World Village Festival, the multicultural framework produces representational erasure in two main ways: through the framework of heritage and the production of alterity. These frameworks are not totalizing, however. As I explore below, they can be subverted by Native performers using a kind of "trickster activism," to paraphrase Gerald Vizenor (1988). Through humor, performers can unmask the hidden settler-colonial logics that undergird the multicultural celebration/white Christian nationalist dichotomy.

Heritage Production

According to the World Village website, the festival "gives people an opportunity to listen, watch, learn, feel and interact while learning and teaching cultural aspects of Idaho's diverse heritage."[13] Much like the Nation of Immigrants frameworks that goes askew at the national level, the possessive nature of heritage as somehow belonging to Idaho is problematic for people who predate the state of Idaho by thousands of years.

In this slippage, we can see what noted folklorist Barbara Kirshenblatt-Gimblett has long pointed out: that heritage is never a given but rather a type of cultural production—an act—that happens in the present and has "recourse" to the past but is not in and of itself the same thing as the past (1995, 369–70). The World Village Festival produces a particular type of Native American heritage—one that is both factually incorrect and perpetuates long-standing settler-colonial patterns that erase and replace Indigenous presence. As theorist Patrick Wolfe points out, this replacement is often a refraction of Indigenous actualities through settler lenses (2006, 389). The "plains Indian" lens, shaped by Hollywood movies, dime novels, and racist mascots, forms one important aspect of what Pauline Strong (2013) calls the "American Imaginary" about Native people. This is how Lakota come to represent "Idaho's Native American heritage" despite the fact that Idaho is in the mountains and the Lakota did not live there.

This kind of replaced heritage production is only possible once the actual stories of the Native people of the Boise Valley are erased. And this erasure is startlingly pervasive. Very, very few settler Boiseans know anything about Boise's history before white settlement. Very few Boiseans can answer: Who lived here, what happened to them, and where are they now?

Told in the conventional settler narrative, Boise's history begins with the discovery of gold in the Boise Valley in 1863.[14] Increasing (violent) settler pressure on Boise bands of mixed Shoshone (*Newe*), Paiute (*Numu*), and Bannock families living in the valley led to the signing of a treaty with the territorial governor that same year. The Treaty of Fort Boise stipulated payment in exchange for the removal of the Boise bands to Fort Hall, 250 miles to the east. The band leaders signed the treaty and agreed to removal, but the treaty was never ratified, and no payment was ever made for the land. After several years of living in terrible conditions (characterized by menial labor, restricted travel, measles, and consumption) at camps in the foothills above Fort Boise and without a ratified treaty, the Boise bands were removed to Fort Hall in 1869. Around 300 Boise Band Shoshone-Paiute, 850 Bruneau Shoshone, and 150 Bannock were marched for over a month into what is now eastern Idaho. The unratified treaty made this case a prime candidate for settlement through the Indian Claims Commission, formed in the 1940s to deal with underpaid and unsettled land claims. However, because the Boise bands were mixed Shoshone, Paiute, and Bannock, the claims commission found that Boise constituted a "Joint-Use Area," and therefore the US government was not responsible for payment for this land seizure. No payment has ever been made for the Boise claim (Wells 1972).

While the obvious injustice of this story of dispossession and loss follows familiar patterns, it is stunning how few people in Boise know *any* of its outlines.[15] And by presenting a "Lakota people drum circle" in place of raising awareness of the removal story, the festival perpetuates settler-colonial patterns of erasure and replacement to fit more cleanly into the American imaginary of what Native cultural production looks like.[16] It signals that the specific histories of the mixed Newe and Numu bands that thrived in the Boise Valley are an irrelevant detail rather than the foundational dispossession that makes all settler life in the valley possible.

One way that representational erasure is practiced, then, is through multicultural heritage production at the World Village Festival that creates a representational trope that White Earth Ojibwe scholar Jean M. O'Brien (2010) calls "firsting" and "lasting." This element of the US American imaginary places Native people first in local histories, but only to the extent that they "give way" to settler modernity. The extinction of authentic Native culture is both produced in settler heritage performance and mourned as an unfortunate necessity on the way to "modern" America (O'Brien 2010).[17] Through this reading, it becomes quite significant that in both 2016 and 2017, "Native American" performers occupied the first slot on the World Village program.

The Production of Alterity

Another way that the World Village Festival promotes representational erasure is through a type of cultural "othering" known as alterity production. *Alterity* comes from the Latin for a type of otherness—specifically the other of two (the alter). Productions of alterity are a form of othering activity that posits an *other* in relation to a *self*—it is the partnering of these two into a dichotomy. Othering creates a fictional inversion of the familiar, such as between the Occident (West) and Orient (East) in the work of Edward Said (1978). This fictional dichotomy is self-serving, producing the discursive superiority of the imperial powers by describing them in contrast to the inferiority of the colonized. In anthropology specifically, alterity has been adopted by Michael Taussig (1993) to refer to the construction of "cultural others" and tied directly to the production of the American imaginary of Native Americans by Strong (2013).

According to cultural theorist Barbara Kirshenblatt-Gimblett, cultural festivals are sites of alterity production that, like ethnography, promise a type of "visual penetration" to the back region of other peoples' lives, essentializing them at play as an image of when they are "most themselves" (Kirshenblatt-Gimblett 1995). These tendencies encourage us to think seriously about what is, at root, a form of cultivated entertainment, carefully considering who benefits from this form of entertainment, in what ways, and at the expense of whom.

For example, during the "Lakota" drum performance in 2016, a group of mainly settler Boiseans got up and began to dance in a circle in the area in front of the stage. Well intentioned or not, this dancing sits dangerously close to a longstanding form of settler alterity production: mimesis. According to Taussig, mimesis is a type of mimicry that represents the enacted production of difference. Following Philip Deloria, it is suggestive of larger American cultural patterns of "playing Indian" through things like mascots, fraternal orders, or children's groups like campfire girls (Strong 2013). The danger of these mimetic processes is that they are embodiments of the American imaginary: none of the participants come out of participation knowing anything more about actual Native lives, priorities, or struggles. Participation in this kind of mimesis only produces a kind of other that reflects back the majority culture for itself (Deloria 1999).

And while alterity production is a peril within the multicultural framework, performers have the agency to enact their own kind of activism, which I (Marshall) call *trickster activism*. According to Anishinaabe literary scholar Gerald Vizenor (1988), the trickster is a comedic figure that can upset settler-colonial structures from within by mocking them rather than directly confronting them.[18] The 2017 performance of one of the drum group organizers—a Lakota man by the name of Dallas Gudgell—is an example of this kind of festival activism. Gudgell has lived in Boise for over two decades and is a well-known local community leader.

In 2017, Gudgell was invited to open the World Village with his drum group and welcome people to the festival. Gudgell showed up without a drum group and, instead, began his performance by saying, "I can't welcome you to this," because his people are not from Boise. In a trickster way, this opening challenged settler "firsting" and "lasting" tropes of Native Americans. But it also challenged the alterity production inherent in firsting/lasting logics that pit American modernity against Indigenous premodernity. Second, Gudgell mentioned the Boise Valley people gathering happening down the road, again emphasizing that local histories are specific, demonstrable, and continue to have relevance in the present. Third, Gudgell talked a little about the Native history of the valley, that it was a "valley of peace" and that "nobody could war here." He mentioned Boise's mixed-band past, saying that it was an area used by many tribes, and described the ways tribes would use the local warm springs for healing, tying specific Native histories to concrete places on the landscape. Thus, he used his platform to perform a bit of education—something out of the frame for festival organizers who aim to celebrate multiculturalism without contextualizing it historically, economically, or politically.

Once he had established this locally specific historical context, Gudgell continued his trickster activism by announcing that instead of singing, he would be telling a Coyote story. Following the typical pattern, Gudgell's Coyote plays a trick on the other animals and ends up getting fooled and looking ridiculous. The Coyote story acts as a metanarrative of the way Gudgell flipped the script on the festival frame. Coyote is the consummate trickster in much Native American lore. So the telling of a Coyote story is clever because it is, of course, an appropriate piece of culture to showcase. Finally, he closed by saying, "They asked me to do a blessing, but I'm not going to do that." And then he commented, a bit offhandedly, "They always ask the Indian guy to do the blessing. Why is that?" Thus, we ended with Gudgell's flat-out refusal to lead a blessing, again refusing to perform as the alter, the spiritual other that blesses the rest. Through trickster activism, Gudgell introduced a critical question into the remainder of the celebratory weekend. He asked the audience to pause and consider, "*Why is that?*" (emphasis added).

Conclusions

Because of broad patterns of representational erasure through settler-colonialism (erase/replace, firsting/lasting, modern/premodern, and other forms of alterity production), producing a multicultural festival is always going to be perilous. But the other peril facing multiculturalism—doing nothing in the face of very real and rising white nationalism—has encouraged us to try to knit our two perspectives on the World Village Festival together. Is it possible that broader awareness of the perils of the multicultural framework in specific, local contexts of our settler-colonial world can help us to better meet the goals of the heterotopic festival? Can interrogating social inequality be incorporated into the celebration somehow? It is never very fun to pair discussions of genocide with music, art, and culture, but refugees came to Idaho for a reason, and Idaho is undeniably founded on Indigenous land dispossession. The World Village Festival is such a diverse mix of things to begin with. So perhaps the establishment of teach-in tents or sites for ally training would not be completely outside the framework of the festival.

Alternately, how can the honed critical edge of academia be used in such a way that it opens rather than completely forecloses possibilities for constructive collaboration—both within festival production and with actual performers on the ground? As Bob McCarl, Idaho's third state folklorist, penned in 1989 when reflecting on the years he had spent helping curate the Smithsonian Folklife Festival: "As my experience grows, my confidence in both the theories and the practice of these presentations falls under greater scrutiny by myself and the people I present. Increasingly, I see my job as providing a forum within which conflicting and often highly emotional issues of personal and community value and power are being worked out. I am much less confident or interested in academic assessments of these dramatizations, and much more interested in the reactions of the tradition-bearers themselves" (McCarl 1989). These words read relevant and true for all of us engaged in cultural production work. It is easy to forget about the level of trust at play and at risk when a performer begins her traditional dance from Veracruz before a live audience of strangers or the trust it takes to buy a plate of food from a vendor whose country you could not locate on a map—or the trust propagated when the threshold between prevailing social order and heterotopia is breached and you feel compelled not only to spend the rest of the day but also to return year after year.

Both of these perspectives take seriously the direct action potential of the festival framework as a type of artistic production that can and should be used to intervene in the received social order. The fostering of a heterotopia through festival models how we might live together differently. Trickster activism models how Indigenous and other festival performers do not just enact multicultural frameworks; they use the microphone and stage to advocate for their communities and their place within the broader Idaho community. Taken together, they model the messy working out of broad-based coalition building necessary to face Idaho's rising divisions. Although diverse in our training and experiences, we agree that the stakes are too high and the peril too great to the actual lives of multicultural performers—and the communities they represent—to freeze in fear of academic critique. Multicultural festivals have room for improvement, but singing, dancing, eating, and shopping together remain important tools for creating space to be human together.

Notes

1. "World Village Festival," accessed September 28, 2023, https://www.globallounge.org/world-village-festival.

2. In 2017, Boise was ranked twelfth in best places to live out of one hundred US metro areas in *US News* and *World Report*.

3. Ruby Ridge was an eleven-day standoff between the Weaver family and the FBI. Randy Weaver was caught in a larger investigation of white supremacist groups for selling shotguns to an undercover agent. Weaver's wife and son were killed in the standoff, as was an FBI agent.

4. For a documentary about the birth of the modern human rights movement in Idaho and successful efforts to evict the Aryan Nations from northern Idaho, see Idaho Public Television, "Color of Conscience," 2011, https://www.idahoptv.org/shows/specials/colorofconscience/.

5. The closest folklife festival is Salt Lake City's Living Traditions Festival (350 miles away), the Montana Folk Festival in Butte (425 miles and a byproduct of the National Folklife Festival), and the Northwest Folklife Festival in Seattle (500 miles away). The Tucson Meet Yourself Festival is just over 1,000 miles (a sixteen-hour car ride) away.

6. The national headlining groups are sponsored and paid for by local booking agent Duck Club Presents, better known for hosting the Treefort Music Festival in Boise each year.

7. Dayo Ayodele and Donna Kovalesk, interview by K. Marshall, July 7, 2018.

8. The festival was not held in 2020 or 2021 due to the COVID-19 pandemic but was held again in June 2022.

9. Alex Jones's *InfoWars* spread the story, promoted on Twitter, under the headline "Idaho Yogurt Maker Caught Importing Migrant Rapists" (Hauser 2017). Chobani (which employs many refugees at its Twin Falls factory) experienced protests and boycotts. A defamation lawsuit by Chobani eventually produced a retraction from Jones.

10. Global Lounge receives annual funding from the Idaho Commission on the Arts, so Hatcher cannot account for hours worked at the festival as part of his duties as the folk arts director at the risk of conflict of interest. However, the two jobs are deeply related.

11. The critique of multiculturalism from an Indigenous perspective has been well articulated by Glen Coulthard's (2007) reading of Hegel's politics of recognition. Couthard (also following Frantz Fanon's critique in *Black Skin, White Masks*) argues that recognition is almost always implemented by colonizers and so will ultimately be used to benefit them.

12. According to Tuck and Yang, settler moves to innocence are "those strategies ... that attempt to relieve the settler of feelings of guilt or responsibility without giving up land or power or privilege" (2012, 10).

13. "World Village Festival," accessed September 28, 2023, https://www.globallounge.org/world-village-festival.

14. Out of respect for the descendants of the Boise Valley people, who are understandably frustrated that non-Natives like me keep telling their stories for them, I have attempted to limit my outline of these events to broad strokes widely available in printed histories. I am not qualified to speak about the personal impacts of removal on generations of Native families.

15. To be absolutely clear, Marshall is a fifth generation Idahoan, grew up in Boise, and did not know any of the outlines of this story either.

16. In fairness to festival organizers, *Newe* and *Numu* people generally live far away from Boise, are very difficult to get a hold of, and are overtaxed by the requests of settler Boiseans for information, speakers, and cultural experts. This distance from Boise and from any kind of reciprocal and interdependent relationship was, in fact, an objective of removal in the first place.

17. Within this post-1950 framing of modernity, multiculturalism plays a large role. See Pfister 2004.

18. Vizenor says of the trickster that he-she is "a comic *holotrope*, an interior landscape 'behind what the discourse says.'" In regard to Native (mis)representation in particular, "the trick, in seven words, is to *elude historicism, racial representations, and remain historical*" (Vizenor 1988, xi).

Bibliography

Alvarez, Maribel. 2021. "Producing Festivals." In *What Folklorists Do: Professional Possibilities in Folklore Studies*, edited by Timothy Lloyd, 156–9. Bloomington: Indiana University Press.

Anderson, Izaak. 2021. "Anti-semitic Graffiti Discovered Near Anne Frank Memorial in Boise." *Idaho News 6*, December 4, 2021. https://www.kivitv.com/news/anti-semitic-graffiti-discovered-near-anne-frank-memorial-under-ninth-street-bridge.

Ayodele, Dayo, and Donna Kovaleski. 2018. Interview with K. Marshall. July 7, 2018.

Camp, Charles, and Timothy Lloyd. 1980. "Six Reasons Not to Produce Folklife Festivals." *Kentucky Folklore Record* 26(1–2): 67–74.

Coulthard, Glen S. 2007. "Subjects of Empire: Indigenous Peoples and the 'Politics of Recognition' in Canada." *Contemporary Political Theory* 6(4): 437–60.

Deloria, Philip J. 1999. *Playing Indian*. New Haven, CT: Yale University Press.

Foucault, Michel, and Jay Miskowiec. 1986. "Of Other Spaces." *Diacritics* 16(1): 22–27.

Goodwin, Shaun. 2022. "Hate Crimes Continue to Trend Upward in Idaho, Particularly Against African Americans." *Idaho Statesman*. February 14, 2022. https://www.idahostatesman.com/news/local/community/boise/article258389958.html.

Gardiner, Dustin, and Mark Olalde. 2019. "These Copycat Bills on Sharia Law and Terrorism Have No Effect. Why Do States Keep Passing Them?" *USA Today*, July 17, 2019.

Hauser, Christine. 2017. "Alex Jones Retracts Chobani Claims to Resolve Lawsuit." *New York Times*, May 17, 2017. https://www.nytimes.com/2017/05/17/us/alex-jones-chobani-lawsuit.html.

Hetherington, Kevin. 2002. *The Badlands of Modernity: Heterotopia and Social Ordering*. New York: Routledge.

Kirshenblatt-Gimblett, Barbara. 1995. "Theorizing Heritage." *Ethnomusicology* 39(3): 367–80.

Marshall, Kimberly Jenkins. 2016. *Upward, Not Sunwise: Resonant Rupture in Navajo Neo-Pentecostalism*. Lincoln: University of Nebraska Press.

Mathias, Christopher. 2022. "Living with the Far-Right Insurgency in Idaho." *Huffpost*, May 17, 2022. https://www.huffpost.com/entry/far-right-idaho_n_628277e2e4b0c84db7282bd6.

McCarl, Robert. 1989. "The Folklorist as Dramatist." In *Time and Temperature: A Centennial Publication of the American Folklore Society*, edited by Charles Camp, 30–31. Washington, DC: American Folklore Society.

NEA Office of Research and Analysis. 2010. *Live from Your Neighborhood: A National Study of Outdoor Arts Festivals*. Washington, DC: National Endowment for the Arts.

O'Brien, Jean M. 2010. *Firsting and Lasting: Writing Indians out of Existence in New England*. Minneapolis: University of Minnesota Press.

Pfister, Joel. 2004. *Individuality Incorporated: Indians and the Multicultural Modern*. Durham, NC: Duke University Press.

Povinelli, Elizabeth. 2002. *The Cunning of Recognition: Indigenous Alterities and the Making of Australian Multiculturalism*. Durham, NC: Duke University Press.

Rose, Andy. 2022. "31 People with Ties to White Nationalist Group Arrested for Conspiracy to Riot Near a Pride Parade in Idaho." *CNN*, June 13, 2022. https://www.cnn.com/2022/06/11/us/31-people-arrested-for-conspiracy-to-riot-near-idaho-pride-parade/index.html.

Said, Edward. 1978. *Orientalism*. New York: Pantheon Books.

Singer, Milton B. 1972. *When a Great Tradition Modernizes: An Anthropological Approach to Indian Civilization*. New York: Praeger.

Strong, Pauline Turner. 2013. *American Indians and the American Imaginary: Cultural Representation Across the Centuries*. Boulder, CO: Paradigm Press.

Taussig, Michael. 1993. *Mimesis and Alterity: A Particular History of the Senses*. New York: Routledge.

Toelken, Barre. 1996. *The Dynamics of Folklore*. Logan: Utah State University Press.

Tuck, Eve, and K. Wayne Yang. 2012. "Decolonization Is Not a Metaphor." *Decolonization: Indigeneity, Education & Society* 1(1): 1–40.

Turner, Victor. 1969. *The Ritual Process: Structure and Anti-structure.* Chicago: Aldine.
van den Berg, Karen, Cara M. Jordan, and Philipp Kleinmichel, eds. 2019. *The Art of Direct Action: Social Sculpture and Beyond.* Berlin: Sternberg Press.
Vaugeois, Lise. 2007. "Social Justice and Music Education: Claiming the Space of Music Education as a Site of Postcolonial Contestation." *Action, Criticism, and Theory for Music Education* 6(4): 163–200.
Vizenor, Gerald. 1988. *The Trickster of Liberty: Tribal Heirs to a Wild Baronage.* Minneapolis: University of Minnesota Press.
Wells, Merle. 1972. *The Boise Claim.* Idaho State Historical Society Reference Series. Boise: Idaho State Historical Society.
Wilks, Linda, and Bernadette Quinn. 2016. "Linking Social Capital, Cultural Capital and Heterotopia at the Folk Festival." *Journal of Comparative Research in Anthropology and Sociology* 7(1): 23–39.
Wolfe, Patrick. 2006. "Settler Colonialism and the Elimination of the Native." *Journal of Genocide Research* 8(4): 388.

Afterword

The Work That Music Festivals Do

ERIC FILLION AND AJAY HEBLE

In "Ally: From Noun to Verb," a conversation between historian Robin D. G. Kelley and pianist and scholar Vijay Iyer published in the *Boston Review*, the latter recalls San Francisco's Asian American Jazz Festival, where he had some of his first gigs as a leader. Referencing one such gig, Iyer remembers, "It was a pan-ethnic kind of thing, based in the idea that we could somehow find a common cause. We could do something together, we could ally around something." Riffing on a range of topics related to the responsibility of artists, Iyer explains to Kelley that he takes his cue from Martin Luther King Jr., who, in 1957, asked a most urgent question: "What are you doing for others?" "That's the question I pose to myself in every context," Iyer explains in relation to his work in the classroom and on stage. "You want to actually open a conversation and activate people's imaginations, and allow them to imagine a different world than the one we're in. And that's the kind of work that an artist can do." He continues, "We're there to stir something up, and also to offer an alternative to the reality that we're inhabiting" (Kelley and Iyer 2019).

 Activating people's imaginations.
 Stirring things up.
 Enacting alternatives to the reality that we inhabit.

In the summer and fall of 2022, we staged a two-part international conference—"Curating for Change: The Work That Music Festivals Do in the World"—that, in its own way, opened up a similar set of conversations with a range of participants operating across the boundaries between academia and the broader cultural sector. Instead of focusing on "the kind of work that an artist can do," our conference, as the subtitle suggests, set out to examine the work that music festivals do in the world. Exploring these events as resonant —if at times contested—sites of activism, equity, environmental stewardship, pedagogical intervention, and community building, "Curating for Change" called attention to a particular vision of curatorial practice as a vital source for social change. With an eye and an ear on the histories and futures of music festivals, we encouraged consideration of how these events function in our communities, how they can stir things up—and with what impact.[1]

As we were preparing for the conference, we were excited to receive a message from the coeditors of this volume. Noting our shared research interests in festivals as strategic forms of social action, they invited us to consider possible ways in which we might collaborate. Think of this afterword as a first step in such a collaboration. Think of it, too, as part of a larger effort to participate in an ongoing conversation about the role festivals have played, play, and will continue to play in activating diverse energies of creativity, awareness, care, and inspiration. Think of it as a prompt for continuing intersectional and dialogical exchanges that reflect a shared commitment to principles of social justice, inclusive engagement, and what the coeditors of *Festival Activism* refer to as the "agential world-making capacities of festival practice" (p. 21).

As the case studies in this volume make clear, music festivals inhabit the cultural landscape of the communities in which they take place (and impact the communities that receive them) in varied and complex ways. It is important to note that not all (or even most) festivals function as sites of activist intervention—it might be difficult, for example, to imagine large-scale, corporate-run initiatives engaging in anything akin to a sustained critique of dominant systems of power and privilege. There is, however an illustrious history of events from around the globe serving as catalysts for political engagement, inspirations for resistant practice, and powerful agents of social change. From celebrated gatherings such as the music-filled Pan-African Cultural Festival held in Algiers in 1969 to today's Accra-based Kwame Nkrumah Pan-African Intellectual Cultural Festival, from the Monterey International Pop Festival of 1967 (a precursor to the rock charities of the 1980s) to the more recent Amsterdam-based DGTL Festival (an eco-friendly celebration of electronic music) and New York's Vision Festival (an artist-run festival of avant-garde jazz and free improvisation that frames its curatorial practices in explicitly activist terms), there is no shortage of examples of music and arts-based festivals that have strategically sought to mobilize resources in an effort to ally around something, to find common cause, and to imagine—and, indeed, to enact—a better world.

We write this afterword from our position as musicians, scholars, event curators, activists, and festivalgoers. We also write from our position north of the United States–Canada border, mindful of our collective responsibility to confront the legacies of settler-colonialism and engage in allyship with the Indigenous peoples on whose traditional territories we reside. Attuned to the potentialities of festivals as "crucial instruments of political transformation... as structural forms manifest in the participatory, pleasurable, enactment of a desired future" (p. 21), to echo this volume's coeditors, we consider it important to reflect on continuums between past and present as well as present and future. In our work and practice, we draw inspiration from the energy, spirit, and agency demonstrated in the alternative institution-building strategies of community-based, independent, artist-run, or what have sometimes been called boutique music festivals.[2] *Festival Activism* discusses many such festivals as well as others that have expanded in surprising ways while traveling from one locale to another—the various iterations of Ladyfest (Barrière) and WOMAD (Nissen) come to mind. Among the key resources and tactics of intervention discussed in these chapters and elsewhere in the book, *assembly* and *deliberation* strike us as particularly valuable for thinking about two moments in the making of Canada's festivalscape: the 1975 edition of the Mariposa Folk Festival, held on Toronto's Centre Island, and IF 2020, the inaugural edition of a worldwide festival of improvised music and arts launched online during the pandemic and hosted by the International Institute for Critical Studies in Improvisation (IICSI) in Guelph.

One of the longest-running folk festivals in North America today, Mariposa was founded in Orillia in 1961 by Ruth Jones-McVeigh, a frequent visitor to Toronto's bohemian Yorkville neighborhood and champion of the folk music revival in Canada. A victim of its success and of rowdy youth, the festival was forced to relocate after its third edition. Itinerant for a few years, it settled in 1968 on Centre Island, a short ferry ride from downtown Toronto. At a time when the music industry and broader cultural sector were dominated by men, Mariposa was a noteworthy initiative. The brainchild of Jones-McVeigh, the event blossomed in the early to mid-1970s in the hands of two equally accomplished women: Estelle Klein (a cultural worker who became a folk music enthusiast after attending a leftist, secular Jewish children's camp on the outskirts of Toronto) and Alanis Obomsawin (an Abenaki singer-activist and, later, documentary filmmaker who spent parts of her childhood on the Odanak Reserve, near Montreal). Mariposa was by then known for its egalitarian ethos and audience engagement through participation, discussion, and demonstration workshops. The festival's yearly schedule began to reflect a more internationalist orientation thanks to Klein's efforts as artistic director, and it prominently featured a program of Indigenous artists, which Obomsawin carefully curated, starting in 1970.[3] As Klein explained to attendees in 1975, "Knowing how things in folk 'connect' with each other has become an increasingly important programming factor at Mariposa." "For some of you, this idea of 'connection' will be communicated in an unconscious sort of way," she noted, adding that others will "want to consciously pick up the threads and weave the cloth in their own minds" (1975, 9). With Obomsawin and her other colleagues, Klein evidently sought to stir things up, to activate people's imagination, and to enact other possible futures.

The edition that best encapsulated that project was arguably the one from 1975. Intended as a celebration of the United Nations' proclamation of 1975 as the International Women's Year, the festival included more female performers than in previous years. Two workshops stood out in the program. The first, "Bread and Roses," took its name from a 1912 Industrial Workers of the World strike that saw Massachusetts workers, many of them women from different diasporas, unite to demand better salaries and working conditions. It was about "women and industry," which all the participants—musicians and nonmusicians alike—understood as also meaning "working mothers" ("Bread and Roses" 1975). The second, "Strong Women: Purpose and Protest," riffed on a prompt from "The Tendrils of the Vine," a 1905 poem by French writer Sidonie-Gabrielle Colette, which muses on the meanings of liberation and the difficulties of freedom. That the festival took place from June 20 to 22, while delegates from around the world gathered in Mexico City to launch the first World Conference on Women, might have been coincidence, but it nonetheless gave those who had assembled on Centre Island a sense of momentum. It gave their deliberation added urgency and hope. At play here was an "active process of recombination," to borrow from Ron Eyerman and Andrew Jamison (1998, 22), one that cut across both time and place and aligned with Klein's desire to see the festival foster connections and inspire new forms of solidarity amid efforts—notably in Canada—to make headway on women's rights issues.[4]

Through assembly, as this volume's coeditors pertinently note, "festival participants embody a kind of coalitional politics and activist potential" (p. 7).

This process was apparent at Mariposa, where organizers, artists, and festivalgoers deliberatively gestured toward alternative models of knowledge generation—allyship too. Take, for example, "Strong Women: Purpose and Protest," which brought together Rosalie Sorrels, an Idaho-born folklorist and single mother who spent the greater part of the early 1970s on the road with her five children; old-time North Carolinian singer and banjo player Ola Belle Reed; Sarah Ogan Gunning, a folk singer born in a Kentucky coal-mining family who made a name for herself recording for Alan Lomax in 1930s New York; African American activist Bernice Johnson Reagon with her a cappella ensemble Sweet Honey in the Rock; and Mariposa's own Alanis Obomsawin. They were an eclectic group, but they came together around issues they and the audience cared about. Taking her cue from Sorrels's reading of "The Tendrils of the Vine," Gunning spoke of—and sang about—the importance of labor militancy but also family and religion in surviving poverty. Obomsawin then broke into a song, "Bush Lady,"[5] which moved the conversation to questions of anti-Indigenous racism, mobility, and decolonization. Sweet Honey in the Rock joined in with a moving rendition of "Joan Little," a song of support for an imprisoned African American woman who had ten months earlier killed a prison guard to keep him from sexually assaulting her. Everyone there, including Reed, who self-identified as a "free spirit," listened with empathy, learning from each other and sharing stories of resilience. The songs they sang in unison—or clapped along to—were an invitation to cultivate their capacity for togetherness. If Sweet Honey in the Rock's "A Woman" energized those in attendance, the vibrant applause that punctuated Reed's "Only the Leading Part Will Do" best captured the transnational and transgenerational resolve that bound the group together that summer ("Strong Women: Purpose and Protest" 1975).[6]

Efforts to cultivate togetherness through assembly and deliberation also informed the inaugural edition of IF 2020, an improvisation festival launched during the COVID-19 pandemic by the team at IICSI (which included one of the authors of this afterword).[7] Featuring over 150 artists from around the globe, this twenty-four-hour online festival, live streamed in real time, connected disparate communities and sought to showcase the power of improvised art and music during a time of crisis. Taking place at the end of a summer during which practically all music festivals, concerts, and gatherings around the world had been canceled, IF 2020 put forth alternative ways of being together and collaborating at a time when we were unable to assemble in face-to-face settings. Based, in part, on the all-night "Nuit Blanche" model in which artists are commissioned to present multimedia works in public spaces across a city (see Marchessault and Nagam 2022) and inspired by the ways in which communities around the world were maintaining social connection through the power and inspiration of music and art, the festival sought to curate and present spontaneous moments of artistic intervention within a shared digital environment. Recognizing the ways in which the pandemic had made it clear to us that human connection is vital to our well-being and feeling the heartache of a summer without live music, organizers saw an opportunity to use the online festival as an alternative way to assemble.

IF 2020 was not, however, a mere substitute for in-person festivals that were forced to cancel or pivot that summer. It featured a wide range of highly acclaimed improvising musicians—such as William Parker (United States), Satoko Fujii (Japan), Sandy Evans (Australia), and Evan Parker (United Kingdom)—and was presented with the support of partnering organizations in Canada, Greece, Norway, Mexico, the United States, Wales, Northern Ireland, and Singapore. It was watched by people from fifty-one countries, making for a truly global affair. The live stream also significantly featured a live chat staffed for the full twenty-four hours by the IF team. The importance of this component cannot be overstated. As arts presenter Christos Carras and philosopher Eric Lewis point out in a coauthored essay on arts making published during the COVID-19 crisis, chatroom features played "a crucial role in pandemic performance, helping build connections between artists and audiences, and create spatially dispersed communities of the type that live performances cannot." They continue: "A spatially distanced and isolated fan of a particular performer can now 'attend' a performance wherever they may be and interact with the performer and other fans. One often gets to see performers in their living rooms and gain a sense of intimacy and familiarity different from that of staged live performances. If you follow the chatroom feeds during performances you often discover that they supply background information about the performances, advertise future performances, and introduce individual fans to each other—you can witness community-in-formation" (2021, 35). A core component of the IF 2020 experience, the live chat made it indeed possible for the participants assembled to forge a vibrant and powerful sense of community and even to transcend some of the limits associated with in-person festivals.

The community-in-formation experience that we witnessed during IF 2020 compels us, as with our discussion above of Mariposa, to think more about the activist potential of music festivals. As we reflect, we are reminded of the work of the artist and community-based educator Deborah Barndt. In *Wild*

Fire: Art as Activism, she questions—as, we suggest, do the contributors to this volume—"a narrow understanding of activism that frames mass protests as the primary mode of political action." Although Barndt is not writing specifically about music festivals, her words about activism seem pertinent to our argument here. "How we think, converse, write, draw, sing, move," she writes, "can unveil power relations and transform knowledge production and everyday actions" (Barndt 2006, 15). "In challenging narrow definitions of art and activism," Barndt continues, "we reframe art *as* activism. Whether the modes are verbal or non-verbal, artmaking that ignites people's creativity, recovers repressed histories, builds community, and strengthens social movements is in itself a holistic form of action" (18). Together, the chapters that comprise *Festival Activism*—many of which deploy resonant concepts such as *sentipensante* (Gubner), dissensus (Bonini Baraldi), acessibilifolia (Snyder), alter-politics (McDonald), and heterotopia (Marshall and Hatcher)—make a similar argument. Music festivals, we contend, can amplify or act as catalysts for such art making.

The need to recover repressed histories, build community, and strengthen social movements proved to be an important focus at IF 2023, the fourth iteration of IICSI's improvisation festival, organized as a hybrid (in-person and live-streamed) event.[8] This focus was particularly apparent in a moving performance by Mali Obomsawin and her quartet on Saturday, October 21.[9] A community activist dedicated to land justice and tribal sovereignty, the Indigenous bassist performed material from her stunning debut album *Sweet Tooth*. Drawing on field recordings of Abenaki songs and stories she discovered at Dartmouth College in New Hampshire, Mali Obomsawin, as a review in *The Guardian* puts it, repatriated some of this archival material "into a suite of resistance" (Rogers 2022).[10] In taking this music onto a festival stage, she engaged the work that Alanis Obomsawin—a relative with whom she shares a connection to the Odanak First Nation community—began decades earlier. Alanis Obomsawin first performed at Mariposa in 1967, an experience that led her to curate the festival's Native People's Area from 1970 to 1976.[11] The following year saw her involved in organizing and documenting a multiday festival in support of Cree First Nations around James Bay, where state-funded plans for the expansion of hydroelectric dams were underway. Staged in Montreal, the event was—in the words of Alanis Obomsawin—the first time that "people [in the city] became aware of the strength and richness of our culture and [that] we became aware of the unity of our people" (Obomsawin 1977b). At IF 2023, an equally inspiring form of sound commitment could be heard in the music of Mali Obomsawin and her quartet. The group was stirring things up, enacting their own vision of coalitional politics while inviting the audience to listen otherwise.

Incidentally, Mali Obomsawin's performance with her quartet was preceded earlier that day by a stimulating dialogue between the saxophonist and scholar Hafez Modirzadeh and Vijay Iyer, with whom we opened this afterword. Presented as part of IICSI's Big Ideas in Improvisation series,[12] their conversation focused for the most part on cultural stewardship and the constraints institutional thinking places on creative imagining. Inevitably, it eventually circled back to a question Iyer had explored as part of his *Boston Review* exchange with Kelley: What is the work an artist can do? An artist is someone who "synthesizes truths from different places," he remarked with deep conviction (Iyer and Modirzadeh 2023). That he deliberated that point among those who had assembled in person and online for IF 2023—a festival that, like Mariposa, sought to make meaning and build something new out of momentous conjunctures—gave it added resonance. Iyer and Modirzadeh returned and took the stage that same evening to improvise together and continue to sound the audience, so to speak. Mali Obomsawin and her quartet had just finished their brilliant set. The fact that these performances followed each other, bringing IF 2023 to a vibrant close, is, we suggest, more than simply coincidental. If we take into account the vital role played by the narrative arc of any festival lineup; the movement of artists and audiences from one act to the next; the beginnings, middles, and endings that form a crucial part of any curatorial vision; and the overlapping—and often unexpected—histories, narratives, and communities activated through these moments of encounter, we recognize just how much the sequencing of events at a festival can be understood as a powerful source of intervention, itself a way of synthesizing truths from different places—a world-making intervention—or, to put it differently, another instance of much-needed festival activism.

Notes

1. For details about the conference program and related resources, visit https://www.whatmusicfestivalsdo.ca/ (accessed March 15, 2024).

2. As Roxy Robinson explains, boutique events, in offering "alternatives to lineup centric festivals," constitute "a counter-trend to the exorbitant commercialism" that characterizes much of today's festivalscape (2015, 67, 167–8). We note, however, that the boutique model has its own dissenters, some of whom decry that "many of these festivals seem tailored to a certain kind of middle-class lifestyle, to which music is merely the soundtrack" (Wray 2023).

3. See Michael Hill (2017) and Sija Tsai (2013) for general histories of the Mariposa Folk Festival.

4. In 1970, the Royal Commission on the Status of Women in Canada tabled a report that listed 167 recommendations to address gender-based inequality and discrimination, prompting widespread grassroots efforts—from the early to mid-1970s and beyond—to do more, faster across all sectors of society.

5. This was an early version of a song that would appear on Alanis Obomsawin's 1988 album *Bush Lady*, reissued thirty years later by Constellation Records (2018).

6. Unless stated otherwise, all quotes and details about "Strong Women: Purpose and Protest" are from the recording of the workshop. Note that excerpts from Alanis Obomsawin's contributions also appear in *"For What Time I Am in This World": Stories from Mariposa* (1977, 71).

7. For details about the artists who presented their work during IF 2020, visit https://improvfest.ca/archive/if2020-archive/ (accessed March 15, 2024).

8. For details about IF 2023's hybrid programming, see https://online.anyflip.com/zkzcm/dqls/mobile/index.html (accessed March 15, 2024).

9. At IF 2023, Mali Obomsawin performed with Magdalena Abrego, Allison Burik, and Mili Hong.

10. The liner notes for *Sweet Tooth* explain that the ballad "Odana" (The Village) is "likely as old as the early 1700s"; it is meant as "an homage to the Abenaki reservation in Quebec, Odanak," a community founded by Mali Obomsawin's "Sokoki and Abenaki ancestors in 1660." The artist had heard Alanis Obomsawin sing the ballad and decided to revisit it for her debut album (2022).

11. Alanis Obomsawin cocurated the 1970 edition with Mildred Ryerson ("Native People's Festival Widens Craft Area at Mariposa" 1970).

12. Big Ideas in Improvisation is an ongoing series presented by IICSI in partnership with Musagetes. The series aims to showcase provocative artists and thinkers in a public forum where they share insights and ideas about the force and urgency of improvisational practices.

Bibliography

Barndt, Deborah. 2006. *Wild Fire: Art as Activism*. Toronto: Sumach Press.

"Bread and Roses." 1975. Tape recording. Mariposa Folk Foundation Fonds, 2007-009. York University Clara Thomas Archives and Special Collections.

Carras, Christos, and Eric Lewis. 2021. "'A Gateway between One World and the Next': Performance-Based Arts in Covid Times." In *Pandemic Societies*, edited by Jean-Louis Denis, Catherine Régis, and Daniel Weinstock, with the collaboration of Clara Champagne, 30–53. Montreal: McGill-Queen's University Press.

Eyerman, Ron, and Andrew Jamison. 1998. *Music and Social Movements: Mobilizing Traditions in the Twentieth Century*. Cambridge: Cambridge University Press.

Hill, Michael. 2017. *The Mariposa Folk Festival: A History.* Toronto: Dundurn Press.

Iyer, Vijay, and Hafez Modirzadeh. 2023. "Big Ideas in Improvisation 2023: Vijay Iyer and Hafez Modirzadeh in Conversation." International Institute for Critical Studies in Improvisation, October 21, 2023. https://improvisationinstitute.ca/document/big-ideas-in-improvisation-2023-vijay-iyer-and-hafez-modirzadeh-in-conversation/.

Kelley, Robin D. G., and Vijay Iyer. 2019. "Ally: From Noun to Verb." *Boston Review*, December 2, 2019. https://www.bostonreview.net/articles/robin-d-g-kelley-ally-noun-verb/.

Klein, Estelle. 1975. "Mariposa: An Introduction." In *Mariposa '75*, souvenir program, 9. Mariposa Folk Foundation Fonds, 2007-009. York University Clara Thomas Archives and Special Collections.

Marchessault, Janine, and Julie Nagam, eds. 2022. *Holding Ground: Nuit Blanche and Other Ruptures.* Waterloo, ON: Wilfrid Laurier University Press.

"Native People's Festival Widens Craft Area at Mariposa." 1970. In *Mariposa Folk Festival*, souvenir program, 22–23. Mariposa Folk Foundation Fonds, 2007-009. York University Clara Thomas Archives and Special Collections.

Obomsawin, Alanis. 1977a. "Alanis Obomsawin." In *"For What Time I Am in This World": Stories from Mariposa*, edited by Bill Usher and Linda Page-Harpa, 71. Toronto: P. Martin.

Obomsawin, Alanis, dir. 1977b. *Amisk.* Montreal: National Film Board of Canada. https://www.nfb.ca/film/amisk/.

Obomsawin, Alanis. 2018. *Bush Lady.* Montreal: Constellation Records, CST 133. LP.

Obomsawin, Mali. 2022. *Sweet Tooth.* Richmond, VA: Out of Your Head Records, OOYH017. CD.

Robinson, Roxy. 2015. *Music Festivals and the Politics of Participation.* London: Routledge.

Rogers, Jude. 2022. "Mali Obomsawin: *Sweet Tooth* Review—Proud, Vital Marriage of Folk and Far-Out Jazz Improv." *The Guardian*, November 18, 2022. https://www.theguardian.com/music/2022/nov/18/mali-obomsawin-sweet-tooth-review.

"Strong Women: Purpose and Protest." 1975. Tape recording. Mariposa Folk Foundation Fonds, 2007-009. York University Clara Thomas Archives and Special Collections.

Tsai, Sija. 2013. "Mariposa Folk Festival: The Sounds, Sights, and Costs of a Fifty-Year Road Trip." PhD diss., York University.

Wray, Daniel Dylan. 2023. "Festivals Now Feel Like a Cross between a Spa and a Gastropub—What about the Music?" *The Guardian*, June 6, 2023. https://www.theguardian.com/culture/2023/jun/06/festivals-now-feel-like-a-cross-between-a-spa-and-a-gastropub-what-about-the-music.

CONTRIBUTORS

Oladele Ayorinde is Research Fellow at the Africa Open Institute for Music, Research, and Innovation, Faculty of Arts and Social Sciences, Stellenbosch University, South Africa. He has held teaching and research positions at Tübingen University and the University of Bonn in Germany; Indiana University Bloomington in the United States; the University of the Witwatersrand and Stellenbosch University in South Africa; and Mountain Top University in Nigeria. Oladele's research, located primarily in South Africa and Nigeria, explores the intersections of music/sound, politics, technology, economy, environment, and the daily experiences of African/Black people in Africa and across Black diasporic communities. He has published in reputable academic journals including *Ethnomusicology Forum*, *Jazz and Culture*, *South African Music Studies* (SAMUS), *Leeds African Studies Bulletin*, and *Musik & Ästhetik*. Oladele's work promotes social justice, public-facing work, music industry practices, community outreach/advocacy, and the empowerment of marginalized people.

Louise Barrière is Associate Professor of Cultural Policy at Aix-Marseille Université. In 2022, she defended a PhD thesis titled "If You Feel Like a Lady... Feminist Mediations of DIY Music in a Globalized Scene." She has published several articles on the French and German Ladyfest networks. More broadly, her research focuses on the fight for equality in cultural industries. She is an editorial board member of *Volume! The French Journal for Popular Music Studies* and the French reviews editor of *MUSICultures*.

Filippo Bonini Baraldi is Principal Researcher at the Instituto de Etnomusicologia—Centro de Estudos em Música e Dança at the Universidade NOVA de Lisboa, where he leads the research group Ethnomusicology and Popular Music Studies. He is author of *Roma Music and Emotion*, which was awarded the William A. Douglass Prize in Europeanist Anthropology by the Society for the Anthropology of Europe.

Eric Fillion is Director of the International Institute for Critical Studies in Improvisation and Assistant Professor at the School of Languages and Literatures at the University of Guelph. He is author of *JAZZ LIBRE et la révolution québécoise: Musique-action, 1967–1975* and *Distant Stage: Quebec, Brazil, and the Making of Canada's Cultural Diplomacy*. He is editor of *Statesman of the Piano: Jazz, Race, and History in the Life of Lou Hooper* (with Sean Mills and Désirée Rochat) and *Ripple Effects: The Active Histories and Possible Futures of Music Festivals* (with Ajay Heble).

Jennie Gubner is a socially engaged scholar, violinist, and visual ethnographer with a PhD from the UCLA Department of Ethnomusicology. She works at the University of Arizona as Assistant Professor of Music and Chair of a Graduate Interdisciplinary Program in Applied Intercultural Arts Research. Her research specializations include Latin American popular music with a focus on the politics and poetics of intergenerational tango music scenes in Buenos Aires, creative and applied approaches to the study of music and dementia and aging, and ethnomusicological filmmaking.

Deonte L. Harris is Assistant Professor of Musicology at the University of North Carolina at Chapel Hill. His research interests include global Black studies, African diasporic music studies, critical race studies, and the anthropological study of value. Harris is currently working on a book project on music, race, and value in the African diaspora, which focuses on the cultural production of London's Caribbean carnival arts scene and its value, meaning, and significance among Black Caribbean Britons.

Steven Hatcher is State Folklorist and Director of the Folk and Traditional Arts Program at the Idaho Commission on the Arts. A public sector folklorist with twenty-two years of experience, he spent a decade living in four countries and on as many continents. Overseas, his experience focused on the educational side of public folklore through contract positions awarded by the state department and as an expatriate hired in the local economy. At the Idaho Commission on the Arts, Steven documents, supports, and celebrates the folklife of Idaho through public programs and grant funding.

Ajay Heble is Professor Emeritus at the School of English and Theatre Studies at the University of Guelph. He was founding Director of the International Institute for Critical Studies in Improvisation (IICSI) and founding Artistic Director of IICSI's Improvisation Festival. His research has covered a range of topics in the arts and humanities and has resulted in sixteen books and numerous articles and chapters. He was founding Artistic Director of the award-winning Guelph Jazz Festival and Colloquium and is a founding coeditor of the peer-reviewed journal *Critical Studies in Improvisation/Études critiques en improvisation* (www.criticalimprov.com). He is editor of *Ripple Effects: The Active Histories and Possible Futures of Music Festivals* (with Eric Fillion).

Serene Huleileh is a cultural activist, dancer, musician, writer, editor, and translator active in the cultural and community education scenes in both Palestine and Jordan since 1990. She was an active member of El Funoon dance troupe in its founding years, and, from 1990 to 1998, she worked with the Tamer Institute for Community Education in Palestine. In her capacity as cultural manager, she organized and coordinated several cultural festivals and events in Palestine and Jordan, both as a volunteer and on a consultancy basis, as of 1992. From 2000 to 2020, she was the regional director of the Arab Education Forum. She cofounded and serves on the board of the Arab Education Forum, al-Balad Theater, and Bayt al Nai in Jordan, as well as serving on the general assembly of El Funoon dance group. She has translated and authored several books and articles on culture, art, and education.

Kimberly J. Marshall is Associate Professor of Anthropology and Faculty Director of the Arts & Humanities Forum at the University of Oklahoma. An anthropologist of religion and expressive culture with a specialization in Native North America, she is author of *Upward, Not Sunwise: Resonant Rupture in Navajo Neo-Pentecostalism*. Her work has been supported by the National Endowment for the Humanities and the Wenner-Gren Foundation, and her current project focuses on the contemporary erasure of Native people from the Great Basin with a focus on the public humanities and cultural infrastructure in Idaho.

David A. McDonald is Associate Professor of Folklore and Ethnomusicology at Indiana University Bloomington. Since 2002, he has worked closely with Palestinian refugee communities in Israel, Jordan, the West Bank, and North America. While trained in ethnomusicology, he has published widely on Palestinian popular culture, focusing specifically on the dynamics of trauma, violence, exile, and media. He is author of *My Voice Is My Weapon: Music, Nationalism, and the Poetics of Palestinian Resistance*. He is an editor of *Palestinian Music and Song: Expression and Resistance since 1900* (IUP, 2013) and *At the Crossroads of Music and Social Justice* (IUP, 2023).

Ruthie Meadows is Associate Professor of Ethnomusicology at the University of Nevada, Reno. Her research focuses on music and sound in Cuba and the Spanish-speaking Caribbean, with special attention to gendered and sexual subjectivities, ritual and popular music, jazz, and ecology. Recipient of the Society for Ethnomusicology's Jaap Kunst Prize (2021), her first book, *Efficacy of Sound: Power, Potency, and Promise in the Translocal Ritual Music of Cuban Ifá-Òrìṣà*, explores music and sound in the Nigerian-style Ifá-Òrìṣà ritual movement in Cuba.

Miguel Moniz is an anthropologist and Research Fellow at the Instituto de Ciências Sociais at the Universidade de Lisboa. His publications on the cultural and political role of associations and associativism include explorations of alternative brass bands in Portugal. Other research includes anthropological and historical studies on state policy and progressive activist movements, cultural diplomacy and the Estado Novo propaganda apparatus, the racialization of labor, and immigrant place-making processes.

James Nissen is a British Academy Postdoctoral Fellow at the University of Sheffield. He completed his PhD at the University of Manchester, and his work focuses on music festivals, multiculturalism, the music industry, gender, and music education. He is a founding and executive member of the ICTMD Study Group on Music, Education and Social Inclusion. As a musician, he is a member of the Manchester-based Migrant Voices collective and the transnational Yiddish Café group.

Jeremy Reed received his PhD in ethnomusicology at Indiana University Bloomington. His dissertation explores Jordanian festivals as sites of cultural and political performance. The fieldwork period that produced his chapter was funded by a Fulbright IIE grant in 2018–2019. During that time, he volunteered as a programming assistant with al-Balad Theater and as stage manager for the Jerash Festival of Culture and Arts.

Andrew Snyder is Research Fellow in the Ethnomusicology Institute—Center for Studies in Music and Dance at NOVA University Lisbon in Portugal. He is author of *Critical Brass: Street Carnival and Musical Activism in Olympic Rio de Janeiro* and *Postcolonial Intimacy: Brazilian Music and Carnival in Portugal* (forthcoming). He is an editor of the *Journal of Festive Studies*, *HONK! A Street Band Renaissance of Music and Activism*, and *At the Crossroads: Music and Social Justice* (2023). He is also a trumpeter and guitarist who plays a wide variety of popular music styles.

INDEX

Aachen, 106, 107, 112, 117n5
Abenaki (indigenous people), 303, 307, 309n10
ableism, 13, 20, 77, 79, 89, 94–95, 97n21, 98
Abu-Khafajah, Shatha, 145, 156, 157, 162
Abu Kwaik, Tareq, 157, 162n10
accessibilifolia, 76, 83, 94, 307, 98
access(ibility), 76, 77, 78, 80, 81, 82, 84, 85, 86, 91, 92, 93, 94, 95, 96n2, 96n5, 97n14, 97n20, 99, 101, 152, 204, 234, 241, 243, 255, 256, 268, 282; attitudinal accessibility, 89; culture of, 13, 75, 88
accommodation, 78, 89, 250
Accra, Ghana, 248, 249, 252, 302, 257
activism, 1, 2; academic activism, 256; trickster activism, 290, 291, 294, 295, 296, 298n18
activist coordination, 17, 204, 207, 209
aesthetics, 15, 70, 106, 126, 138, 139, 140, 145, 199, 200, 212, 213, 249, 257
Afonso, Jose "Zeca" (Portuguese singer-songwriter), 173, 174, 175, 182, 183
African American, 116, 251, 305, 298
African diaspora(s), 20, 30, 31, 32, 33, 34, 44, 47, 48, 49, 50, 51, 114, 185, 215, 224, 236, 238, 249, 304, 313
Afropolitanism, 202, 213
agency, 5, 18, 39, 40, 167, 177, 193, 200, 202, 212, 235, 243, 245, 276, 294, 303
Alarcón, Alexis, 217, 218, 221, 222, 234, 236, 236n2, 237

ala(s) (sections of carnival parade groups), 85, 86
alienation, 147, 161, 168, 207
Allen, Erin, 22n2, 23, 80, 92, 99, 177, 187, 214
Almagro (Buenos Aires neighborhood), 129, 136, 137, 138, 142n9
alterity, 291, 299; production of, 293, 294, 295
alter-politics, 275, 307
Alvarez, Maribel (folklorist), 288, 289
Alves, Camila, 13, 76, 77, 84, 85, 86, 89, 90, 94, 95, 96n5
"American imaginary," 292, 293, 294
Amireh, Mohammad, 149
Amman, 15, 16, 144–145, 146, 147, 148, 149, 150, 151, 152, 154, 155, 156, 157, 158, 159, 160, 161, 161n6
Añá (consecrated drums), 228, 232, 233, 236n6
Ansell, Gwen, 244, 246
Anyaa Arts Quartet (Ghanain musical ensemble), 248, 249, 250, 252
apartheid, 193, 195, 240, 241, 243, 244–245, 246, 248, 256, 256n1
appearance, 6, 11, 17, 89, 150, 159, 268, 269, 274, 276, 277; as a "political effect of assembly," 8; politics of, 9
Arab Education Forum, 154, 155, 163
Araújo, Samuel (ethnomusicologist), 243, 252, 255, 257
Archer, Gerry, 30–31
Arendt, Hannah, 22, 275, 278

317

INDEX

Argentina, 6, 125, 130, 135, 141n2, 142
Armstrong, Piers, 31, 50
Arnaud, Lionel, 30, 49
Artaud, Antonin, 55, 58
artivism, 4
Artists United Against Apartheid, 193, 195
Asfour, Raed, 144, 150, 153
assembly, 1, 2, 6, 9, 11, 17, 22, 191, 224, 264, 265, 268, 269, 271, 277, 303, 304, 305; as an "act of sovereignty," 8
"assexybilidade," 86, 87
"associativism," 165, 166, 177, 179, 180, 186, 187
audibility, 11, 29, 159
Auslander, Philip, 103, 108
authoritarian(ism), 21, 171, 172, 264
Avenida da Liberdade, 165, 181, 182

babaláwo (male Santeria priests), 215, 228, 231–232, 233
baile (Brazilian dance concert), 109, 112, 125
Bakhtin, Mikhail, 3, 31, 78, 108, 193
Baladk Street and Urban Arts Festival, 145, 147, 150–154, 156, 158, 159, 160, 161
al-Balad Music Festival, 145, 146, 147, 156, 157–158, 159, 161
al-Balad Theater, 15–16, 144, 145, 146, 147, 148, 149–150, 151, 152, 153, 154, 155, 156–157, 158, 159–160, 161, 162n7
Bal des Pianos, 53, 58, 59, 61, 63, 64, 68
Barndt, Deborah, 306–307
batalera(s) (female ritual percussionists), 215, 232
Beatón, Ramiero Herrero (Cuban theater director), 219, 221, 223–224, 224–226, 236n2, 236n4
Beaudet, Jean-Michel, 52, 57, 66, 69n9
Beliso-De Jesús, Aisha M., 228, 230, 236n5
Berlin, 106, 107, 108, 110, 112
Black, Indigenous, and People of Color (BIPOC), 103, 114, 116
Black Lives Matter movement, 49n6, 193, 199
Black music, 113, 245
Black radical tradition (BRT), 31, 34
Blagrove, Ishmahil, Jr., 33, 34, 42, 43–44, 45, 46–47

bloco(s) (musical ensembles), 75–83, 84, 85, 86, 87, 88, 89, 90, 91, 93, 94, 95; list of blocos practicing accessibility, 92
Bodenheimer, Rebecca, 215, 216, 218
Boise, Idaho, 280–285, 287–288, 289, 290–291, 292–293, 294, 295, 297n2, 297n6, 298n14, 298n15, 298n16
Boise Valley, Idaho, 281, 283, 288, 289, 290, 292, 293, 294
Boliche de Roberto, el (Buenos Aires tango bar), 137–138
Bordallo, Antônio, 88, 91
Boston Review, 301, 308
Bourdieu, Pierre, concept of habitus, 10, 56, 66
Brazil(ian), 13, 32, 76, 79, 80, 84, 92, 94, 95, 96n2, 108, 109, 112, 169, 227
Buenos Aires, Argentina, 15, 123, 124, 125, 126, 128, 129, 130, 132, 133, 134, 136, 139, 141; as "The Tango City," 127
Butler, Judith, 1, 8, 9

Cabildo Teatral Santiago (Cuban theater troupe), 218, 219, 220, 223, 224, 225
Cacho, Lisa Marie, 265, 267, 278n10
calypso, 30, 37, 48n4, 49, 49n4
Canada, 106, 220, 303, 304, 306, 309n4
Candomblé, 32, 44
capitalism, 32, 89, 97n21, 211, 217
Caribbean Performing Arts Festival, 217, 219, 223
Carnation Revolution, 165, 167, 173
carnival, 3, 4, 11, 12, 13, 20, 22n1, 29, 30, 31, 33, 34, 35, 36, 37, 38, 39, 40, 42, 44, 45, 46, 47–48, 48n1, 48n3, 48n4, 49n7, 55, 66, 75–77, 78–79, 80, 81, 82, 83–84, 84–85, 85–86, 89, 90, 91–92, 92–93, 94, 95, 96n2, 97n5, 97n14, 108–109, 193, 195, 196, 205, 206, 207, 210, 215, 216, 226, 227, 236n1
carnivalesque, the, 31, 34, 55, 95, 97n14, 108, 109, 193, 196
carnival studies, 3, 31, 48, 216
Casa del Caribe (Cuban research institute), 215, 216, 217, 218, 221–222, 223, 224
cinema(s), 144–145, 160, 265
cisgender, 13, 101, 111
cityscape, 15, 147, 150

INDEX

coalitional performance, 276, 277
coalitional politics, 8, 304
Cohen, Abner, 34
collective action, 5, 7, 33–34, 40, 68, 192
collective identities, 3, 16, 17, 54, 57, 66, 69n5, 80, 98n21, 100, 103, 106, 108, 111, 112, 113, 114, 115, 116, 117n8, 131, 147, 148, 150, 153, 155, 156, 158, 161, 168, 177, 193, 202, 215, 217, 218, 222, 228, 247, 298
Collins, Patricia Hill, 40, 111, 114
Colombia, 124, 142n1, 227
colonialism, 12, 30, 32, 46, 47, 89, 175, 200, 203, 218, 268, 281, 290, 291
commons, the, 67, 68, 70n13
Communist Party of Cuba, 220, 222, 224
communitas, 3, 6, 7, 21, 31, 34, 273, 281, 288, 289
Compton, Fiona, 39
ConCiertos Atorrantes (tango concert series), 137–138
consensus, 6, 53, 56, 66
consumerism, 4, 67
Coplan, David, 244, 245
Corbani, Alberto "Pata" (Argentinian musician), 133, 134
Corbett, Elena, 146, 153, 156
corda (rope), 76, 85, 86
cosmopolitan(ism), 161n6, 180, 192, 210, 240, 266, 267, 271; jazz cosmopolitanism, 248, 249, 251, 252, 255
costume(s) (*fantasias*), 35, 76, 108, 109, 110, 115, 207
COVID-19 pandemic, 76, 77, 79, 91, 92, 93, 95, 104, 250, 252, 297n8, 303, 305, 306
creative adaptation, 167, 170, 183–184
crowd(s), 4, 8, 30, 42, 60, 76, 84, 85, 90, 91, 109, 139, 159, 182, 191, 209, 260, 262, 263, 266, 276, 283
Cuba(n), 6, 18, 20, 215–217, 218–219, 219–222, 223–224, 225, 226, 227–228, 229, 230–231, 231–232, 233–234, 234–235, 236n5, 236n6, 254; Cubanidad (Cubanness), 217, 218
cultural politics, 31, 123–126, 131, 134, 141
cultura poular, 165, 166, 167, 168, 169, 170, 171, 173, 176, 181, 182, 183; definition of, 16

Dardot, Pierre, 68, 70n13
Dauvergne, Peter, 194, 211

Debord, Guy, 64
decenter(ing), 15, 129, 147
Delanty, Gerard, 152, 242
Del Caribe (academic journal of Casa del Caribe), 216, 217, 218
deliberation, 17, 19, 189, 263, 303, 304, 305; as a "tactic of intervention," 10; as a motif, 191–258
deliberative action, 17, 18
De Waal, Alex, 210
dialogic(s), 19, 79, 240–241, 243, 250, 252, 255, 256, 302
diga, 19, 252, 254–255
direct action, 1, 21, 265, 269, 274–276, 280, 281, 284, 285, 289, 290, 296
disability(ies), 13, 73, 75–78, 79, 81–82, 84, 85, 86, 87, 88, 89, 91, 92–94, 94–95, 97n5, 97n7, 97n8, 97n13, 97n20, 97n21, 111
discourse, 9, 12, 15, 90, 101, 104, 105, 108, 109, 110, 111, 112, 114, 115–116, 117n8, 136, 140, 141, 146, 173, 200, 201, 202, 218, 245, 256, 268, 298n18
disruption, 10–11, 11–12, 14, 16, 19, 145, 152, 264, 269, 270, 271, 276, 287; as a "tactic of intervention," 10; as a motif, 29–71
dissensus, 66, 70, 307; definition of, 10; efficacy of, 10, 67
diversity, 2, 22n1, 52, 64, 65, 69n8, 86, 177, 195, 196, 201, 202, 211, 221, 248, 270, 272, 280, 282, 283, 284, 285, 288, 289, 290; Festa of, 177, 184n3
do-it-yourself (DIY) music, 13, 100, 102–103, 108, 109, 111, 112, 115, 116, 117n8, 207
Dornelles, Patricia, 75, 77, 82

Edmondson, Belinda, 216, 235n1
electronic dance music (EDM), 106, 113
embodied practice, 201
emotion, 4, 14, 15, 17, 37, 56, 68, 85, 113, 124, 139, 203, 204, 296
equity, 58, 64, 248, 302
erasure, 10, 14, 268, 274, 290, 291, 292, 293, 295
escapism, 8, 21, 272, 276
espiritismo (mediumship), 222, 224, 225, 227, 234
essentialization, 109, 113, 115, 270, 294

Estado Novo (the corporatist Portuguese state of 1933–1974), 167, 169, 171, 172, 174, 185n8

ethnography, 29, 31, 33, 34, 47, 52, 59, 103–104, 123, 166, 172, 181, 194, 216, 218, 294; ritual ethnography, 217, 231

ethnomusicology, 5, 52, 54, 56–57, 58, 59, 64, 66, 67, 79, 103, 105, 113, 142n9, 196, 216, 218, 226, 235, 241, 248, 255–256, 281

European Festival of Diversities and Antidiscrimination, 53, 62, 64

European Union (EU), 37, 63, 69n8, 167, 170, 171, 179, 180

exclusion, 9, 16, 18, 19, 81, 82, 95, 147, 160, 233, 240, 241, 244, 246, 247

Expósito Álvarez, Benita (religious studies scholar), 231, 236n2

Extinction Rebellion (UK-founded environmental movement), 191, 199, 207, 208–209

Farra Fanfarra (Portuguese brass band and civil society organization), 165, 180, 182, 184n4

Fasheh, Munir, 155

Feld, Steven, 79, 248–249, 250, 251, 252

feminism, 13, 35, 40, 90, 97, 100–102, 102–103, 104, 105–106, 106–107, 108, 109–110, 111, 114, 115–116, 168; third-wave, 97n21, 101

festa(s), 117n5, 166, 167, 170–171, 175, 176, 177, 178, 179–180, 183, 184n2, 184n3; definition of, 2, 16

Festival Activism, 1, 3, 4, 6

Festival del Caribe, 18, 215, 216, 217, 218, 221, 223, 224, 226, 230, 234, 235

Festival do Avante!, 175–176, 180, 183, 184n2

festival experience(s), 7, 8, 13, 53, 194, 199

festivalization, 4, 100, 108, 111, 116, 235n1; of activism, 17, 207

festival practice, 5, 6, 7, 8, 9, 13, 15, 18, 19, 20, 21, 95, 166, 215, 248, 264, 274, 302

festival studies, 4, 5, 235, 242, 243, 247

festive culture, 165, 168, 170

festive studies, 1, 2, 4

festivity, 2, 10, 12, 75, 76, 77, 78, 80, 95, 97n5, 159, 199, 265, 269

Fiesta de Fuego, 215, 226

Figarola, Joel James, 215, 217, 218–219, 220, 221, 222, 223, 224, 234, 236n2

filarmónica (traditional Portuguese band), 166, 170, 171, 176, 177, 178, 180, 181, 184n4

foliona (female reveler), 83–85, 88; definition of, 76

folklife, 285, 287, 288–289, 290, 296, 297n5

folklore, 5, 165, 170, 174, 220, 262, 281, 290

47Soul (Jordanian-Palestinian musicians and activists), 158, 201

Foucault, Michel, 2, 281, 286, 287

Fractura Expuesta (underground radio station), 129–131, 142n4, 142n8

France/French, 6, 54, 57, 66, 68, 70n11, 80, 100, 103, 105, 106, 113, 115, 116n2, 137, 174, 200, 217, 219, 254, 304

Franco, Marielle, 89, 90

Frauenfest, 101, 106

freedom dreams, 20, 29, 33, 34, 48

"Full Extreme" (carnival party song), 38

funk, 108, 109, 112, 201

futurity, 19, 22, 269, 272; festival futurity, 20, 21, 95, 261, 264, 265, 272, 275, 276, 277; as a motif, 261–300; as a "tactic of intervention," 10

Gabriel, Peter, 195–196, 197, 198

Galeano, Eduardo, 124, 139

Galí Riverí, Milián (percussionist), 219, 224

Garofalo, Reebee, 22n2, 80, 92, 177

German(y), 6, 100, 101, 103, 105, 106, 107, 112, 114, 115, 116n2, 118

Ghana(ian), 248, 250, 252, 254

Global Lounge, 284, 297n10

Goldschmidt, Martin (music festival organizer), 261, 265, 265–266, 271

Graeber, David, 21, 274, 275

"Grândola Vila Morena" (popular Portuguese song associated with the Carnation Revolution), 165, 173, 174, 182

Greater Amman Municipality (GAM), 150, 152, 153, 156, 157

griot, 61, 203

Gudgell, Dallas (Lakota activist), 294–295

Guelph, University of, 4, 303

Guilbault, Jocelyne, 3, 30; on pleasure, 7

Guss, David, 3, 17, 159, 160, 161

GYM TONIC (synth-punk band), 109, 110

Habermas, Jürgen, 242, 243

Hagedorn, Katherine, 225, 228, 230

Haiti(an), 32, 49n9, 202, 215, 219, 220, 221, 224, 227, 234
Hakaya Storytelling Festival, 145, 154–155, 155–156, 158, 159, 161
Hauser, Christine, 284, 297n9
Hayes, Eileen, 22n2, 102, 116
Hechavarría, Ibrahim (Cuban *santero*), 224, 225
Hennion, Antoine, 102
heritage, 35, 106, 113, 126, 145, 153, 154, 241, 242, 286, 290, 291–293
heteropatriarchy, 32, 40
heterotopia, 20, 281, 285, 286–287, 288, 296, 307; as artistic activism, 288–290
Holton, Kimberly, 172, 184n1
Homens da Luta (Portuguese satirical musical troupe), 182, 183
HONK! Festivals of Activist Brass Bands, 80, 92
Hourani, Najib B., 145, 147, 157
hypersexualization, 107, 109, 112

Idaho, 20, 280, 281, 282, 283, 284, 285, 286, 288, 289, 290, 291, 292, 296, 297n4, 297n9, 297n10, 298n15, 305; Idaho Commission on the Arts, 285, 286; Folk and Traditional Arts Program, 285–286
Ifá-Òrìṣà, 18, 216, 230
IF 2020 (festival), 303, 305, 306, 309n7
improvisation, 302, 303, 305, 307, 308, 309n12
inclusion, 16, 18, 20, 77, 81, 82, 89, 151, 201, 240, 241, 243, 255, 256
Inclusion and Revelry (documentary series), 77, 81, 82–83
intercultural interaction, 13, 17, 199, 202, 203, 204, 209
International Course-Workshop on Popular Religiosity, 227, 228, 231
International Institute for Critical Studies in Improvisation (IICSI), 303, 305, 307, 308, 309n12
intersectional(ity), 6, 89, 91, 97n21, 101, 111, 112, 114, 116, 272, 302
intersex, 13, 101, 105, 177
intimacy, 3, 8, 15, 97n20, 128, 139, 141, 306
inversion, 3, 31, 34, 108–109, 293
Irbid, 155, 156, 158
Iseed, Mu'ath, 149, 150, 151, 160, 161n4

Israel(is), 20, 21, 153, 158, 201, 262, 264, 267–268, 271, 274, 275, 276, 277, 279
Iyer, Vijay, 301, 308

Jackson, Peter, 29, 34, 197
Jamaica(n), 39, 42, 201, 215, 227, 235n1
Japan(ese), 157, 231, 283, 286, 306
Jardim, Marcelo, 75, 77, 82
Jasper, James, 4, 275, 279
Jassey, Victoria Rosemary, 232, 233, 234
jazz, 18, 19, 61, 240, 241, 243, 244–245, 246–247, 248–249, 249–250, 251, 252, 253, 254–255, 283, 301, 302; jazz clubs of Johannesburg and Pretoria, 240, 245, 250, 253
Jazz Cosmology: Not Another Jazz Festival, 18, 19, 240, 241, 248, 249, 250, 251, 252, 255, 256
Johannesburg, 240, 245, 246, 249, 250, 251, 252, 253, 254
Jones, Alex, 280, 284, 297n9
Jones, Claudia, 34, 35
Jones-McVeigh, Ruth (founder of Mariposa Folk Festival), 303
Journal of Festival Inquiry and Analysis, 4
Journal of Festive Studies, 4
Joy of Jazz (music festival), 245, 246, 248
jumāhīrī(yya) (populist), 146, 160
Juqqa, Lubna, 149, 150, 151, 160, 161n3

kaiso (calypso song), 37, 49n4
Karkabi, Nadeem, 157, 269
Keil, Charles, 67–68, 70n12
Kelley, Robin D. G., 31, 33, 301, 308
Kirchner, Christina Fernández de, 125, 130, 140
Kirshenblatt-Gimblett, Barbara, 292, 294
Klein, Estelle, 303–304
Koskoff, Ellen, 105
Kovaleski, Donna, 284, 285
Kurikindi (Ecuadoran shamanic healer), 208
Kwame Nkrumah Pan-African Intellectual Cultural Festival, 302

La Boca (Buenos Aires neighborhood), 129, 133, 136
LaDIYfest Berlin, 108, 109, 112
Ladyfest, 13, 100–101, 101–102, 102–103, 104–105, 105–106, 107, 109, 110, 111, 112, 114, 115–116, 116n2, 116n4, 117n5, 117n8, 117n11, 303

Lakota (Native American people), 290, 291, 292, 293, 294
Larduet Luaces, Alberto (researcher, Palo and Santería priest), 221, 224, 227
Latour, Bruno, 102, 110, 111; and the concept of translation, 102–103
LeBaron, Genevieve, 194, 211
Le Bon, Gustave, 4
Lisbon, 95, 96, 165, 177, 180, 181, 182, 184n3, 185n7
Lloyd, Timothy, 288
Lortat-Jacob, Bernard, 58
love song(s), 123, 124, 125
Luis, Heitor (saxophonist), 84, 87, 90

Mace, Ronald, 78
Machín Hernández, Enrique (Cuban Ifá priest), 231, 233
Macri, Mauricio (Argentinian politician), 125, 126, 130
Mahlangu, Jennifer (dancer), 240, 241, 244, 245, 247, 256
map(s), 17, 129, 151, 168, 296
marginalization, 7, 9, 11, 12, 13, 33–34, 37, 63, 65, 80, 89, 91, 100, 102–103, 111, 112, 135, 152, 168, 177, 184n1, 203, 221, 240, 241, 242, 286, 288
Mariposa Folk Festival, 303, 304, 305, 306, 307, 308, 309n6, 309n11
Martínez Betancourt, Julio (ethnobotanist), 231, 236n2
Marxism, 4, 32–33, 153, 216, 220, 221
Mathias, Christopher, 280, 282, 284, 285
McCarl, Robert (folklorist), 296
McKay, George, 22n2, 193, 197, 209
MC Xuparina (funk singer), 108–109, 112, 114, 117n7
mediation, 57, 102, 103, 104, 115–116, 242
Mexico, 202, 227, 282, 304, 306
migration, 11, 113–114, 173, 219, 282
Millet, José, 217–218, 219, 221, 234, 236n2
Mismar, Yazan, 151, 161n5
Mitwally, Dalal, 152–153, 162n8
Modirzadeh, Hafez, 308
multiculturalism, 48, 54, 195, 197, 280, 284, 289, 290, 295, 297n11, 298n17
Muñoz, José Esteban, and "disidentification," 109, 112, 115, 117n8

Murad, Bashar (Palestinian singer), 261, 262, 263, 264, 270, 271, 272, 273, 274, 276, 277n1, 277n3
mural(s), 16, 150, 151, 152, 153, 154, 158, 159, 160, 162n8, 162n9
music festivals, 5, 53, 57, 59, 61, 64, 100, 101, 102, 103, 116n1, 131, 145, 146, 147, 156, 157–158, 159–160, 161, 166, 170, 173, 174, 175, 177, 193–194, 195, 196, 200, 207, 209, 244, 266, 267, 301–302, 303, 305, 306, 307; megafestivals, 139–140, 193, 196; politics of, 2–7
musicking, 67, 195
music making, 6, 123, 124, 125, 127, 128, 136, 137, 138, 141, 168, 176, 251, 252, 277n1
myth(s)/mythology, 3, 75, 100, 173, 183, 204, 232

Nabulsi, Aya, 149, 158
National Arts Foundation (FUNARTE), 76, 93
Native American(s), 280, 290, 292, 293, 294, 295
neoliberal(ism), 15–16, 54, 123, 124–125, 128, 136, 138, 140, 141, 144–145, 146, 148, 149, 155, 192, 194, 197, 199, 200, 210, 211, 246; post-neoliberal, 123–125, 128, 138, 140
Nigeria(n), 6, 18, 216, 226, 228, 230–231, 231–232, 233, 234, 247, 248, 254, 284
NOISEAUX (singer and musician), 112–114, 115, 117n12; and her song "I Have a Loaded Voice," 113–115
nonbinary, 13, 101, 105
nostalgia, 15–16, 16–17, 123, 138
Notting Hill (London neighborhood), 29, 42; Notting Hill Carnival, 29

Obomsawin, Alanis, 303, 304, 307, 309n5, 309n6, 309n10, 309n11
Obomsawin, Mali, 307, 308, 309n9, 309n10
O'Brien, Jean M., 291, 293
Odanak (First Nations people), 304, 307, 309n10
Odeon Amphitheaters, 145, 152, 156
odú (divinatory signs), 232–233
oficina(s) (music classes), 79, 80, 81, 87, 94
Oliveras, Jofre, 152, 153, 162n8
Olympia, Washington, 100, 106
oricha (Yoruba deity), 224–225, 228, 233

INDEX

Orozco Rubio, Enrique (Cuban drummer), 232, 233, 236n2
Orquestra Voadora (Brazilian musical ensemble), 13, 20, 75, 76, 77, 79, 80, 84, 85, 89, 90, 91, 92, 94, 95

Pachamama (Mother Earth), 208–209
palero (*palo* priest), 221, 224, 227
Palestine Music Expo (PMX), 20, 21, 261, 263, 264, 265, 266, 267–268, 268–269, 269–270, 271–272, 273, 274, 275, 276, 277, 277n1, 278n4, 278n5, 278n6, 278n8
Palestinian(s), 21, 148, 153, 158, 160, 201, 262, 265, 266, 267, 268, 269, 270, 271, 272, 274, 275–276, 277, 277n1, 277n2, 278n11
Palmié, Stephan, 220, 228, 230
palo monte (Afrodiasporic ritual practice), 224, 227, 234
parade(s), 13, 16, 20, 66, 82, 84, 85, 86, 87, 88, 89, 90, 91, 95, 96, 165, 166, 167, 170, 171, 176, 179, 180, 181, 182, 183, 196, 210, 288
Paris, 10, 53, 54, 55, 57, 59, 63
participatory action, 6–7, 141n1, 269
pedagogy, 87–88, 124
performance, 4, 5, 7, 11, 14, 15, 18–19, 21–22, 30, 31, 42, 47, 48n4, 52, 55–56, 57–58, 59, 60, 61, 64, 69n1, 75, 79, 92, 93, 97n8, 102–103, 107–108, 109, 110–111, 112, 115, 116, 124, 126, 128, 133, 139–140, 141, 149, 154, 155, 156, 158, 159, 165, 166, 167, 168, 169, 170, 171, 173–174, 175, 176–177, 178, 179–180, 181–182, 184, 197, 200–201, 203–204, 208, 220, 223, 224, 226, 235n1, 245, 249, 255, 261–262, 263–264, 265–267, 269, 270–271, 272, 275, 276, 277; performative spaces, 181, 263
plaza(s), 123, 128, 129, 130, 136, 137, 138, 139, 142n9, 145, 157
pleasure, 6, 7, 8, 9, 17, 21, 22, 40, 67, 86, 275, 276, 289; as a "force of power," 7; politics of, 7–8
poetry, 148, 158, 192, 235n1, 276
political action, 7, 9, 13, 17, 181, 205, 271, 273, 276, 284, 307; "key resources" for, 6
political intervention, 1–2, 5, 7, 11, 19, 21, 241, 265, 271, 272
political transformation, 6–7, 21, 35, 277, 303
polymusic(s), 65, 66, 67, 68, 69n9
Portugal, 2, 6, 16, 95, 165–176, 178, 181, 182, 183, 184, 184n4, 185n7, 185n8

Pouymiró, Nagybe Madariaga (female percussionist), 18, 232, 233, 234, 236n2
praxis, 18, 154, 230, 235
Pretoria, 240, 245, 247, 249, 250, 253, 254
Pride, 95, 96, 138, 177, 285, 289
PRO (right-wing political party), 125–127, 131
protest(s), 1, 2, 4, 8, 12, 16, 20, 30, 35, 43, 48, 49n4, 80, 95, 107, 123, 124, 127, 148, 157, 165, 166–167, 169–170, 171, 172, 173–174, 177, 179, 180, 181–182, 182–183, 184, 184n4, 185n7, 191, 192, 195, 199–200, 201, 202, 204, 208, 242, 264, 265, 269, 275, 289, 290, 297n9, 304, 305, 309n6; protest music, 17, 168, 169, 175, 193, 199, 200, 207, 209
public spaces(s), 8, 9, 11, 12, 19, 54, 55, 57, 75, 80, 109, 147, 150, 151, 155, 158, 159, 160, 161, 166, 176, 306
punk, 61, 64, 100, 105, 106, 109, 110, 112, 113, 114, 195, 202
Pyper, Brett (scholar), 244, 245, 246–247, 248, 249

queer, 13, 97n21, 101, 102, 105, 111, 112, 115–116, 181, 262, 263, 271–272, 276
Quinn, Bernadette, 287, 289
Quinteto Negro La Boca (tango ensemble), 133, 136

Al-Rabady, Rama, 145, 156, 157
Ramallah, 262, 265, 266, 267, 269, 271, 275
Ramos André, 75, 76, 77, 78, 79, 81, 82, 83, 84, 85, 86, 88, 91, 82, 93, 94, 95, 96n1, 96n3, 97n10–12, 97n15–19, 98n22–26
Rancière, Jacques, 9, 10, 11, 53, 56, 66
Recife, 94, 96
refuge, 12, 13, 14, 16, 210, 264, 270, 271; as a "tactic of intervention," 10
Regla de Ochà (Santería), 44, 215, 216, 219, 224, 225, 228, 230, 232, 233, 234
relational geometry(ies), 11, 53, 56, 57, 58, 59, 64, 67, 69n1; definition, 52
renewal, 14, 15, 16, 19, 121; as a "tactic of intervention," 10
resistance, 12, 32, 33, 35, 42, 44, 45, 89, 90, 113, 125, 141, 156, 168, 172, 180, 183, 196, 197, 198, 199, 200, 201, 202, 210, 211, 221, 231, 248, 255, 274–275, 307

revisionism, 18, 216, 228, 230, 231
Rio de Janeiro, 13, 75, 76, 80, 83–84, 92, 94, 96n1–2, 97n16–18, 109
Riot Grrrl movement, 100, 106–107, 115
ritual revisionism, 18, 216, 228, 231
Robinson, Dylan, 22n2, 220
Robinson, Roxy, 7, 22n2, 31, 32, 33, 193, 308n2
Roma, 12, 52, 53, 57, 61, 63, 69n5
Ross, Stacey Leigh, 33, 35, 36, 37, 39, 40, 47
Rouget, Gilbert, 56, 58
rupture(s), 10, 66, 67, 159, 167, 168, 169, 171, 172, 179, 183, 235

Said, Edward, 278n11, 293
samba school(s), 75, 80, 84, 85, 92, 96n2, 97n14, 205
Santería, 32, 215, 222, 224, 225–226, 227, 228, 230
santero (Santería priest), 221, 224, 225, 227, 228
Santiago de Cuba, 18, 215, 216, 217, 218, 219, 220, 223, 224, 227, 229, 231, 233, 234
Sassatelli, Monica, 152, 242
scenography, 60, 65–66
Schwedler, Jillian, 147, 148
semiotic(s), 167, 168, 169
sensoriality, 10–11, 21, 22, 66–67, 161, 276, 277
sentimental(ism), 123, 124, 136, 138, 140, 141; as a "tool for activism," 15
sentipensante (tango performances), 15, 123, 124, 136, 138, 141, 307
settler-colonialism, 220, 267–268, 278n10, 281, 291, 292, 293, 294, 295
sha'bī(yya) (popular), 146, 160
Shami, Seteney, 144, 147, 161
Shcolnik, Fernanda, 13, 83, 88–89, 91, 97n20
shemagh (scarf), 153
slave trade, transatlantic, 32, 46, 47, 228
SlutWalk movement, 107, 115, 117n6, 119
soca (musical genre), 38, 49n7
social action, 15, 144, 146, 192, 263, 302
social justice, 17, 40, 43, 124, 179, 192, 240, 241, 243–244, 245, 246, 247, 248, 255, 256, 302
social media, 39, 104, 105, 132, 156, 165, 182, 199, 205, 278n9
social movements, 33, 95, 105, 107, 115, 125, 179, 192–196, 205, 207, 209, 210, 307; theory of, 2, 4

social order, 3, 4, 168, 287, 288, 290, 296
Sorrels, Rosalie, 305
South Africa(n), 18–19, 240, 241, 243–244, 245, 246, 247, 248, 250, 252, 253, 254–255, 256, 256n1, 257
Spirit of Resistance (interactive art piece), 33, 44, 45; and Tate & Lyle (sugar manufacturer), 45–46
storytelling, 16, 49n4, 145, 148, 203; as a component of heritage, 154
Strong, Pauline Turner, 292, 294
"Strong Women: Purpose and Protest" (workshop), 304, 305, 309n6
subjectivities, 103, 242, 262, 263, 271, 272, 276
subversion/subversive, 3, 30, 75, 79, 110, 158, 174, 175
Sunday in Plaza Almagro (short film), 138, 142n9
Szwarcman, Alejandro (poet, lyricist, journalist), 133, 135

tactics of intervention, 6, 9–10, 17, 303
Taha, Raeda, 158–159
al-Tal, Shima, 152, 153
Tamimi, Basem (Palestinian journalist), 275, 278n12
tango, 15, 123, 124, 125, 126, 127, 128–131, 131–134, 135–137, 137–138, 138–140, 140–141, 141n2, 142n4, 142n7, 142n8; neighborhood tango festivals, 15, 123, 124, 125, 126, 127, 128, 129, 131, 132, 133, 134, 135, 136, 137, 139, 140, 141
Tanzanian Albinism Collective, 13–14, 203–204
Taussig, Michael, 293–294
Taylor, Jodie, 4, 101, 108, 242; on festivals and feminism, 100–101
temporality, 59, 272
"Tendrils of the Vine, the" (poetry workshop), 304, 305
theorizing, 1, 2, 3, 6, 31, 33, 34, 96n5, 103, 251
Toukan, Hanan, 152, 158, 159
tourism, 15, 29, 54, 123, 124, 125, 126, 127, 130–131, 133, 134, 141n2, 145, 146, 156, 157, 160, 230, 235n1, 246, 247
transgender, 12, 13, 62, 63, 69n5, 101, 105
transgression/transgressive ideas, actions, and objects, 3, 4, 9, 13, 14, 19, 21, 108, 174, 196, 204, 263, 264, 265, 269, 271, 272

INDEX

translocal, 17, 106, 166, 215
transnationalism, 17, 18, 80, 157, 161, 193, 195, 196, 198, 200, 202, 203, 204, 209, 211, 305; definition of, 192; politics of, 5, 17, 193–194; transnational activism, 17, 191, 192, 193, 194, 195, 198, 199, 201, 202, 209, 210, 211
Transylvania, 12, 52, 57, 61, 63
Trinidad(ian), 35, 36, 38, 39, 227, 235–236n1
Tuck, Eve, 291, 297n12
Turino, Thomas, 6, 53, 55, 273, 277
Turner, Victor, 3, 31, 281

UNESCO, 125, 127
unimaginable, the, 20, 95, 264, 273
United States, 6, 80, 101, 192, 193, 196, 234, 278n10, 303, 306
urbanism, 15, 124–125, 145

Valentín Alsina (Buenos Aires neighborhood), 129, 132, 133, 135, 136, 140
Vargens, Joana, 84, 85
Vazquez, Marisa (Argentinian singer), 133, 136
violence, 1, 12, 20, 34, 37, 38, 39, 40, 107, 171, 174, 175, 201, 203, 245, 263, 264, 265, 272, 276, 277
visibility, 11, 12, 14, 18, 29, 63, 128, 130, 131, 132, 137, 138, 140, 141, 158, 159, 234, 235, 246, 277; "politics of," in Jordan, 153
Vizenor, Gerald, 291, 294, 298n18
vodú (religion), 219, 220, 221, 222, 224, 227, 234
volunteer(ism), 146, 149, 160, 166, 178, 252, 283, 284, 285, 290

Wast al-Balad, 144–145, 156–157, 160, 161
wedding(s), 69n1, 242, 261, 262, 263, 270
wheelchair, 76, 84, 87, 88, 95
Wilks, Linda, 287, 289
Windrush, 42
Wits Festival Study Group (WFSG), 18, 241, 242, 247, 248, 251, 255
Witwatersrand, University of the, 240, 241, 247, 249, 250, 252, 252–253, 254, 255, 256
Wolfe, Patrick, 268, 291, 292
Woodward, Ian, 4, 108, 193
Woolgar, Steve, 102, 111
world making, 19, 20, 21, 48, 95, 264, 302, 308
world music, 30, 53, 57, 58, 59, 64, 66, 79, 194, 196, 197, 209, 211
World of Music, Arts and Dance (WOMAD) Festival, 13–14, 17–18, 191, 194, 196–197, 197–198, 199, 200, 202, 203, 204, 205, 206, 207, 208, 209, 210, 211, 211n1, 303; WOMAD foundation, 195, 201
World Village Festival, 20, 280–293, 295–296, 297n1, 298n13

Yaghi, Amro, 147
Yang, K. Wayne, 291, 297n12
Yemayá (Yoruban deity), 228; festival to, 228, 229
Yorùbáland, 18, 228, 230, 231
Younis, Rami (music festival organizer), 265, 266, 267, 278n4, 278n7

Zulu, 249, 253, 254

For Indiana University Press

Sabrina Black, Editorial Assistant
Allison Chaplin, Acquisitions Editor
Anna Garnai, Production Coordinator
Sophia Hebert, Assistant Acquisitions Editor
Samantha Heffner, Marketing and Publicity Manager
Katie Huggins, Production Manager
Darja Malcolm-Clarke, Project Manager/Editor
Dan Pyle, Online Publishing Manager
Michael Regoli, Director of Publishing Operations
Pamela Rude, Senior Artist and Book Designer

www.ingramcontent.com/pod-product-compliance
Lightning Source LLC
Chambersburg PA
CBHW021343300426
44114CB00012B/1057